Deer & Deer Hunting
Book 3

Deer & Deer Hunting
Book 3

Robert Wegner

Stackpole Books

Published by
STACKPOLE BOOKS
Cameron and Kelker Streets
P.O. Box 1831
Harrisburg, PA 17105

Printed in the United States of America

10   9   8   7   6   5   4   3   2   1

First Edition

Some of the chapters of this book originally appeared in *Deer & Deer Hunting* magazine. They are published here in revised form with the permission of the Publisher and the Editors of *Deer & Deer Hunting* magazine.

Library of Congress Cataloging-in-Publication Data
(Revised for vol. 3)

Wegner, Robert.
     Deer & deer hunting.
     Includes bibliographies and indexes.
     Contents: v. [1] The serious hunter's
guide—bk. 2. Strategies and tactics for the advanced
hunter—bk. 3. [without special title]
     1. Deer hunting.   2. Deer.   I. Title.   II. Title: Deer
and deer hunting.
SK301.W35   1984   799.2′77357   84-2413
ISBN 0-8117-0434-3 (v. 1)

*The whitetail is the American Deer of the past,
and the American Deer of the future.*

—Ernest Thompson Seton
Lives of Game Animals, 1929.

Dedication

For my friend and colleague Al Hofacker, one of the
most enthusiastic students of the whitetail, who understands
better than anyone else how much time
first-class, in-depth, feature magazine writing requires.
Deer & Deer Hunting Books 1, 2, and 3 owe you a
considerable debt and I want to say thanks.

Contents

Part IV   THE DEER HUNTER

Part V   WHERE TO FIND MORE INFORMATION

Acknowledgments

I would like to thank my colleague Jack Brauer, publisher of *Deer & Deer Hunting* magazine, for enticing me to leave the University of Wisconsin in 1979 for a job that paid $50 a week and all the road kills I could eat. Thank you Chet Fish, executive vice president of Stackpole Books, for accepting and editing Books 1 and 2 and for initiating Book 3. Thank you Jay Cassell, senior editor of *Sports Afield* magazine, for your superb job in editing all three volumes, a finer editor no author could have! Thanks Maren Wegner for editing everything that I have ever written. And finally, thank you Lennie Rue for allowing me to use your magnificent photos for all three volumes. You once told me never to get into book publishing, and you know what, Lennie? Even though I didn't listen to you, you were right as usual.

Robert Wegner
Deer Foot Road
June 4, 1990

PART I

GIANTS AMONG DEER HUNTERS

Flintlock: A Dixie Deerslayer

In discussing deer hunting as a sport, it seems to me that we must never lose sight of the fact that its interest is due chiefly to the nature of the game pursued. . . . I hope to be a stag follower as long as I can see a sight. This feeling I attribute to the character of the deer—that noble, elusive, crafty, wonderful denizen of the wilds, the pursuit of which is surely the master sport of the huntsman.

—Archibald Rutledge, *Days Off in Dixie,* 1924

Archibald Rutledge (1883–1973), known to his deer hunting partners as "Old Flintlock," ranked the white-tailed deer at the top of his hunting passion. He studied and observed whitetails all his life. He philosophized and wrote poetry about them. From his deer stand in a century-old live oak, he watched white-tailed bucks travel along moonlit trails; later he captured their mystic radiance in high-level prose. From his plantation records that date back to 1686, Flintlock learned that whitetails had been using the same trails and crossings through the woods of his home for more than three centuries.

Rutledge killed his first white-tailed buck in December of 1894 at the 2000-acre Hampton Plantation, along the banks of the Santee River, near the town of McClellanville, South Carolina. He was only eleven years old at the time, but this isn't surprising for someone who when only eleven months old swung on the antlers of a pet buck named "Ben." He began to hunt deer at the age of six, and at the tender age of ten he guided President Cleveland. The 2000 acres that formed the Hampton Plantation would remain his favorite hunting haunt throughout his long and amazingly productive life.

When Flintlock died at the age of ninety, his deer-kill statistics reached a total of 299 white-tailed bucks. "If 299 bucks seem just too many for one man," Rutledge tells us, "I will remind the reader that South Carolina is a good deer state and that some of its zones have the longest season in the United States. A hunter is allowed five bucks a season and I have hunted for seventy-eight years." Following

Archibald Rutledge (1883–1973) with his deer hound.

are samples of some of Flintlock's more memorable buck hunts together with a brief look at an individual who certainly ranks well to the forefront of those who perused the gallant animal and described their adventures in print.

Like most white-tailed deer hunters, Flintlock acquired his keen interest in the sport from his father, Colonel Henry Rutledge II, who spoke of deer and deer hunting, as Flintlock puts it, "with a gravity that gauged his feeling." As they tramped the great pine barrens and cypress swamps around the Hampton Plantation, the Colonel, who killed more than 600 whitetails and attained a remarkable record of thirty double shots on deer (one with each barrel), would suddenly stop and point out to the young boy the very spot where several years earlier he had dropped a magnificent 10-point buck. On

their numerous journeys through the deep pinelands, the Colonel taught the boy to recognize the track of a buck from that of a doe: "A buck walks heavily, is blunt-toed and wears a number ten shoe; a doe is a lady. She minces along in high-heeled slippers."

Yet, Flintlock himself believed that his great love of deer hunting was not only born in him, since the men of his family always hunted deer, but that a curious happening which occurred when he was only eleven months old deeply instilled in him a profound love of the animal and an intense interest in the hunting of them. The incident took place one day after his mother left him alone in his crib in a large room in the plantation house. Up the cypress steps of the front porch and through the front door came "Ben," a magnificent, full-antlered buck that the Colonel had raised on a bottle. Old Ben bent over the little boy and nuzzled him intently. Unafraid of the buck, the infant reached up his tiny hands and seized the wide, beaded antlers. The buck suddenly snorted and when Flintlock's mother entered the room, she saw her baby swinging on the rack of a white-tailed buck. "I have always felt sure," Rutledge writes in a story entitled "That Christmas Buck," "that the old stag (since he knew that his own hide was safe) passed me the mystic word concerning the rarest sport on earth. He put it across to me, all right!" Thus inspired from the cradle, Archibald Rutledge would spend his whole life doing his best to pass on the glad tidings to all deer hunters.

As the young Archie grew up, he became accustomed to seeing portraits of famous sportsmen and the antlers of many a white-tailed buck hanging on the walls of the old plantations. While visiting one plantation with the Colonel, he saw a collection of more than 400 white-tailed racks. The antlers gazed down at the boy and deeply affected his lifelong interests. While eating dinners at the Hampton Plantation, the boy enthusiastically admired the rack of one great chestnut-colored buck that hung in the dining room; its massive antlers carried twelve points. Later in life Flintlock recalled his early fascination with antlers:

"A plantation home without its collection of stag horns is hardly to be found, and in passing I may say that some of the collections, dating back almost to the time of the Revolution, are of remarkable interest. . . . In some families, there is a custom, rigorously adhered to, that no deer antlers must ever leave the place, so that the antlers of every buck killed find their way into the home's collection. Such a frieze in a dining room seems to fill the place with woodland memories and serves in its own way to recall the hunts, the hunters and the hunted of long ago."

During his school days, the young boy longed to climb into the crotches of live oaks at Hampton and watch whitetails. Reading tales about giant, legendary bucks and being wise in the ways of the woods and whitetails intrigued the boy more than formal lessons in the classroom.

In his early years, Archie listened to the Negro huntsmen tune up their hunting horns and he heard the joyous yowling of the staghounds as they responded to the mellow blasts. For a young boy on the Hampton Plantation, white-tailed-deer hunting with these sounds on Christmas Day was as much a part of the season as a Christmas tree. By the age of nine, deer and deer hunting had become one of the most serious things in the life of Archibald Rutledge. Later in life, he would acknowledge that "there is no grander sport in the whole world than riding to hounds after deer; and this is a sport typical of a plan-

tation Christmas. With my Colonel, throughout his long life, it was almost a religious rite, and it never failed to supply the most thrilling entertainment for visitors. Indeed, I do not know exactly what the rural South would be without deer hunting as a diversion."

Beginning in 1730, deer hunting became an essential, integral ingredient of life at the Hampton Plantation, especially at Christmastime. "For a period of twenty shining years," notes Irvine Rutledge, the youngest of Flintlock's boys and now a retired judge living in Maryland, "there was The Hampton Hunt." The Hampton Hunts began in 1923, when Flintlock's sons Mid, Arch, and Irv were old enough to look down the barrel of a shotgun. They ended in 1943, when Mid was killed in a car accident and Arch and Irv went off to fight in World War II.

"The Hampton Hunt," circa 1940. *Left to right:* Flintlock, Archibald Rutledge Jr., Henry Middleton Rutledge IV, Irvine Hart Rutledge. *Courtesy Judge Irvine Rutledge*

Yes, Flintlock taught his three boys to be deer hunters, believing if more fathers taught their sons to be hunters, many of the so-called father-son problems would be eliminated. Quite often ladies and "lollypop sentimentalists" who came to visit the Hampton Plantation would be somewhat dismayed to learn that Flintlock and his boys enjoyed deer hunting. In defense of the sport, Flintlock would take them to his living room and show them that famous picture of naturalist John J. Audubon holding his shotgun of awesome proportions. "Teach the young how to shoot," Flintlock would tell his guests. "There is something inherently manly and homebred and truly American in that expression 'shooting straight.'"

Flintlock's eloquent defense of hunting culminated in his essay "Why I Taught My Boys to Be Hunters," a classic statement of hunting that stands with Roosevelt's hunting works, Leopold's "Wildlife in American Culture" and Ortega y Gasset's *Meditations on Hunting* (1972).

"Hunting is not incompatible with the deepest and most genuine love of nature. Audubon was something of a hunter; so was the famous Bachman; so were both John Muir and John Burroughs. It has always seemed to me that any man is a better man for being a hunter. This sport confers a certain constant alertness, and develops a certain ruggedness of character that, in these days of too much civilization, is refreshing; moreover, it allies us to the pioneer past. In a deep sense, this great land of ours was won for us by hunters."

During the time of the Hampton Hunts, Rutledge and his boys coined many nicknames: Arch, Jr. they called "Buckshot," and Irvine was "Gunpowder." They referred to Flintlock's beloved twelve-gauge Parker shotgun with the thirty-inch barrel as "Annie Oakley." In his lifelong correspondence with his deer hunting cronies, Flintlock signed his letters with the drawing of a flintlock. Their deer stands acquired such names as the Crippled Oak Stand, the Shirttail Stand, the Six-Master Stand, and the Seven Sisters. They christened the wild bucks of the woods they pursued with such names as Bushmaster, the Blackhorn Buck, Old Clubfoot, and the Gray Stag of Bowman's Bank. They called their deer hounds Old Buck, Old Bugle, Driver, Blue Boy, and Red Liquor. The immense and inviolate swamp where many of their bucks often escaped they called the Ocean, and their deer drives were the Long Corner, the Huckleberry Branch, Boggy Bay, and the Turkey Roost Drive.

Flintlock holding his beloved Parker 12-gauge double barrel, which he used "to roll" many a white-tailed buck.

The Christmas Day deer hunt reigned supreme in the litany of the Hampton Hunt. It was a religious rite, an exhilarating affair in and of itself, never to be matched in the history of American deer hunting. "Not to have a stag hanging up on Christmas Eve," Rutledge once admitted, "is to confess a certain degree of enfeebled manhood — almost a social disgrace." According to an old English custom, instead of going to church on Christmas morning Flintlock and his boys went deer hunting. In an article titled "A Christmas Hunt," Flintlock makes the argument for adhering to this custom:

"Quaintly, and very humanly, the chief business on Christmas Day on an old Southern plantation is not going to church. While the women naturally think religion should come first, they do not greatly demur when their husbands, brothers, and lovers, like the attractively boyish barbarians men always really are, decide to take to the woods."

Buckskin, buckshot, horses, clamoring hounds, echoing horns, blaring shotguns, and antlers and white tails flashing in the breeze gave the whole business an aura of religiosity and the appearance of a minor military campaign. "To ride up deer in the open woods," Flintlock confessed in *An American Hunter* (1937), "and to shoot them from horseback, sometimes when both the deer and the horse are running at full speed, is to prove that deer hunting has not completely degenerated."

Old Flintlock and his Dixie deerslayers took deer hunting seriously. If you have any doubts in this regard, consider the telling expressions Rutledge used in his writings. Bucks were not shot, killed, or harvested, they were "rolled." In a letter to his son Irvine, then a senior in college, Flintlock used the expression "to roll one" to mean bringing down a buck:

Forget life's triumphs and defeats,
Forget your Coleridge and your Keats;
Forget whatever you have *saw* —
Old Mercersburg and Old Nassau.
Forget your girl, but don't forget
Old Flintlock's going *to roll one* yet.
And if you think one is too few,
Old Flintlock's going to roll you *two.*
He's going upon a killing spree —
Old Flintlock's going to roll you *three!*

Flintlock received this reply from his son:

When red leaves fall in October days,
Tis then I change my peaceful ways.

To shoot and kill I'm all Hell bent
By heredity and environment.

To peace and love I'm fully blinded —
I'm full-capacity killer minded.

These Dixie deer hunting comrades loved antlers on the wall but they also shot venison for the pot. When Old Flintlock shot, the boys and their Negro companions joyously cried, "Put on the pot!" These legendary Hampton Hunts remind us of the deer hunting campaigns and expeditions of Philip Tome, Oliver Hazard Perry, Meshach Browning, and Judge Caton. Following in the tradition of these giants among deer hunters, Flintlock takes his place in the picturesque gallery of American deer hunters.

Christmas deer hunts at the Hampton Plantation ended at the barn, where the quarry was hung, skinned, and butchered by flickering lanterns and red-flaring lightwood torches. After the deerhounds received their portions, a hunting horn sounded and all the participants of the Hampton Hunt received their share of the venison. "With me deer hunting is a kind of religion," Flintlock writes in his essay "Blue's Buck," "and I have worshipped at this shrine ever since a grown oak was an acorn."

Flintlock did not know of any other sport that would whet the appetite more keenly than the sport of deer hunting. And no American writer ever more keenly expressed the ultimate excitement of a Christmas Day deer hunt in the South than Rutledge in this autobiographical excerpt from his book, *My Colonel and His Lady* (1937).

As we ride our mounts down the sandy road, we are on the lookout for deer tracks; and these are seen crossing and re-crossing the damp road. The hunters who have charge of the pack have to use all their powers of elocution to persuade the hounds not to make a break after certain hot trails. The horses seem to know and to enjoy this sport as well as the men and the dogs do. No horse can be started more quickly or stopped more abruptly than one trained to hunt in the woods.

We start a stag in the Crippled Oak Drive, and for miles we race him, now straight through the glimmering pinelands, sun-dappled and still, now through the eerie fringes of the Ocean, an inviolate sanctuary, made so by the riotous tangle of greenery; now he heads for the river, and we race down the broad road to cut him off. . . . There is a stretch of three miles, perfectly straight and level, broad, and lying a little high. Down this we course. But the crafty buck doubles and heads north-ward for the sparkleberry thickets of the plantation. I race forward to a certain stand, and just as I get there, he almost jumps over me! The dogs are far behind; and the stag gives the appearance of enjoying the race. Away he sails, his stiffly erect snowy tail flashing high above the bay bushes. I await the arrival of the dogs, and soon they come clamoring along. I slip from my horse and lead him into the bushes. I love to watch running hounds when they do not observe me. They always run with more native zest and sagacity when they are going it alone.

A rather common dog, of highly doubt-ful lineage, is in the lead. The aristocrats come last. I am always amused over the manner in which full-blooded hounds per-form the rite of trailing. This business is a religion with them. They do not bark, or do anything else so banal and bourgeois; they make deep-chested music, often paus-ing in the heat of a great race to throw their heads heavenward and vent toward the sky perfect music. Their running is never pell-mell. A good hound is a curious combination of the powers of genius: he is Sherlock Holmes in that he works out in-fallibly the mazy trail; he is Lord Ches-terfield in that he does all things in a man-ner becoming a gentleman; and he is a grand opera star, full of amazing music. I get a never-failing thrill out of listening to hounds and out of watching them at close hand. To me it appears that the music they make depends much upon their environ-ment for its timbre. And as they course over hills and dip into hollows, as they ramble through bosky water-courses or trail down roads, as the leafy canopies over them deepen or thin, their chorus hushes and swells, affording all the "notes with many a winding bout" that the best melody offers.

Our stalwart buck makes almost a com-plete circle, outwits us, enters the mysteri-ous depths of the Ocean, and is lost. But perhaps — at any rate, on Christmas Day — for us to lose his life is better than for him to have lost it. Yet his escape by no means ends our sport.

Their Christmas Day deer hunt would end in the dining room with antlered bucks from previous campaigns looking down from above on the candlelight dinner with its wild rice, brown sweet potatoes, roasted rice-fed mallards, and venison tenderloins fattened on acorns. At twilight, the boys would form a great semicircle before the fireplace to watch the giant yule log and to "rehunt" the chases of that day. The pres-ence of several of their deerhounds lying on the rug before the fireplace added sub-stance and reality to their tales. As the deer came out of their coverts again to roam the darkness of the plantation's woods and as the cold moon of December cast its silvery glamor over the Hampton Plantation, the echoes of the laughter and merriment of the Hampton hunters faded into the shadows of the past.

As the master of the Hampton Hunts, Flintlock remained an incurable optimist who always believed in the possibility of last chances. In his splendid essay "A Buck in the Rain," he wrote that "men who know deer nature best know that the element of chance is perhaps about as great in the pursuit of this superb game animal as it is in the following of any other game in the world."

Old Flintlock steadfastly maintained that each deer hunt should make sporting history, not create mystery with hunters giving faulty, elaborate reasons why missing that buck seemed altogether reasonable. No, Rutledge didn't care much for refined dissertations on how the buck successfully escaped into the eternal, inviolate sanctuary. Instead, he wanted to see the Old Boy fall to the forest floor with his last race run as if he had been struck by lightning. Then and then only could the hunter get that special thrill out of the possibility of wrenching success from failure at the last minute of the game. As a pragmatist, Flintlock wanted the buck on the meat pole, not a masterpiece in the way of a Great Excuse. In this regard, a primordial element of blood lust drove him until his dying day.

The object of the game for the Rutledge boys was to stick with the deer hunt until the black dark sky set in on the very last day of the season. Old Flintlock rightly believed that many deer hunters go home defeated because they stop too soon.

"So often has the very last chance afforded me the best luck that I have become almost superstitious about this business of last chances. . . . Faith, supersti-

tion, persistence—call it what you will; but I know that the luck of the last chance has often taken the empty cup of bitterness and disappointment and brimmed it with the wine of achievement. I can recall killing no fewer than sixteen bucks on last chances. . . . The actual shooting of them is usually a thing of the moment; the only question is whether you have patience to wait for the moment. Often, the last moment *is* the moment."

Such was the case with "Old Clubfoot," a mysterious buck, crippled, wiser than most buck hunters, gallant and seemingly immortal. Not even Joel Mayrant, a prominent buck hunter of the pinelands, could shoot this 300-pounder with the four-inch track. Rutledge and his boys hunted this particular buck for three years. They also managed to collect a set of his shed, freak antlers the year before the last chance came.

Most hunters could easily recognize Old Clubfoot because of his antlers. The bases of the beams were heavily encrusted with ivory and brown beading. His antlers were unique and atypical: The right antler, heavily palmated, pitched forward, while the left antler towered over the right and leaned curiously toward the rear. This buck ran with an unusual rocking gait due to an old injury. During his lifetime, this wise and seasoned strategist of the deer woods waved a mocking farewell to many a buck hunter, including Archibald Rutledge.

His downfall came one morning when Rutledge had to leave Hampton early to return to the Mercersburg Academy in the mountains of Pennsylvania, where he taught English for thirty-three years. Believing in last chances, Flintlock and his boys arose early that morning and left for the big wooded pasture east of the house; they were dressed in their traveling clothes to get in one last hunt. The morning broke clear, warm, and still. Traveling to the wooded pasture, Flintlock wondered to himself why a reasonable man would leave the South in midwinter and travel northward into the blizzards of Pennsylvania to teach English at a boy's academy. While leaning against a pine tree and enjoying the sunshine, Flintlock suddenly saw a superb buck take flight.

"From the moment I first saw him I knew not only that he was a deer of remarkable size and beauty, but also that he was an ancient acquaintance of mine. Identification was made immediately possible by his freak antlers."

After an abrupt takeoff, Old Clubfoot stopped in an old logging road about 130 yards away—clearly out of range for Flintlock's "Annie Oakley." The buck next made a splendid leap away from the startled hunter. The whole affair seemed over; the last chance was gone. Watching Old Clubfoot's rapid departure, Flintlock seemed ready to take, as he admits, "a long pull from the flask of saints' delight and call the business off." But as Flintlock always told his boys, you can often count on the unexpected to happen. Suddenly, and most unexpectedly, Old Clubfoot made a sharp slant to the right and came running toward the hunter full bore.

"Out of the corner of my left eye I saw the stag coming like a Barnegat breaker. He was going to give me a fair chance. I started breathing hard, as you may well believe. I steadied myself as best I could, and as the splendid old fugitive sailed by broadside I let him have the choke barrel. I saw him flinch—a sure sign that he had been struck. But he went on without apparent effort, and a myrtle thicket swallowed him, horns and all.

"Within half a mile, stretched beneath one of the pines under which I doubt not, he had often roamed, lay the rugged old veteran, his last race over. He had been struck by nine buckshot."

This victory in the last moments of the deer season inspired the triumphant return to the plantation. Old Clubfoot's strange rack looked down at Flintlock from the walls of his den for many years as a fine reminder of the possibilities of last chances; that the great chance does in fact come to the faithful, that the buck hunter's insane faith often results in the greatest reward.

Like most serious students of whitetailed deer behavior, Rutledge knew that no one really knows white-tailed deer unless he studies them after dark, especially under a full moon. So Flintlock built himself a large platform sixteen feet up in the forks of an oak tree, overlooking a heavily used deer crossing. In this deer stand in the oak, Flintlock spent countless hours studying and watching the secret lives of white-tailed deer under moonlight. He did this during October, November, and December and quickly learned of the great difficulty involved in watching whitetails in the moonlight, for they are sometimes visible and then vanish as quickly as you see them. In his book *Home By The River* (1941), he describes the excitement of discerning the shadowy outlines of two whitetailed bucks under the moonlight.

"I have a long wait, but who will not wait amid deepening peace and increasing loveliness? At last they come: two fairy shapes, silent, elusive, beautiful. The mild night air is drifting from them to me, so that they do not detect my presence. Here are two great silver stags with silver horns, moving with unpostured grace through a silvery world. They pause, as if posing for an urgent picture. Nearer they come, and I notice that at certain angles in the moonlight they are almost invisible; at others they are vividly visible. Past me they glide like spirits of the wilderness, having all the meaning connoted by the night, by stillness, and by the unwearied charm of nature. Into the silver silences they vanish."

While George Shiras III, a friend and a contemporary of Flintlock's and the founder of deer photography, captured the magnificent radiance of white-tailed deer in the moonlight in his award-winning photos, Flintlock immortalized the animal in the moonlight in his great nature essay "My Friend the Deer," first published in *The New Country Life* in May 1918.

No other creature of the forest seems more a shape of the moonlight than does the deer. It is apparently possible for the largest buck to move through the dense bushes and over beds of dry twigs with no perceptible sound. A movement rather than a sound off to my left had attracted my attention; another glance showed me the glint of horns. A full grown stag was in the act of jumping a pile of fallen logs. He literally floated over the obstruction, ghostlike, uncanny. I noticed that he jumped with his tail down—a thing he would not do if he were startled. Behind him were two does. They negotiated the barrier still more lithely than the buck had done. . . . All three of them were feeding; but at no one time did all of them have their heads down at the same moment. One always seemed to be on watch, and this one was usually the buck. For a few seconds at a time his proud head would be bowed among the bushes; then it would be lifted with a jerk, and for minutes he would stand champing restlessly his mouthful of leaves, grass, and tender twigs. Often he would hold his head at peculiar angles—often thrust forward—as if drinking in all the scents of the dewy night woods. After a while, moving in silence and in concert, the shadowy creatures came up on the space of white sand which stretched away in front of me. Now they paused, spectral in the moonlight, now moved about with indescribably lithe grace, never losing, even amid the 'secure

delight' of such a time and place, their air of superb readiness, of elfin caution, suppressed but instantly available. The steps they took seemed to me extraordinarily long; and it was difficult to keep one of the creatures in sight all the while. They would appear and reappear; and their color and the distinctness of their outlines depended on the angle at which they were seen. Broadside, they looked almost black; head-on, they were hardly visible. At no time could I distinguish their legs. When they moved off into the pine thicket, whither I knew they had gone to eat mushrooms, they vanished without sound, apparently without exerted motion, and I was left alone in the moonlight.

Flintlock killed many white-tailed bucks in his long life, but his most thrilling deer hunt occurred in December of 1942, when he decided to drive Wambaw Corner, a famous hangout for bucks. While sitting on a pine stump at a deer stand called Dogwood Hill, Flintlock had a premonition that something unique would happen on this drive, and it did. As the drivers neared the end, he suddenly heard twigs breaking and the sound of deer hooves. Then he saw tall tines rising and falling before him. A buck of gigantic proportions came running straight for him and abruptly stopped, almost wedging itself between two pines fifty-five yards in front of the startled hunter. At the blast of Flintlock's Parker the buck reared straight up and then fell backward. Four buckshot struck the deer.

Flintlock stood in awe when he came up on the dead buck lying at the foot of a huge cypress. The buck carried thirteen symmetrical tines; seven on one side and six on the other. Some of the tines reached eighteen inches in length with a basal circumference of five inches. The antlers exhibited a beautiful chestnut color, with heavy beading and a twenty-five inch inside spread. The buck weighed 287 pounds; Flintlock never shot a better one.

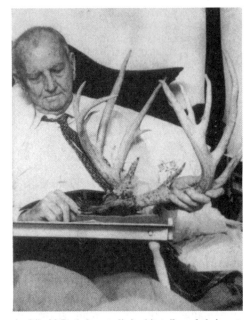

Archibald Rutledge studied whitetails and their antlers for more than seventy-eight years. Here he examines one of his best racks, a 13-pointer that he shot in December 1942.

He called the buck "Flora's Buck," since his daughter-in-law, Flora, had missed the same buck on the same drive two weeks earlier.

Who of Rutledge's readers will ever forget the strategic and dramatic tactics of the Jasper Hill Buck that charged straight into four guns, eleven deerhounds, and four drivers mounted on horses. At first glance it looked as if the buck were hunting the hunters. Flintlock describes the wild scenario for us in his essay, "That Hunt at Jasper Hill."

"The buck, seeing the hounds but apparently not aware of us, lowered his head and charged straight through the whole pack of waiting dogs. And they were so amazed that they dodged, skulked, and ran. We, too, made way. Here then, was the singular spectacle of a stag scattering dogs and men before him.

"In a moment the stag had passed us, entering a pine thicket beyond the road. As he was vanishing, four guns blared out, giving him a special salute of honor of eight barrels, speeding after his broad white tail about a hundred and fifty buckshot. I saw the tops of several little pines jump off. But so did the deer. As far as I could see, he was heading for the tangled wilds of Jasper Hill, and for freedom."

One-half mile from where the four gunners poured two barrels of buckshot apiece at the old boy, the Hampton Hunters found the great Jasper Hill Buck stretched out on the forest floor with only two buckshot out of the 150 fired at him, but dead nonetheless. While deer hunters might forget the name of the church in which they were married, they never forget the most minute details of the shooting of each and every buck.

Old Flintlock and his Dixie deerslayers loved to reminisce about the splendid, grandiose strategy and the "shadowy subterfuge," as Rutledge called it, of the famous 12-point Blackhorn Buck. This whitetail, like the Jasper Hill Buck, had a pronounced tendency to do the unexpected, to charge the shouting drivers and clamoring hounds shortly before the drive would end regardless of the manpower involved. When the Blackhorn Buck decided to ram Rutledge's boys one day in early October, not even five men, nine hounds, and three horses could turn the wild fugitive back. "He never changed his direction," Flintlock reported, "never altered his stride. He won his safety by as bold and gallant a maneuver as the greenwood ever saw. There was about it a superb uncertainty, —wayward, sagacious, and splendid."

Rutledge estimated the inside spread of this buck at two feet. While the antlers of most white-tailed bucks take on a chestnut, gray, or ivory color, this buck's antlers were ebony, almost like those of a water-buck or an ibex. Flintlock took a special interest in this unique buck, the life of which he soon came to view as one prolonged series of masterful stratagems.

The fame of this buck, not surprisingly, spread dramatically and deeply stirred the imagination of the Hampton Hunters. Many deer hunters saw this buck and shot at him; but the buck with the ebony antlers lived on into old age. Flintlock never killed this buck and perhaps, deep within his innermost being, he never wanted to, as we learn in reading his essay "The Blackhorn Buck," for which he very nearly was awarded the Nobel Prize for literature.

"Whenever a hunting season passes without proving disastrous to him, I rejoice that his magnificent ebony crown is not drying out at some taxidermist's, but is thrusting aside dewy pine boughs in the moonlight or, deep in a fragrant bed of ferns and sweet-bay, is affording the shy moonbeams something really mystic on which to sparkle."

In Flintlock's many years of deer hunting, this buck stood out as having no equal. On numerous occasions Flintlock thought he had this buck helplessly cornered, only to learn that no one ever corners a white-tailed buck, not even Archibald Rutledge. While Rutledge studied the forest around the Hampton Plantation for a half-century, he admitted that this buck knew the terrain far better and more intimately than he. In his heart, Flintlock was often on the side of this master tactician. Of this buck, Flintlock once remarked, "When you get in antlers craggy massiveness, a twenty-three-inch spread and twelve points—Man, what more do you want?"

Flintlock's curious and never-failing fascination with antlers lasted throughout his life. Becoming one of the first antler collectors in this country, his collection consisted of more than 300 sets, most taken from his own plantation, some dating back almost 100 years. One 26-pointer sported a twenty-eight-inch spread. When he heard of an unusual rack in his area, he would travel miles to see it. He traveled all over the country, visiting museums of natural history to view famous bucks. He not only collected sheds, but studied in detail the Boone and Crockett record books of his time as well as Roland Ward's *Records of Big Game*. In short, he liked to "tamper with kingly crowns," as he put it in his inimitable way. One wonders what Old Flintlock would think of the current antler mania in this country, of the thousands of trophy bucks that decorate the deer classics of our time. (He would probably be both thrilled and appalled; thrilled by the massive heads, appalled by the crass commercialization.)

Rutledge greatly admired the famous Strohecker Buck, which he often referred to in his writings and in conversations with old backwoods buck hunters. Killed in the High Valley of Centre County, Pennsylvania, in 1886 by Samuel Strohecker, Rutledge considered this 26-pointer to be the most beautiful and magnificent buck of his time. His friend, Colonel Henry Shoemaker, an authority on Pennsylvania deer, characterized the beauty and the mental image of that buck:

"The length of the longest antler on the Strohecker head was thirty-one inches. It was twenty-one inches at its widest point, sixteen inches from tip to tip; the circumference taken above the brow point was five and half inches. The buck carried fifteen points on the right, eleven on the left. The sweep of the antlers was graceful in the extreme, they were still not top-heavy, and the excess points on the right antler were not large and did not detract from the harmonious effect of the whole.

The antlers were of a rich chestnut brown in color, ivory at the tips, and very sharp. The beading was uniform, and the head singularly free from rudimentary points. The expression of the head was most strikingly lifelike."

For buck hunters interested in shooting bucks of this stature, Flintlock offers short and simple advice:

"Always be willing to go the second mile and to do the hard thing; don't quit and take the backtrack to camp. Punish yourself a little; use more strength from your body and more patience from your mind and more cool-headed determination from your brain than you have ever used before. You are playing a hard man's game against no mean antagonist; and you need all you have to play it right. The greatest deer hunters have always been second milers; men of tireless energy and infinite patience; men who would follow a trail all day, and who would, when the game was close, do the serpent act over a rocky hillside for the distance, however great, that would bring them within shooting range." In short, when it came to deer hunting, Rutledge believed in the full-scale application of what Teddy Roosevelt called the strenuous life.

During his lifetime, and unlike most deer hunters, Flintlock observed thousands of deer in the wild; he once estimated the number at about 7000. But like most deer hunters, he never got over the amazing appearance of them. There was always something new, special, and dramatic about the appearance of each one of them. After seventy-eight years of hunting and watching deer, he came to view the life of the whitetail as one long, strategic maneuver. "Successfully stalking one of these heavy-shod, burly-horned, seasoned old strategists," Flintlock writes in "Stalking Your Buck," "is a woodland victory of the

It's the buck with the wide-branching horns! *Mike Biggs photo*

first order. . . . No other creature so large lives so silently, so secretively and so self-effacingly."

Following his death in 1973, *The New York Times* reported that after spending more than a half century in the deer woods in pursuit of whitetails, Flintlock still managed to find time to write eighty books and accept twenty honorary degrees and thirty gold metals for his literary efforts. He missed winning the Nobel Prize for literature by one vote to another diehard buck hunter from the South named William Faulkner.

Bucks with wide-branched antlers, whether hunted during the daytime or studied in the beauty of the moonlight, haunted Old Flintlock's dreams, as we learn from the last stanza of "Hunter's Choice."

It's the buck with the wide-branching horns!
His beauty the wildwood adorns,
His wonder the wildwood adorns.
He is haunting my dreams
Of the mountains and streams,
My evenings, my nights, and my morns,
The buck with the wide-branching horns!

His countless articles and books on white-tailed deer and deer hunting stand as precious possessions and vast warehouses of natural lore that time will never diminish in appeal.

As long as the American deer hunter stalks the old, noble buck in the forests of fall, the deer and deer hunting tales of Old Flintlock based on the famous Hampton Hunts, illustrated with the sporting art of Lynn Bogue Hunt, and highlighted with the great deer photos of George Shiras III, will live forever. We will always remember Archibald Rutledge as the most eloquent chronicler of American white-tailed deer hunting, as a master huntsman-narrator, as the deer hunter's buck hunter—the storyteller of buck hunting tales par excellence. I have met many incurable buck hunters in my life, but none with the flair and religious enthusiasm of Archibald Rutledge; he lived and breathed deer and deer hunting

White-tailed deer, whom Rutledge fondly referred to as "the masterminds of the wildwoods," also owe Flintlock a considerable debt, for no one better expresses the real meaning and the ultimate value of this animal for American cultural history. Every deer he saw left him with a sense of awe; in the presence of every white-tailed buck, Flintlock perceived America in prehistoric times, and he captured that view best of all in his poem "The Stag." His lines stand as a singular tribute to the animal he loved, revered, and immortalized.

Today in the wild pinelands a stag I saw,
A noble buck in the lone pinelands today.
I was walking upwind. At the end of a swampy draw,
Bounding from his bed of ferns, he fled away.
It was not for long I saw him, but long enough
To see his lithe and powerful grace, to mark
His craggy antlers, beaded and brown and rough,
And his flag that glimmered white through the forest dark.

It was more than a deer I saw in the wildwood green,
And the presence of him filled me with awe; for I,
In that shaggy, proud, primeval stag had seen
America under a prehistoric sky;
A tawny sleeping empire, boundless, blest,
Before Columbus dreamed there was a West.

Chapter 2

A Woman Buck Hunter

The deerskin rug on our study floor, the buck's head over the fireplace, what are these after all but the keys which have unlocked enchanted doors, and granted us not only health and vigor, but a fresh and fairer vision of existence.

—Paul Brandreth, *Trails of Enchantment,* 1930

In 1930, publisher G. Howard Watt of New York published a unique book on deer and deer hunting titled *Trails of Enchantment.* In the introduction to the book, naturalist and explorer Roy Chapman Andrews noted that Brandreth knew the white-tailed deer as few hunters know any game animal. He ranked the book as a standard contribution to the natural history of the animal.

I recall our enchantment when the managing editor of the *Deer & Deer Hunting* magazine and I first encountered this blue-chip deer book in the early 1980s, fifty years after its publication, and how we read, re-read, and cherished the great one-liners found therein. I also recall my surprise, when, after a great deal of deep-digging research, I learned that Paul Brandreth was the pen name for Paulina B. Brandreth (1885–1946), a buckskin-clad deer hunter from the Adirondacks who not only loved to shoot big bucks with such noted deer hunters as Roy Chapman Andrews, General Pershing, and famed Adirondack guide Reuben Cary, but who loved to photograph deer, illustrate them for her own writings, and tramp the deer-yards at every opportunity to observe and study them in every detail.

As a naturalist and conservationist, Brandreth was a woman way ahead of her time. By the age of nine, she had already published articles on whitetails and wolves in 1894 issues of Charles Hallock's *Forest and Stream,* the most prestigious sports-men's journal of its time. Editor Hallock listed her material as coming from Camp Good Enough, Brandreth Lake, and considered her to be "one of the most skillful of the *Forest and Stream* family of hunter naturalists."

Brandreth and her deer hunting cronies. *Left to right on top of the buckboard:* **Reuben Cary, Frank Cary, Mary McAlpine, and Barbara McAlpine. Paulina is standing against the buckboard with her cherished 40/65. Kempton Adams and Adam Lafoy kneel beside her.**

Although a good number of women hunted deer at the turn of the century and although the early issues of various outdoor magazines such as *Forest and Stream, Outing,* and *The American Field* offered stories about or by these modern Dianas, Brandreth remained isolated in this male-dominated recreational activity. Not wanting to be an outsider, she chose to write with the pseudonym of Paul Brandreth, which undoubtedly facilitated the publication of her byline. Of the more than 800 books written on the subject of deer and deer hunting, only five are written by women. Not only is *Trails of Enchantment* the best of this group, but it reigns supreme as perhaps one of the best books ever written on the subject of white-tailed deer and deer hunting. As usual the book, like the other classics, remains out of print. List number forty-eight of Dutchman Books dated January, 1990 advertises the book for $48.

Brandreth was born in Ossining, New York, in 1886. In 1851 her grandfather, Dr. Benjamin Brandreth, a wealthy pharmaceutical manufacturer, bought Township 39 in the Town of Long Lake, Hamilton County, in the heart of the Adirondacks, for the exclusive purposes of fishing and hunting. It consisted of 26,000 acres, for which he paid fifteen cents an acre. The area became known as the Brandreth Tract, and contained Brandreth Lake. As lumber operations prospered in the area, the deer population responded and eventually exploded. Within this well-known deer hunting mecca, the young buck hunter came of age while hunting with her father, Colonel Franklin Brandreth, and two prominent Adirondack deer guides: Wallace Emerson and Reuben Cary.

At her father's hunting lodge at Brandreth Lake she read the deer and deer hunting tales of Meshach Browning, Philip Tome, T. S. Van Dyke, Judge Caton, and Archibald Rutledge. Antlered bucks graced the walls of the lodge, as did the classic deer photos of George Shiras III and the deer and deer hunting paintings of A. F. Tait, Winslow Homer, and Sir Edwin Landseer.

Like T. S. Van Dyke and William Monypeny Newsom, two of her contemporaries, Brandreth preferred to still-hunt whitetailed bucks. "Personally, I would rather a thousand times tramp the woods and get a buck that way than freeze on a deer stand, or sit near a runway. Driven deer are usually traveling fast, and running shots are the rule, thereby greatly increasing the risk of wounding and losing an animal. Sometimes, however, a specimen killed in this fashion looks as though it had been bombarded with a machine gun!" Brandreth compared deer drives and stand hunting to catching speckled trout with bait; she clearly preferred flyfishing and still-hunting and did both with a great deal of style, energy, and enthusiasm. Outwitting and overcoming a white-tailed buck's tactics of escape gave her the ultimate satisfaction of beating them at their own game. She admiringly viewed the white-tailed buck as "a shadow lurking in a shadow." Like all diehard still-hunters, she loved the elements of expectancy and uncertainty that still-hunting whitetails affords.

No one ever better defined the true art of still-hunting than Paulina Brandreth in her *Trails of Enchantment*.

"There is a charm about still-hunting that no method of circumventing the wiles of the whitetail can compete with. It re-quires patience, skill, forethought, good judgment, and often a sort of subtle intuition that brings into play the ancestral hunter that is in you. It is an active red-blooded game with the odds greatly in favor of the hunted. Time and again you will suffer disappointment, or be done out of a good shot by some infinitesimal slip, or lack of proper foresight. Yet, the difficulties encountered—an ill-chosen gust of wind, a branch cracked underfoot, a trail on freshly fallen snow lost in a maze of other tracks—only serve to increase your energies and add fuel to your enthusiasm. And sooner or later, the desired opportunity will present itself and another ten- or twelve-pointer be added to your collection."

Under the expert tutelage of Reuben Cary or "Rube," as she called him, Brandreth learned the business of still-hunting trophy bucks as she followed in the footsteps of this tall, picturesque figure with the silvery beard and penetrating blue eyes. Of this memorable guide, Brandreth wrote as follows in her hunting journal. "Unhurried and tranquil, full of dry humor and witty sarcasm, his personality and companionship form an indispensable part of our trips."

On one of her more memorable still-hunting trips with old Rube, Brandreth came across the track of a good-sized buck along a ridge that overlooked North Pond. Although somewhat discouraged as a result of a long day's still-hunt coming to an end, the size of the track seemed to put new life in the two weary hunters. Like Old Flintlock, both Rube and Brandreth believed in the possibilities of last chances.

"Never cuss yer luck till yer git home," Rube remarked.

The wisdom of that remark soon became reality. As the hunters reached the top of the ridge, Rube suddenly stiffened and stood still, gazing ahead for a patch of gray, the flicker of a white tail, or the glimmer of an antler. "The buck is here somewhere," Rube insisted. Brandreth explains what happened:

"Suddenly we glimpsed a mighty set of horns as the buck burst cover and fled up the ridge. He did not bound, but seemed to slip like a shadow over the ground, his head carried low, his great dusky antlers laid back on his shoulders. Twice we obtained a fair view of him, and twice I tried to get a shot, but each time with almost uncanny precision, he managed to put a barrier of lopped tree tops between us. The thing happened so quickly that we just stood there and looked at each other."

Refusing to accept defeat, Rube and Brandreth ran down into the valley in an attempt to get the wind in their favor. In her book, she describes the taking of this trophy buck.

With his keen eyes covering the woods ahead, Rube fell into a swinging gait. There was no chance for any pussy-footing or cautious still-hunting. It was getting dark too fast. Coming to a skid trail which led down the hill, he followed it a short distance, and then striking a logging road, turned to the left again. Just at that moment I caught the outline of a deer moving at a walk down the ridge in our direction.

The next few seconds were crammed with excitement. Looking back on the experience, it seems always to assume more and more, an element of the ridiculous. Certainly it proves like many other incidents, that the game of hunting is more often than anything else a game of chance. Here were we, the hunters, being literally hunted by the deer which a short time previous we believed had given us the slip. In other words, we had been whisked around within fifteen minutes from the extreme of bad to the extreme of good luck.

Side by side, we knelt in the snow, waiting for the buck to appear from behind the intervening trunk of a big birch. The suspense was harrowing. And then at last he loomed suddenly before us.

Enough of daylight still remained for us to see him in detail, and certainly he was a magnificent creature. He came at a swinging walk, his head lowered, his nose close to the ground. There was something almost formidable in his appearance, and I believe that, not having winded us the first time he was scared out, he had gotten the idea that another buck was in his area, and was therefore returning to administer a sound thrashing to the intruder.

I have seen a number of large heads during the years I have spent in the Adirondack woods, but the head of this buck overshadowed all the others. The horns were so massive they made the animal look top-heavy. As he came towards us, he swung them from side to side with a motion similar to that of a belligerent bull.

When he had passed a few feet beyond the birch, I gave a loud whistle. Instantly he froze into rigid suspicion, and threw up his head. He stood facing us, slightly quartering and offered a deadly shot. At the crack of my rifle he plunged forward in his tracks, struggled a few paces, and just as Rube fired a second shot, rolled over stone dead.

The buck carried thirteen tines, several of which were heavily palmated. The blunt tips of the tines suggested that the old warrior had done a good deal of rubbing and thrashing. The buck weighed 245 pounds dressed.

When Roy Chapman Andrews examined the buck as a possible addition to the American Museum of Natural History's collection, he concluded that the buck had the largest and heaviest antlers of any whitetail that he ever observed. All of the deer on display at the Museum of Natural History at that time were shot by Andrews on the Brandreth Tract. The backgrounds for the whitetail displays were made by Brandreth's brother Courtenay, a well-known bird painter and ornithologist.

Brandreth and Rube generally breakfasted under the stars and traveled from sunup to sundown. During deer season, they roamed for miles each day in the vast and picturesque wilderness of the Adirondacks. "Being young and enthusiastic," she confessed, "I wanted to eat up the miles, and eat them up we did in spite of Rube's argument against such overstrenuous methods." In their travels they found many unique places that they put a stamp of ownership on by constructing special deer hunting camps. One of her cherished camps was located near a sheet of water called Panther Pond.

Its unique character never faded from her mind. She described it in *Trails of Enchantment.*

> In shape it resembled a large Indian tepee. Great rolls of spruce bark had been ingeniously wrapped around a framework of poles, and a wide opening in front faced the fireplace. In many ways it was warmer and more comfortable than a lean-to. Inside three people could sleep without crowding on the thick fragrant mat of balsam boughs.
>
> The tepee stood on a knoll sown thick with big balsams. They were not the kind that snapped off easily in a windstorm, but were trees of antiquity, and their aromatic spires towered high above the camp. On the south side of the knoll at the bottom of a shallow ravine coursed a clear spring-fed brook, which emptied and lost itself a little farther on in the heart of a dense black spruce swamp. Beyond this swamp a spacious beaver meadow reached to the brink of Panther Pond and extended for almost the entire length of its easterly shore.

While still-hunting at Panther Pond early one morning during the 1912 deer season, the year New York initiated its controversial Buck Law, a law prohibiting the shooting of antlerless deer, Brandreth and her guide encountered a 10-pointer standing broadside and motionless as a statue in the misty sunrise, with his head partially hidden behind a small spruce tree. She knelt on the ground and placed the bead of her old model 40/65 Winchester repeater on the buck's fore shoulder and pulled the trigger. When the smoke cleared, she saw the buck standing exactly in the same place.

"You didn't touch him," groaned Rube. "Shoot again!"

As the buck dashed off, she fired three more shots in rapid succession. At the last report the buck veered to the right and vanished into a vast array of alders.

The blood trail that they quickly found led up through a steep slope of spruces. Halfway to the top, the blood trail sharply swung off at a right angle. Following the sharp turn in the trail, Rube stepped forward, shouldered his rifle, and fired the final killing shot. Behind the roots of a fallen spruce lay a trophy 10-pointer.

"Let's see where you hit him," he said to her.

"I held for his shoulder on those shots," she insisted.

When they turned the buck over, they "found a bullet hole in a place that makes even a tyro blush with shame," Brandreth admitted.

"Held for the shoulder and shot the buck through the ham," the old guide remarked in a frowning and unsympathetic manner.

"The mist and the fog did me in," she quickly exclaimed.

Brandreth later admitted that human nature often provides us with a theory about how we should handle such a situation. That theory, in Brandreth's own inimitable style, goes like this: "The best thing to do if you make a fluke shot, when without doubt you should have made a good one, is to retire discreetly into the profundities of silence, and blame the con-

Reuben Cary, an Adirondack deer guide, is pictured with Brandreth's best buck, a 13-pointer weighing 245 pounds dressed.

ditions—blame anything so long as it eases your conscience."

But Brandreth never took the problem of wounded deer lightly. As a matter of fact, this pioneer woman deer hunter represents the conscience of our sport with regard to clean kills and the problem of losing deer. Who will ever forget this one-liner that originally appeared in an article titled "Clean Kills" in *Forest and Stream* in November 1928?

"If you are of the right stamp you will take pains to learn where the vital spots are located on a deer's anatomy, instead of blazing away helter-skelter, and maiming several individuals before you happen, through a stroke of graceless luck, to knock one over."

Experienced deer hunters with humanitarian interests, Brandreth insisted, don't take chances. They don't shoot at deer unless the deer is in the right position. They don't shoot at deer standing in thick cover. They don't take excessively long-range shots. And they don't shoot at running deer. In other words, experienced hunters use sound judgment and prefer to let a buck pass rather than to run the risk of wounding him. Brandreth cherished the idea of getting a trophy buck with one clean shot. She attributed the high wounding rates to bad judgment, ignorance, and poor marksmanship.

Brandreth knew that a wounded buck will resort to every known subterfuge to throw the hunter from his trail: He will backtrack, circle windfalls, hide, and take the hunter through a maze of sapling undergrowth. She gave little credence to the theory that wounded deer always run with their tails down. She saw some wounded deer with flags flying while other wounded bucks bolted like rabbits with their tails down.

Her advice for solving the problem of losing deer is simple: "Learn to shoot and where to shoot and avoid taking chances. . . . Still-hunting is a clean, vigorous sport, and it could be made still cleaner if every one who practiced it made a principle of cultivating judgment and control and eliminating carelessness in the trailing of a wounded deer, and too hasty decision over the matter of a possible miss. A person with the proper sporting spirit should prefer to leave the woods without his trophy rather than make a mess of things by putting in shots where they don't belong."

Later in life, with her still-hunts at Panther Pond but a memory, she bemoaned the fact that the tepee at Panther Pond gradually moldered away beneath winter snows, but Panther Pond, she believed, would always be a favored haunt of the whitetail, and the stars above it would never be commercialized.

For more than twenty years, Brandreth hunted bucks in another fascinating place called Cathedral Meadow, an old beaver meadow consisting of 600 acres of swampland filled with lush aquatic food. Deer in this area attained a size that was larger than other whitetails within a radius of several miles. Not only were the bucks in this area larger in weight and antler mass, but they also had a wider range of color variation. Bucks—especially older bucks—in Cathedral Meadow displayed a distinct tendency to stick to the thickest part of the swamp and feed chiefly after shooting hours. This desolate place gave Bran-

dreth and her campmates a sense of utter detachment and afforded them a truly challenging prospect for still-hunting whitetails.

At Cathedral Meadow, Brandreth and her friends constructed a small, picturesque log cabin. When covered with snow, its high pitched roof made the cabin look like a miniature cathedral. Even when deer season was closed, Brandreth and her hunting partners would snowshoe to Cathedral Meadow to cook venison tenderloins at the little camp half buried in snowdrifts and enjoy the magnificent scenery of the rugged Adirondacks.

At this cherished deer camp, Brandreth would hold forth on shooting bucks in the magic area of the swamp. And a magic area it was. In an essay titled "Bucks of Cathedral Meadow," she characterized the setting. "The skeleton figures of dead trees have toppled over decayed and formed a rich seed bed for semi-aquatic plants. Black spruce, tamarack, balsam, and clumps of alders have replaced the original stand of mixed timber. There are blueberry bushes and sweet-scented grasses. You walk on cushions of sphagnum and reindeer moss, conscious of dense aromatic shade or the delicious warmth of the sun. What was once a scene of devastation has become transfigured into one of exquisite beauty and enthrallment."

To the west of her camp was a hardwood promontory that extended into the meadow. Bucks traveled along well-worn runways on this hardwood promontory. These runways led from protective haunts to the timbered flats where the deer searched for acorns and beechnuts. Brandreth spent many days of her life stillhunting whitetails along this hardwood promontory. One November morning, just at daylight, Brandreth and Curt Hall, a guide at Brandreth Lake, left camp for a hunt on the promontory. Rain had fallen the night before. As they walked along in a drizzle, Curt suddenly stopped.

"I smell a buck," he whispered, as a strong musky odor of the rut greeted his nose.

As they stood there in the rain-drenched forest, they had a fleeting glance at a magnificent rack in motion. They heard a crash and a sharp snort, and caught a glimpse of a white flag. The sudden realization that this buck had been quietly studying them as they walked along the old logging road seemed like a hard pill to swallow. Yet Brandreth readily admitted that for every buck killed at Cathedral Meadow, four evaded her.

"The swamp whitetails are seldom or never caught napping. They are wilder than any deer I have ever hunted. Suspicious, skulking, constantly testing the wind, they venture out from the dense sanctuary of the meadow only when conditions seem to preclude danger. If they see you first, the game is up. They never wait. Curiosity does not appear to be one of their failings; and, of course, this adds greatly to the sport and fascination of the chase."

Brandreth believed that whitetails exercise a highly developed telepathic instinct: They will stand motionless for a great length of time if they feel they are not seen, regardless of how close you are to them. They seem to know when you do not see them, and instantly know when you do — at which point they immediately take flight. Even when you look straight at them but do not see them, they seem aware of this fact and will not move. The instant you see them, they're gone!

She and Curt worked a level hardwood stretch of the promontory for several hours and jumped only one doe. Two days remained of the open season, and they both wanted one of those Cathedral Meadow bucks. The rain gradually turned to sleet

and the heavy, northwest wind made the prospects of success far from encouraging.

But as is so often the case in the game of still-hunting, the unexpected suddenly occurred. Through the driving sleet Brandreth saw a huge set of antlers, then the vague outline of the deer's body. She fired her 40/65 at the buck bedded not more than sixty yards ahead but never cut a hair. With the wind in his face, the buck stook up, looking in the opposite direction. As he began to move broadside, she fired a second shot. The buck jumped and disappeared over a rise. Fifty yards ahead, she found the buck lying dead at the bottom of a deep depression.

"Well, there's a head worth workin' for," Curt remarked as he examined the 8-pointer.

Was it worth working for, this pioneer of the mythical minority of women who hunt asks. "Yes, that's the way I have always felt about Cathedral Meadow bucks. They're worth working for. Moreover, of all places I have ever hunted, the promontory leading to this magic area of swamp holds the greatest charm."

Still-hunting white-tailed bucks in Cathedral Meadow in 1927 entailed a great deal of hard work, for after studying the deer population on the Brandreth Tract intensely, Townsend and Smith in their classic study, *The White-tailed Deer of the Adirondacks* (1933), conclude that the population only approximated five deer per square mile.

All deer hunters have their special places in deer country despite the number of deer per square mile. Cathedral Meadow in the heart of the Adirondacks captivated Paulina Brandreth and all who hunted with her.

Like her Dixieland contemporary Archibald Rutledge, Brandreth readily acknowledged that deer hunting success in any given year is largely due to luck. Actually, scientists view the role of luck as a major part of deer hunting success in any given year. After reading countless accounts of the demise of trophy white-tailed bucks, I am of the opinion that 50 percent of all trophy bucks killed during the gun season are killed as a result of what Brandreth calls "a stroke of graceless luck." Throughout her life, she insisted that you grasp more opportunities than you make. In other words, the candid rifle hunter will admit that the trophies he works the hardest for are the very ones he never gets; that good luck is frequently the greater value in the chase of white-tailed bucks than a detailed, thoughtfully planned-out campaign.

"You may be the best kind of a hunter," she writes in *Trails of Enchantment,* "practiced, careful and an excellent shot, but if luck shuns you entirely, as it sometimes does, you will certainly fail where another less experienced will succeed. Luck may mean a number of things but primarily I should say it means a well-timed coordination of your own movements, and· those of the animal you are hunting."

Brandreth cites a memorable buck hunt with General Pershing, a frequent visitor at the Brandreth camp, as an illustration of being in the right place at the right time. The night before the hunt, they retired to the "shop" to discuss strategy and select the territory to be hunted. They decided to start at the "flow," a body of water loggers used as a storage ground for pulpwood. From there they would still-hunt the old railroad track.

The morning of the hunt dawned clear, calm, and cold. For breakfast they ate broiled venison and pancakes. From Brandreth Lake they followed the trail to North Pond, which they crossed with a guide boat. After landing at the mouth of the inlet they took up the trail to the "flow," and arrived at the old railroad track. Several hours of still-hunting passed with neither a sign nor sound of a white-tailed buck.

"But had we only known it," Brandreth tells us, "the gods of good luck were at that very moment preparing for us in their inscrutable way a most enlivening little drama."

The drama began to unfold when Ivan Stanton, a caretaker and guide at Brandreth Lake, came across a very large buck track and a freshly rubbed sapling, still green in color. Ivan decided to take the track, with Brandreth and the General cautiously still-hunting along both sides of the tracker. It soon became impossible to continue to follow the track.

Several hundred yards beyond where Ivan lost the track, they topped a low hillock. While standing still and facing into the wind, they heard a loud crashing in the brush in front of them and the thud of bounding hooves. Shouldering his rifle, the General tried to get a shot at the buck—which had a splendid set of antlers—but couldn't since the big deer ran low to the ground through a tangle of brush and thick briar bushes. As luck would have it, the buck suddenly landed on a little knoll and presented a standing broadside shot. The General's Winchester echoed throughout the woods as the 10-pointer toppled to the ground, against an old log.

All three hunters remained uncertain about what had caused the buck to stir in the first place, since the hunters could have easily gone around the animal without seeing him, much less did they know why he stopped on the knoll and looked in the opposite direction. No one ever will know.

Brandreth came to this conclusion with regard to the incident: "Luck in the hunt-

ing field is as variable as the winds of
heaven. Some years it will be your constant
companion, again it will pass you by, until
you commence to feel as though you were
haunted by malevolent spirits."

In *Trails of Enchantment,* she gave us
another illustration of how the Red Gods
smiled on her one cold, bright October
afternoon as she followed a tote road
through a section of country traditionally
associated with large antlers. The leaves
that day were very crisp and noisy underfoot as she hurriedly walked along in an
attempt to reach a certain ridge. Approaching a shallow ravine, she experienced a dramatic shock.

In her blue-chip deer book, Brandreth exhibits a visionary quality that one seldom sees in the field of
outdoor literature.

Out of the thicket of briars where he had
been feeding was thrust the startled head
of a gray-faced buck. I don't know which
one of us was the most surprised, the deer
or myself. I worked just about as fast as
was possible, and as is often the case when
there isn't time to get shaky or overexcited
from waiting, the result was entirely satisfactory.

Scrambling hastily across the ravine, I
reached the top of the knoll ready to plant
another bullet if the buck jumped. But he
was dead with a shot through the neck,
and when I saw how big he was, I dropped
the rifle and did a war dance. Although
carrying a moderate-sized pair of antlers
with only nine points, the weight of this
animal was far above the average, as I soon
came to find out when I tried to hang him
up. The following day he tipped the scales
at 197 pounds dressed.

Like Old Flintlock, Brandreth remained
literally fascinated with white-tailed deer
antlers. Antlers painted by Allan Brooks,
the great Canadian hunter, artist, and naturalist, graced the dust jacket of her book.
Photos of antlered bucks illustrated the
text. She continuously talked about the
great variation in the color of antlers, as
well as their shape, spread, and symmetry.

She probably dreamed about antlers.
Thoughts of seeing antlers moving through
the brush accompanied her on every hunt.
Like Flintlock, she viewed antler collecting
as one of the chief charms of hunting the
white-tailed deer.

The sport of deer hunting is still a final
frontier for women to explore. Paulina
Brandreth led the way on conquering that
frontier in this country. I cannot think of
any other woman of Brandreth's time who
did more to break down the barriers of
this male-dominated sport in this country.
In England, however, one thinks of Lady
Breadalbane of Argyllshire who once shot

six stags with six shots in one day. Brandreth read her classic book, the *High Tops of Black Mount* (1935), and underlined the following passage that emphasizes practice at the target:

"All the years I have been deer stalking, throughout the whole season I have gone regularly to the target, holding that no amount of trouble is too great which will lead to fewer wounded stags, fewer misses and fewer disappointments to the hunter."

Both Brandreth and Lady Breadalbane preferred the strenuous activities of tramping the hills in pursuit of stags and the wholesome lessons of endurance in deer stalking to the self-indulgencies that beset modern daily life. *The High Tops of Black Mount* and *Trails of Enchantment* stand on many deer hunters' bookshelves as two great books on deer hunting written by two great women buck hunters—or stag hunters, as the English prefer.

Other women deer hunters have been carrying on the tradition of Diana the Huntress since Brandreth's day. One thinks of Justine Kerfoot and her deer hunting adventures at Gunflint Lodge in the Boundary Waters region of Minnesota. We also think of Frances Hamerstrom, who is one of only five women to become a wildlife biologist before Women's Lib. In her book *Is SHE Coming Too? Memoirs of a Lady Hunter* (1989), Hamerstrom, a former fashion model turned wildlife researcher, writes that each year "when sighting in my rifle, a 250-3000, I dream of shooting an enormous swamp buck with a rack that would make everyone marvel."

In her memoirs, this contemporary huntress gives us a sensitive and eloquent description of what hunting means to her as a woman. If Brandreth were alive to read these memoirs today, she too would underscore the passage.

"For me, hunting is so much more than the high point of delight of any one sense.

I use all five senses—and all the knowledge I have accumulated up to that time—and besides I hunt with my man. For me hunting is not a symphony, not a painting, not to be defined. It is a long, fascinating road leading to moments of ecstasy."

More and more women are experiencing these "moments of ecstasy" in the deer hunt. I see it in the adventures of Marci Cunningham, who lives in the heart of southwestern Pennsylvania's deer country and who wrote *Deerhunters' Guide to Success* (1985), and in Kathy Etling's deer hunts in Missouri.

According to the United States Department of the Interior's 1985 *National Survey of Fishing, Hunting and Wildlife Associated Recreation,* issued in November 1988, women constitute 9 percent of hunters sixteen years old or older. That means that we now have approximately 1.5 million female hunters in the woods—up 1 percent from the 1980 National Survey and growing, though very slowly.

Women hunters today still face the same obstacles that Paulina Brandreth had to cope with in her day. Too often do they hear that non-welcome comment: "Is SHE coming too?" Too frequently the attitudes of men reflect indifference. Not only do women lack enthusiastic role models and proper education but outdoor clothing and guns designed to fit them well. Nevertheless, more and more women are beginning to enjoy a sport that has too long been a bastion of masculinity. It is high time we welcomed women deer hunters into our midst.

During the late 1930s, Brandreth traveled and hunted throughout the western states with her father. On that hunting trip, she contracted a serious fever from which she never recovered. She died on April 18, 1946 in Bethel, Connecticut, after a prolonged illness.

What prompted a woman such as Paulina Brandreth to pursue white-tailed bucks with such vigor and relentless gusto? The same things that prompt all deer hunters, men and women alike: a love of nature and a desire to study the magnificent whitetail in its natural habitat and to ultimately experience the charm and freedom of life in the wilderness.

In her writings on deer and deer hunting, Brandreth exhibited a visionary quality that one seldom sees in the field of outdoor literature. No one in the history of this sport expresses the real meaning and significance of hunting more eloquently than does this prominent buck hunter, a giant amongst deer hunters.

"Hunting is a recreation and an invigorating pastime that never should, through a super-civilized, over-artificialized state of living, be allowed to die out. In this age of neurotic haste it means rest and renewed health to the man whose brain and energies are being constantly overtaxed. It means stronger muscles, a more vigorous constitution, self-reliance, hardihood. A real man does not care for sport that does not involve difficulty, discomfort, and sometimes danger. The trouble with modern life is that physically it is terribly softening. We need something to counteract the effects of luxury and too easy living. Hunting does this because it takes a man to places where he has to depend on first principles, and where he comes in contact with obstacles that tend to build up and strengthen his natural abilities and manhood. It makes his eyesight keener, teaches him patience, and unfolds many natural laws and beauties and wonders that otherwise would remain to him unknown. We all need something of the primitive in us in order that we may have a rock bottom on which to stand."

Chapter 3

A Master of Whitetail Woodcraft

The hunter makes the highest type of soldier and the whitetail makes the highest type of hunter that is widely possible today. The whitetail trained the armies of the Revolution . . . and may supply the vital training of the country's armies in the future. When this people no longer has need of armies, when the nations learn war no more, and men cease to take pleasure in beautiful wildlife — then only can we afford to lose the white-tailed deer.
— Ernest Thompson Seton, *Lives of Game Animals,* 1929

Like his contemporary, Archibald Rutledge, whose writings he greatly admired, Ernest Thompson Seton (1860–1946) viewed deer hunting as a school for manhood — and no one became a greater master of whitetail woodcraft than did Seton. In his *Book of Woodcraft,* originally published in 1912 and reprinted in 1988 by the Creative Arts Book Company, this great hunter-naturalist noted that the hunter not only needs woodcraft in its highest form to successfully outmaneuver the white-tailed deer, but that woodcraft may very well save man from civilized decay.

Mastering whitetail woodcraft for Seton meant spending a lifetime in pursuit of every detail of this animal's remarkable natural history — whether with the bow or rifle, camera or sketch pad. He used all of the above and while doing so read the great blue-chip deer books of his time: Caton's *The Antelope and Deer of America* (1877), Van Dyke's *The Still Hunter* (1882), Roosevelt's *The Deer Family* (1902), as well as the deer and deer hunting tales of Archibald Rutledge as published in the pages of *Forest & Stream.*

No one worked more enthusiastically in sketching deer and making notes on their social behavior than this eccentric, strong-willed, eminent Victorian. The journals that he kept religiously for more than sixty years attest to his meticulous recording of deer behavior. His numerous drawings of

"Group of White-tailed Deer" (1906) by Ernest Thompson Seton. *Seton Memorial Library, Philmont Scout Ranch, Cimarron, New Mexico*

white-tailed deer antlers underscore his insatiable curiosity for understanding every facet of this animal's natural history; he became as enamored with antlers as Old Flintlock. Seton's famous "Group of White-tailed Deer" (1906) captured the spiritual essence of the animal in a way that few artists ever accomplish; his *Trail of the Sandhill Stag* (1899) is one of the most thoughtful and provocative deer hunting tales ever written.

Seton's lifelong passion for studying animals in general and deer in particular culminated in his four-volume *Lives of Game Animals* (1929), which took more than twenty years to complete. In this classic work, Seton rightly classified the white-tailed deer as "the American deer of the

past and the American deer of the future." During his lifetime, Seton—known to his friends as Black Wolf—became one of America's best-known men of the woods, the American woodsman supreme. In his deer hunting stories, he taught several generations of American boys how to hunt deer, myself included.

Like most deer hunters, Seton never forgot his first encounter with a deer. It occurred in the autumn of 1866, when his brother Joe shot a doe through the heart at thirty yards on the Seton farm in Toronto. While examining the deer, his older brothers showed him the interdigital gland between the deer's toes. "The scent between the deer's toes," Seton later wrote in his

Like most deer hunters, Seton had a famous buck
that he greatly admired. His choice was the famous
"Caesar Whitetail" that once reigned supreme as the
world record of the species. It sported forty-two tines
and a basal circumference of six inches with an outside spread of 27¾ inches. *Seton Memorial Library,
Philmont Scout Ranch, Cimarron, New Mexico*

autobiography, *Trail of an Artist-Naturalist* (1940), "had a strange musky smell that
I never forgot. My nose must have been
better than common, for my memory was
more gripped by smell than by appeals to
other senses." Seton would probably agree
with the modern-day deer doctors who insist that hunters with a refined sense of
smell can actually detect the presence of
deer, especially rutting bucks, with their
noses alone.

By age fourteen, Seton had already built
his own secret cabin in the Don Valley near
the family farm. In his best-seller, *Rolf in
the Woods* (1911), a historical novel for
boys about the adventures of a Boy Scout
living and hunting with an Indian named
Quonab, Seton describes his first bout

with buck fever and documents the killing
of his first deer. The incident occurred near
his little cabin and was viewed through the
eyes of the novel's hero, Rolf Kittering.

While still-hunting in a southwesterly
direction one day near sunset, he came
across a small forest opening. As he proceeded to cross it, he caught movement in
the brush on the other side. He stood still
and waited for several minutes. He tested
the wind by throwing a handful of dried
grass into the wind. "Yes, it was from the
southwest," he thought to himself as he
began a slow, stealthy stalk in the direction
of the movement. After approaching to
within twenty yards of the spot, he
stopped and watched for several minutes.
He again tested the wind and gradually
moved slowly west. Seton documents what
happened as Rolf approached the spot.

Ernest Thompson Seton in his hunting clothes at the
age of forty-six. *Seton Memorial Library, Philmont
Scout Ranch, Cimarron, New Mexico*

After a long, tense crawl of twenty yards he came on the track and sign of a big buck, perfectly fresh, and again his heart worked harder; it seemed to be pumping his neck full of blood, so he was choking. He judged it best to follow this hot trail for a time, and holding his gun ready cocked he stepped softly onward. A bluejay cried out, "jay, jay!" with startling loudness, and seemingly enjoyed his pent up excitement. A few steps forward at slow, careful stalk, and then behind him he heard a loud whistling hiss. Instantly turning he found himself face to face with a great, splendid buck. . . . There not thirty yards away he stood, the creature he had been stalking so long, in plain view now, broadside on. They gazed each at the other, perfectly still for a few seconds, then Rolf without undue movement brought the gun to bear, and still the buck stood gazing. The gun up, but oh, how disgustingly it wobbled and

Seton in the woods near his DeWinton estate, around 1917. *Seton Memorial Library, Philmont Scout Ranch, Cimarron, New Mexico*

shook! and the steadier Rolf tried to hold it, the more it trembled, until from that wretched gun the palsy spread all over his body; his breath came tremulously, his legs and arms were shaking, and at last, as the deer moved its head to get a better view and raised its tail, the lad, making an effort at self-control, pulled the trigger. Bang! and the buck lightly bounded out of sight."

Seton found the bullet hole in a tree, five feet above where the buck's head had been. He tramped back to camp filled with disgust and self-contempt; a big buck standing broadside at thirty yards and a clear miss! Unable to stop thinking about the incident, he slept very little that night.

The next day he still-hunted the same area. As he crossed through a willow thicket, he caught the flash of a deer's ear. Slowly raising his gun, he issued a short, sharp whistle. A doe suddenly rose, then another, and then a small buck stood up. They all stood still for a moment and gazed in his direction.

"Up went the gun, but again its muzzle began to wobble. Rolf lowered it, said grimly and savagely to himself, "I *will not* shake this time." The deer stretched themselves and began slowly walking toward the lake. All had disappeared but the buck. Rolf gave another whistle that turned the antler-bearer to a statue. Controlling himself with a strong *"I will,"* he raised the gun, held it steadily, and fired. The buck gave a gathering spasm, a bound, and disappeared. Rolf felt sick again with disgust, but he reloaded, then hastily went forward."

After following the buck for about twenty yards, he found bright-red stains of blood. One hundred yards from where he shot at the buck, he found it dead on the forest floor with a heart shot. Imitating his Indian friend Quonab, he gave out a long war cry as he stared down at the buck with his eyes fixed on the antlers.

Like his friends T. S. Van Dyke and Archibald Rutledge, Seton devoted a great deal of time to antlers and antler collecting. He filled his journals with pictures, drawings, and illustrations of typical, atypical, and freak antlers. Like Flintlock, who greatly admired the famous Strohecker head, Seton also had his favorite: the Caesar Whitetail, shot by Henry A. Caesar of New York while hunting in Maine during the 1910 deer season. This one-time world record of its time sported 42 tines, a 6-inch basal circumference, and a 27¾-inch outside spread.

The crowning glory of a white-tailed buck is his antlers, and the finest white-tailed buck has antlers befitting his stature and dignity. No one romanced deer antlers in greater depth and artistic detail than Seton. "I am out to fight," Seton writes in the January 1906 issue of *Scribner's Magazine* of the rutting buck with polished antlers during the madness of November. "My antlers are clean and sharp, I am big and strong, I fear no living thing. On this fight I will stake my range, my family, my social position, my limbs and life." In staking everything on the outcome many bucks lose their lives.

In his *Lives of Game Animals,* Seton notes that bucks dying as a result of locked antlers is very common among whitetails. He also reports two instances of three bucks locking antlers and perishing in their struggles. Seton believed that 1 percent of all white-tailed bucks perish with interlocked antlers. Texas deer biologists estimate buck mortality as a result of fighting as high as 15 percent.

In his *Lives,* he also gives us countless examples of wild bucks battling with the hunters themselves. If the buck becomes the conqueror in these battles with man,

he will ferociously trample his victim as long as any sign of life exists. Some hunters reported to Seton that they only saved their lives by playing dead.

When one reads Seton's deer hunting tales, one is overwhelmed with his wanderlust for hunting deer. His hunts during the early 1880s take on the dimensions of minor military campaigns, in the tradition of Oliver Hazard Perry, Meshach Browning, Philip Tome, and Judge Caton. On one of these vigorous campaigns, known in the annals of American deer hunting as "the Carberry deer hunt," Seton traveled about 300 miles on foot through deep snow. The hunt ended successfully, but only after nineteen days of toil.

The Carberry deer hunt began on October 27, 1884, when Black Wolf vowed that he would not cease to hunt in the hills around Carberry, Manitoba, until either he downed a deer or the season closed before he succeeded. With snow on the ground that day, he took to the hills with high hopes, for he believed that when you find a track, as he wrote in his diary of that hunt, "it is only a question of time and perseverance before one comes up with the track maker." But he traveled fifteen miles that day without seeing a deer or a track.

The next day he traveled even farther, without faring any better. On the third day he found two old elk tracks and again returned empty-handed and weary after tramping through deep snow for twenty miles. He determined the distances he traveled each day by watching survey stakes.

On the fourth day of the hunt, he walked even farther in a new direction. Although he saw no deer, he discovered new and abundant deer sign.

Several of his friends joined him on day five and laughed at his incurable optimism. Black Wolf saw no deer that day, but his friend James Duff missed several chances due to the limited range of his shotgun.

Early the next morning Seton set off for the hills with his brother. He saw seven deer that day and wounded a buck with buckshot, but he was unable to retrieve it. While tracking the wounded animal, he stopped and made detailed sketches of the tracks, measuring their length and width and the spacing between them. In his hunting diary he wrote, "these effortless bounds covered a space of eighteen to twenty-five feet. Ye gods! They do not run at all, they fly, and once in a while come down again to tap the hilltops with their dainty hooves." Like some buck hunters I know, Seton believed that the hunter can determine the sex of a deer by examining the track and analyzing other deer sign as well. In his journal, he carefully illustrated the drag mark of the buck's track.

Day seven passed without Black Wolf seeing a sign of deer, but he remained even more determined and enthusiastic. On the next day, Seton and his friend Duff took several shots at three antlerless deer near Smith's Lake but to no avail. They followed the tracks until sundown and then tramped twelve miles back to camp.

On this hunt, Seton met a Cree Indian named Chaska, with whom he hunted for a week. In Seton's mind, Chaska seemed to represent the spirit of the land and the ideal deerslayer. Seton's description of him, published in an article titled "A Carberry Deer Hunt" in *Forest and Stream* (June 3, 1886), reminds us of James Fenimore Cooper's deerslayer.

"He was about six feet tall in his moccasins, straight and well-built, his features decidedly aquiline. His hair hung in two long black braids, ornamented with a bunch of brass rings and thimbles. He was dressed in the customary white blanket and leggins. A scarlet handkerchief covered his ears. He carried the usual fire-bag, knife, and gun. He was a minor chief and evidently a man of experience, for he spoke excellent English.

"We took to each other from the beginning. There was an indefinable charm about his quiet dignified manners — and I knew that he could teach me much about woodcraft."

During that week, Chaska taught Black Wolf many of the practical methods and tricks used by his tribe for hunting deer. While hunting with Chaska, Seton felt himself to be in harmony with the wolves, the deer, the Indians, and the spirit of the land. But still he killed no deer in the Carberry sandhills that week.

By the fifteenth day of his hunt, after walking approximately 265 miles, Black Wolf still remained an unsuccessful deer hunter. By this time he had lost weight and the confidence of his friends, injured his knee in a fall, and suffered frostbite on his feet. His knee injury grew worse, so he took a week off from the hunt.

During his reprieve from the Carberry hunt, he built a life-sized deer target, placed it 250 yards from his shanty, and blazed away at it until he could consistently hit the heart area three out of five times.

His shanty was an eight-by-twelve-foot log structure with split strips of wood that he plastered with tempered mud. He built the roof with prairie hay one foot deep and covered it with six inches of clay. In the lintel over the door, he carved "E. T. Seton, 1884."

In his diary he describes his general disposition. "I longed to be free again, but my knee was still very painful. I felt like a hawk with a broken wing, but knowing the danger of overworking a strained knee, I stayed at home for the full week. This was the only time when I almost repented having said I would fetch out a deer, the only time when I felt my confidence shaking. Lying still went hard against the grain, for the only athletic exercise that I delight and excel in is this fast traveling. So far, I have not met with one that I cannot leave behind. Duff is the fastest man with whom I have hunted and often I have to wait for him to catch up."

The fifteenth day of the Carberry deer hunt resumed in late November as the young Nimrod took to the hills again to run deer trails. His friends smiled derisively, refusing to participate due to the scarcity of deer. Although mule deer were common in the area, their density per square mile remained very low. Despite this, Seton loved to run deer trails all day and came home fresh.

"Ten miles is to me now no more than half a mile to most persons. I can run all day and come home fresh, and always when alone in these lonely places I feel running through me so strong a gush of glorious exhilaration that no trouble in my mind can stand before it, and since a man's troubles are nowhere but in his mind, my troubles all are blotted out and my happiness complete."

As the red sun set on the fifteenth day, he crossed Kennedy's Plain. He stopped and turned to the east. While watching a majestic full moon rise in the eastern sky, he heard wolves.

"I mimicked their howling and noted by the sound that they were gathering together, doubtless hunting. Then as they responded to my howls, I noticed that they were rapidly coming nearer. 'H'm,' I thought. 'It's me you're hunting, is it?' I was just leaving the woods and as the sounds bore down nearer on my trail, I turned and stood perfectly still, thinking, 'Well, if those wolves are foolish enough to attack a man armed with a Winchester rifle, just let them come on.' And so I waited. Nearer and nearer they came until

I heard them at the edge of the timber only fifty yards away. They must have seen me then; there was a low growl, a snarl or two, and all was still. I heard them no more, and went on my way."

As he tramped toward the shanty that evening, he understood what a deer senses when it hears a moccasined hunter in the trail behind it. On the next day, he tramped twenty-five miles alone without experiencing the slightest trace of a deer.

On day seventeen, he still-hunted a large spruce swamp and followed the track of four moose until sunset. That night he entered the following entry into his diary. "What a fascination there is about deer tracks in the snow; what endless stories one will read and learn from the telltale snow; there is something fantastic about the thought that just at the other end of that row of dots is the beast that made them, and it is only a question of time for one to overtake it. The record of every movement is so perfect that it affects one most strangely."

But would he overtake a deer before the season ended? Would the season pass in one long series of failures?

On the eighteenth day, Black Wolf resolved to waste no more time returning to the shanty each evening. He now packed three days' provisions in his bobsleigh and left for the hills with his friend Duff. That day ended unsuccessfully, with the young hunters tirelessly following the tracks of three moose until sunset. They then made a wind screen of spruce boughs and slept on the ground that night.

After an early breakfast on the nineteenth day, they picked up the moose tracks of the day before and continued the chase. A tedious tramp of about two miles led them into dense poplar brush and willow sloughs where the signs of the three moose grew fresh. Continuing to follow the tracks, they suddenly heard a faint "bang, bang" in the distance. Seton describes what happened in "A Carberry Deer Hunt."

We stopped and gazed blankly at each other, perfectly disgusted to think that we had driven our moose right into the fire of some other hunters, probably Indians.

Then dejectedly we started again, hoping that it was not so. But suddenly the idea struck me, the chances are the moose will only be turned by the shots, and they will come back on their tracks. Jim agreed with me, so we then proceeded more cautiously. Scarcely two minutes had elapsed before I saw in a clearer space some two hundred yards ahead, a great rusty red beast charging through the bush toward us. Into the snow I dropped like a shot; my companion saw nothing but dropped because I did. On came the whirlwind of red hair, his body swaying inward as he rounded the trees, like a racer turning a corner. Nose up, horns back, mane erect, a vision of tremendous brute strength as he dashed on toward us with that speed, which is his greatest safety.

Thousands of thoughts of moose-killing rushed into my mind as I crouched on the snow, right on the trail, right in the path of the maned monster that was tearing through the timber toward us. It several times occurred to me that it was most likely he would kill me, but I lay and bode my time. Then, just as he was within twenty yards of trampling on us, I sprang to my feet.

With two awful snorts that I shall not soon forget, the moose sprang to one side, and for a moment stood and stared, uncertain what to do.

Bang, Bang!

With a plunge the monster started off again, crashing through the woods. . . . With feelings of mingled hope and fear we crossed over to his trail, and there — oh! savage glee, at every stride was a jet of blood. What a thrill of hope and triumph.

Away we ran on the trail of the crimson splashes like wolves, fairly gloating over the continued jets of blood.

There are glorious dyes in the sunset skies
There's splendor in heaven's fair bow,
There's noblest color in beauty's bright eyes,
To kindle our feelings, I know.
But to stir up the inmost soul of a man,
And to fire him with frenzied glow.
To double his manhood, yet prove him a brute,
There never were richer, brighter dyes,
Than the spotless white where it crimsoned lies,
With a life being spilt on the snow.

Four hundred yards ahead, they found the moose lying dead in a large pool of blood.

"We stood for a few minutes gazing on the magnificent beast with feelings of rapture and triumph; feelings, in my case, not unmingled with regret that what was once such a noble animal should be lying at our feet, shorn of its majestic beauty and now no more than a great load of butcher meat."

And so the Carberry deer hunt ended on the nineteenth day in the thrill of triumph, but not without a certain ambivalent feeling in Seton's mind toward killing deer. After traveling 300 miles on foot through heavy snow, Seton kept his hunting vow and killed one of the grandest beasts of the chase. Was the reward commensurate with the labor?

"I never had the slightest doubt on the subject, and both Mr. Duff and myself will not cease to look back on the days of our hunting together, with pleasurable emotion that can be understood only by the sportsman or the naturalist, who appreciates the chase not by the avoirdupois return, but rather by seeing therein a real elixir of life for the present, and a fountain of delightful memories for the future."

But that ambivalent feeling remained in the back of Seton's mind throughout his life. Later in life, in his autobiography *Trail of an Artist-Naturalist* (1940), he again reflected on the moment as he gazed at the dead animal lying in the pool of blood.

"Another thought possessed me as I gazed on that superb animal, turned into a pile of butcher's meat, for the sake of a passing thrill. The thought was much like remorse—so that I then and there made a vow, which I have lived up to ever since—that so long as they are threatened with early extermination, I will never again lift my rifle against any of America's big game."

Killing was never the real fascination of a Seton deer hunt, as we learn from his wife, Grace Gallatin Seton, who accompanied her husband on his many hunting safaris. In *A Woman Tenderfoot* (1900), this feminist and outdoorswoman summed up the real meaning of deer hunting for her husband, whom she called Nimrod.

"Of the many, many times I have watched deer and left them unmolested, and of the lessons they have taught me, under Nimrod's guidance, I have not space to tell, for the real fascination of hunting is not in the killing but in seeing the creature at home amid his glorious surroundings, and feeling the freely rushing blood, the health-giving air, the gleeful sense of joy and life in nature, both within and without."

The memories and experiences of the Carberry deer hunt on the Big Plain of Manitoba had a lasting and profound impact on Nimrod. He referred to those days of his life as "the best days of my life . . . my golden days." The experiences of the Carberry deer hunt surfaced in his great novella, *The Trail of the Sandhill Stag* (1899), one of the most thought-provoking, sensitive, moving tales ever written of the long, endless pursuit of a black-tailed buck. If you have not read this Seton story, you still have a lot to learn about the real meaning and significance of deer hunting, for the story challenges and questions the

basic philosophy of the chase to its very foundations.

This little volume of less than 100 pages will arouse the spirit of any deer hunter. It is a fascinating record of long searches that usually end unsuccessfully; it captures the spell of the deer forest and the joy of the hunter. When this blue-chip deer book appeared in 1899, the *New York Times* instantly recognized it as a classic: "It is in every way thoroughly pleasing, both through the beauty of the story—one which once read, we think, can never be forgotten."

Unlike what happens in most tales of early American deer hunting, when Yan, the main protagonist of this tale—the young Seton of the Carberry deer hunting days—finally encounters the Sandhill Stag in his rifle sights, after several years of intensive study and elusive chase, he refrains from shooting. As he stands in front of the magnificent monarch of the woods with his nerves and senses taut, he says to himself, "Shoot, shoot, shoot now! This is what you have toiled for!" But shoot he does not. Instead, he says to himself while staring into the soul of the stag:

"We have long stood as foes, hunter and hunted, but now that is changed and we stand face to face, fellow creatures looking into each other's eyes, not knowing each other's speech—but knowing motives and feelings. Now I understand you as I never did before; surely you at least in part understand me. For your life is at last in my power, yet you have no fear. I knew a deer once, that, run down by the hounds, sought safety with the hunter, and he saved it—and you also I have run down and you boldly seek safety with me. Yes! you are as wise as you are beautiful, for I will never harm a hair of you. We are brothers, oh, bounding Blacktail! only I am the elder and stronger, and if only my strength could always be at hand to save you, you would never come to harm. Go now, without fear, to range the piney hills; never more shall I follow your trail with the wild wolf rampant in my heart. Less and less as I grow do I see in your race mere flying marks, or butcher-meat."

During his late teens, Black Wolf spent endless days following deer trails in the glades and groves of the Sandhill wilderness around Carberry. His description of Yan was really a portrait of himself.

"He was a tall, raw lad in the last of his teens. He was no hunter yet, but he was a tireless runner, and filled with unflagging zeal. Away to the hills he went on his quest day after day, and many a score of long white miles he coursed, and night after night he returned to the shanty without seeing even a track."

He pitted their wits against his, their strength against his, their speed against his Winchester. He sketched their tracks and scat and measured them in great detail. He photographed deer at every opportunity and read every scrap of information he could find on deer behavior in the popular press and the scientific journals. He compared his own enthusiasm and exhilaration for deer hunting to that of the instincts of the wolf in hot pursuit of whitetails. When Black Wolf describes Yan's strength, he clearly presents a picture of himself: "He gloried in the independence of his strength, for his legs were like iron and his wind was like a hound's."

Trigger itch, buck fever, or wanderlust — call it what you will — but Seton expresses it best of all in his story. "How the wild beast in his heart did ramp — he wanted to howl like a wolf on a hot scent; and away they went through the woods and hills the trail and Yan and the inner wolf."

Seton read James Fenimore Cooper's *The Deerslayer* and could quote whole passages of Natty Bumpo's hunting wisdom from memory. Dressed in buckskin and wearing deerskin moccasins, Seton played the role of the deerslayer to its full extent. Tall, active, and sinewy, with dark hair, dark eyes, and his skin tanned to a deep copper color, he looked more like an Indian than a white man. Seton actually desired to be an Indian and learned a great deal about deer hunting from his Indian friends. In the ritual of the hunt, Seton found himself to be at one with the deer and the wolves, with the Indians and the spirit of the land.

For more than two years, Black Wolf followed the tracks and trails of the Sandhill Stag. The fascinating and endless tracks and behavior of this particular buck literally mesmerized the young buck hunter. No one can follow deer trails, he argued "without feeling a wild beast prickling in his hair and down his spine. Away Yan went, a hunter-brute once more, all other feelings swamped." He likened the pursuit of this particular buck to the search for the Holy Grail. After endlessly chasing this deer, Seton learned that a hardy man can in fact run a deer down.

"From a hunter, perfectly equipped, one who knows the secrets of the trail," he writes in his *Animal Tracks & Hunter Signs,* published posthumously in 1958, "a deer cannot escape. The trails may seem to end, but the trailer knows that it does not, except at the victim. It may elude him for a few hours, or even a day. It may puzzle him by side tracks and doubles, and may distance him by sheer speed, but it cannot shake him off. Sooner or later the tracker will run it down." The mystery and mystique of this buck's trail overwhelmed the young hunter. He noticed that the buck often backtracked for 100 yards or more and then would bound off in another direction.

Seton adds to our knowledge of wood-craft the interesting notion that the blue jay is the deer's greatest tattletale, crying out in the forest, "Deer there—deer, deer, deer!" One day while following the Sand-hill Stag on the downwind side, Seton observed the buck bed down. After watching the bedded buck for awhile, he imitated the cry of the blue jay. The buck waved its ears and lunged forward, and then stopped abruptly. There it stood sniffing the wind while watching its back trail. Seton could have shot the big buck with the bronze and ivory antlers at fifteen feet, but he chose not to.

Like Archibald Rutledge, Seton wished to perpetuate the mystique and myth of the mighty stag that always gets away and fades into oblivion. In an article titled "The Big Buck We Didn't Shoot," Seton indicated that often he preferred the animal to live so that it would continually tempt man to take up the chase.

"Again I see that glorious head against the sky, as often I did—more often in early days than now, for he appears most often to the tyro in the woods—see him give one great bound when cracks the ready rifle, and know from the miraculous way in which the unerring ball was turned aside that this was indeed the Mighty Stag again, the Spirit of the Race, and that no bullet cast of lead can ever graze his hide—and again he fades away.

"Long may he roam and spurn the hill-tops with his flying feet and dash the dew drops from the highest pine tops as he clears the valley at a bound; long may he live and tempt a perfect hail of harmless lead."

Seton was not always on the side of the deer, of course. In fact, he played a prominent role in the revival of hunting deer with the bow and arrow at the turn of the century. In his imagination, Seton longed for a different type of hunt in which shadowy figures moved silently through the timber as they stalked their prey with bows and arrows. He believed that woodcraft declined dramatically with the emergence of the rifle and argued that the limitations of the bow make the success of the hunt depend solely on the skills and abilities of the hunter.

"The modern hunter with a rifle that kills as far as he can see or farther," Seton wrote in an article titled "The Revival of the Bow and Arrow," published in *Country Life,* "has little need of that infinite knowledge of times, seasons, winds localities, habits, sounds, signs, kinds of ground, silent walking, deft approach, telltale footing, or the eternal endurance and patience exacted of the hunter who must secure his quarry with a bow whose farthest deadly range is perhaps fifty yards."

In 1905, Seton designed a game for boys called "the Deerhunt" that received wide publicity in the press and became a basic element in the manuals of the Boy Scout movement, a movement that Seton helped to launch. He designed the game to be more exciting than mere target practice. The game consisted of a life-sized deer built on a wire frame and covered with burlap. It was made to be as realistic as possible. A large oval shape marked the heart-lung area, and a smaller oval shape represented the heart.

The boy who plays the deer for the first hunt hides the dummy wherever he chooses. As he goes through the forest, he leaves a trail of corn that represents the scent of the deer. He also wears an iron deer hoof attached to his shoe to leave a trail similar to that of a deer. The boy playing the role of the deer places corn on the trail where the iron hoofmark might be difficult or impossible to see. Seton gives us the rules of the Deerhunt in *The Book of Woodcraft.*

The hunters now hunt for this deer just as for a real deer, either following the trail or watching the woods ahead; the best hunters combine the two. If at any time the trail is quite lost the one in charge shouts 'Lost Trail!' After that the one who finds the trail scores two. Any one giving a false alarm by shouting "Deer" is fined five.

Thus they go till someone finds the deer. He shouts "Deer!" and scores ten for finding it. The others shout "Second," "Third," — etc., in order of seeing it, but they do not score.

The finder must shoot at the deer with his bow and arrow from the very spot whence he saw it. If he misses, the second hunter may step up five paces, and have his shot. If he misses, the third one goes five and so on till someone hits the deer, or until the ten-yard limit is reached. If the finder is within ten yards on sighting the deer, and misses his shot, the other hunters go back to the ten-yard limit. Once the deer is hit, all the shooting must be from the exact spot whence the successful shot was fired.

A shot in the big oval is a body wound; that scores five. A shot outside that is a scratch; that scores two. A shot in the small oval or heart is a heart wound; it scores ten, and ends the hunt. Arrows which do not stick do not count, unless it can be proved that they passed right through, in which case they take the highest score that they pierced.

If all the arrows are used, and none in the heart, the deer escapes, and the boy who was deer scores twenty-five.

The one who found the dummy is deer for the next hunt. A clever deer can add greatly to the excitement of the game.

Seton believed that the Deerhunt offered the same exercise for marksmanship, eyesight, muscle, and trailing as that of real deer hunting. The game had the added advantage of providing boys with woodland sport throughout the entire year.

No hunter-naturalist worked harder or more persistently in educating young boys in deer hunting and woodcraft and in deciphering and recording the mysteries of deer tracks, trails, and behavior than did Ernest Thompson Seton. His vast knowledge of deer trails, tracks, scat, behavior, and the animal's natural history culminated in his *Lives of Game Animals,* which contains a multitude of drawings of deer tracks, trails, and antlers. When the book first appeared, *Forest & Stream* called it the most important book on the subject since the days of Audubon and Bachman. Today, it remains a standard reference work for anyone interested in deer and deer hunting. In this monumental work, Seton's love for the whole deer tribe manifests itself on every page. It documents in a unique way the innumerable curiosities of deer life. In it Seton portrays the whitetail as the wisest and most exceptional animal of the entire deer clan and immortalizes the animal in the process.

"This is the only one of our deer that can live contentedly and unsuspectedly in a hundred acres of thicket. It is the only one that can sit unconcernedly all day long while factory whistles and bells are sounding around it; and yet distinguish at once the sinister twig-snap that tells of some prowling foe, as far away, perhaps, as the other noises. It is the only one that, hearing a hostile footfall, will sneak around to wind the cause, study its trail, and glide, cat-like, through the brush to a farther heaven, without even trying to see the foe, who thus gets no chance for a shot. It is the least migratory, the least polygamous, the least roving, as well as the swiftest, keenest, shyest, wisest, most prolific, and most successful of our deer.

"It is the only one that has added to its range; that, in the North and West, has actually accompanied the settler into the woods; that has followed afar into newly opened parts of New England and Canada; that has fitted its map to man's; and that can hold its own on the frontier."

PART II

DEER HUNTING LORE
AND
NATURAL HISTORY

Chapter 4

In the Moonlight

A favorite time for [feeding] forays is in the moonlight; and the rising of the moon is, in all much-hunted regions, a signal for the deer to go forth. Many supposed irregularities in their habits will be explained by reference to the lunar calendar.
— Ernest Thompson Seton, *Life Histories of Northern Animals,* 1909

In his life history of the white-tailed deer, Ernest Thompson Seton, that great student of deer, observed that whitetails under heavy hunting pressure dispense with noonday visits to water holes and daytime feeding forays altogether; they become nocturnal. Secret and silent like the raccoon, they go forth with the rising of the moon. Other deer researchers, as well, link the daily rhythm of deer with the various phases of the moon. Arthur Carhart, a leading American conservationist, while studying the mass migration from the winter to summer range of the famous White River deer herd of Colorado, found a definite relationship over several seasons between the phases of the moon and the movement of deer. He reported that deer moved in greater numbers as the moon reached and passed the point of being full. While I have never studied the migration

patterns of deer, like Carhart, at the end of each Rutting Moon one eternal question always lingers in the back of my mind: Does the lunar cycle affect deer movement and, if so, to what extent?

The popular literature in this regard abounds with references to deer activities and the lunar cycle and its implications for the deer hunter striving for the optimum results. Acclaimed wildlife photographer Erwin Bauer suggests in his *Deer in Their World* (1983) that whitetails move more during the early mornings and the late evenings of the new moon. He hastens to add, however, that the moon's influence on deer movement remains mysterious and confusing at best, since no solid, scientific statistics exist on the question. In his 1986 edition of *The Modern Deer Hunter,* John Cartier, a Michigan deer hunter, states

When the full moon rises at sunset or sets at sunrise, the deer hunter frequently encounters white-tailed bucks silhouetted against the sky. *Richard P. Smith photo*

this point of view even more emphatically when he insists that deer feel more secure in the open during the dark of the moon. Consequently, the degree of luminosity at night, Cartier tells us, will probably have little bearing on the success of your next deer hunt.

Reading further in the popular literature, we find the opposite point of view expressed by such deer hunters as Byron Dalrymple, the master deer hunter from Texas, who argues, unlike Cartier, that during bright nights whitetails feed more avidly than on dark ones. According to Dalrymple, they move around in the moonlight without inhibition. Consequently, the hunter experiences poor hunting at dawn and dusk. By and large, Dalrymple reports, "the dark of the moon

and the small slivers of moon furnish the best hunting."

Like many deer hunters, Dalrymple never scoffs at the old backwoods-business of the "full of the moon." His fifty years of deer hunting experiences indicate that deer feed more heavily on moonlit nights when no other weather influences interfere, perhaps because it's more convenient. Conversely, during the new moon deer become much more active at dawn and dusk. After studying the influence of bright moonlight on deer movements, Dalrymple reaches the conclusion that daytime deer activity becomes more pronounced during the moonless periods than during moonlit periods. In *Deer Hunting with Dalrymple* (1978), he reports on the implications of his experiences.

"I'm not suggesting that you should refuse to hunt deer except in the dark of the moon. What I mean is that your chances of killing a good deer may be better then—perhaps only 1 percent better. My hunting philosophy always has been to give yourself every break. If you can hunt during a dark period, by all means time your hunting to include this advantage."

Like many American sportsmen, Dalrymple gives credence to the solunar theory of John Alden Knight, which states that animals move and become more active during solunar periods; he remains convinced that the major and minor feeding periods Knight worked out apply for deer hunters as well as fishermen. Actually, a good number of American deer hunters find Knight's solunar theory to be more than a colorful piece of Georgia backwoods sophistry. Not surprisingly, *Field & Stream* still publishes Knight's solunar tables.

Red Freeman, a rugged, old-time deer hunter from Maine, also believed that the feeding times of the white-tailed deer change with the phases and the rising and setting of the moon. As the moonlight changes, according to Freeman, the deer simply change their feeding patterns. Unfortunately, this reformed backwoods deer poacher never gave us any documentation or statistical evidence for his belief.

Regardless of whether we have significant scientific documentation of the moon's effect on white-tailed deer behavior or not, deer hunters across America seem to believe that the full moon exercises a dynamic effect on deer behavior. In his *Stalking Deer* (1986), Don Groves, a New York deer hunter, tells us that "the woods come alive like gang busters" during the full moon. He reports that he stayed in the woods one night to watch deer in the moonlight.

"The moon was bright and the deer started running all over the place. The young ones were calling like there was some kind of panic. Everybody was running everywhere. First one direction and then the other. The deer would run in groups or separately, not too far in any direction and right back to the starting point. Just all round high jinks. I had never seen anything like it and I was enthralled with the activity. I was situated on a high spot and they were not aware of my presence. I had a ringside seat. I've heard deer call before but that night was like the hooting and hollering at the fireman's fair."

While I've experienced deer play and rutting behavior in the moonlight, I have never experienced such a degree of moonlight frenzy.

Nationwide, deer hunters seem to agree that a full moon represents the poorest time to hunt deer while the best time occurs during the dark of the moon. Tom Hayes, a widely recognized deer hunting authority from Texas, notes in his *How to Hunt the Whitetail Deer* (1977) that when the moon rises during the daylight hours deer hunting will be above average. But when the moon rises during the hours of darkness, you will encounter below-average results. According to Hayes, "the lunar month contains one excellent hunting week, one good week, one fair week, and one poor week for hunting, although weather conditions and food scarcity can cause marked variations in the whitetail's activity levels. Any man who refuses to regard the moon's position when planning his strategy is not now and never will be a top whitetail hunter. Yes, this includes you."

Perhaps no one agreed with this position more than Ken Heuser, a Colorado deer hunter, who believed that the dedicated buck hunter always insists upon being in the woods during the week of the first quarter. In his outdoor musings, Heuser recommended the dark of the moon as the best time for deer hunting. His many years of experience indicated that the week before and the week after a full moon provide the poorest times to hunt deer. By the time it's light enough to shoot in the morning, the deer are already bedded down; worse, they won't move again until it's too dark to shoot in the evening.

While studying the lunar effect on deer activity in Alabama, my friend Kent Horner reached similar conclusions: Deer remain more active in their daily activity patterns during the new moon and half-moon phases and less active during the full-moon period. Kent points out in his *Art and Science of Whitetail Hunting* (1986) that since the white-tailed doe's sexual heat cycle is based on a twenty-eight-day lunar month, it stands to reason, "that the doe's sexual activities are influenced by lunar phases. Thus indirectly, during the rut, the buck is affected also, if for no other reason than the influence of the doe's sexual activity." He goes on to suggest that when the peak of the rut coincides with the dark of the moon or the new moon, deer become more active, even though we do not understand the complex physical and biological mechanisms.

In his study of deer movements on the Burnt Pine Plantation in Georgia, David Morris, a game biologist and outdoor editor, adds a significant point to the discussion when he says that moon phases greatly influence deer movements *if all things are equal.* The problem, he hastens to add, is that all things are seldom equal. Most bow hunters know that during the summer and early fall, with stable weather patterns and little or no hunting pressure, moon phases play a very prominent role in governing deer movement patterns. But when the cold fronts start sweeping down from the North and as gun hunting pressure mounts, moon phases take on a more secondary role. Morris concluded his study titled "Deer Movements," published in the *Georgia Sportsman,* by observing that "the full moon does have a direct impact on deer movement, and *when* hunting is likely to be best."

Other deer hunters disagree. Dwight Schuh, for example, a western bow hunter, emphasizes the fact that deer exhibit excellent nighttime vision, and lunar luminosity or the lack thereof represents no limitation to nighttime activity. In an article titled "A Weather Eye for Whitetails," he states that deer become most active on cloudy and moonless nights and speculates that they feel more secure in the open during dark nights, since they remain less visible to predators. Schuh suggests that we forget about the moon when planning our next deer hunt.

Francis Sell, that great Oregon backwoodsman, tells us the exact opposite in his *Art of Successful Deer Hunting* (1964).

When a full moon hangs low in the late autumn sky, touching the scarlets, browns and gold of the woodlands with an overlay of silver, this experienced hunter is not only mindful of the beautiful setting for his hunt, he also knows the effect of that moon on plans.

Rain, shine, storm, all these have their effect on deer hunting, regardless of whether you plan to drive, still hunt or trail watch. Given a full moon over the deer cover, your quarry feeds during the entire night, then is securely bedded in the thickets before good morning shooting light.

Deer hunting plans based on normal morning and evening feeding periods, under the circumstances, are futile. You must appraise chances in accordance with changed conditions. With the full moon in the autumn sky, they travel at night, feeding, playing, holding high revel on the ridges and in the open glades.

No one pursued deer more vigorously on the ridges and in the open glades than T. S. Van Dyke. After observing deer in the moonlight for many years, he concluded that whitetails during the dark of the moon, if submitted to little or no hunting pressure, often feed during the middle of the day. But, he added, we must remember that whitetails can do whatever they need to do with or without the moon or anything else.

In his *Practical Deer-Stalking* (1986), G. Kenneth Whitehead, an acknowledged authority on English deer and deer hunting, urges deer hunters to take the periods of full moon into consideration when planning hunts, especially in areas where deer are subjected to human disturbance since they respond by becoming nocturnal in their habits, especially during a full moon, thus delaying their emergence from cover until well after darkness.

Michael Brander, a well-known historian of hunting, agrees. In his *Deer Stalking in Britain* (1986), he tells deer hunters that a full moon and a cloudless sky overnight force deer to feed freely throughout the hours of semi-darkness. "The stalker who wishes to stalk after such a night may well find that many of the beasts he would expect to find have already departed." Brander recommends scheduling your deer hunts on days following cloudy overcast nights when the moon is not to be seen.

Lew Dietz, a deer hunter from the woods of Maine, agrees: "The native hunter avoids the full phase of the moon. Even a superficial examination of deer-kill records indicates that fewer deer are shot during the full-moon period than during its dark phases. There is no great mystery here. When a deer is able to feed by the light of the moon, the hunter won't see much of him during the shooting hours."

John Wootters' advice in his *Hunting Trophy Deer* (1977) summarizes the general consensus of opinion in the popular domain on the subject of deer and lunar influence: "I've seen scientific correlations, which tended to show that the phase of the moon has nothing to do with whitetail activity if all other things are the same. Which convinces me that either the deer haven't seen the same charts or all other things are never the same. I will go to my grave unshakably convinced that exactly the opposite is true, and that moon phase is critical to a hunter's plans." Indeed, on no other question do deer hunters and deer biologists disagree more vehemently.

When we turn our attention to the scientific literature, we find no *conclusive* evidence to support the idea that the moon directly influences deer movements and/or behavior. Conflicting data, however, exist on the subject, suggesting the possibility of lunar influence at least — thus keeping the question of how deer respond to lunar cycles alive even though the waters at times seem quite muddy, especially when we delve into the cosmic connections between hydrographical and meteorological phe-

nomena, between lunar cycles and game populations.

While investigating the intensity of moonlight on mule deer movements and bedding patterns in the Yosemite region of California, Joseph Dixon, an early deer researcher, found a definite tendency for mule deer to bed down in the moonlight in dense shadows under thickly foliaged trees, chiefly cedars. He found no deer in meadows during moonlit periods. During the dark of the moon, however, he searched these same meadows and found them well-populated with grazing deer. He made frequent investigations on dark, moonless nights and found deer numerous and bedded down in the open meadows; but they bedded down in the shadows under trees in thick cover on bright moonlit nights. His nighttime experiments revealed the fact that in bright moonlight deer bedded in the deep shadows were relatively difficult to see. While thus concealed, they maintained an excellent chance of detecting the approach of any intruder through the moonlight zone surrounding them.

Other deer researchers, on the other hand, have found a striking correlation between periods of bright moonlight and the occurrence of mule deer at salt licks. Still other observers, such as deer researcher Frank Barick in North Carolina, report that whitetails also appear to feed more heavily on clear, moonlit nights. He qualifies his observation, however, by adding that "seeing more deer on these nights may be due to better visibility."

Perhaps no one has spent more time watching deer in the moonlight and documenting specific information in this regard than Linsdale and Tomich, deer researchers at the Hasting Natural History Reservation in California. Desiring specific information about the possible effect of moonlight on deer feeding and movement patterns, they spent the last three nights before the full moon of July (referred to as the Buck Moon by the Indians because buck deer were fat at this time and their meat could be quickly dried in the hot July sun) and three nights after the full moon at their nighttime research station, watching for and listening to deer activity. They reached the conclusion that moonlight does not regulate deer foraging and movement. In fact, based on their nighttime watching of deer, they suggested that moonlight is not essential to any nighttime activities.

In a similar study, James Elder, a wildlife researcher, noted that the phases of the moon had no discernible effect on the watering patterns of desert mule deer in Arizona.

In examining the various meteorological factors influencing the spotlighting counts of white-tailed deer, wildlife researchers in South Dakota reported that whitetails were more easily spotlighted on dark nights; during the dark of the moon they

remained less wary and failed to flee to cover as readily as on bright, moonlit nights. The early wildlife photographers such as George Shiras III and Tappan Gregory, who worked extensively at nighttime deer photography, reported similar findings. In his deer research in Georgia, Larry Marchinton also observes that whitetails apparently feel more secure in exposed habitats under cover of darkness.

Texas deer hunters generally applaud when their deer season opens at the dark of the moon and groan when the opening falls during the full-moon period. But as Texas Parks and Wildlife Biologist Gary Spencer reports, studies done by the department have found no correlation between lunar phases and nocturnal deer movement.

Spencer explains:

"When we began to use nighttime spotlight counts as a tool in deer census work, we ran a statistical analysis on factors that could affect the accuracy of the method.

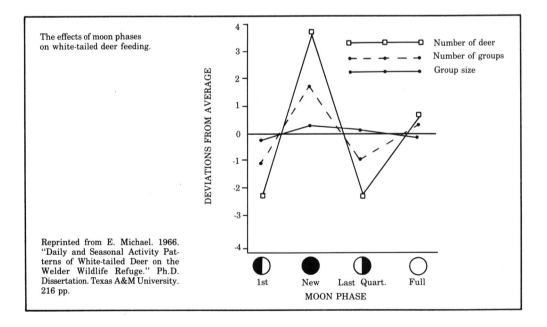

The effects of moon phases on white-tailed deer feeding.

Number of deer
Number of groups
Group size

DEVIATIONS FROM AVERAGE

Reprinted from E. Michael. 1966. "Daily and Seasonal Activity Patterns of White-tailed Deer on the Welder Wildlife Refuge." Ph.D. Dissertation. Texas A&M University. 216 pp.

1st   New   Last Quart.   Full
MOON PHASE

We considered such factors as moon phase, relative humidity, barometric pressure, cloud cover, wind direction and speed.

"We ran a lot of spotlight counts all over Texas and were never able to prove that moon phase or any of the other factors affected nocturnal deer movements. From personal experience on spotlight counts, I've seen just as many deer on pitch-black nights as I've seen on a full moon."

Similarly, while studying the nighttime activity of white-tailed deer in the Adirondacks, Don Behrend, a wildlife researcher, found no definite relationships between deer activity and moon phases. Florida deer biologists reached the same conclusion when analyzing the possible effect of moon phases on deer movement in the Crandall Pasture, an area of approximately 15,000 acres near Fernandina Beach, Florida.

Edwin Michael, another deer biologist, also arrived at the same result after studying the nocturnal activity patterns of whitetails in southern Texas. According to Michael, "The overall effect of moon phases on deer activity was not statistically significant and moon phase had no significant effect on deer feeding at different times of the twenty-four-hour period." He noted that deer activity tended to decrease during periods of full moons and that this trend held true for both the number of deer and the number of groups of deer. (See accompanying figure.) His findings, however, indicate a slight increase in the number of active deer between the hours of 2:00 to 4:00 A.M. during the full moon phase. He detected no decrease in the number of active deer during the daylight hours of the full-moon phase. His data also indicate that the dark-moon phase does not result in an increase in the number of deer feeding during the daytime hours. In fact, his data indicate the direct opposite. Michael added one interesting

point: Deer activity seemed to increase during the first and, to a lesser extent, last quarter when the moon is neither full nor completely dark.

In a similar study, Keith Thomas, a wildlife researcher, reached comparable conclusions: Nocturnal white-tailed deer feeding occurs less frequently during the full moon period than during the first quarter and last quarter of the moon. Using the spotlight method to study nocturnal deer activity on the Crab Orchard National Wildlife Refuge in southern Illinois, Thomas found that whitetails appear more skittish and quickly seek cover on bright moonlit nights. His 2050 nighttime observations of deer indicate that during the full moon whitetails feed more before the moon appears and after it sets during the period of bright moonlight. In general, he found the full moon more unfavorable for nighttime deer feeding than the other moon phases.

Unlike Thomas, Richard Prior, one of Britain's leading deer biologists and deer stalkers, reports that roe deer, based on his five-year study, remain unwilling to move or feed on very dark nights and that lack of moonlight actually remains a limiting factor on the nighttime movement at least for this species of deer. He summarizes his findings in *The Roe Deer of Cranborne Chase* (1968): "Peaks of feeding occur between full moon phases with sufficient regularity to indicate that moonlight, or the lack of it, has a profound effect on the movement of roe deer at night." Prior points out that the question of lunar phase and deer activity remains a promising field for experimentation in deer observation at night but that little has been done in this regard.

In the March 1987 issue of *Deer: Journal of the British Deer Society,* Dr. Frank Holmes, a natural historian of roe deer, reports that "when the moon is full both

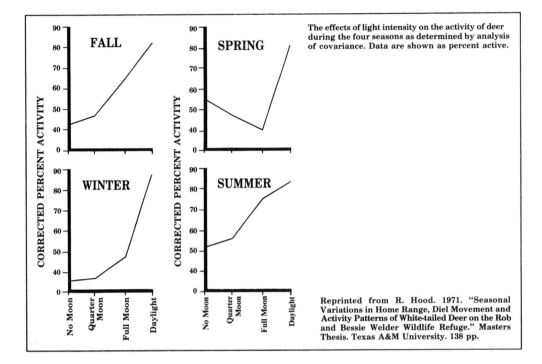

The effects of light intensity on the activity of deer during the four seasons as determined by analysis of covariance. Data are shown as percent active.

Reprinted from R. Hood. 1971. "Seasonal Variations in Home Range, Diel Movement and Activity Patterns of White-tailed Deer on the Rob and Bessie Welder Wildlife Refuge." Masters Thesis. Texas A&M University. 138 pp.

the morning and evening stands are usually unproductive even when there is cloud cover." In his observations on roe deer movement relative to the phases of the moon, Holmes came to believe that while the phases of the moon modify normal deer movement patterns, they exercise no influence on deer movement during the rut.

Some American deer biologists who studied light intensity and white-tailed deer activity reached conclusions similar to those of the English deer biologists. Ronald Hood, for example, a wildlife researcher at Texas A&M University, found whitetails to be more active under a full moon than when no moon was shining. Hood concluded that deer activity increased with an increase in light. Radio-tagged whitetails became most active at night in his study during a full moon in

summer, fall, and winter and least active during the dark of the moon. (See accompanying figure.) Hood could not explain the great deviation of spring data from this pattern. Similarly, Kent Kammermeyer, a deer biologist with the Georgia Game and Fish Division, observed more white-tailed deer feeding in fields on bright moonlit nights; his radio-tracking data indicated greater deer movement overall when the moon was in the light phase. (See accompanying figure.)

Yet other scientists disagree. Wildlife researcher Michael Zagata, for example, reports that lunar phase did not affect the number of deer sighted in his study on the influence of light on the observability of Iowa deer. Likewise, Wain Evans — while studying deer movements in New Mexico — notes that neither moonrise nor moonset exercised any observable effect on

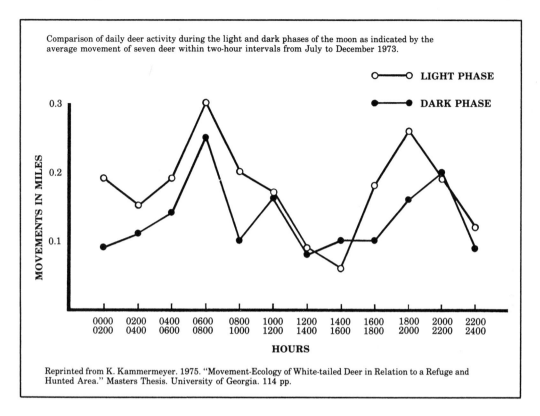

Comparison of daily deer activity during the light and dark phases of the moon as indicated by the average movement of seven deer within two-hour intervals from July to December 1973.

Reprinted from K. Kammermeyer. 1975. "Movement-Ecology of White-tailed Deer in Relation to a Refuge and Hunted Area." Masters Thesis. University of Georgia. 114 pp.

the activity of his radio-tagged deer. Moon phase, according to Evans, had no apparent effect on deer activity.

Pennsylvania deer researchers reached the same conclusion while studying the distribution and nocturnal activity of white-tailed deer along a Pennsylvania interstate highway: No definite relationship existed between the number of deer sighted and the presence or absence of moonlight. Deer researcher Arthur Hosey also found no significant correlation between deer movements and moon phases while studying the activity patterns of white-tailed bucks during the rut in Alabama.

On the other hand, in his study of the effects of weather on the behavior of white-tailed deer of the George Reserve, located northwest of Ann Arbor, Michigan, deer researcher Stephen J. Newhouse reports seeing more adult bucks on brighter nights and few bucks at all on darker nights.

During the late 1970s, my colleague Al Hofacker examined deer activity in relation to the lunar cycle as determined by analyzing the data sheets submitted by more than 1000 deer hunters from thirty states and one Canadian province. In August 1981, he published the results of his survey in an article titled "The Lunar Cycle and Deer Activity" in *Deer & Deer Hunting* magazine. Deer hunters participating in the collection of his data spent a total of 13,516.75 hours stand hunting and ciate editor of *Deer & Deer Hunting* magazine, kept careful records of daytime deer sightings based on moon phases during fifty-eight days of the 1982 bow season. He found a striking correlation between the lunar cycle and deer activity. His deer sightings consistently peaked between the new and the first quarter for September and October; he found stand hunting to be the most productive at that time.

Trophy buck hunters also find a direct correlation between moon phases and deer activity. Gene Wensel, for example, expresses his opinion on the subject in *Hunting Rutting Whitetails* (1984): "I have a lot of faith in moon phases controlling whitetail movement. Moon phases will not play any part in determining the rut but they most assuredly will play a big part in affecting it. Whitetails are definitely lunar. Their activity is extensively controlled by the position of the moon. They will get up when the moon rises and they will bed down when the moon sets. Observation of domestic cattle will prove likewise. When

Using the spotlight method to study the nocturnal movement patterns of white-tailed bucks, some deer biologists report increased nocturnal deer activity during the full-moon period; other researchers, however, have reached the opposite conclusion. One deer researcher notes that the eyeshine of the whitetail appears white from the frontal view and red-orange from a profile view. The greater distance between the eyes of bucks causes their eyeshine to be wider than that of the does. *Leonard Lee Rue IV photo*

recorded 7148 deer sightings for an average of 52.9 deer per 100 hours of stand hunting. Hofacker correlated their information with moon phases and reached the following conclusion: "The effect of the lunar cycle on deer activity, based on this study, is so minimal that it can probably be ignored as a variable which affects deer activity." (See accompanying figure.)

Yet, individual deer hunters maintaining records of their own reach the opposite conclusion. Randy Schwalbach, the asso-

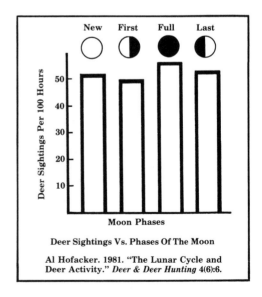

Deer Sightings Vs. Phases Of The Moon

Al Hofacker. 1981. "The Lunar Cycle and Deer Activity." *Deer & Deer Hunting* 4(6):6.

cattle are bedded down, so are deer. There are periods when insects, man, birds, and all wildlife will be active right along with domestic animals. This activity can be directly related to the position of the moon. In my country at least, the absolute best time to be in the woods is during the third week of November if a full moon at perigee rises during *daylight* hours and coincides with cold, clear weather and very little wind. If you don't believe a full moon can effect the libido of all living creatures, prove it to yourself by holding a cocktail party during a full moon sometime and another during a new moon. See which one proves to be the best party."

And so the debate continues on the lunar cycle and deer activity in the scientific literature and in deer camps alike. As Larry Marchinton writes in the Wildlife Management Institute's *White-tailed Deer* (1984): "There is still some question as to how deer respond to lunar cycles." Indeed. The lingering question became apparent as I listened to the paper "Censusing Deer by Plot Removal using SPOTLITE" at the 1987 Southeast Deer Study Group Meeting in Gulf Shores, Alabama. In that paper David Urbston, a wildlife researcher with the USDA Forest Service, underscored the importance of minimizing the lunar influence by spotlighting five nights after the full moon, thus acknowledging at least indirectly a lunar influence on deer movements, even though some scientists suggest that the moon exercises no influence on deer movement.

The addition of the lunar element to deer hunting never fails to add a dash of mystery to the sport; the association of the moon and the white-tailed deer always conjures up in my mind a hint of mystery, perhaps based on my own uneasiness at wandering the deer forest in the moonlight. Few deer seasons pass without giving me a dose of extraterrestrial enchantment when thinking about whitetails and moonshine. Indeed, exultation always reigns supreme when bringing into camp a deer and hanging it on the limb of a sheltering tree to cool in the moonlit shadows of the deer shack.

As I stare at the deer in the glow of the campfire and fill my nostrils with the savory smell of venison loin, the Hunter's Moon rises golden and full of strange excitement through the starry sky of October. I know that the Hunter's Moon will always come and go and so will deer hunters and whitetails. The beauty and mystery of hunting moons and whitetails move me to ponder their deeper meanings and relationships.

Regardless of how technical and sophisticated the modern-day deer hunter becomes, when everything else fails in the deer forest, many of us reach for *The Old Farmer's Almanac* and hope that the "zodiac secrets" found within will help us hang that buck on the meat pole. Whatever influence the moon might exert on white-tailed deer behavior, that influence seems to lie in the mysterious realm of the unexplainable. Who wants to deny that influence and its inherent mystery? As one redneck deerslayer from Scottsboro, Alabama, indicated: "To take the myth and mystery out of deer hunting would be to destroy it."

The opinions concerning the influence of the moon on the feeding habits and the nocturnal and diurnal movement patterns of deer remain diverse in both the popular and the scientific literature. I believe that every deer hunter should determine for himself, based on his own experiences and field notes, whether or not moon phases need to be considered when planning his next deer hunt. My personal experiences and field observations indicate that various periods of the lunar cycle affect white-tailed deer movements and feeding patterns and consequently need to be considered for optimum success.

Periods of full moon in my experience result in curtailed daytime deer activity. I experience an increase in deer activity in the pre-dusk and post-dawn hours during the last quarter of the old moon and the first quarter of the new moon. The rising of the moon and the gradual increase in nighttime luminosity seem to signal, as Ernest Thompson Seton believed, a start of feeding activities and commencement of deer movement toward feeding areas. When the moon rises during the daylight hours and can be seen in the late afternoon sky from my tree stand, I experience more deer activity than when the moon rises after dark. Yes, I place a great deal of faith in moon phases influencing white-tailed deer movement, especially during the early bow season, before the peak of the rut and before hunter density peaks.

No one in the history of American deer hunting spent more solitary hours studying and observing whitetails in the moonlight of November and December than Archibald Rutledge, the most eloquent chronicler of deer and deer hunting in South Carolina. Near his plantation house in McClellanville, he built a platform in an oak tree so that he could observe white-tailed deer behavior in the moonlight. In his opinion, moonlight dramatically influences deer movements and feeding patterns.

My advice for those deer hunters and/or deer biologists who deny the effect of moon phases on white-tailed deer activity is to spend *less* time in the lab, the library, and the experimental pens and *more* time in the deer forest. I live in the deer forest and my moonlight wanderings indicate that whitetails definitely respond to the lunar cycle. While pre-season scouting in July and August, I often see some of the largest, antlered white-tailed bucks in alfalfa fields on full moonlit nights, bucks that seem to be far out of their bailiwick. If every deer hunter would walk the deer forest once a month in the moonlight, he would soon agree with Arthur Carhart in *Hunting North American Deer* (1946): "Wherever you see him, especially in the bright illumination of the full moon, and with heart beating fast, the whitetail is a woods spirit, graceful, wary, trim-limbed, and the incarnation of wild places."

Chapter 5

The Scrape

Signposts produced by male white-tailed deer function to assist in terminating seasonal anestrus (a prolonged period of inactivity between two periods of heat in cyclically breeding does) and synchronizing estrus, in addition to their role in mate selection and as aggressive displays among bucks.
— Karl Miller, Larry Marchinton, and Matt Knox,
White-tailed Deer Signposts and Their Role as a
Source of Priming Pheromones: A Hypothesis, 1987

Deer hunters from time immemorial have been familiar with scrapes and the peculiar odors emanating from the various scent glands of deer. Research into the chemical composition of the secretions from deer glands dates back to 1906, when perfume chemists identified muscone as a major component in the secretion from the abdominal gland of the male musk deer of central Asia. But up to this day, we remain virtually ignorant of the functions these odors fulfill in the social life of deer. White-tailed deer researchers have only begun to scratch the surface in their investigations of scrapes and scent communication; they have only begun to explore the social mechanisms involved in signpost communications. We know very little about scrapes and pheromonal communication despite all the hype and sensationalizing of the modern-day deer hunting chemists to the contrary. The history and development of scraping patterns remains virtually unexplored. After a thorough examination of the scientific literature on the subject, we encounter more questions than answers.

In reading the sporting press of our day, we find more verbiage on white-tailed deer scrapes than on any other deer sign known to man. Perry Riley, a rather irate deer hunter from Indiana, recently complained in his self-published pamphlet *Bowhunting the Fake Scrape* (1985) that "sports writers have exaggerated scrape analysis into a complicated, confusing theory, making themselves look like geniuses." Indeed, we read about primary scrapes, breeding scrapes, territorial scrapes, secondary scrapes, hub scrapes, ground scrapes, pause scrapes, open-terrain scrapes, trail scrapes, scrape areas, fake scrapes, regular scrapes, mock scrapes, scrape enhancement, scrape elimination, scrape lines, scrape savvy, scrape watching, scrape mapping, scrape hunting, and who knows what else. One would think that the writers who use all this terminology in their enthusiastic discourse all graduated from high-powered research institutes with graduate degrees in deer "scrapology."

But what do we really know about scrapes and scraping? How many bucks are killed over scrapes? Can we determine the size of the buck from the size of the scrape? Can we smell scrapes? Where do we find scrapes? How do we hunt scrapes? How do mature bucks approach scrapes? How many scrapes do mature bucks (3.5 years or older) make? Do all bucks scrape? Do does make scrapes? Is scraping an innate or a learned behavior? Is scraping behavior predictable? Inducible? How have scrapes evolved over time? Will they evolve out of existence? How are they related to habitat characteristics, mast production, population density, sex, and age structure? Does the age of the bucks dramatically affect scraping patterns? Do bucks make scrapes to attract does or to establish dominance among other bucks? Or as deer biologist/bow hunter Arnold Haugen phrased it, "Is it to mark territory to warn other bucks to stay away or is it to add irresistible lure to does or both?" Attraction of does or intimidation of bucks? Despite the numerous assumptions and hypotheses, that question still remains unanswered.

Other questions go unanswered as well. In what way do scrapes function in phero-monal communication between the sexes during the rut? What information do certain scents from various glands carry in differing social situations? What is the chemical nature of the sex gland product? How is the white-tailed deer's pheromone (any chemical substance released by an animal that serves to influence the physiology or behavior of other members of the same species) transmitted from one deer to another? What is the chemical composition of the secretion from the tarsal gland? What happens when it unites with urine, the soil, and the interdigital gland? Does it encode information about sex and maturity? What is the sexual attractant for white-tailed does?

Despite the inability of scientists to answer many of these questions, or to even identify the chemical nature of white-tailed deer pheromones or to fully understand the behavioral function of pheromones in signpost behavior, the marketplace remains saturated with an incredible volume of "estrous doe" scents. One wonders how many white-tailed deer we would need in captivity to produce this fine array of chemical juice? Probably more deer than we have in the wild. It doesn't take a certified member of the International Society of Chemical Ecology to ask whether any of these artificial stimulants make sense. I wonder.

T. S. Van Dyke, the well-known deer-hunting naturalist who still-hunted white-tails without the aid of fragrant chemicals, undoubtedly emerges as the first deer hunter in America to document the "pawed circles" that appear during the rut in woods frequented by white-tailed deer. While he assumed that white-tailed bucks make these pawed circles as part of their rutting behavior, he apparently did not observe bucks in the act of scraping and consequently failed to give us a detailed description of scrapes and white-tailed deer scraping.

Other deer-hunting naturalists who followed Van Dyke, such as William Monypeny Newsom, referred to scrapes as "stamping places which you will immediately recognize by the patches of freshly torn up and trampled earth several feet in diameter." Ernest Thompson Seton called them "odoriferous cesspools" of the forest. He freely admitted his ignorance as to their function: "What pleasure it gives the animal, or what purpose it serves, no one knows; but every hunter who finds one of these odoriferous cesspools of the forest, knows at once that the bucks have begun to bestir themselves for the good of the next generation. Whether the wallow is a sex or sanitary institution is not known." Deer hunter/naturalist Art Carhart referred to them as "mud wallows" where white-tailed bucks ease their sexual hunger during the fall fever. He characterized scraping as a "strange and wild practice" about which we know little or nothing.

It wasn't until the fall of 1952, seventy years after Van Dyke's early notation of bucks pawing the ground, that Bill Pruitt, a naturalist working at the Museum of Zoology at the University of Michigan, clearly saw and fully described the behavioral sequences associated with a white-tailed buck in the act of making a scrape. While on one of his daily tramps through the E. S. George Reserve in southeastern Michigan on November 14 of that year, Pruitt spotted a large 8-pointer whose weight he estimated at about 225 pounds pass through a second-growth, oak-hickory woods and approach an abandoned field at about 8:00 A.M. Clear weather prevailed with a light southeast wind; the air temperature was twenty-seven degrees Fahrenheit with a relative humidity of 80

percent. In a general note published in the February 1954 issue of the *Journal of Mammalogy,* Pruitt recalls what happened.

> He rattled his antlers on low oak limbs and uttered several low grunts. He reached up and grasped low-hanging oak limbs in his mouth, pulled them down, and, by twisting his head, raked his antlers through them.
>
> Alternating with this activity were spells when he pawed the ground with his forefeet, throwing soil and leaves up over his back, and raked his antlers, first one side and then the other, through the leaves and loose soil.
>
> Occasionally the buck would wheel in a circle, flash his flag, grunt and then resume his antler-rattling and pawing. The whole procedure was strongly reminiscent of the actions of a domestic bull when he smells a cow in heat or is working himself into a frenzy preparatory to a charge.
>
> Inspection of the spot immediately after the buck had left revealed the presence of a typical pawed circle about three feet in diameter, where all the leaves had been removed and the soil torn and trampled, with hoof and antler marks plainly and deeply imprinted. Loose soil was scattered for several feet around the circle on top of the leaf litter. No evidence of fresh urine was noted. The lower limbs of the tree immediately over the circle were torn, scarred and broken.

Pruitt's landmark description, however, did not deal with either the social significance or the functions of these activities nor did he use the term "the scrape." Joseph Batty, a taxidermist and hunter for the U.S. government surveys, first coined the term in his instructions for hunters, *How to Hunt and Trap* (1882), when he wrote that "bucks make scrapes in open woods which they visit at night to see if the does have crossed and follow any trails that may be found." The term was first used in the scientific literature so far as I know by

James Teer and other researchers in a publication of The Wildlife Society entitled "Ecology and Management of White-tailed Deer in the Llano Basin of Texas" (1965). They defined the term as places where bucks paw shallow depressions in the ground and in which they urinate.

Considerable time passed before Pruitt's observations percolated down to the deer hunter, especially the gun hunter. During the 1960s, deer hunters from the South still referred to scrapes in romantic terms as "buck pawings" and "love traps." Texas deer hunter Tom Hayes, for example, talked about "Romeo Buck making bee-lines back to scrapes with undiminished ardor to renew his love potion." In 1969, Wisconsin's George Mattis summarized the general state of knowledge about scrapes among deer hunters: "This is the trademark of the sire claiming these grounds, and it serves notice to all intruders that this area belongs to the lord whose seal is here displayed. These dirt pawings bear a little study for they are not a mere work of exuberance without some purpose."

During the next decade, Larry Marchinton and his graduate students at the School of Forest Resources at the University of Georgia set out to determine the scientific purpose underlying these dirt pawings at their Whitehall Deer Research Facility. Supported by McIntire-Stennis funds, the Keeper Bait Company, Super-Synt Inc., and the Georgia Forest Research Council, Marchinton and his students began to unravel the intricate details of scrapes and scraping.

In one of the first studies titled "An Investigation into the Existence of Signposts and Their Relationship to Social Structure and Communication in White-tailed Deer" (1971), Athens 1, a radio-equipped 4.5-year-old buck played a prominent part in their scientific search for the social significance of scrapes and scraping. Gerald Moore, the principal author of the study, observed Athens 1, a dominant 11-pointer weighing 175 pounds, make twenty-seven scrapes one fall. The buck marked the surrounding foliage (including the overhanging branch) in all twenty-seven scrapes. He urinated in 16 percent of them and defecated in 7 percent of them. "When the animal urinated at the scrape," Moore reported, "an olfactory signal was left that even the investigator could detect for a short period of time."

Athens 1 exhibited aggressive behavior at the scrapes 11 percent of the time. He located his scrapes in a clumped distribution around his rubs; they existed in a total area of three square miles. He returned to some of his scrapes every two to five days and "reworked" them. He scraped most often just before dark, although he occasionally scraped throughout the day and shortly after dark.

His scrapes generally approximated one to two square feet in size, although some were somewhat larger. While scrape size varies, the scrapes of Athens 1 never exceeded the immense sizes frequently reported in the popular literature. For example, Texas deer hunter Bill Grusendorf reports in his *Fifty Years of White-tailed Deer Hunting in Texas* (1961) that during the deer hunting season of 1940, he found a scrape ten miles east of Leakey, Texas, measuring twelve feet across that was used year after year. One deer hunter from Alabama named Courtney "Foots" Lumpkin notes in his *100 Deer* (1980) finding a "scrape as large as a car." That's a bit larger than the scrapes found in the bailiwick of Athens 1.

Athens 1 usually made his scrapes in such conspicuous places as the intersection

When pawing in a scrape, a buck becomes aggressive and the hair on his back stands erect. *Leonard Lee Rue III photo*

of deer trails, in old logging trails and roadbeds and near the edges of forest openings. He made them under water oaks, southern red oaks, and live oaks. They most often occurred in feeding and bedding areas. Moore also observed Athens 1 in the act of what he termed "pawing variations and unusual scraping behavior"—something deer hunters often refer to as the "false rut." These pawing variations occurred near the beginning of the rut and were not located in conspicuous places. Athens 1 made them in a hurried manner and they consequently remained small and hardly noticeable. While pawing in this manner, according to Moore, "the animal became aggressive and dug his antlers into the exposed soil. The hair on his back became erect, but after he walked away from the pawed area, his hair resumed its normal position. Urination rarely occurred near pawed areas of this type." Athens 1 also frequently engaged in this type of behavior after making buck rubs.

After observing Athens 1 for 154 telemetric-contact days as well as studying thirteen other bucks for 350 hours, Moore concluded that bucks make scrapes to communicate a threat in the animal's absence and that scrapes function to allow bucks to maintain a dominant position in a given area during the rut. In addition, he speculated that scrapes may provide a form of visible communication between the sexes to ensure the presence of a buck when a doe reaches estrus. He further noted that the scrape represented a complex signpost including everything from tracks left in the scraped area, secretions from the interdigital gland, the soil, deer urine, secretions from the tarsal gland, visual stimuli presented by the scraped area and the overhanging branch, and olfactory signals on both the branch and the soil, as well as grunting and sneeze-like vocalizations.

Moore noticed that young bucks seemed ill at ease and disoriented near scrapes and quickly left the scene when larger, more dominant bucks approached. He also speculated that licking the tarsal glands may allow bucks to transfer the scent to other signposts such as rubs and overhanging branches that they mouth.

During the rut, Athens 1 exhibited three forms of territoriality or areas of defense: dominance territory, scrape territory, and the territory around estrous females. Moore's data showed that white-tailed bucks express a form of territoriality during the rut "at least in moderate or low deer population levels and where heavy hunter harvest does not disrupt population structure." Moore's evidence indicated that sexually mature bucks may physically defend the area immediately around their scrapes and that scrapes serve to delineate and identify specific territories in an animal's absence. This type of territoriality, Moore and Marchinton carefully point out, depends upon the population structure and density and tends to break down at higher population levels, especially in

heavily hunted populations where sex ratios strongly favor females.

Building on Moore's study, Terry Kile continued to study white-tailed deer scrapes on a 200-acre tract in the Georgia Piedmont. He systematically examined the entire tract every two weeks for a period of one year for the occurrence of new scrapes. He recorded the date, location, various measurements, and the various tree species involved for seventy scrapes. He found most scrapes in habitat types where the understory was relatively open. Eight-six percent of the scrapes Kile observed had overhanging branches above the pawed area. Sweet gum, eastern red cedar, dogwood, and loblolly pine were the tree species most frequently associated with the overhanging branch in the area he studied.

Sixty-six percent of the overhanging branches revealed various types of mutilations such as scarred bark and broken limbs. The distance from the overhanging branch to the ground ranged from thirty-one to sixty-nine inches. The length of scrapes ranged from fourteen to forty-nine inches and the width from ten inches to forty-two inches. Seven scrapes of the seventy scrapes studied contained fecal pellets within the pawed area; thirty percent of them revealed distinct tracks of smaller deer in the pawed area as well, possibly indicating visits by does.

The number of scrapes increased from the beginning of September until the end of December and were generally clumped independently of buck rubs. Since scraping and breeding frequencies began and peaked at the same time, Kile suggested that scrapes "apparently" facilitate communication between bucks and does during the rut, but that more research was needed in this regard.

At the second annual meeting of the Southeast Deer Study Group Meeting at Mississippi State University, Marchinton, in summarizing the research done by him and his students, referred to areas of high scrape densities as "dominance areas" that are spatially defended by dominant bucks. While dominant bucks allow subordinates to pass through these dominance areas, the latter must maintain a subordinate posture. Bucks often assert dominance by making scrapes in the presence of subordinate animals. This type of behavior I have experienced on many occasions in my hunting area. Marchinton found that dominant bucks spend several days in each dominance area before moving on to another. The length of time spent in each area probably depends upon the number and breeding conditions of the does in the area.

In the paper "Signpost and Pheromone Communication: What We Know (Or Think We Know) Now?" Marchinton summarized his findings by saying, "Scrapes have a communicative function. Bucks often return to scrapes and sometimes 'freshen' them or make another scrape nearby. Scrapes also are visited by does, which leave an olfactory message and trail for the buck to follow. How this trail is left is not clear. Possibly they urinate and step in the urine. In any case, a buck returning to a scrape that has been visited by a doe makes grunting sounds and moves off at a fast walk with his nose near the ground following the doe's trail."

The Georgia research continued with Tim Sawyer focusing his attention on the behavior of does at scrapes with special emphasis on pheromonal communication. Sawyer found that even white-tailed does scrape to a limited extent and that doe scraping does not confine itself to the rut. In August 1979 he observed one radio-tagged doe paw out a scrape and urinate directly into it. She then licked each of her tarsal gland tufts several times and then bedded down within a hundred yards of

the scrape. Sawyer underscored the fact that we know very little about how female scrapes function in social communication.

While observing deer from his tree stand along an old logging road in a mixed hardwood and pine woodlot in Georgia's Taliaferro County one October morning, Sawyer recorded the following unique observation of doe scraping: "At 7:00 A.M. a female, apparently an adult, emerged from a thicket. A few minutes later, a six-pointer approached her. He stopped twenty yards from the female at a small scrape, which was at least two days old and was near a rubbed sapling. He thrashed some bushes with his antlers and pawed the old scrape into a larger one approximately twenty-eight inches in diameter. The female watched him intently and, apparently in response to his actions, pawed an almost identical depression where she stood. The male then joined her, and they moved off together browsing. Neither deer urinated in association with their scraping."

I have never seen a doe make a scrape or scrape in an existing scrape nor have I read or listened to anyone clearly and adequately explain in an in-depth manner how a doe responds to a scrape. No clear, scientific documentation exists on this question. In order to understand the role that the doe plays in scrape initiation and/or maintenance, we need to set up infrared, motion-sensitive cameras near scrapes in the wild to photograph at pre-set intervals all motion present near or at scrape sites.

After studying four radio-tagged does for approximately 1400 hours during a two-year period, Sawyer reported that does sniffed and walked through the pawed depressions and urinated in the vicinities of scrapes made by bucks. He speculated that their sniffing of the scrapes may represent their perception of pheromones deposited by bucks but hastened to add that this was mere speculation since the actual chemical identities of white-tailed deer pheromones and their specific social functions remain unknown.

Pheromones at the scraping site may come from many possible sources: the tarsal glands, the interdigital glands, the preorbital glands, the forehead scent gland, the sac-like nasal gland, urine and saliva, or a combination of any or all of these sources. No one knows for sure despite all the marketplace bull and hype to the contrary. Sawyer reached the conclusion that his research did not strongly support the hypothesis that scrapes even function in pheromonal communication between bucks and does but that it did not preclude the plausible idea that white-tailed deer pheromones, whatever they may be, are somehow transferred from bucks to does and in the process communicate sex, breeding status, age, individual recognition, physical condition, and dominance status.

At the fifth annual meeting of the Southeast Deer Study Group Meeting in Charleston, South Carolina, Marchinton again stressed how little we know about white-tailed deer pheromones, glands, and scent communication: "Deer live in a different world from us. They use their many scent glands in ways that we do not yet comprehend — we don't even know how many glands they have. Only when we understand more about what these scents mean to deer will we have hope of achieving complete insight into deer behavior."

The University of Georgia's deer behavior research program next began to focus its attention on the scent-producing glands of the whitetail and in the process discovered two previously unidentified skin glands: the forehead scent gland and the sac-like nasal glands, found just inside the nose connected to the nostril by a short

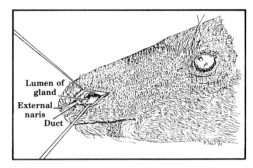

THE LATERAL VESTIBULAR GLAND. This figure shows the lateral view of the whitetail's sac-like nasal glands. Each gland empties to the exterior via a short duct. While the function of these nasal glands remains unknown, by drawing chemicals from female urine that a buck licks, sniffs or inhales into the sensory pit of the vomeronasal organ he may be able to detect the state of readiness of a doe. Deer biologists believe that whitetails have a well-developed vomeronasal organ capable of functioning in the act of flehmen as a sensor of non-volatile, water-soluble chemicals.

Reprinted from Thomas Atkeson. 1983. "Aspects of Social Communication in White-Tailed Deer." Ph.D. Dissertation: University of Georgia, Athens. 63 pp.

duct. (See accompanying figure.) Although the precise social function of these lateral vestibular nasal glands remains a mystery, their very presence underscores the significance of scent communication as associated with flehmen, scraping, and other forms of white-tailed breeding behavior.

During the peak of the rut in 1981, I once observed an 8-pointer chasing antlerless deer around an alfalfa field; when he approached the scrape under my tree stand, he snorted in such a dramatic way that I could actually see what deer researcher Tom Atkeson calls "a visible expulsion of atomized material" come from the buck's nose. After sharing this experience with my taxidermist, he immediately showed me the inner structure of these nasal glands.

After examining seventy-eight white-tailed deer, Tom Atkeson found that twenty-two of them contained visible accumulations of a white, fatty secretion within the lumens of these nasal glands. Although not studied exhaustively, he noted no apparent differences in this unknown secretion between seasons, sexes, or ages. Atkeson speculated that these secretions may be kept sequestered within these nasal glands and emitted only during snorting behavior.

While the function of these nasal glands in pheromonal communication remains unknown, deer researchers now believe that the white-tailed deer's well-developed vomeronasal organ may function as a sensor of non-volatile water-soluble chemicals, especially when deer exhibit the flehmen (or "lip-curl") posture. Actually, these nasal sebaceous glands may serve as pheromone producers on a year round basis. In his unpublished paper "Scent Communication in White-tailed Deer" (1982), Marchinton speculated on the pos-

sible significance of these nasal glands and flehmen behavior: "White-tailed bucks will sniff the spot where a doe has urinated and lick it or lick the doe's vulva if he can get close enough. The buck then wrinkles his nose, licks his lips and inhales. By doing this he draws chemicals from the urine into his mouth and then into the sensory pit of the vomeronasal organ where he can detect the state of readiness of the doe by the presence of unknown substances that apparently are not detectable by the nose itself. The nerve connections of this organ do not go to the olfactory lobe of the brain, but rather, go directly to the part that controls sexual behavior. The behavioral significance of this alternative mode of scent communication is not yet understood but it is possible that there is a com-

"White-tailed bucks will sniff the spot where a doe has urinated and lick it or lick the doe's vulva if he can get close enough." — Larry Marchinton. *Leonard Lee Rue III photo*

plex interaction between the sexes, and their scent marks and body scents serve to induce and synchronize breeding."

Perhaps deer, unlike humans, think through their noses. Indeed, generations of biologists, field naturalists, and deer hunters have marveled at the whitetail's acute sense of smell and cursed it as well when it thwarts the still-hunter at the mere hint of a breeze. As deer hunters, we are barred from the whitetail's whole range of smells that Kenneth Grahame in his classic *The Wind in the Willows* calls "those delicate thrills which murmur in the nose of the animal night and day, summoning, warning, inciting, repelling." Unlike the whitetail, we cannot think through our noses. We cannot recognize those faint traces of scent, those conspicuous signals transmitted from one deer to another; the whitetail's social odors are quite beyond our powers of detection. Yet, our own dismal and ill-equipped sense of smell spurs us to great heights of curiosity in trying to learn more about how whitetails communicate.

In trying to learn more about how whitetails communicate, Karl Miller, another deer hunter/researcher from the Georgia School of Forest Resources, continued to study the importance of scrapes and scraping as a communicative mechanism and developed a technique for evaluating a whitetail's scraping history by assessing the differential wear between the front and rear hooves of the animal. He soon learned that not all bucks scrape, and that it is important to know "who" makes scrapes in populations with varying densities, sex ratios, age structures, and differing habitats. His research, based on a three-year-study of scrape behavior, indicates that yearlings and 2.5 year-olds scrape later in the rut than older, prime-aged bucks and that a higher percentage of

them scrape in areas under-represented by older bucks.

According to Miller, "dominance, testosterone levels, and the maturational state of the male apparently interact to promote the expression of scraping behavior." In other words, scraping appears largely dependent on the maturational state of the male. Miller found that the more mature, dominant bucks (i.e., mature age, large-bodied animals with darkly stained tarsal glands and swollen necks) were most expressive of scraping behavior. Yearlings demonstrated delayed scraping and less scraping than prime-age bucks. Miller's data suggest that bucks may have to reach a certain threshold of testosterone before scraping may occur.

In one of the most fascinating studies to date, titled "Social and Biological Aspects of Signpost Communication in White-tailed Deer" (1985), Miller tells us that if scrapes are made primarily by dominant males, estrous females may seek out these scrapes in search of the best reproductive partner, since natural selection favors females who choose to breed with the "most fit" male. He recommends that future research be directed toward elucidating the effects of different harvest strategies on scraping activity and ultimately on white-tailed deer breeding performance. I could not agree more with this suggestion.

Future research continues at the White-hall Deer Research Facility on such topics as the seasonal variations in the marking behavior of both sexes of white-tailed deer and the artificial manipulation of the estrous cycle of adult white-tailed deer as well as all aspects of white-tailed deer communication, especially rubs, scrapes, and pheromones. Marchinton's research has profound implications for deer populations and the future of deer hunting all across this land. I find it very disturbing, given the great popularity of this animal and the intense interest in deer hunting in America, that no one has come forth to fund this significant research. Unfortunately, their progress is greatly hampered due to lack of funding. Any individuals and/or sportsmen's organizations interested in contributing tax-deductible funds for this greatly needed white-tailed deer research should contact: R. Larry Marchinton, School of Forest Resources, University of Georgia, Athens, GA 30602. 404/542-3932.

In a paper titled "White-tailed Deer Signposts and Their Role as a Source of Priming Pheromones: A Hypothesis" presented at the International Congress of Game Biologists in Krakow, Poland, in August of 1987, Miller, Marchinton, and Knox synthesized their findings and reported that glandular secretions and urinary deposits left on rubs and in scrapes act as a source of priming pheromones (i.e., pheromones that act upon an organism to modify development or physiology) to assist in terminating seasonal anestrus and synchronizing estrus to coincide with the buck's peak condition. According to the report, the licking of rubs, overhanging branches, and tarsal glands may involve the vomeronasal organ as a mediator of priming pheromones. They also reported that, in certain areas, reduced acorn production results in a dramatic decrease in antler rubbing.

While Marchinton and his colleagues continue to study scrapes and scraping in the South, John Ozoga continues his deer research on the social role of scrapes in the whitetail's northern range. While studying the comparative breeding behavior and performance of yearlings versus prime-age bucks near Shingleton in Michigan's Upper Peninsula, Ozoga noted that, un-

like their southern colleagues, prime-age bucks in the North begin making scrapes nearly two months prior to the onset of breeding and that scraping peaks during the first two weeks of November, declines gradually thereafter, and ceases in early December. Yearlings in his study made only 15 percent as many scrapes as did mature bucks. While mature bucks reworked

Nearly half of all scrapes are reused year after year. Given uniform habitat conditions, certain favored scraping sites may be used for generations of time. It is important to search out early scrapes and pay close attention to them because many of them will become breeding scrapes during the peak of the rut. *Richard P. Smith photo*

about half of their scrapes, yearlings only reworked from 31 to 44 percent of their scrapes. Almost half of the scrapes were reused year after year. Given uniform habitat conditions, certain favored scraping sites, like deer trails, may show use for generations of time.

Ozoga found, as did Marchinton, that compared to mature bucks yearlings demonstrate delayed scraping and less overall scent marking in general. Despite these differences, however, no scientific evidence suggests that yearlings are inferior breeders. Although Ozoga's study does not reveal any deleterious effects of intensive buck harvesting, he does not recommend the complete harvest of bucks each fall as a wise practice, since the lack of superior males may reduce the herds's genetic fitness in the long run.

Ozoga's findings generally agree with those of Marchinton and his researchers. According to John, "scrapes serve as important means of communication between the sexes and enhance the maker's breeding success. We also found scrape-making a specialized trait largely dependent upon male physical/behavioral maturity, not merely high dominance rank. Because does may visit scrapes selectively, such communication behavior may allow them to solicit attention from preferred mates when a choice exists."

Ozoga believes that scrape making is clearly an inherited, innate trait that improves with time and experience, and that scrape making varies tremendously even among the most mature bucks. He found in his research that some mature bucks are avid scrape makers while others are not. He once watched an exceptional scraper make five scrapes and two buck rubs within a thirty-minute period. That buck probably made hundreds of scrapes during a single breeding season. The number of scrapes a buck makes varies greatly — remaining a puzzle at best. Virginia deer hunter Riley Puckett reports that he once found thirty-one scrapes in an area of about 200 yards.

Deer hunters frequently ask, "How often does a buck return to his scrapes?" Ozoga studied hundreds of scrapes; he reports that few, if any, were ever consistently used day after day for extended periods of time. This revelation remains exceedingly important for the deer hunter, since John studied a stable deer population in an unhunted area. One can only imagine the inconsistency of use in heavily hunted terrain. Yet, some deer hunters insist that bucks return to their scrapes several times a day. "Even those sites that showed repeated use for five or six consecutive days were often-times abandoned," John reports, "or at least not reopened, for periods of a week or more at a time. Some very respectable looking scrapes were never reused."

Where do we find scrapes? Ozoga found most of the scrapes he studied in areas with an open understory. The most frequently used sites he found on "easily bared soil (not sod-bound)." He located most of the scrape sites in areas of heavily concentrated deer use. White-tailed bucks in his study preferred soils that were neither too wet nor too dry. Most of the scrape sites he found also contained that "truly mystifying feature of the scrape" — the scent-marked overhanging branch. Ozoga's data indicates that bucks prefer deciduous species over conifers when choosing overhanging branches, although he did find some overhanging branches on jack pines.

As most observant deer hunters know, the real drama at the scrape revolves around the overhanging branch. "When the overhanging limb consists of little more than a single slender stem," Ozoga observes, "bucks tend to rub more gently, carefully guiding the stem's feathered tip along the side of their face, beginning at the base of the nostril. To watch a buck engaged in this type of behavior is a treat in itself. He stands as if in a trance, outstretched, as he meticulously and delicately anoints the fragile twig with some magical ingredient."

After studying hundreds of scrapes and countless scraping incidents, Ozoga concludes that scrapes and pheromonal communication remain largely a mystery. Indeed, the subject remains highly complex and controversial. As he puts it, "The exact chemical compounds, behavior, and physiological mechanisms involved are poorly understood at best. . . . Even the scientific community knows relatively little about the chemical signals, called pheromones, that are exchanged between whitetails."

In attempting to learn more about white-tailed deer pheromones, Ozoga confined adult white-tailed does with individual bucks in permanent buck pens measuring twenty yards by twenty yards. He learned that the constant presence of a rutting buck in a tight enclosure with does

Most scrapes include that "truly mystifying feature"—the overhanging branch. Here a rutting white-tailed buck rubs his forehead scent gland on the overhanging branch. *Leonard Lee Rue III photo*

resulted in what deer researchers call a "biostimulation" effect that induces an overt estrus and early successful breeding in what would otherwise constitute an early but "silent" estrus. In speculating on the results of his experiment, Ozoga noted that "this reproductive response stemmed mainly from buck-doe interaction or excitation; i.e., females in the permanent-buck pen could not elude the rutting male's close and constant attention. Behavioral-physiological studies are needed to ascertain the respective influence of olfactory, auditory, visual, or tactile stimuli in triggering the temporally advanced breeding season we noted in crowded penned deer."

At the Whitehall Deer Research Facility in Georgia, Karl Miller, Matt Knox, and Larry Marchinton are also conducting experiments utilizing a synthetic analog of a prostaglandin f-2a (Lutalyse) to artificially manipulate the estrous cycle of adult white-tailed deer in their efforts to learn more about rubs, scrapes, and priming pheromones. Using this luteolytic enzyme, they have been able to bring does into estrus within seventy-two to eighty hours at a success rate of 60 percent. The main thrust of their research now focuses on understanding the key role played by the pheromones of bucks in terminating seasonal anestrus and synchronizing estrus and learning how scrapes function in this regard. These researchers report that the mechanism by which pheromones induce ovulation remains unknown. And so the questions continue: How do the priming pheromones from the male alter the physiology of the female? How do rubs and scrapes assist in this process?

Historically, it seems strange that few, if any, deer biologists really studied or analyzed scrapes before the 1950s. Perhaps the increase in deer populations since then and the marked increase in the popularity of bow hunting paved the way. With more and more bow hunters watching scrapes and reporting on their observations in the popular literature, more and more deer biologists became interested in these centerpieces of breeding activities as well. This occurrence represents a fine example of what Judge Caton called combining the sport of deer hunting with the science of natural history in such a way that "the hunter, who seeks and takes the game in its native fastnesses, may thus, I say, give the scientist valuable assistance."

While observing scrapes throughout the year, the white-tailed deer enthusiast will experience almost every form of deer behavior known to man: pawing, urinating, rub-urinating, flehmen, overhead-branch-marking, chasing, striking, flailing, sidling, hard-look threats, butting, licking, sniffing, grunting, alert-snorting, snort-wheezing, sparring, fighting, rubbing, thrashing, and scraping.

One of the most dramatic incidents of rubbing, thrashing, and scraping that I have ever heard about occurred on the Rob and Bessie Welder Wildlife Refuge in San Patricio County, Texas, on the evening of November 3, 1969, as Bennett Brown, a deer researcher at Texas A&M University, observed an 8-pointer walk into a small depression, densely vegetated with spiny aster. The buck, according to Brown, swept his head rapidly from side to side against saplings and stems. He then increased the intensity by thrashing the vegetation vigorously with his antlers — feinting and thrusting as if goring an opposing buck in real combat. After six minutes of doing so, his excitement increased; he now bounded about in circles, pivoting on his forelegs and hooking and thrashing sapling stems and vegetation.

Four more minutes of this activity passed. He had bent flat most of the vegetation in the immediate area; the stems and

During the rut, aggressive bucks sometimes want to rip up the entire woodlot. *Tom Edwards photo*

saplings lay broken and frayed to ribbons. The buck then thrust his antlers into the downed vegetation—thrashing and throwing stems, branches, and pieces of plants into the air over his head. On several occasions he fell to his "knees," snorting, sniffing, licking, and wheezing. He then plunged his antlers into the soil and with a great deal of strain and stress sniffed and smelled the low-lying vegetation in the process. Brown indicated that the incident lasted for almost twenty minutes before the agitated buck left the scene. In surveying the scene, Brown found that the buck flattened an egg-shaped area, measuring approximately seventeen feet on the long axis and almost nine feet at the widest axis. Brown could detect the smell of the aromatic spiny aster twenty to thirty yards downwind from the thrashed site.

Deer camp discussions frequently raise the question whether the deer hunter can determine the size of the buck from the size of the scrape. Louisiana deer hunter Ronnie "Big Buck" Glover insists that larger bucks make the largest scrapes. "I can guarantee you," he writes in his *More Than Luck: A Guide for Hunting the Trophy Buck* (1980), "that there is a direct relationship." Other deer hunters maintain that the size of the scrape depends upon the number of deer using it.

Ohio deer hunter John Weiss believes that the size of a buck's scrape accurately represents a clue to the buck's size: Small scrapes signify small bucks, according to

Weiss. He once found an incredibly large scrape in Gallia County in southeastern Ohio. The buck responsible for the scrape weighed 300 pounds and sported a 12-point rack. This buck, according to Weiss, "began making one scrape about three feet in diameter. Then a few days later he apparently began making a second scrape. It was about five feet away from the first and about twenty inches in diameter. This double-scraping characteristic of trophy deer is not unusual. Then the deer began work on a third scrape, this one right between the first two. By the time this sex-crazed buck was finished with his mating invitations, the ground had been pawed into a mammoth scrape. It was shaped somewhat like a football and measured four feet wide by seven feet long."

Weiss concludes that mature bucks make scrapes measuring at least two feet by three feet and that tine marks often appear in the scrape where the buck drags his rack through the dirt. He recommends that when we find this type of evidence that we carefully examine the distance between the individual tine drags and the width of each drag furrow. He observes that if "five inches or more separate the tine drags, with each furrow three quarters of an inch or more in width, you can be sure there is a large deer in the area."

While other deer hunters disagree, I must say the idea seems plausible, although I have never seen any scientific evidence to prove or disprove it. Dr. Dave Samuel, an avid bow hunter and a wildlife biologist at West Virginia University, claims in an article on scrapes, that "scrape size is irrelevant."

Some hunters like to insist that the direction of the leaves, dirt, and debris thrown back from the scrape by the buck indicates what time of day the buck visited the scrape. According to this theory, debris thrown toward the bedding area tells us that the buck scraped in the evening or late afternoon while on his way to his feeding grounds; while debris thrown toward the feeding area suggests that the buck scraped early in the morning while returning to his bedding area. I think this theory may well lay in the realm of myth and behavioral gibberish.

Can the deer hunter smell scrapes? Some hunters suggest that we can. Larry Marchinton tells me that he "sometimes smells them but more often smells the buck himself, especially after the buck rub-urinates. *Yes,* up to 100 yards!" John Wootters also says that "a recently freshened scrape has a strong, musky odor which is easily detected even by the feeble human nose." On the other hand, Lennie Rue and his friend Joe Taylor report that after carefully sniffing a number of scrapes they could only detect the "odor of the fresh earth."

I have often seen more than one buck use the same scrape, especially in July and August when white-tailed bucks establish social dominance in my hunting area. When this situation occurs, a social pecking order usually remains quite obvious at the scrape. I once had the rare opportunity in the early bow season of killing an 8-pointer while he stood with five other bucks at a scrape beneath my tree stand. I have located the most active and productive scrapes in my hunting area high up on white oak ridges running in an east-west direction. I have often hunted bottomland scrapes that look like choice sites to no avail; too often bucks detect my human odor in this type of situation.

If you are interested in scrape hunting, find an area where you not only have a one-to-one buck/doe ratio, but an area where you have more bucks than does. Remember that the more equal the buck/doe ratio becomes, the greater the breeding competition and hence the greater number of scrapes. It is hard to even find scrapes in areas where the buck/doe ratio is way out of balance and in areas with a very young age structure among the buck population. In such areas white-tailed scrapes virtually lose their function. One can also seriously question the real significance of scrapes for the gun hunter in areas of heavy hunting pressure, especially in the North where the rut peaks before the gun season even begins and where scraping activity tapers off drastically before the gun season opens.

Bow hunters, in particular, frequently raise the question of how bucks approach scrapes. How bucks approach scrapes depends upon many variables such as wind direction and velocity, light conditions, hunting pressure, habitat conditions, and available cover. Some bucks circle the scrape so they can approach it from a downwind position; others will scent-check the scrape from as far away as fifty yards or more. As daylight fades some bucks suddenly appear at the scrape as ghosts from nowhere. While few mature bucks charge right into a scrape along a main deer trail, I have seen this behavior. Others use less distinct trails in their approach.

Whether the best method for scrape hunting entails hunting over a particular scrape, stand hunting on the downwind side of a group of scrapes, or standing hunting in a well-chosen breeding area really remains a question of personal preference. I have shot bucks doing all of the above.

Deer hunters will try every trick in the book to encourage bucks to come to a specific scrape on the forest floor—doing everything from using deer decoys and making artificial scrapes and building their own overhanging branches, as deer researchers did as early as the 1970s, to urinating in the scrapes themselves. Trophy deer biologist Professor James Kroll at the Stephen F. Austin State University admits that "I even urinate in existing scrapes myself. You would not believe how it drives a big buck crazy to encounter one of his scrapes treated in such a fashion. I once tried this tactic and watched the scrape from afar for several hours. Not only was the scrape visited by more than one buck—each of which renewed the scrape—but a coyote also added his two cents' worth to the area!"

I have found through the years that the overhanging branch that bucks lick and sniff in July and August often becomes a main breeding scrape during the peak of the rut. While observing pre-rut socialization at scrapes and overhanging branches in July and August, it has appeared to me that deer of both sexes prefer open habitat so that they can see buck combat and antler display, as well as dominance formation, and so that they can acquire an individual recognition of dominant bucks through sight as well as odor.

In my mind, the unique curiosity of the scrape remains the individual hoof print visibly left in the fresh, black dirt. Why is it there? What is its significance? Why is it a smaller print than our imagination would hope for? Does this individual print indicate that the doe purposely stepped in the urine she deposited in the scrape in order to transfer scent to the interdigital glands to facilitate a rutting buck in following her scent trail? Or do all deer automatically place one of their front hooves forward to balance their weight as they place their nose on the ground to sniff the urine in the scrape? Or is this distinct deer track in the middle of the scrape made by the hind hoof of the buck as he leaves the scrape? Is it a single deer track? Or a double overlapped deer track? Does it indicate the direction from which the buck left the scrape?

While the scrape serves many functions such as facilitating communication in determining mate selection, delineating breeding areas, assisting somehow in the termination of seasonal anestrus, and the synchronization of estrus, it serves *above all* as an aggressive display among bucks in establishing and maintaining social dominance. I clearly saw the aggressive nature of this function on Wednesday, November 12, 1986 in such a dramatic way that I will never forget the day, the incident nor the importance of this function of the white-tail's scrape.

On that day, with the Beaver Moon approaching fullness, I arose at 5:00 A.M. and found three inches of newly fallen snow on the forest floor, a rather unusual event in my area for the closing days of the early bow season. I turned on my weather-band radio and listened to the announcer give the wind direction and velocity: eight m.p.h. from the northwest. An ideal situation for my tree stand near Doc's Rock, I thought. I left for my stand at 6:00 A.M. At 8:10 a young 4-pointer passed by my tree stand, heading for a scrape approximately twenty-five yards from me on the top of a small knoll. The white spruce trees that I had mistakenly planted on the knoll had been obliterated by the hooves and antlers of aggressive bucks in their creation of a large scrape atop this lookout point.

The young buck stopped broadside and stood within fifteen yards of my stand. In the interest of choice venison for the pot, I shot a Gamegetter 2117 through the animal. Instead of a dramatic lunge toward cover, he just stood still, as if nothing happened. I raised my field glasses to take a closer look. I could see blood in the snow on both sides of the animal. I learned later

A 7-pointer charged this young buck as he lay peacefully dying in a scrape and chased him literally to his death. *Maren Lea Wegner photo*

that the arrow passed through the pyloric artery leading from the heart. The buck slowly ambled toward the scrape, leaving a profuse blood trail behind him. Upon reaching it, he peacefully bedded down right in the scrape. Several minutes passed, he gradually nodded as though falling asleep, his last race run—no kicking, thrashing, or any abrupt movements of any kind. It seemed to be the most peaceful death imaginable—something I had never before observed after firing an arrow.

Usually the animal vanishes into the underbrush leaving the dazed hunter wondering.

Suddenly, a large 7-pointer appeared on the scene. When he reached the blood trail, he put his head down like a bloodhound and followed the trail to the dying 4-pointer. He stopped at the scrape where the buck lay, studied the buck in the scrape, turned around and again followed the blood trail, with his nose to the ground, back to where I hit the animal. He then returned to the scrape, put his head down and thrust his antlers into the back of the dying buck. The 4-pointer seemed oblivious. The 7-pointer again thrust his antlers into the back of the dying buck, who stumbled to his feet and staggered down the backside of the knoll with the 7-pointer in hot pursuit.

They both ran downhill for fifteen yards into a dense scrub oak thicket, where the 4-pointer expired in his tracks as if struck by lightning. The 7-pointer towered over the dead animal; he then proceeded to lay a fresh scrape that measured two feet by eighteen inches adjacent to the dead buck. He pawed until all the snow, leaves and forest debris were visibly absent from the wet, bare ground and then dashed out of sight with his antlers gleaming in the sunlight.

I crawled out of my tree stand and approached the dead buck. In surveying the scene, I kept thinking to myself what an incredible example of territorial dominance, especially in a heavily hunted area with a very young age structure among bucks and in an area where the sex ratio strongly favors females. As I stood there in bewilderment, staring at that intimidating scrape in utter disbelief, territorial black-capped chickadees poured out their melancholy, clearly whistled two-note phrases — fee-bee, feeee-bee — like a final salute to a fallen victim of a territorial skirmish.

Chapter 6

Death in the Deeryard

They are likely to die in March. And they die unmourned, untended, unnoted.

— Curtis Stadtfeld, *Whitetail Deer,* 1975

Webster's Third International Dictionary defines a "deeryard" as "a place where deer herd in winter." But it is also a place where deer die in a slow and agonizing manner as a result of the grim specter of winter hunger, starvation, malnutrition, disease, and predation. A two-week delay in the spring green-up after a severe winter may mean lingering death to hundreds of thousands of white-tailed deer nationwide. The consequences of these deaths in the northern deeryards dramatically affect the subsequent fall's hunting prospects for white-tailed deer hunters who hunt in such states as Minnesota, Wisconsin, Vermont, New Hampshire, Maine, New York, Pennsylvania, Michigan, and the southern Canadian provinces.

What we know about deeryards and how they affect the hunter's prospects of getting a deer dates back to the winter surveys and detailed maps of deeryards in the Upper Peninsula of Michigan by Ilo "Bart" Bart-

lett, the famous Michigan deer biologist who followed more deer trails and tramped through more deeryards than any other man, dead or alive. Snowshoeing twenty to thirty miles a day in his pursuit of knowledge of wintering whitetails in their northern latitude, this "indomitable figure"—as the *Detroit News* once called Bartlett—slept under a lean-to of hemlock boughs and cooked his coffee in a lard can over a sputtering campfire in sub-zero temperatures. His selfless concern for understanding the deer problem in the animal's northern region inspired many deer researchers ever since.

After trudging over thousands of miles of trails and yards in whitetail country and braving the stormy blasts of winter to live with deer during their hard times, "Mr. Deer," as he was known in the Great Lakes area, raised several basic questions regarding deeryards that remain in the minds of deer hunters and biologists to this day.

Snowshoeing twenty to thirty miles a day in his pursuit of knowledge of wintering whitetails in their northern latitude, Ilo Bartlett, known as "Mr. Deer" in the Great Lakes area, followed more deer trails and tramped through more deeryards than any other man, dead or alive. Here he measures a very high browse line in the famed Hulbert yard. *Alice Bartlett photo*

Why do whitetails concentrate in certain areas when there appears to be more and better food only a short distance away that is easily accessible? Does the availability of running water play a significant role in the location and formation of deeryards? Do whitetails return to the same deeryard each year? Do they maintain a homing instinct in this regard? How does overbrowsing affect young cedars? To what degree does a given style of cutting damage or improve deeryards of a given type and condition? To what extent does winter mortality affect the number of deer available for hunting?

In attempting to answer some of these questions, Bartlett intensively trapped and tagged hundreds of whitetails bunched in yards during severe winters in Michigan's southwestern Alpena County. At one of his Stephenson box traps alone, in the Hulbert deeryard, he caught eighty-seven deer in sixty-two days of deer trapping for an average of 1.4 deer a day. He tagged all deer in the right ear with a standard Fritz ear tag used in marking cattle. He numbered them serially and stamped "Notify Dept. Con. Lansing" on each tag.

After transferring one buck more than five miles by truck and setting the animal free in a swamp well supplied with food and water, Bart re-caught the animal three days later in the same trap in the same browsed-out deeryard. He soon discovered that whitetails not only return to the same yard winter after winter but when their food supplies fail they stay on and starve in these foodless ghettos rather than migrate a few miles to a swamp where plenty of browse awaits them. He once broke a snowshoe trail from an intensely overbrowsed cedar swamp to an area with adequate deer browse; he baited the trail with white cedar to lure the whitetails to the new feeding site. As soon as his bait-trail ended, the deer returned to the overbrowsed yard to resume the process of starvation.

But why? Why do they exhibit an apparent suicidal tendency to return winter after winter to the same graveyards of starvation? Why whitetails stay on and perish when an abundance of food is readily accessible not a mile distant remains a mystery. The presumption exists, but with insufficient proof, that natural predators once tended to distribute wintering whitetails more evenly over their winter range by breaking up their congestions.

Deer hunters shot a buck in November, which Bart had tagged in the same year, fourteen miles from Bartlett's trap. Hunters shot another buck that traveled fourteen miles from its release site and twenty miles from Bart's deer trap. In studying his returns, however, Bart observed that whitetails transferred more than twenty miles from their trap site seemed to be in strange country and showed no apparent homing instinct.

Whether trapping whitetails in the Cusino deeryard, the Johnswood Swamp on Drummond Island, the Fletcher Swamp in Alpena County, the famed Hulbert yard, or in the countless deeryards in the Turtle Lake district with its private deer hunting clubs, Bart experienced the disastrous swath cut by winter hunger: deer dying in their beds as a result of Nature's grim execution. After studying reports from 573 deeryards covering nearly 2000 square miles, Bart came to believe that whether white-tailed deer live or die in the yard depends upon many complex and interrelated factors and cannot be attributed to any one factor. The relationship between the summer range and the winter range, the number of deer using both types of ranges, the amount and quality of winter food, the interspersion of areas of summer and winter range, the length of the deer-yarding season, the depth and condition of the snow, the time of the spring breakup, the extent of disease and predation, wind conditions, winter temperatures, barometric pressures, and the very habits of the deer themselves can all be contributing factors.

Bart learned the ways of the whitetail and the vicissitudes of their wintry exis-

tence as no other man learned and cared about them. From his deep, personal communion with whitetails, he worked tirelessly as a disciple of antlerless deer hunting as a merciful measure for managing deer and balancing the herd to the carrying capacity of the winter yards. He fought bitter battles with the public on this issue in Michigan, as did Aldo Leopold in Wisconsin, Richard Gerstell in Pennsylvania, and Bill Severinghaus in New York, for the common man refused to accept (and some still do) the idea of killing surplus does and fawns before they starve to death in the yards during severe winters.

Speaking out for antlerless deer hunting, Bartlett fought the "deer war" to the finish

Too many hunters still fail to understand that if we don't shoot antlerless deer, they will perish along with the bucks in the deeryards. *Richard P. Smith photo*

and won. Yet the opposition to shooting does remained fierce, as he recalls in an article in the Michigan *State Journal*. "We would get hundreds of letters. They hung us in effigy and I remember once that a caravan drove down from the north country to Lansing. They had a funeral for a deer—they claimed it was the last one left in Michigan." Despite public pressure, he insisted that deer hunters must forget about sentiment and resign themselves to the fact that they will have to kill antlerless deer as well as bucks or they will starve in the deeryards. He put it succinctly in his *Michigan Deer* (1950), now a collector's item: "Either the herd must be cut down to fit its natural food supply or it will go down naturally. If we wait for Nature to act, the result will be browsed-out deer range and small deer herds in the future."

Deer going down naturally in the deeryards remains one of the most pathetic sights of nature. Their deaths in over-browsed yards might be likened to the process of slowly drowning: As the height of their browse line recedes above them, snowdrifts gradually consume the animals from below as they stand belly deep in it. Some just stand and stare in the cedar thickets, in the midst of narrow, well-trampled, winding, interconnecting deer trails, silhouetted against what Sigurd Olson calls the "frozen beauty of silver and blue." As the snow and bitter cold continue, only the strong will see spring return.

Bartlett repeatedly watched the slow, ugly process of deer starving to death. Eighty to ninety percent of the starving victims were fawns from the preceding summer. They staggered and floundered in the snow until they could no longer get up. Once their loss of weight progresses beyond a specific point, no amount of food will reverse the process. The majority of them reach their lowest point in their an-

Starving white-tailed deer fawn. *Leonard Lee Rue III photo*

nual weight curve usually during the last week of February. Many deaths occur between February 20 and March 5. It's a tragic sight to watch a sixty-pound fawn lying on the snow trying to lift its wobbly head and move its legs and to see its big dark eyes stiffen and die. These weak and emaciated animals often curled up on the lee side of a tree and died in front of Bart as he detailed the process of starvation in his notebook.

"First the fat over the rump and the saddle disappears. Shortly afterward the deer begins to lose that slick early fall appearance. As the fat under the skin is lost, the skin hangs loosely. Fatty tissue around the heart and in the abdomen around the lower organs is used and the animal has now developed a typical fuzzy-faced look. The final stage is an almost complete loss of fat from the normally creamy-pink bone marrow with the fat completely gone—proof of starvation."

Bartlett considered it ironic that starvation in the deeryard causes so little excitement, but that the harvesting of antlerless deer by hunting creates headlines. He knew that this senseless waste reflects a dramatic symptom of long-standing illness—wanting more whitetails than the range can accommodate. He also realized that the real and deeper issue underlying the problem of starving deer in the yards revolves around the question of whether prejudice or science will prevail: Will the deer biologists manage the herd on scientific principles and evidence or will public sentiment, wishful thinking, and parochial prejudice do the job based on "grandma's mustard plaster" as it emerges from barbershop biologists and politicians of the cracker barrel league. I for one prefer the advice from the men of science.

As a meticulous note-taker, Bart spent forty-two years gathering every possible scrap of information on white-tailed deer and their yarding patterns. Ray Schofield, Bartlett's former co-worker in the wildlife division, recalls that all of Bartlett's peers "learned that they could check dates and happenings from his field notes. When working deeryards with Bart you could always be a little sloppy with your own record-keeping, because you knew he would have all the vital information written down."

He recorded every minute observation of life in the deeryard. After finding a hemlock tree one day near the edge of a deeryard that five deer visited for several days until they established a well-beaten deer trail leading to it from their yard, he recorded in his field notes that the somewhat lowly regarded and despised porcupine should be credited with providing welcome relief for white-tailed deer in winter. While they eat hemlock in the winter, they often spend several days in the top of the same tree without descending. While climbing in the upper branches, they gnaw and break off twigs and small branches of hemlock that drop to the forest floor. Whitetails quickly find this source of food, a welcome break in their diet, and return to the spot daily so long as the porcupine remains in the tree—trimming hemlock and chewing away.

Whether on snowshoes in the deeryards and swamps or with slide rule in the office, or on the floor of the legislature or at sportsmen's meetings, whether with caliper, typewriter, rifle, or scalpel, Bart realized that deer and deer management are almost synonymous with controversy. With regard to the controversial issue of artificial feeding, Bart took a strong stand.

"Starvation of deer is waste and needless cruelty, but it is still more serious as a symptom of ruined range. Trying to cure starvation by emergency feeding is like giving an aspirin for a disease that needs surgery. To cure a sickness the doctor must strike at the cause, not the symptom. Saving a few deer one winter by emergency feeding means more deer to starve or feed next year. It does not help to balance the deer population with its food supply."

Bartlett frequently estimated the annual winter loss at 70,000 to 100,000 deer for Michigan alone during severe winters. Yet, prolonged malnutrition does not always result in death. It does, however, frequently leave its mark on individual deer as well as on the herd taken collectively. Adults and fawns often become so weak that various diseases and parasites gain a secure foothold in the animal's body. Pregnant does that are starving frequently lose their fawns. The fetuses are reabsorbed and returned as food to the female body. Fawns that manage to survive a winter of intense starvation and malnutrition frequently remain stunted for the rest of their lives. After a severe winter of starvation, white-tailed bucks seldom produce a normal rack the first year. Sustained chronic starvation year after year gradually affects the entire herd in terms of body size, weight, and antler development. Weakened deer are also more readily killed by wolves, coyotes, bobcats, and free-running dogs.

While Bartlett snowshoed through the inaccessible deeryards of Michigan, Sigurd Olson, one of America's foremost backwoodsmen, often snowshoed the deeryards of the Quetico-Superior wilderness while studying the predatorial relationships between wolves and whitetails. One night while snowshoeing through a yard in the moonlight, with temperatures well below zero, he encountered an old white-tailed buck that timber wolves had pulled down on the ice of a small lake. As he studied the scene, he could hear "the long-drawn quavering howl" of timber wolves over the next ridge. The buck had obviously been run to exhaustion and been sliced at his hamstrings. Olson could see the long red spurts of blood where the wolves ripped the jugular. Bits of mangled deer hide lay strewn on the snow around the carcass. Despite the buck's large and broad palmated antlers, the trampled bloody circle indicated that the buck did not last long in the struggle. In his great nature essay, "Timber Wolves," Olson tells us that "he might have died slowly of starvation or disease, but he died as he should when his time had come, fighting for his life against his age-old enemies, dying like the valiant warrior he was out on the ice."

Although a gruesome site, Olson viewed it gladly, for it meant to him a wilderness in balance, a primitive country untamed.

He viewed that death on the ice as part of the age-old cycle of dependency between whitetails and wolves. By eliminating the old, weak, and diseased deer, Olson argued that wolves improved the actual character of the herd by keeping the younger and more virile breeders alert and aware of danger. There on the ice he found evidence of the completed cycle, gruesome though it might be.

It was cold, bitterly cold that moonlit night; he hurried back to his cabin and struck a match to the waiting birch in his potbellied stove. He knew that many deer hunters in that region would not agree with his interpretation.

Encountering a hunter the next morning in the same swamp, he explained to the hunter how the wolves had dragged the buck down on the ice.

"Those critters," the hunter retorted. "We'd have a lot more deer if they was all killed off. They kill a deer every few days and sometimes just for fun. They're the ones that make hunting tougher and tougher in this country."

He could have argued with the hunter, but he did not, for he knew well the attitudes of many deer hunters in the Quetico-Superior region regarding wolves and whitetails.

"I could have told him," Sigurd thought to himself, "about ecological balances and how wolves and deer, moose, and caribou had lived together for centuries in the North; that what determined survival was not predation but the amount of winter food available; that during winters of extreme cold and heavy snow, 10 to 20 percent of the deer herd might die of starvation; that the wolves had actually done the race a favor by eliminating an aged and crippled sire and that the doe, who no doubt was bred, would replace it in the spring."

But he did not. Instead, he snowshoed across the ice to the mouth of a creek and then disappeared into the deeryard to resume his observations. Snowshoeing along, he wondered to himself if man will ever understand the importance of *Canis lupus.*

Perhaps no one studied the killing of whitetails in deeryards by wolves more than David Mech, a wildlife biologist with the United States Department of the Interior. Mech found that wolf predation in the central Superior National Forest in northeastern Minnesota is the main direct mortality agent on deer but that wolf density itself appears to be secondary to winter weather in influencing the deer populations. He observed that wolves kill a significantly higher proportion of adult males. Bucks, based on his telemetry studies, live more along the edges of deeryards and wolves tend to kill proportionately more deer along the edges of yards. Older white-tailed bucks also incur leg arthritis to a greater extent than other deer, which probably affects their ability to escape predation as well.

Few direct observations of wolves actually hunting and killing whitetails in the yards exist, but those that do indicate most of the deer encountered by wolves escape unless special circumstances such as disease and emaciated condition work against the deer. While following a pack of seven wolves by aircraft one January afternoon, Mech watched the wolves come to within 100 feet of a standing whitetail. For several minutes the deer and the wolves stared at one another. When the deer bolted, the wolves immediately began the chase. After flushing another deer in the process, most of the pack got sidetracked. The lead wolf, however, continued after the first deer. But the deer quickly outdistanced the wolf, and the animal gave up after 250 yards.

Mech's aircraft observations of wolves hunting whitetails in and around deeryards leads him to believe that snow hinders the wolves more than the deer and that their pursuit of deer becomes virtually useless in snow depths greater than sixteen inches. While they can travel as far in one bound as a deer, they come up and back into the snow at a lower angle and thus meet greater resistance. Mech believes that wolves do not easily catch whitetails and that their success rates in trying to do so remain quite low. But once caught, whitetails are virtually defenseless. Their main defense is their ability to detect wolves at great distances and to execute short, speedy dashes to safety. Mech found most wolf-killed whitetails on the frozen lakes, rivers, and beaver ponds as Sigurd Olson's observations indicate as well.

Given the whitetail's vulnerability to wolf predation during the wintertime, one would naturally expect the species to develop a strategy to promote survival. The deeryard represents just such a strategy. In the yard individual deer can spend less time maintaining their defensive alert and more time eating and searching for food. In addition, herding naturally increases the ratio of whitetails to wolves in the yard, thus decreasing, as Mech says, "the relative predation level through a sheer mathematical effect." Yarding together also exposes the older and more vulnerable individuals when wolves confront the herd. And finally the congregation of many deer creates a vast and complex system of deer trails, providing escape routes during difficult chases.

After twenty-five years of intensive research on wolf-whitetail interactions, Mech one day superimposed some maps of individual deer ranges and yards over plots of wolfpack territories and discovered to his great surprise that almost all of the deer studied lived along the very edges of wolf territories. Mech was obviously elated when he suddenly saw the significance of the fact that the deeryards in his study all lay along wolfpack-territory edges or "buffer-zones," i.e., demilitarized zones that all wolves tend to avoid since the inevitable result of traveling through them seems to be serious fights ending in the death of one of the top-ranking pack members. Through instinct, habit, and tradition whitetails learn to take advantage of this spatial requirement of wolves and survive in a remarkable way by yarding in these buffer zones.

The only other example Mech ever found of a buffer zone acting as a prey-reservoir involved humans, ironically enough, as the predators. "From 1780 to 1850," Mech reports, "a buffer zone existed between the Chippewa and Sioux tribes in Minnesota. Members of both tribes ventured into the zone, but neither tribe spent much time there because of the threat of an attack by the other. According to anthropologist Harold Hickerson, this buffer zone became the main area where white-tailed deer survived. However, European traders eventually affected a truce between the two tribes. The result? The deer were soon exterminated from the buffer zone."

Despite the whitetail's incredible ability to adapt to most circumstances as the establishment of deeryards in the wolf's buffer zone well indicates, when we consider the desperate life of the white-tailed deer in its winter ghetto, its unremitting drift toward death from disease, lung-worms, liver flukes, nose bot infestations, starvation, debilitation, and predation, it's remarkable that the animal even exists in the northern latitude. In tramping through winter deeryards during the whitetail's most critical time of ultimate stress, one

soon realizes that they have no real options for self-preservation. They cannot store food like beavers, squirrels, or chipmunks. They must live off their fat reserve. Indeed, during the most severe weather body fat actually becomes the sole source of energy when deer bed down and stop eating for days at a time. The animal furthermore maintains no secure "home" in which to hibernate, as do black bears. Whitetails also exhibit no instinct to migrate to a better food supply a short distance away. When pursued by wolves, coyotes, bobcats, or dogs, they cannot climb into trees or escape underground. "The whitetail is forever above ground and on the ground," as Hugh Fosburgh, an Adirondack deer hunter, describes the animal's dilemma in his deer hunting diary. "It is subject to the

The deeryard — the whitetail's winter ghetto. *Leonard Lee Rue III photo*

whims of winter and an oscillating, sometimes nonexistent food supply. It can't escape, it can't hide, ever; it is vulnerable twenty-four hours a day, all days of the year. Its sole option is to live, usually in misery, or die. Of all mammals, I would least like to be a deer of the northern wilderness."

Just how miserable life can become for whitetails in the deeryard is perhaps best characterized by Bill Stokes, a newspaper reporter who spent one haunted night in sub-zero temperatures in the Bad River deeryard in northern Wisconsin. In his

This deer is practically reduced to skin and bones. Many deer barely stagger out of the cedar swamps at spring break-up, which often doesn't occur until mid-April. *Leonard Lee Rue III photo*

chronicle of that chilling night afield, Stokes notes that a "deeryard at night is like the attic of a haunted house—full of strange noises, festooned with shadowy movement and immersed in periods of deep expectant silence. The night creeps into the Bad River deeryard on the Odanah Indian reservation on feet that are moccasined in cold and quiet. . . . After branches as big as broom handles have been gnawed away, winter's long arm of deep snow and severe cold reaches down into the guts of the deer and pulls the life out of them. They lay in rows on the trails, frozen in frigid death beds."

Many deer barely stagger out of the cedar swamps at spring break-up, which often does not occur until mid-April. In dispersing from their yards for their summer range some deer seem confused, disoriented, and indecisive in their movement patterns. For example, while radio-tracking one mature buck labeled buck #515, my friend Orrin Rongstad observed that this buck left the Cedar Bog Lake deeryard in east-central Minnesota the night of April 15 but returned the next night. He again left the night of April 19, returned April 26, and left the yard again on April 28. A semitrailer killed buck #515 on May 11, seven miles south of his traditional yarding area. (See accompanying figure.)

Ultimately, the animal not only remains at the mercy of semitrailers but at the mercy of natural forces that seem whimsical to man because they remain beyond our control. Nevertheless, for the past sixty years deer researchers have intensely studied the deeryard dilemma and every minute aspect of the whitetail's vulnerability in the deeryard setting.

They developed the bone marrow test as an index of malnutrition. They know the capacity of rumen microorganisms of deer to digest alfalfa hay when in a starved con-

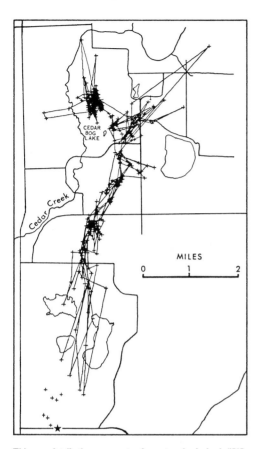

This map details the movements of a mature buck, buck #515, that left the Cedar Bog Lake deeryard in east-central Minnesota the night of April 15, but returned the next night. He again left the yard the night of April 19, returned on April 26, and left again on April 28. The star at the lower edge of the figure indicates where a truck killed buck #515 on May 11, while crossing a road seven miles south of his winter deeryard.

Reprinted from Orrin J. Rongstad and John R. Tester. 1969. "Movements and Habitat Use of White-tailed Deer in Minnesota." Journal of Wildlife Management **33(2)**: 366–379.

dition. They have measured the animal's energy-conservation adaptations during the winter months to the precise kilocalories per day per deer. They continue to map and survey many of the deeryards in the whitetail's northern region. They proceed with their experiments in trapping

and translocating deer from overbrowsed yards to other areas with adequate food supplies. They conduct countless artificial feeding experiments and encourage antlerless deer hunting. In managing the deeryard losses they argue with themselves as well as with foresters, loggers, farmers, resort owners, and the general public as a whole. "Managing the over-winter losses," as Patrick Karns, a Minnesota wildlife researcher maintains, "has provided the battleground between wildlife managers and the populace since the deer moved north."

Deer researchers measure the exact extent to which deer nip and crop preferred browse. They examine rumens to determine the preferred winter food of the whitetail and construct innumerable tables, charts, and graphs in this regard. They measure the amount of deer browse produced from felled trees. They monitor the daily intake of browse consumed under penned conditions in search of clues to the whitetail's adaptation to the extremities of winter. They know the air temperatures at the ground level in relationship to canopy closure. They conduct massive dead deer surveys. Descriptions of the spatial distribution of the yards exist as well as detailed information on the movements to the yards, dispersal from the yards, and the duration of confinement. We know the number of deer that die per acre in certain areas. Detailed analysis also exists on the character of the snow cover, its insulation effect, depth, and texture.

While Aaron Moen measured the surface temperatures and radiant heat loss of whitetails and such major factors contributing to heat loss as conduction, convection, radiation, and evaporation at the Cedar Creek Natural History Area in Minnesota, Lou Verme, a deer biologist at the Cusino deeryard complex in northern Michigan, developed an index of winter weather severity for whitetails and invented the "chillometer," a calorimetric device designed to provide a continuous record of atmospheric chill production. One research scientist at the State University of Environmental Science and Forestry at Newcomb, New York, even equipped deer in the Adirondack Mountains with aluminum respiratory masks in order to calculate the whitetail's energy expenditure while lying, standing, walking, and running in deep snow to the specific kilocalories per grams per minute per foot. The animals with their respiratory gas masks on looked like survivors of worldwide germ warfare.

After studying the movements of deer from their winter yards, Verme tells us that 211 hunter-killed deer yielded a mean dispersal distance of 8.6 miles between their yards and the kill site during the November gun season. His study indicates that the colder the weather in November the closer the shot-deer are to their yards. Verme remains convinced that whitetails possess a strong homing instinct and return to the same yards annually.

A deeryard study in the Clam Lake area of northern Wisconsin, under the direction of Orrin Rongstad, is again measuring the homing instinct of whitetails while focusing on the effects of winter feeding on white-tailed deer movements. The Wisconsin study, supported by funds from Whitetails Unlimited, focuses on four basic questions. (1) Can winter feeding affect the factors that now limit the deer population in that area? (2) How does winter feeding affect the home range size, habitat use, and seasonal movements of white-tailed deer? (3) How much does a white-tailed deer winter-feeding program cost? (4) How many deer will a single feeding site attract and what is the size of the area involved?

Another large-scale field project involving supplementary feeding and white-tailed deer harvest allocation is currently underway in several areas in Ontario. This Cooperative Deer Study, funded in part by the Ontario Federation of Anglers and Hunters, is trying to determine (1) the number of deer feeders required in an area, including the distance between them; (2) the number of deer using the feeders, including a percentage of the herd reached; (3) the acceptability by deer of feed rations such as a pelleted total diet and corn/oats; (4) the best basic design for deer feeders; and (5) a basic schedule of feeding during winter based on the winter severity index and the capacity of deeryards to maintain a number of deer.

Their preliminary results indicate that large adult bucks are in very poor condition during the winter months. "It appears that after the rut they have insufficient time to build up fat reserves and consequently, by mid-winter, are in very poor condition," says Dennis Voigt, one of the principle deer researchers of the project. "Similarly, many fawns are in poor condition by late winter and we are seeing more evidence of this than in earlier winters." Fawn mortality rates in their study remain much higher than for yearlings and adults.

One of the most fascinating anecdotes in the whole deeryard story—epitomizing the real dilemma of American deer hunting in general—revolves around Professor Orrin Rongstad at the University of Wisconsin, who in realizing that fawns in the deeryards suffer the highest rate of mortality (over 90 percent in some deeryards), in the late 1960s issued a university extension news release entitled "Shoot Fawns to Help the Deer Herd!"

The release stated "that an ideal deer season would concentrate harvesting efforts on fawns. There would be a reward system for shooting fawns such as guaranteeing a party permit (either-sex, bonus deer permit) for the next season. And there might be a penalty for shooting adult does, like a forfeiture of a deer license for the next hunting season. A lottery system could be devised to limit killing of older bucks. . . . We have to start eliminating the guilt feelings deer hunters have about shooting fawns."

The news release went on to suggest that shooting fawns would help reduce the starvation losses because fawns are usually the first to succumb. But because deer hunters with hunter's choice permits frequently shoot larger animals, "the ages of the animals hunters kill differ from the age structure of deer dying during a severe winter. So, killing a deer under these circumstances during the hunting season doesn't necessarily prevent one from starving during the winter."

The news release also emphasized the fact that age distribution affects total herd productivity. "Fawns are either nonproductive or less productive than older does. If they dominate the population, it is more difficult for herd numbers to bounce back or increase the next year."

The release concluded by noting that antlerless permits allow hunters to legally shoot all ages of deer, but that deer hunters who kill fawns often leave them in the woods to avoid criticism or call them "yearling does" and "spike bucks," thus hampering the recordkeeping system of our deer-kill statistics.

One can readily imagine the sentimental and emotional response that this seemingly sensible scientific news release generated from the public, especially after United Press International picked up the story and turned it into the Bambi syndrome revisited. Headlines such as "Bul-lets for Bambi" appeared in newspapers all across the country by the next day. Radio stations from Chicago to Philadelphia interviewed the professor for his opinions on the subject. One radio commentator prefaced his introductory remarks by reminding his listeners that Disney's Bambi was currently playing at the local theaters and said, "Thank God our kids are in school, for you won't believe what my next guest is going to tell you!" And tell them he did.

"Not only should hunters shoot fawns, but they should be rewarded for doing so, not condemned," said the outspoken ecology professor. "Public sentiment, the laws, and deer hunting attitudes are all working against the deer population. An ideal deer season should concentrate its effort on the fawns. Fawns are the most likely to die during the winter anyway. If the hunter is happy with one-third less meat he shouldn't be criticized. We shouldn't call him names because he shot 'Bambi.' He should be praised, not scorned! If people only knew that the agony and slow death of starvation in the woods is so much worse."

The man on the street responded: "Good grief! What manner of man would encourage deer hunters to slay Bambi? For that matter, what manner of man would go so far as to say so in public?"

"Bambi, beware!" wrote Bruce Ingersoll in the *Chicago Sun Times*. "A guy who sounds more like a wildlife heretic than a wildlife ecologist is advocating an early death for you and many of your brethren."

An article in the *Los Angeles Times* reporting that "a university professor is gunning for Bambi" sparked a flood of anti-hunting letters directed toward the chancellor's office. "If people only knew," wrote one bleeding heart from Glendale, California, "the agony and slow death that accompanies the amateur shot of a nondescript hunter, the agony and slow death of a crippled deer, bleeding inexorably in the woods, for as long as it takes to die unmercifully."

Another woman responded from California by threatening the professor: "I wonder if you would like me to get a gun and hunt you down!"

Another letter told the professor, "I'm glad you can take the flak but can the deer?"

One irate deer hunter, in a commentary in *The Whitehall Times,* responded by saying, "I have talked to many hunters, and I'm sure there are thousands I haven't talked to, that shriek at the attitude of harvesting the unaware fawns that trail and depend upon the adult doe. It's like taking the chicks before the hens. All sportsmen are out there for the thrill of the deer hunting season, and want to bag the biggest rack, and also fill their freezer with venison. Who wants to bring home a fifty-to-sixty-pound fawn to brag about? These accidents happen without creating them. Who wants to hang a medal on their fireplace along with their trophies saying 'I Shot a Fawn'?"

The most incredible letter — underscoring the real dilemma of the matter — came from another professor of wildlife management who gave a brief sermon on the situation.

> What makes good sense theoretically often makes no sense at all at the human level. Your plan for hunting fawns would, after all, strip the hunters of their most treasured illusion; that they are engaged in an equal contest with an adult wild animal (the fearless hunter who, having been tested to the limits of his endurance, emerges victorious over the nameless terrors of the wilderness). To allow the shooting of fawns would cause most (if not all) hunters to appear as they really are — overfed suburbanites out for the thrill of

Species	
Preferred	Readily eaten
White cedar	White ash
Apple	Sugar maple
Striped maple	Choke cherry
Red maple	Black cherry
Witchhobble	Hazelnut
Second-choice	Starvation
Honeysuckle	Beech
Wild raisin	Aspen
Silky dogwood	Balsam fir
Round-leaver dogwood	Tamarack
	Alder
	Red spruce

Principal browse species according to white-tailed deer preference and maximum use in the Deer River and Brown Road wintering areas in northern New York.

watching something die and the novelty of laying away a chunk of venison in the freezer.

> Don't misunderstand me — I am not anti-hunting and I favor good game management. But any rational game management plan must take account of the often irrational, but nevertheless very real, emotional responses of the people. Maybe Bambi doesn't exist in the wild, but to those convinced that animals have feelings and that it is a cowardly act to kill an innocent 'baby,' your theoretical arguments will not be at all persuasive. What politician would put his career on the line to support the 'slaughter of the innocents,' as the headline would undoubtedly portray it?

> I am afraid that your comments may seriously harm the cause of game management and alienate people even further against their natural resource agencies. The sentiment here in the U.P. against the Michigan DNR is already virulent enough, as indicated by the popularity of bumper stickers saying SUPPORT THE DNR — WITH A ROPE! and the like.

> You may very well be right, from a scientific point of view, in your analysis of the deeryard situation; but it was not very bright of you to say so.

Given the sheer amount of research materials and documentation in existence on the problem of winter mortality in the deeryards, one would think the problem would no longer exist; but it does, for winter weather and its climatic variations ultimately continue to be the strongest controller of the overall size of our North Country white-tailed deer herd. Deaths in the deeryards continue to occur when deep snow prevails, for whitetails can do little to reduce the cost of a minimum amount of travel.

"Northern deer face a potentially serious energy crisis," John Ozoga reports from the Cusino deeryard complex, "due to inadequate nutrition each winter, as the combined effects of forest maturation, years of overbrowsing, and inadequate forestry practices push deeryards past peak carrying capacity for deer. Today, more so than in the past, the bulging deer population depends highly upon humans, in one way or another, for survival during crucial winter weather. In the future, human actions (or lack thereof), will likely impact even more upon the behavior and well-being of wintering whitetails."

As hunters and landowners, we should strive to prevent unnecessary losses by disturbing wintering whitetails as infrequently as possible, by eliminating snowmobiling in or near winter concentration areas, and by eradicating free-running dogs. We should also strive to provide natural food and cover whenever possible. While we cannot fully understand all the intricate scientific details of the problem we can acquire an understanding of the winter food habits of deer and an ability to identify individual plants and classify them as preferred, second-choice, readily eaten, and starvation foods.

When afield we should learn to identify browse lines and the typical clipped appearance of heavily-browsed plants and realize that as the availability of preferred foods gives way to stuffing foods, whitetails approach their range capacity, thus necessitating more adequate antlerless deer hunting, whether it be the shooting of does or fawns, so that we no longer experience white-tailed deer bones and deer hides strewn along the manure-stained deer trails of the yards, so that we no longer witness hundreds of thousands of white-tailed deer nationwide turning into dull-eyed, listless racks of bones, clothed in rough, shaggy coats, stoically awaiting death in their wintering ghettoes.

Red maple sprouts heavily over-browsed by white-tailed deer. *Leonard Lee Rue III photo*

Chapter 7

Deer Tracks

Tracks made by deer are of outstanding interest both to the field naturalist and to the hunter, since they frequently tell a great deal that men wish to know.

— Joseph Dixon.
*A Study of the Life History and
Food Habits of Mule Deer in California,* 1934

Deer tracks in the snow of a mountain forest, in the soft mud along an October stream bank or in the sand under a stand of white pines offer man a thrill that only nature can grant. Deer tracks tell stories, and the observant hunter learns to read and interpret these stories as nature's sign language. To the eye of the skilled tracker, deer tracks do not merely indicate the direction of travel, but they often indicate the sex of the animal, whether it passed in a leisurely manner or in great haste, whether wounded, seeking a mate, or escaping a predator.

Not only does the skilled tracker become more knowledgeable in deer tracks if he follows them throughout the year, but he soon realizes more and more that deer write their autobiographies for the hunter in endless manuscripts found on the forest floor—in the oldest of all writing. He also realizes the real meaning of the old adage, "The thing I am seeking is seeking for me." This adage, when placed in the hunter's context, means that the more you devote yourself to studying deer tracks and practicing the art of tracking deer, the greater the opportunities you will encounter of making contact with your quarry, opportunities unknown to those blind to the pursuit of tracking.

So far as I know, no other field naturalist and avid buck hunter worked longer and more persistently in studying, deciphering, drawing, photographing, and recording the endless mysteries of deer tracks and tracking problems than Josef Brunner during the first decade of the twentieth century.

One day while hunting deer in the Big Snowy Mountains of Montana, Brunner spotted a buck galloping broadside at a distance of 120 yards. He fired one steel-jacketed .30 caliber U.S. bullet. After several jumps, the buck stopped behind a clump of small trees, preventing another shot. He remained hidden for a short time, and then finally trotted off. "If ever I would have sworn that a deer was missed," Brunner wrote in his field notes, "I would have done so then." Force of habit compelled Brunner to follow the tracks of the buck. Two hundred yards from where the buck stopped, he found the animal dead with a heart shot. Not one drop of blood existed on the trail. In his diary, he wrote: "Moral — follow the deer even if you think you have missed!"

Brunner followed deer tracks at every opportunity. In his field notes, he kept accurate measurements of the size of the tracks, their distance from an imaginary center line, the degree to which the hooves point outward, whether hillocks exist in

The track of a white-tailed doe. Note how the track of the hind hoof comes down on top of the track of the front hoof. *Leonard Lee Rue III photo*

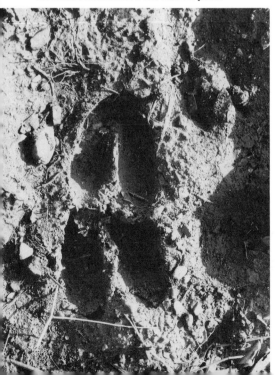

the track, whether drag marks exist and their length; he recorded the clearness of the track, the roundness of the toes, the size and form of the dewclaws and whether the tracks were accompanied with the "blazing of trees and the pawing of ground." He measured the distance between the tracks, observed the breaking of twigs, studied and sketched deer droppings, and noted whether the deer watched from cover. All of this information he placed into tables comparing the data for whitetails, mule deer, elk, moose, bighorn sheep, and antelope.

From his detailed observations on white-tailed deer tracks, Brunner learned that when deer walk the track of the hind hoof comes down on top of the track of the front hoof of the same side. He noticed that sometimes the hind hoof lags, that is, it does not quite reach the track of the front hoof. This sign, he believed, indicates the presence of an old buck that's rather stiff with age. Brunner found that the hind hooves of deer are usually smaller than the front hooves.

While following deer tracks before and after the rut, Brunner documented the tendency of white-tailed bucks to drag their feet. During the rut, he noticed that the drag marks reach a climax. (See illustration.)

Like most deer hunters, Brunner constantly tried to distinguish buck tracks from the tracks of does. He listed seven signs to help the hunter distinguish a buck's trail from that of a doe's: (1) the presence of rubs, (2) scrapes, (3) the distance of the tracks from the center line — buck tracks exhibit a greater distance, (4) the pointing outward of the toes from the center line, (5) the lagging back of the track of the hind hoof, (6) drag marks, and (7) the greater tendency of bucks to watch the hunter from heavy cover.

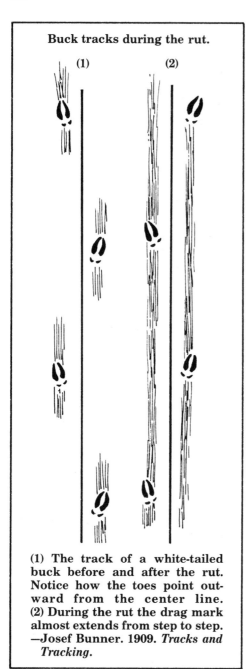

Buck tracks during the rut.

(1)   (2)

(1) **The track of a white-tailed buck before and after the rut. Notice how the toes point outward from the center line. (2) During the rut the drag mark almost extends from step to step.** —Josef Bunner. 1909. *Tracks and Tracking.*

Brunner's greatest contribution to our knowledge of deer tracks appeared in his unique diagrams of track configurations based on wounded deer behavior. After extensive tracking of wounded deer, Brunner found that the configuration of tracks often reveals the nature and seriousness of the wound.

In 1909, the Outing Publishing Company of New York published Brunner's data in a slender, forest-green colored volume for $1.25. The book, titled *Tracks and Tracking,* went through several editions and now remains out of print — frequently listed in out-of-print book catalogs for $60 or more.

The story of deer tracks in many ways begins with this unusual volume of practical significance. In it, Brunner not only summarizes man's knowledge of tracks and tracking, but stresses the importance of interpreting deer tracks when hunting, especially when following wounded deer. The deer hunter, Brunner writes, "who is unable to interpret the meaning of tracks he encounters, however many deer he may have killed by chance, luck, or with the assistance of others, will be considered a tyro in woodcraft by companions who have learned their lessons in this art."

Perhaps, no one studied Brunner's lessons more and consequently taught us more about deer tracks and the art of tracking as a basic element of woodcraft and hunting than Ernest Thompson Seton, a contemporary of "Old Bruno's" and one of America's greatest naturalists. Like Brunner and most diehard buck hunters, Seton believed that man can determine the sex of the deer by examining the track as well as taking other deer signs into consideration, especially the drag marks following the track. In his *Game Animals and the Lives They Live* (1929), Seton suggests that the drag mark is the only "true way" to determine the track of a buck from a doe in the snow. He further notes that older bucks exhibit a more pronounced drag mark than yearlings. According to

Seton, the oldest bucks drag the strongest with their toes inclined to turn out.

A buck cannot escape, Seton insists, from a determined hunter well versed in the secrets of the trail. While the trail may seem to end, the tracker knows that it does not except at the victim's feet. It may elude the hunter for days on end, but sooner or later the deer hunter will run it down. To successfully do so, the hunter must know the animal's natural history — its tracks, trail characteristics, scatology, and social behavior. In his *Book of Woodcraft* (1912), Seton suggests that we confer the Degree of Hunter on those individuals who can clearly discriminate the tracks of twenty-five of our common wild quadrupeds and who can track a deer for a mile and secure it without the aid of snow.

While Brunner tracked deer in the snowy mountains of Wyoming and Seton in the snowy forests of Manitoba, Joseph Scattergood Dixon, a contemporary of Seton's and a well-known man of science, argued that the size and shape of deer tracks when taken in conjunction with other trail sign aid man in determining the sex of the deer. After carefully studying the tracks of both sexes of mule deer while working as a field naturalist and curator of mammals at the Museum of Vertebrate Zoology at the University of California, Berkeley, Dixon reported that tracks made by mature bucks are broader and larger than those made by yearling bucks and does. He noticed, however, that antlered does frequently make buck-like tracks but nonetheless believed that if the hunter follows deer tracks in the woods and studies them in great detail as they relate to urine deposits in the snow, he can arrive at definitive conclusions as to the sex of the animal that made the tracks: urine deposited well *forward* of the hind hoof tracks indicates a buck while urine deposited *behind* the hind hoof tracks indicates a doe.

Yet, despite Dixon's early observations, the argument between sportsmen and biologists over whether the sex of a deer can be determined from its tracks persists. Some deer hunters say yes; others say no. In his classic *Shots at Whitetails* (1949), Larry Koller, a deer hunter from the Catskill Mountains, says "yes." After examining the carcasses of more than 1000 white-tailed bucks during two decades, Koller remained unconvinced that the largest bucks carry the largest hooves, but he points out that heavy-bodied bucks show a marked tendency to walk with their front hooves wider apart than does and yearling bucks. They also show an inclination to "toe-out" with their front hooves as their toes turn out from the center line. (See accompanying illustration.)

In Koller's opinion, buck tracks exhibit more purposeful and direct movement as opposed to the aimless wandering of doe tracks. They often show a marked tendency to stray off to one side or the other from a group of deer tracks. Like Brunner and Seton, Koller believed that in snow of less than four inches in depth, bucks consistently give away their sexual identity by dragging their front hooves. But in heavy snow, all deer exhibit drag marks. The tracks of sick, weak, and wounded animals, regardless of sex, also show drag marks. Evidence of drag marks frequently becomes difficult to detect unless the soil over which the deer travels is soft, muddy, or covered with snow. The experienced woodsman, however, can detect drag marks in the absence of snow by observing disturbances in ground litter.

Before drawing any hasty conclusions about deer tracks, Koller issued the following words of caution for deer hunters nationwide.

"Much has been said about the spreading of a buck's toes as a distinguishing characteristic. To me a spread-toe print

Buck and doe tracks differ.

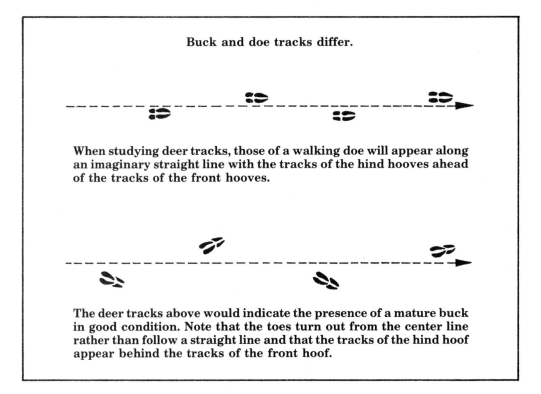

When studying deer tracks, those of a walking doe will appear along an imaginary straight line with the tracks of the hind hooves ahead of the tracks of the front hooves.

The deer tracks above would indicate the presence of a mature buck in good condition. Note that the toes turn out from the center line rather than follow a straight line and that the tracks of the hind hoof appear behind the tracks of the front hoof.

means only a heavy deer, whether it be buck or doe. Any running or loping deer will leave a spread-toe print, particularly in firm soil. Neither does the shape of the hoof itself have a definite bearing on the sex of the deer. Short, broad hooves and long narrow hooves will be found at random on both bucks and does. The nature of the terrain underfoot has much to do with slight differences in the shape of hooves. Hard rocky ground and generally rocky deer-areas contribute to wearing off the front of the toes. The swamp areas and coniferous timberland allow the hoof to grow a much more pointed toe."

While Koller studied deer tracks in the Catskills, Dr. Frederick Weston, a legendary figure on the deer hunting ranges of southern Texas, studied deer tracks in the whitetail's southern range and greatly added to our knowledge of deer tracks and trail-craft lore. Like Koller, Weston found that the different soils alter the size and shape of white-tailed deer hooves. In his hard-to-find *Hunting White-tailed Deer in Texas* (1954), Weston tells us that whitetails living on ranges of clay, sand, and other softer soils exhibit longer and more pointed hooves than deer living on rocky ranges. Weston's research indicates that the great variation in hoof size and shape also depends upon food, age, the effects of the various seasons, as well as heredity.

Weston, known as "The Oldtimer" to many of his Texas readers, spent a great deal of time examining buck tracks and hooves during the rut. He found that before bucks mate their hooves are generally longer and more pointed. But their front hooves change with maturity and excessive pawing in scrapes. Because mature bucks carry the weight of their antlers and a swollen neck during the rut, they place more weight on their front hooves than does do. As a result, their front hooves spread more and show more wear than the front hooves of does. Consequently, bucks leave tracks with deeper toe imprints. "The older he gets," Weston argues, "and the heavier his antlers and the more swollen his

neck becomes, the more obvious is this wear. Larger and older bucks, therefore, generally have a wider and more rounded front foot than do does, and thus leave tracks with deeper toe imprints. In contrast, does leave tracks without deeper toe imprints. . . . The tracks of the front feet, then, should be used by the hunter in any attempt to identify the sex of the maker."

Many deer hunters believe that the print of the dewclaw in the track indicates the sex of the animal that made the track. But we must exercise caution when discussing the clear imprint of the dewclaws, the auxiliary weight-bearing units aiding the animal when running at a rapid gait. While the dewclaws show up in the tracks of very heavy deer when walking on soft ground, they are always present in the tracks of running deer granting the animal a wider and stronger landing gear. Yet, Weston rightly believed that they may indicate the sex of the animal.

"The heavier a deer gets, the smaller the angle between the pastern and the ground. This brings the dewclaws closer to the ground. Heavier deer, then, are likely to leave the imprints of dewclaws. Dewclaws on the front legs of bucks are normally closer to the hooves than they are on does. Thus bucks, which are usually larger than does and whose dewclaws are anatomically closer to the ground, are more likely to leave the imprint of dewclaws with the tracks of their front feet while walking." Since the dewclaws on the front hooves of bucks are closer to their toes than on does, deer hunters should study the tracks of the front hooves, as mentioned earlier, when trying to identify the sex of the maker of the tracks.

After a lifetime of deer hunting and studying white-tailed deer, Weston, like Koller, remained somewhat ambivalent of man's ability to identify the sex of the animals by track analysis *alone*. "No man,"

Like the fingerprints of man, deer hooves have individual characteristics. In (A), this hind hoof of a buck has shell-like edges to make the hoof concave, while one toe is abraded and shorter than the other one and turns in. The outside toe on the left has an oval depression just forward of the sole pad and a circular growth near the edge of the cleft line at about its center. All these characteristics would show up in the tracks made by this animal. In (B), this front hoof of a buck has well-formed pads on the sole; however, the inside toe on the right has a pad extending forward nipple-like half again as far. It forms a distinct ledge having a Y-shaped depression on its inner side and a serrated one on the outside that joins across its middle to form a saddle. Forward of the saddle is an irregular circular growth. These characteristics would also show up in the tracks made by this animal. *Dr. Frederick Weston photo*

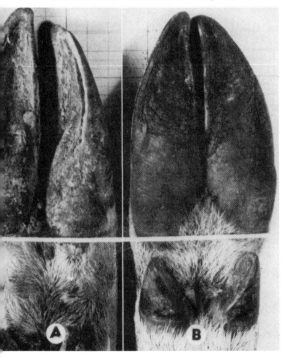

he writes in his scientific treatise on deer hunting, "can positively and consistently identify the sex of white-tailed deer by its track alone, although there are characteristics by which, under certain conditions, tracks of bucks and does can be differentiated. There are simply too many variable factors which, individually or collectively, prevent establishing a fool-proof pattern which can be applied to deer tracks for sex identification." In testing more than fifty deer hunters, Weston found that only one hunter in fifty could correctly identify the sex of the animal based on the track. Most hunters were only right 25 percent of the time.

In 1965, deer researcher Dale McCullough set out to determine if differences do in fact exist in the sizes and shapes of deer hooves (and hence in deer tracks), and to express those differences in quantitative terms. Following in Dixon's tracks, McCullough measured the hooves of 106 freshly killed black-tailed deer while working at the Museum of Vertebrate Zoology at the University of California, Berkeley. He measured the total length and the maximum width at the front one-third of the toe to the nearest 0.5 millimeter; he then aged the deer by tooth wear and replacement. McCullough's findings substantiate Dixon's earlier observations that in adult deer both length and width differences exist between the sexes with bucks exhibiting larger and wider hooves and tracks than does. (See accompanying figure.)

Thus McCullough reports in the *Journal of Wildlife Management* that the tracks of most adult males, including the tracks of larger yearling males, can be identified with a high degree of certainty. In other words, a pattern does exist for the sexual identification of deer via track analysis. I

can already hear my friend Lennie Rue: "Fine, but I defy anyone to detect these differences in millimeters when looking at deer tracks in the wild." Right. McCullough also points out that malformed and broken hooves often show up in such a distinctive way as to constitute individual recognition marks that can help determine the individual movements of certain deer from their tracks.

McCullough's findings also agree with those of Jean Linsdale and Quentin Tomich, who in their compendium of mule deer facts, *A Herd of Mule Deer* (1953), report that buck tracks tend to differ from those of does in that they are larger, relatively broader, and more strongly curved toward the tips than doe tracks, which exhibit straighter sides and tend to be long and thin. While McCullough, Dixon, and Linsdale and Tomich did not extend their studies of the physical differences of deer hooves and tracks to include white-tailed deer, their results are probably valid for whitetails as well.

While hunting whitetails in the deer forests of northwestern Wisconsin, the short, stocky, deerstalker with the ruddy cheeks and white hair named George Mattis, spent more than forty years trying to find a pattern for the sexual identification of the animals making the tracks. His experiences led him to believe, like Weston, that heavy-bodied bucks with weighty antlers make a deeper impression with the tips of the toes of their front hooves than antlerless deer. But he hastens to add that this observation may well be ignored by many American deer hunters, since in most areas 80 to 90 percent of all bucks shot are yearlings, and that few of us ever encounter heavy-bodied bucks in the older age classes. Indeed, in areas of heavy hunting pressure, bucks seldom live long enough to grow to maturity, and consequently their

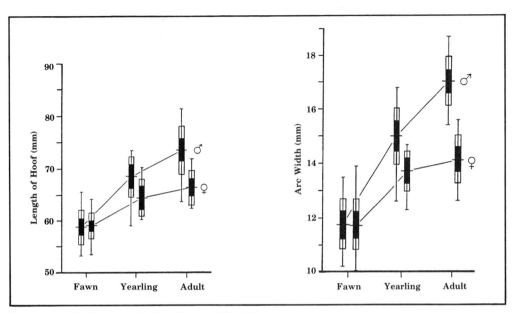

**Comparison of the hoof length and width at one-third of the
length back from the tip, by age and sex of deer. Horizontal
lines indicate the means; open bars, the standard deviations;
and vertical lines, the ranges. Non-overlap of solid bars
indicates statistical significance at the five percent level.
—Dale R. McCullough. 1965. "Sex Characteristics of Black-Tailed
Deer Hooves."** *Journal of Wildlife Management.* **29(1): 211.**

tracks may be indistinguishable from the tracks of does.

Mattis believed that the surest way to recognize the track of a buck results from actually seeing the animal make the track. The second best bet, George says, "is to find where the animal urinated. A doe hunches back and urinates in her tracks, often with a wide and irregular spray, while a buck's urine comes straight down to perforate the unbroken snow. Even as the animal moves on, the snow stains remain to determine the animal's sex. Yet, both of these clinchers are far too remote to be of great use, for one finds a buck's urine stains in the snow about as often as he sees the animal itself."

During the rut, Mattis relied heavily on finding a lone, walking track made at night, especially a track with wide spread toes and toes pointing outward from the center line—a track traveling in a definite direction. Early in the morning, after posting a stander, Mattis would follow such a track. The cross-country traveler often turned out to be a buck shot by his stander.

The best scientific description of the differences in the tracks of bucks from does is found in the British Deer Society's *Field Guide to British Deer* (1971).

"Differences in the tracks of the sexes are slight when young, but become more definite with age. . . . As a rule the tracks and step of a mature male are one-fifth greater than those of a mature female of the same species. His far heavier weight helps to develop other characteristics as well. Thus his tracks are longer and deeper, and in proportion relatively broader. His fore tracks are relatively longer in proportion to his hind, and the fore cleaves (the two halves of the toes) show a tendency to splay. The shape of the cleaves is more obtuse and their edges less sharp. The dewclaws are larger in proportion, more prominent and less sharp; they splay more widely, pointing outwards rather than downwards. His step is not only longer but more regular, the sway is normally greater, and he tends to point his toes outwards."

Yet not all deer biologists agree. "The idea that the number and sex of deer in a woods can be estimated by their tracks," Donald Chapman writes in his *Fallow Deer* (1975), "although still widely believed, is a fallacy."

Not all deer hunters agree with the findings of deer researchers in this regard either, as we learn from the late Ken Heuser, a Colorado deer hunter.

"Size and appearance of deer tracks are not reliable for determining whether the animal is a buck or doe. I know it's been said that a true expert can tell you at a glance whether it was a buck or doe. The buck is supposed to have a huge track with rounded toes from traveling after the ladies. Their dewclaws are supposed to touch the ground much of the time because of their great weight and all that sort of bunk.

"Deer are not made with cookie cutters, so they come in various sizes and weights. Some deer have big feet, some have small feet. . . ."

Heuser found the greatest value of deer tracks as signs indicating the areas that deer currently use and perhaps the number of deer as well. As a youngster, I learned that a small group of antlerless deer can make a large number of tracks in a limited area, giving the hunter the mistaken im-

pression that great numbers of deer exist in his hunting area. I recall the excited manner in which I would talk about all the deer tracks I had seen after returning to the deer shack, only to learn from some of the "old boys" at the shack that we couldn't really do much with "fried deer tracks."

Robert Donovan, a deer hunter from Virginia, also questions the scientific findings. "The hot-stove-league stories that one hears about slenderness of hoof, spread of toes, roundness of toes and other features that are supposed to distinguish between the sexes are so many pipe dreams. Where I hunt, there are more big does than big bucks."

Lennie Rue, the white-bearded white-tailed deer guru from New Jersey, has his doubts as well. "I, personally, cannot tell the sex of a deer by its tracks, though I have been studying and living with deer for more than thirty-five years. The so-called experts would stop claiming they could do so, if they ever managed to see most of the deer that made the tracks."

On the other hand, Texas deer hunter John Wootters tends to agree with the scientists, especially when speaking about exceptional bucks, and so do I. "No doe's hooves can match those of an exceptional buck. Not only are his prints longer and much deeper, but they're usually more splayed, with the hoof tips blunt, far from the dainty heart-shaped tracks of the typical doe. His trail, if you can see it, will be wider; that is, there will be more lateral spread between the prints of his right and left feet, and in a light snow or heavy mud, the walking buck will drag the tips of his hooves into each track."

Larry Benoit, the ridge-running, Red-Man-chewing buck hunter from Duxbury, Vermont, also sees a difference. "There's as much difference between a buck's and a doe's track as between your gnarled old

The toes of most mature white-tailed deer average three inches in length. Tracks measuring more than three inches in length and two inches in width often belong to bucks. *Richard P. Smith photo*

hands and those of a woman. . . . Common sense tells me that a big deer track, eight times out of ten, means a big buck." Benoit also finds a marked difference between the tracks of trophy bucks and light-weight bucks.

And so the debate continues on whether man can determine the sex of the animal by examining the tracks.

Deer tracks have been used since the beginning of mankind to guide hunters to their game and to detect the number of deer in certain areas. The final achievement of the proficient and skilled deer tracker in this regard revolves around man's ability to estimate the approximate

number of deer in a particular cover from deer tracks. But is this procedure possible?

In recent years, deer researchers employed serious efforts to determine population numbers from deer-track counts. Some biologists believe that a definite relationship exists between the number of deer tracks crossing dirt roads and the deer population. Ed Tyson, a researcher with the Florida Game and Fresh Water Fish Commission, concluded that a reliable census may develop from deer track analysis. After traveling along countless miles of dirt roads in a slow-moving Jeep and completing reams and reams of what many of us would consider "mathematical gibberish" at first glance, Tyson reported a 1.6:1 ratio of deer tracks per kilometer of road to deer per square kilometer.

Other deer researchers in Louisiana, however, remain doubtful and believe that deer-track counts are not directly proportional to the population and that they cannot be used as a valid measurement of population size. As one researcher put it, "So many variables are involved such as weather and changing food habits, that I doubt any simple formula can be worked out for estimating deer density from track counts. However, we like track counts for trend information, and they are much better than nothing as an index to densities."

Those deer biologists who use track counts to estimate deer density view their numbers on the conservative side, since it is virtually impossible to find all of the tracks crossing narrow counting strips under varying conditions of soil and weather.

Deer researchers in central Wisconsin found a highly significant correlation between deer-track counts and deer population size on a 406-square-mile study area. They note a remarkably high degree of correlation between the number of tracks counted per mile and the success of the deer season that follows, and view deer-track count information as a valuable index when used with other data. They also demonstrated, like their colleagues in Michigan, a direct correlation between deer-track counts and buck-kill statistics.

Deer biologists in east Texas also use deer-track counts to provide trend information if not information on actual numbers. Their track counts involve locating a soft area of ground in the afternoon, usually a roadside, and then dragging the area with brush to remove all evidence of tracks made earlier. The next morning they make a count to determine the number of deer that crossed the area during the night. Personnel ride the smoothed area in Jeeps and count only the tracks that enter the strip. Since the cleared area is a known distance, deer researchers use conversion factors to determine the number of deer crossing the strip. They do not make counts during the periods of unstable weather, such as approaching storms, cold fronts, or unseasonably hot temperatures, since these factors tend to reduce deer activity.

While deer-track counts have been used in east Texas and elsewhere with varying results in determining deer populations, no documentation exists on the degree of precision achieved in estimating deer numbers by means of deer-track counts.

While counting deer tracks and studying deer trails during the winter in the Adirondacks, New York deer biologist Bill Severinghaus discovered that when individual deer tracks outnumber group tracks and deer trails, deer are able to find enough forage to maintain themselves in good physical condition. But when group tracks and trails outnumber individual deer tracks, their foraging range has become so narrow that they cannot secure adequate nourishment.

The newest and perhaps most interesting research on deer tracks and hooves comes from the University of Georgia, where researchers tell us that yearling white-tailed bucks exhibit narrower hooves than adults and consequently leave narrower tracks. While studying the growth rate of hooves of white-tailed deer during the rut, deer researcher Karl Miller discovered a very interesting, unexplained hoof-length variation in young bucks. He noticed that the length differential patterns—that is, the

A marvel of adaptation, deer hooves change structurally over time to match the varying soil conditions. *Richard P. Smith photo*

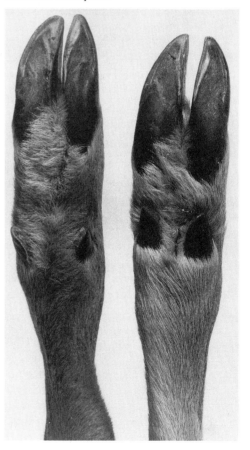

mean difference in length between the front and the rear hooves—of some young bucks changed over time.

In his study of deer hooves, Miller found that the length patterns for some young bucks aged six to fourteen months changed from longer front hooves to longer rear hooves. The hoof-length patterns then reversed this trend, tending again toward the traditionally longer front hooves. According to Miller, "In all three cases where hoof-length patterns changed dramatically, the front hooves became shorter and the rear hooves longer. An explanation for these changes in hoof lengths still remains unclear."

Deer hooves, as a marvel of adaptation, not only provide deer with the best possible traction under changing conditions but change structurally over time to match the varying soil conditions. They are composed of keratin, a type of solidified hair, the same type of substance as our fingernails. The outer rim of the hoof remains much harder than the central portion. During winter the central portion retracts somewhat, giving the hoof a concave appearance. Only the outer rim makes contact with the ground as a result of this retraction. This change provides excellent traction on rough surfaces. During the rest of the year the central portion of the hoof tends to be convex, swelling outward to give the hoof a spongy surface. The hoof grows and changes continuously throughout the deer's life. The abrasion of rock and hard soil affects these changes in growth.

Not only is the deer researcher concerned with the deer's hoof structure and the deer hunter with the animal's track, but the deer themselves show a marked interest in their back track especially before bedding, when wounded, or when being dogged by a persistent deer tracker.

The persistent tracking of deer to their death is not a particularly popular technique of deer hunting in this country for several reasons. First of all, deer for the most part can only be successfully tracked in fresh snow—a situation seldom encountered in many deer-hunting areas. Second, deer tracking takes a considerable amount of time, skill, physical endurance, and patience, all of which tend to discourage the majority of American deer hunters. And third, trying to track deer to their death in areas of heavy hunter-density probably amounts to little more than following deer tracks to gut piles. Many hunters trying to track deer are also stopped frequently by posted signs.

Nonetheless, tracking deer as a traditional method of deer hunting remains widely practiced today in many northeastern states. One such deer tracker is Jim Massett of Chittenango, New York, who tracks down trophy Adirondack bucks under the most difficult of circumstances. Massett, a long-distance runner in great physical shape, knows the remote parts of the Adirondacks well. During the 1986 deer season, Massett traveled 232 miles on foot to see forty-one deer, including fifteen bucks. He finally shot his 137-5/8 Boone and Crockett buck in Hamilton County, after more than nineteen days of steady deer tracking. Many deer hunters would probably consider such tracking exploits as belonging more to *The Last of the Mohicans* and Daniel Boone.

Like Daniel Boone, Massett uses a tent as a base camp and prefers to hunt alone. During the summer months, while fly fishing for trout, he scouts his deer hunting turf; when the rut comes, he heads for the secluded mountains in search of big deer tracks. Once on the track of a big buck, Massett will travel fifteen to twenty miles a day. He will run or jog after a fresh track

Hunting deer by following tracks remains a widely practiced method of deer hunting in the Northeast. After marathon deer tracking sessions in the rugged mountains of the Adirondacks, often going on for fifteen to twenty miles a day, New York deer hunter Jim Massett usually returns to his tent with a buck ranging from 125 to 145 on the Boone and Crockett scale. *Jim Massett photo*

when necessary. The snow-covered woods, the rough terrain, and all types of weather and temperatures merely heighten the marathon deer tracking experience for Massett. Most of his bucks average 7.5 years old or older. Many of them probably never saw a human before encountering Massett.

With at least three inches of snow on the ground, Jim believes that he can tell the difference between a buck track and a doe track within a 400-yard span at least 99 percent of the time. He uses urine marks as a positive key to sex identification and notes than an unmolested doe will usually urinate at least once within a 400-yard trail. White-tailed bucks, Jim observes, often dribble urine while walking, a urination characteristic not common for does.

These yellow-stained lines in the snow clearly reveal themselves to a persistent tracker like Jim Massett.

Like many deer hunters, Jim readily admits the difficulty in properly aging deer tracks and views the ability to age tracks as an acquired skill learned only through long practice sessions and years of experience. Aging deer tracks in areas devoid of sunlight can be particularly difficult, as can aging tracks partially filled with newly fallen snow. A melted-out buck track can also fool many deer hunters.

When tracking deer on dry ground, one needs to study the leaves that deer turn up and ask questions. Are the undersides of the leaves dried compared to the undisturbed leaves? Has dirt crumbled into the

How to make a plaster cast of a deer track.

Carefully remove twigs, leaves or mud that have fallen into the print. Forceps or photographers' blower brush are useful at this stage.

Mix plaster of Paris with clean water in plastic bowl.

Press card (or tin) strip round track and avoid air bubbles by pouring plaster carefully onto side of track.

Check by gentle finger pressure to see if dry. This usually takes 15-30 minutes depending on how much water was mixed with plaster.

Cut out soil round plaster and remove completely. Pull back card and pack carefully inside newspaper.

Very gently wash off mud under tap. When dry, colour track or back-ground and add details.

—Jim Taylor Page. (ed.) 1971. *Field Guide to British Deer.*

track? How does the track compare with your own track? Some deer hunters carry a deer hoof with them and make a fresh track next to the one they are following for purposes of comparison. Is the track hard and rigid? If so, it's probably at least a day old.

A fresh deer track shows a sharp impression with a glaze on the outer edges. Older tracks lose that glaze when exposed to the sun and gradually show drying cracks on the tightly pressed soil. I have noticed throughout the years that when tracking deer, the daily arc of the sun can greatly enhance or hinder tracking conditions. Ideal tracking conditions on bare ground exist while the sun rises in the first one-third arc and when the sun enters the last one-third of its downward arc prior to sunset. During those two periods of the day the sun provides the hunter with light that approaches the forest floor at a low angle causing an accentuation of shadows that make deer tracks in the ground easier to see.

I frequently hear hunters claim that they can tell the age of a track to within an hour. I doubt it. While I have seen some excellent deer trackers in operation, none of them were magicians. None of them can track a deer across solid rock or accomplish any of the other remarkable feats that deer trackers presumably accomplish in the windy tales one hears in deer camp. You would think that some hunters have Master's degrees in deer "trackology."

I do know that if you get down on your knees and scrutinize deer tracks with a magnifying glass, you will be amazed at the unique and intricate detail of each track. Like the fingerprints of man, deer hooves have individual characteristics that show up in their tracks. Learning to make plaster casts of deer tracks can be a meaningful and enlightening experience for the beginning deer hunter.

Learning to distinguish between tracks of different ages on bare ground and being able to read and interpret deer tracks often determines whether the hunter merely airs out his hunting clothes or experiences a successful deer hunt. *Charles J. Alsheimer photo*

Learning to distinguish the difference in the appearance of tracks of different ages on bare ground and being able to read and interpret deer tracks can often make the difference between merely airing out your hunting clothes or experiencing a successful deer hunt. The ability to do so demands a great deal of effort; but it's worth it, for a thorough knowledge of deer tracks and tracking adds a genuine dimension of intrigue and mystery to our sport.

One of the most enduring and unresolved mysteries in the world of the white-tailed deer for me revolves around the ultimate meaning and significance of that sole, indelible, well-formed heart-shaped deer print left in the middle of scrapes. They are obviously placed there with the utmost deliberation and attention to detail. But why? What do they signify? To which sex does the track directly in the center of the scrape belong? A doe? Or is it the result of a buck lightly placing a hoof print down? Perhaps the track belongs to the doe, since new scrape research from Southwest Missouri State University by Grant Woods and Lynn Robbins indicates that does make 47 percent of all scrape visitations, with bucks making only 33 percent and juvenile deer of unknown sex 20 percent.

As I stare at those heart-shaped deer prints in the center of scrapes each October and try to determine their ultimate significance and the sexual identity of their maker, I think of this passage from Larry Koller's *Shots at Whitetails:* "The study of deer prints never loses its charm for a deer hunter. Rather it adds to the fun of a day in the woods."

Chapter 8

Woodland Tragedies

Many a man, on first seeing a deer dash through the dangerous, mazy wreck of a storm track, has wondered how it could escape with its life. As a matter of fact, deer suffer many accidents in their haste.
—Ernest Thompson Seton, *Lives of Game Animals*, 1929

In their great haste to escape man, predators, free-roaming dogs, and man-made hazards, deer frequently panic, and accidents of various kinds take their toll. While accidental mortality of deer—with the exception of deer/vehicle collisions—does not constitute a population-limiting factor, it does take a considerable number of animals nationwide and often in a very traumatic way. Indeed, deer die in many different ways other than from gunshots or arrows—often quite unnoticed; although some diehard buck hunters roam the woods at all times of the year and record these unusual deaths and speculate about their causes. While some of these accidental deaths are quite common, some are very bizarre, with their causes remaining in the realm of mystery. With the exception of Seton, who knew well that the life of a wild deer often ends in tragedy, few of us appreciate the drama, variety, and extent

of these accidental deaths. Sometimes the tragedies occur in the animal's own bailiwick and sometimes the trauma and terror occur when the animal wanders into suburbia and destroys itself in the process of thrashing modern civilization. In both cases the results remain the same: few deer live longer than 2½ years and here are some of the reasons why.

One of the most common forms of accidental deaths involves deer colliding with sticks, branches, and trees. In his *Lives of Game Animals* (1929), Seton speculates that not one adult deer in ten escapes from being snagged many times by sticks and branches, as revealed by the numerous scars on their legs and bellies. In some cases deer survive in a remarkable way; and in others, death occurs immediately.

Montana deer hunter R. Clarke Fisk gives us a remarkable example of survival after stick impalement. After shooting a

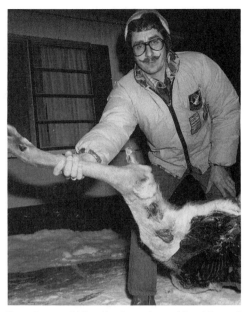

Deer frequently impale themselves with sticks and branches as they dash through the woods. Some die immediately; incredibly, others survive. *Richard P. Smith photo*

white-tailed doe, he found a fir branch measuring one foot in length and a half-inch thick in the body cavity. Entering between the fourth and fifth ribs on the right side and barely missing the lung, the fir branch pierced the top of the diaphragm and the liver and rested against the underside of the backbone. Fisk believed that the doe experienced the accident while quite young.

"That the animal met with this accident while it was yet young, I am thoroughly convinced, for the end at the ribs had been entirely drawn into the opening of the heart and lungs, and had thoroughly healed on the outside. The skin which I now have shows only the faintest trace of a scar. There was not a particle of pus or inflammatory matter of any kind. In fact, the branch, covered as it was with the white skin, exactly resembled one of the

long bones of the leg. The animal was healthy and fat, and the venison was fine."

Charles Gianini, a deer hunter from Herkimer County, New York tells of a similar accident.

"Last fall while hunting in the town of Wilmurt in the West Canada Creek country, we shot a two-year-old buck. On dressing him out, we were surprised to find driven into his chest a piece of poplar limb. This piece measured 5½ inches in length and ⅜ inches in diameter and was encased in a sac of tissue. On the outside the deer's chest there was no sign or scar showing where the wood had entered. The deer was apparently healthy and seemed to be in no way affected by this accident."

When Wilbur Smith of South Norwalk, Connecticut, found a dead doe in an alder patch one day, he studied the area and discovered that while jumping a wire fence, she had caught the top wire. In falling forward, after pulling staples out and sagging the wire, she had struck an alder stub that thrust down her throat. A broken windpipe but no sign of struggle suggested an instant death.

While deer hunting in the Oswegatchie Country, an Adirondack deer hunter jumped a buck in heavy cover. Although he had not fired his rifle, while trailing the animal he soon discovered a very pronounced blood trail. After finally catching up with the buck, he shot the badly wounded animal and discovered a deep gash in its chest. Retracing the buck's trail, the hunter learned that the buck, in leaping into heavy brush, had impaled itself on a dry, spear-like branch of a fallen tree.

Adirondack deer hunter J. A. Henry reports seeing a buck galloping over soft ground and suddenly spiking its belly on a sharply protruding branch imbedded in mud. The buck did a complete somersault. The hunter found the animal motionless with a broken neck; its antlers still embedded in the ground. He tagged the deer without firing a shot.

Some deer die from stick impalements and suffer from severe infectious fibromas, while others survive with no apparent aftereffects. After killing a mule deer in Colorado, Eli Loback discovered, while skinning the deer, that it had badly snagged itself with a spruce branch measuring eight inches in length and three-quarters of an inch in diameter. The branch had pierced the shoulder blade, broken two ribs, and penetrated eight inches into the chest cavity. Eli found the deer fat and healthy, with the spruce branch completely encysted.

While field-dressing a white-tailed buck, a physician from Virginia discovered an extraordinary example of the whitetail's incredible ability to recover from natural accidents. The physician observed that at some time in the animal's life an elder stick had "entirely transfixed" the heart. In his post-mortem examination, the doctor learned that the stick had been imbedded in the heart for a great length of time. The doctor summarized his findings in his journal.

"The wound that the elder stick made in its ingress perfectly healed with no trace of inflammation discernible nor any sign of disease in the substance of the heart through which it penetrated. Nature kindly and effectively cured the wound and preserved the life of that gallant buck that he might die by the hands of a doctor/deer hunter, *secundum artem*."

In a similar case, a deputy game warden from Williamsport, Pennsylvania, killed a white-tailed buck during the 1966 deer hunting season. He cooked the heart for supper that night. While slicing the heart with his knife, he hit something hard. The surprised warden found a piece of bone

one inch long and a half-inch thick imbedded in the heart. Completely surrounded by gristle, apparently the bone had existed in the deer's heart for a long period of time. One can only surmise how it penetrated the animal's body and pierced its heart.

Another deer hunter asked himself the same question when he found a stick that had punctured a lung of the deer he had shot. He noted that the wound had healed, the lung had inflated itself again, and a gristle-like covering had developed over the stick to prevent further damage to the lung.

Darell Saunders of Plymouth, Michigan, knows well that "truth can be stranger than fiction." In a letter to the editor of *Deer and Deer Hunting* magazine, he tells about his "stick deer." While walking along a grassy fence line during the 1980 bow hunting season, he almost stepped on what seemed to be a sleeping deer. The deer showed no sign of movement. He touched the carcass and felt a warm body. He noticed a slight bulge under the skin in the rib area of the right side. While field-dressing the dead doe, he found a ten-inch stick imbedded in the lung cavity. After studying the area, he concluded that the doe had impaled herself with the stick and traveled 300 yards before collapsing. The stick had entered just behind the extended front left leg and the resultant bleeding was mostly internal. He tagged his deer that season without shooting an arrow.

After field-dressing an illegally shot white-tailed doe in 1986, Glen Taylor, a conservation officer in New Hampshire, came to believe as his friend Ernie Robinson put it, "that the vitality of a whitetail is at least as great as the vaunted life-force of the proverbial cat!" He believes so because in thoroughly examining the animal, Taylor found a three-inch stick as big around as a broom handle encapsulated in gristle in the upper chest cavity of the deer. The absence of any wound or outward sign of how the stick got there indicated that it had been there for some time without apparently affecting the animal's behavior, even though it lay only an inch from the spine.

But deer also confront trees in yet another tragic way: They hang themselves. While polishing his antlers one fall day, one mule deer buck became so entangled in the crotch of two birch trees that he strangled himself to death. A conservation officer from the South Dakota Department of Game, Fish and Parks found the buck sitting on his rump with his body in the upright position and his neck caught in the crotch of the two trees.

A mule deer buck caught in the crotch of two birch trees. *South Dakota Department of Game, Fish and Parks photo*

In the *Journal of Mammalogy,* researcher Harvey Gunderson reports an incident of a white-tailed buck in Marshall County, Minnesota, becoming so entangled in bog birch that the animal strangled itself. According to Gunderson, "several pieces of the birch were wound around the bases of the antlers and securely knotted." The antlers and the skull of that heroic buck now bear the Catalog Number 4483 at the Minnesota Museum of Natural History. More bucks than we think might only narrowly escape similar tragic results of hanging and strangling, given the frequency with which deer hunters find fractured antlers (some with brain matter still attached), imbedded in tree trunks and branches during the breeding season.

In a more dramatic instance, one deer hunter from New York's Catskill Mountains, found a buck hanging in an oak tree twenty feet above the ground. Apparently, predators forced the animal to leap off a steep cliff. Hanging from its position of death in the oak tree, the animal stared at the acorns on the ground below through the bony eye sockets.

While studying the winter range conditions of deer, researcher Edwin Caswell found a deer hanging in a yew tree. In his notebook, he documented the accident.

"The yew tree was growing below an abrupt bank at the edge of Deadman Creek. A cover of crusted snow approximately three feet deep recorded the series of events leading to the fatal accident. This deer was able to travel on top of the crusted snow and from the abrupt bank browse parts of the yew otherwise beyond reach. Undoubtedly overzealous in its attempt to get the choice twigs of yew, the deer walked to the very edge of the snow-capped bank, and while it was stretching to reach the twigs the snow gave way beneath the animal. It plunged forward and

This deer, while standing on its hind legs and reaching high to browse, slipped and caught its leg between two trees. It died after an extended struggle. *Ralph Williams photo*

was hanged by the neck in the fork of the yew tree. Bobcats visited the accidental kill and feasted on the hindquarters."

Deer are forced to do many things that often result in accidental deaths. One spring day game manager Issac Baumgardner was tramping the hills of Pennsylvania, when he discovered a young buck hung by its neck in a crack of an old stump. Someone had placed salt on top of a very high stump. Its height forced the buck to stand on its hind feet to reach the salt. Evidently, it slipped and caught its neck in the crack of the stump.

Many deer die while reaching high for browse on their hind legs. If they slip, they sometimes get their front legs tightly wedged in the crotch of two trees and die

after an extended struggle, as deer hunter Ralph Williams discovered one mid-February day while snowshoeing in Cheboygan County in northern Michigan. This type of accidental death is quite common in the whitetail's northern range.

In another incident of deer struggling with trees, one deer hunter found a live doe lying under a tree with exposed roots. Somehow the deer had slipped its hind leg under one of the exposed roots beyond the gambrel joint and could not get up. Not wishing to secure his venison in such a way, the hunter liberated the distressed animal by cutting through the root.

In a recent "Deer Browse" item published in *Deer & Deer Hunting* magazine, Bill Schubert, a deer hunter from Racine,

Wisconsin, documents an even more bizarre case of a deer getting stuck between two trees. After jumping a group of ten whitetails, Schubert ran to the top of a nearby hill. When he reached the top, he found "a doe digging and driving with her front legs but obviously not going anywhere." After taking several pictures of the deer's strange predicament, Bill climbed one of the trees above her and pried the two trees apart, thus setting the animal free from what would surely have resulted in a very traumatic ending had he not intervened.

Another one of the most common and traumatic deaths for deer revolves around their encounters with wire fences. While deer adeptly negotiate fences on a daily basis by crawling under them, many get one of their hind legs caught in a simple half-hitch. Trapped in this manner, they hang by a snared leg until death takes its toll from starvation, exhaustion, and/or predation.

High, woven-wire fences, in particular, prove insurmountable for many deer, especially fawns and animals in a weakened condition. Nationwide, hundreds, perhaps thousands, of deer annually suffer a tragic fate while struggling with barbed-wire fences of one kind or another until violent death eases the pain.

One deer hunter on the Gage Holland Ranch near Big Bend, Texas, found a mule deer skull with twenty pounds of fencing wire wrapped around its antlers. That buck had run into a fence and torn lose hundreds of feet of wire. As he turned, the wires had twisted into a cable; not being able to free himself, the buck had perished in a miserable way.

A. M. Fish, a deer hunter from Powers, Oregon, documents the case of a big black-tailed buck on Eden Ridge in Coos County, Oregon, that entangled itself in some unknown and extraordinary way in the telephone line of the Coos County Fire Patrol Association. In his failing efforts to free himself from entanglement with the telephone wire, the buck pulled 600 feet of the wire down before dying of exhaustion. His gallant head, with part of the tangled telephone wire, hung for many years at the Oregon Department of Fish and Wildlife.

Lennie Rue records an unusual situation of what happened when high-voltage lines broke loose near Erie, Pennsylvania. In touching the wire, three deer—a buck and two does—were instantly electrocuted. Two red foxes that came to pick their bones received the same treatment; two mongrel dogs made the same mistake and suffered the same consequences.

Wire and deer represent a bad combination. I have found whitetails twisted up in woven-wire and barbed-wire fences during the various seasons of the year. One deer hunter even found a piece of 19-gauge wire lodged in the liver of the white-tailed deer he shot on the Archer and Anna Huntington Wildlife Forest Station in New York. Deer break their antlers, jaws, and legs on wire fences, but there isn't much we or they can do about it. Wire fences simply represent another hazard of modern civilization with which deer must contend.

The most dramatic woodland tragedy occurs when bucks decide to slug it out to the finish and lock antlers while at the same time entangling themselves in wire fences. Bill Carey, a deer hunter from Vermillion, Alberta, cites one of the most unusual examples of deer behavior in this regard. In early January 1971, he noticed a dead deer in an alfalfa field. He assumed that someone had shot it and failed to recover it. As he approached the deer, however, he realized that it was in fact two white-tailed bucks with interlocked ant-

Bill Carey, a deer hunter from Vermillion, Alberta, encountered this woodland tragedy in January 1971. *Russell Thornberry photo*

lers, both temporarily entangled in a barbed-wire fence. One buck was still alive; the other buck was dead, partially eaten by coyotes. With the aid of a hunting buddy, Carey roped and hog-tied the buck. He then sawed several inches off the main antler beam, thus freeing the live buck from his burden. Once released the startled buck vanished into the nearby timber, waving the traditional fond adieu.

On November 5, 1971, Edward Wesslen of Blackfalds, Ontario, similarly found two dead bucks with locked antlers along his fence line, ensnared in barbed wire. In their death struggle they had uprooted 100 feet of barbed-wire fence and posts, and torn up the ground around the scene of their tragic battle.

Two mule deer bucks, fighting during the breeding season near Cherry Creek, Montana, engaged themselves in a similar situation. While shoving themselves around, one buck twisted his antlers in a strand of barbed-wire fence. As the bucks twisted and turned, their antlers tragically tied together. After one buck eventually strangled itself, James R. Martin, the landowner, appeared on the scene and dispatched the live one. In the course of their tragic battle, the bucks broke off thirteen fenceposts and pulled loose more than sixty yards of wire.

Dick Farrell, a deer hunter from the Tugaska area of Saskatchewan, experienced a buck fight that proved fatal for one white-tailed buck, although his opponent escaped none the worse for wear. While on his way home from work, Farrell spotted a large buck entangled in a wire fence. A closer look revealed the buck's true predicament: He stood not only helplessly entangled in wire but locked in the antlers of his fallen competitor. After rounding up some friends, Farrell returned to the scene of the battle. The live buck still stood in the same position — completely exhausted — staring at the dead buck, which was half eaten by coyotes. One can only imagine his terror in watching coyotes chew up his half-eaten rival. While two of his friends struggled to hold the buck, Farrell sawed the antler holding them together. When freed, the astonished buck disappeared into the bush.

Other deer researchers and hunters have also saved bucks from tragic situations. Professor Jerry Haigh of the Department of Herd Medicine and Theriogenology at the University of Saskatchewan recalls a similar case of locked antlers in which he saved one of the antagonists. But in this particular buck fight, he found two bucks with only one antler from each animal locked. The right antler of a live buck was quite free of the left antler of a dead buck partially eaten by predators. According to Professor Haigh, "the second and third tines of the live deer had slipped under the main beam of the dead deer near the base. It was impossible to disengage the deer even after the live one had been immobilized. When one pushed down on the live deer's antler to try to disengage it, the tip of the antler jammed against the back of the skull of the dead deer and could not be pushed down far enough. After the animals had been separated, I administered an antidote to the live deer, which shortly thereafter ran off, apparently none the worse."

In another white-tailed buck fight in the Dirt Hills near Pangman, Saskatchewan, a farmer named Lew Darby observed two bucks lying on the side of a small hill. While approaching them, they scrambled to their feet and Darby noticed that their antlers were locked together. After returning to the area with help, Darby eventually roped one buck and, with a friend sitting on the other animal, he sawed one inch off the tip of one antler and gingerly released them. The bucks ran off side by side. Since this buck fight occurred in September, they undoubtedly locked while sparring rather than engaging in rut-related dominance.

Most bucks found in the locked position are not so fortunate, for deer season often coincides with the timing of their brush battles; consequently, a good number of locked bucks end up on the meat pole and later in the taxidermy shop. Judging from the number of photos, newspaper stories, locked antlers on display at deer classics, news releases, and letters to the editor, bucks with locked antlers eventually shot by hunters are not an uncommon occurrence in the fall of the year.

What is uncommon often revolves around the way in which the deer hunter ends these tragic death battles. During the 1984 deer season, Sam Mathews, an Illinois deer hunter, got the surprise of his life while hunting in Pike County, Illinois, during the second half of the firearm season. While coming across the top of a hill, he spotted a 10-pointer grazing, or at least he thought the animal was grazing. He raised his shotgun and put a well-placed slug into the animal. As the buck went down, another 10-pointer stood up right beside it. Only then did Mathews realize that the buck was irreversibly locked with an opponent. His hunting partner, Jerome Martin of Pleasant Hill, Illinois, shot the second 10-pointer. Locked like crossed sabers at the base of their brow-tines, these two 10-pointers would have exhausted themselves in hours or days of futile struggle, only to die of starvation, broken necks, or as victims of opportunistic predators. Martin and Mathews donated the mounted, locked-bucks to the Illinois State Museum.

While hunting in the Chequamegon National Forest in northern Wisconsin during the 1984 deer season, Les Talo decided to still-hunt an old logging trail taken over by young spruce. As he moved along the trail, he saw a tree about fifteen feet off the trail shake violently. Looking at the tree, he spotted the back half of a large deer. Since he carried an either-sex permit with him, he placed a shot just behind the front shoulder, even though he did not see antlers. The deer fell at the report of the rifle. When he pushed his way through the brush and looked at the dead animal, he could hardly believe his eyes! Talo tells us what happened:

"There lay two dead bucks with their antlers locked together and tangled in several two-inch saplings. The buck I shot (a 10-pointer weighing 170 pounds dressed out) had killed the other buck (an 8-pointer weighing 190 pounds) by piercing the heart area with an antler tine. It had dragged the dead buck about fifty yards through the woods before the dead buck became caught in the saplings. The living buck, as a result, couldn't move forward or backward nor raise his head. The one buck had been dead for about two days and was not salvageable as meat."

Not too many deer hunters get two bucks with one shot, especially when they don't even know that they are shooting at a buck in the first place. But then not too many deer hunters wind up sharing their locked-bucks with coyotes either.

Yet, that's exactly what happened to Jack Graham, a deer hunter from Alberta, who on a cold fall day in 1981 chanced upon a pair of interlocked white-tailed bucks being worked over by coyotes and black-billed magpies in an alfalfa field. Graham found that one buck was still alive and saw that it had dragged the partly consumed carcass of the other, larger buck across the field. In his *Trophy Deer of Alberta* (1982), Russell Thornberry documents the Graham case.

"The coyotes had eaten the dead buck to within sixteen inches of the living buck's nose. Graham shot the remaining exhausted buck soon to be another meal for the coyotes. Both bucks had good mature racks but the smaller of the two had killed the larger deer by thrusting a sharp tine into his eye socket. The dead buck was too heavy to move for the smaller buck but coyotes were making the load lighter with each meal. Nature is not gentle in her ways and both deer were destined to die a dramatic death."

On her 1985 deer hunt in the Pease Creek area north of Geddes, South Dakota, Jackie Gau of Lake Andes, South Dakota also learned that nature is not always a friendly provider, for on a fall day she learned a dramatic lesson on just how stern nature can be when she encountered two bucks with locked antlers. One buck, already dead, consisted of only a head, one front leg, the spine, and some hide—the victim of coyotes. She shot the living and exhausted remaining buck, a 5-pointer, which apparently had spent most of his time before she encountered him keeping the coyotes at bay while they took turns eating parts of his opponent.

When deer hunters gather to exchange their tales of the 1984 deer hunting season, they better hope that Ed Hall of Glidden, Wisconsin is not in their midst.

His story of the 10-pointer that he shot with his bow in the Chequamegon National Forest in early December of 1984 almost borders on a "Ripley's Believe It or Not" story. Locked within the 10-pointer's rack was the head of a 19-pointer with a 19.5-inch nontypical spread. The front point of the 10-pointer's left antler had entered the skull of the 19-pointer beneath its right ear, killing it. Exactly how the body of the dead buck became completely severed from the neck remains open to conjecture and/or doubt. In any event, wildlife managers estimated the live weight of the emaciated 10-pointer at around 300 pounds prior to the rut.

Despite the frequent vigorous nature of buck fights, under normal circumstances most bucks resolve their rutting conflicts by a hasty retreat of one antagonist or the other. Yet this is not to imply that bucks do not injure themselves or kill themselves in battle.

While studying the battle scars of rutting bucks, Professor Valerius Geist at the University of Calgary found that on the average a buck deals with twenty to thirty wounds per year. In examining the deer skin of a 3.5-year-old white-tailed buck, Geist found thirty-nine wounds. Many people claim that deer do not injure themselves or kill themselves in antler combat. Don't believe it!

In observing traumatic injuries and accidental deaths of white-tailed deer, G. S. Wobeser, a deer researcher at the University of Saskatchewan, came across a 6.5-year-old white-tailed buck during the rut in a very weakened condition. Bleeding from multiple wounds, the buck—which was blind—soon died. In his post-mortem examination of the buck, Wobeser found multiple deep puncture wounds in the perineal, hip, flank, and head regions. He noted the total rupture and collapse of one eye and severe chronic keratitis and anterior synechia in the other eye. This buck, according to Wobeser, "appeared to have been attacked repeatedly and because of blindness the animal was unable to respond appropriately or escape when threatened by other males."

In 1961, deer hunter Kenneth Stoppleworth discovered the results of one of the rarest occurrences of self-inflicted mortality of which I have ever heard. While deer hunting with his brother near Woodworth, North Dakota, Stoppleworth found a trio of battling bucks—two 8-pointers and a 10-pointer—that had locked in combat to their deaths. This remains one of only three recorded incidents, as far as I know, of three locked bucks destroying themselves in combat while paying the dearest penalty possible for their ambitions.

After being called to examine a dead buck found by a hunter on a deer trail, Gary Lindquist, a Michigan conservation officer, attests to the fact that bucks kill one another. In skinning the animal, Lindquist found four puncture wounds from antler tines under the buck's front leg. One antler tine had punctured the heart and broken a rib. One of the dead buck's antlers had been broken off, but Lindquist failed to find it in the twenty-foot circle of trampled ground.

When bow hunter Richard Van Nostran missed a shot at a 10-pointer, he wondered why the buck didn't run. He then killed the buck with a well-placed second arrow. While skinning the buck, he answered his question.

"There was a large wound in his left hindquarter with three gashes along his flank. The spacing between these wounds made it apparent that they were caused by the antler tines of another buck. The hindquarter wound was so deep that I could insert my forefinger to the knuckle and not hit bottom. This episode convinced me that bucks occasionally inflict serious, if not fatal, injuries on one another."

Buck fights resulting in the death of both participants from injuries or exhaustion, but *not* involving locked antlers, occur very seldom. When you find dead bucks as a result of combat without locked antlers, you may well see the largest animals in your area. Most fights among dominant bucks of equal strength usually last no more than fifteen to thirty seconds—not exactly resembling the massive brush battles in the wild imagination of the novice hunter.

While deer hunting near Woodworth, North Dakota, Kenneth Stoppleworth found a trio of bucks that died after their antlers locked in combat. Two of the bucks were 8-pointers and the third, a 10-pointer. To the best of my knowledge, this is one of only three recorded incidents of three white-tailed bucks locking antlers and all perishing in an endless struggle.

Intriguing tales of buck fights and tragic deaths as a result of intertwined antlers exist as a natural curiosity for deer hunter and naturalist alike. Illustrations and pictures of such natural mortality have graced the sporting journals and tabloids of this country since their inception. With larger deer herds and more hunters afield, more of these kinds of accidental deaths come to our attention. One wonders how often bucks lock their antlers and perish without being discovered. Is it as rare as most deer hunters believe? I doubt it, for the odds of bucks locking their antlers are probably greater than we suspect, especially in

highly managed deer herds where a more equal sex ratio exists, a ratio that increases breeding competition. We do know that in studying the movements of trophy-class bucks, Dr. Steve Demarais, a research scientist at Texas Tech University, found a rather high natural mortality rate (15 percent) for bucks in the upper ages.

Other forms of woodland tragedies take their toll as a result of various kinds of weather-related accidents. When Mount St. Helens erupted, game department officials announced that more than 10,000 deer died in mud flows, steam, ash, and flying trees. Millions of animals perished, and the eruption destroyed hundreds of square miles of deer habitat.

A more common form of death resulting from adverse weather occurs when deer drown in floodwaters from tropical storms. The best example of this kind of natural mortality occurred in June 1982 in Florida's Everglades Wildlife Management Area when two tropical storms forced 5,500 white-tailed deer to high ground or islands where they competed for scarce food resources. Without any abatement of the water level and with heavy July rains, as well as a temporary injunction initiated by antihunters that effectively halted an organized deer hunt, thousands of deer died from trauma, stress, and malnutrition.

Drowning is probably a more common form of miscellaneous mortality than one would suspect, especially in such southern states as Louisiana or in such northern states as Vermont, where free-roaming dogs often force deer to plunge into ice-choked streams. Chased by dogs into the Colorado River, one exhausted fawn became trapped by an ice shelf. Unable to return to shore, the fawn drowned. Deer researchers in Arizona found a mule deer fawn drowned in a water tank installed exclusively for cattle. While studying the Okanogan mule deer herd in the Methow Valley watershed in north-central Washington, researchers reported that 184 deer drowned in irrigation canals during a nine-year study.

Besides using waterways to escape from pursuing predators, whitetails often travel on frozen, windswept lakes, rivers, and streams. Even when not being pursued by predators, they sometimes slip and fall and suffer pelvic, limb, ligament, and muscle damage. Unable to rise, they freeze, starve, or are consumed alive by predators.

While studying how mule deer respond to a highway underpass, deer researcher Dale Reed noted that four deer fell to their deaths from a high precipice created by the construction of Interstate 70 west of Vail, Colorado. In his study, he viewed a buck falling from a high cliff. The buck landed on his back on a small ledge several feet down from the cliff and then on his legs and brisket at the bottom. The buck then limped across four busy lanes of I-70, nearly getting hit by four different vehicles.

Deer fall to their deaths in many different ways. Mule deer migrating over the

Deer hunter Dan Behring found this buck on a small island between two forks of a river after a spring flood. It was hanging in a tree at floodwater level—apparently the victim of drowning. *Dan Behring photo*

crest of the Sierra Nevada often plummet off snowfields that changing weather conditions transform into solid ice by successive thaws and freezes; they land on sharp rocks below. Researchers seldom observe these kinds of accidental deaths. But one deer researcher who did, Fred L. Jones, tells us what he saw.

"Deer attempting to pass the crest of the Sierra Nevada were unable to obtain traction and plummeted into a jumbled area of sharp talus blocks below. The rocks were bloodstained and strewn with splintered antlers and bits of flesh. Limbs, heads, necks, and backs of deer had been fractured in a variety of combinations and some body cavities had been punctured by sharp rocks."

Some deer fall into prospect pits or mine shafts. Cecil Williams, a former director of the Denver Wildlife Research Center, once encountered a fawn in such a pit west of Boulder, Colorado. Had he not rescued the weakened animal, it would have surely died in a miserable manner.

Other deer die as a result of falling into wells, abandoned silo pits, and concrete aqueducts. Some are struck by snowslides and others marooned on mounds in flooding rivers. And some die mired in swampland muck.

Deer also must contend with violent blizzards. On Friday, January 10, 1975, a severe storm started in North Dakota that lasted for several days. Because very little snow covered the ground, large areas of bare ground were exposed to winds that peaked at sixty-four m.p.h. Temperatures reached $-30°F$, creating wind-chill factors approaching $-100°F$. Zero visibility existed due to blowing snow and dirt. This driving snow and dirt forced deer out of their normal cover. During the weeks following the blizzard, Stephen Richards, a disease-research biologist, studied the

Although whitetails often consciously avoid wildfires in a cool and collected manner by running upwind and around the flames, some deer panic and run to their deaths on smoking hooves as did this white-tailed deer in northeastern North Carolina. *Scott Osborne photo*

effects of the blizzard on white-tailed deer and their behavior.

Richards found that most deer stranded in roadside ditches, were iced up, blinded, and readily accessible to man. Dirt soiled their roughened coats and large layers of ice had formed on their heads and legs, resulting in injuries to their eyes, muzzles, and hides and to the muscle, fascia, and tendon tissue of their legs. The "ice helmets" of these struggling, floundering and blinded deer extended from under their lower jaws to over the bridge of their noses, eyes, and back to the ears, or antlers in the case of the bucks.

In this report of this woodland tragedy, Richards documents what he saw: "In addition to the ice on their heads, many of the deer sustained injuries on the inside of the legs at the knees of both front and hind limbs. This was caused by ice forming at the knees when the animal was lying down. When the deer stood up suddenly, the ice held and hide, fascia, and muscle tissue were ripped away. These lesions were further aggravated and infected by plunging through the crusted snow. Some of the deer exhibited cuts on the faces, legs, and flanks, probably caused by running into barbed-wire fences." When some deer jumped up, large portions of their hides remained frozen to the ground. Richards observed one deer dragging a large piece of ice attached to a strip of hide on one leg. One blinded doe, still standing, lost the hide from all four legs. Deer with such severe leg damage died quickly from massive bacterial infections.

Farmers caught some of these deer blinded by the blizzard and penned them in their barns. There they thawed them out by placing them in front of heaters. But most died following their de-icing. Their behavior varied when captured. Some remained docile while others reacted very aggressively.

Richards found one little buck with its head completely encased in ice and its eyes frozen open. He de-iced many deer on the spot and released them. "Some of those that were freed of the ice moved away normally while others continued to stagger, fall, and run into trees, posts, and fences."

Wildfires also injure, blind, and kill deer and force some deer to run on stumps of legs to their death. Although a dearth of eye-witness accounts exist on how deer respond to wildfires, we do have some on-the-scene reports. Richard Beach, a Michigan conservation officer, once observed a doe and a fawn fleeing the path of a serious forest fire that raged in the region of the main Tahquamenon Falls. In approaching the blinded deer upwind, Beach watched them run in one direction and then another in utter panic and confusion. In their bewildering attempts to get away from the flames and smoke, they crashed repeatedly into trees, brush, logs, and stumps—plunging to the ground until finally being consumed by the blazing flames.

In another account of a wildfire in the Apache Forest in Arizona, one observer says, "We saw a white-tailed doe and fawn, apparently terror-stricken, run blindly into a fiercely burning tangle of downed timber. Both were consumed, as we never saw them come out."

While observing extensive white-tailed deer mortality in two wildfires in northeastern North Carolina in May 1981 and April 1985, Scott Osborne, a deer researcher with the North Carolina Wildlife Resources Commission, estimated deer mortality from ground and aerial surveys at 1.4 to 10 deer per square kilometer. Osborne and his colleagues observed that 20 percent of the deer in the burned area died outright and 20 percent of the survivors suffered severe injuries, including burned hooves and legs with secondary chronic infection and malnutrition.

Other observers of deer hemmed in by fire indicate that they escape by jumping high over the blazing flames and running through the burned area, apparently none the worse.

Aldo Leopold was perhaps one of the earliest observers of deer behavior to raise the question of whether deer allow themselves to be surrounded by forest fires; whether they consciously avoid wildfires in a cool and collective manner or stay in their home range and perish. He noted that a great deal of "unreliable romancing" exists on the subject of deer behavior in the presence of smoke and wildfires. In his experiences in New Mexico, he often saw deer feeding peacefully within a half-mile of a large fire and in an area filled with woodsmoke for weeks. In observing deer behavior during forest fires, Leopold reached the conclusion that deer do not usually flee from smoke; but they do keep out of the way of advancing flames in a leisurely manner by going around and upwind as they would do while avoiding deer hunters.

When deer become increasingly alarmed, however, they often stampede and consequently are scorched and burned alive. Leopold provides us with a classic example of this type of behavior. While fighting a forest fire in the Gila Forest, he spotted a black-tailed doe bounding down a mountainside parallel with the front of the blaze just inside the unburned area. She ran straight toward him.

"When she got within ten yards, I thoughtlessly threw up my arms. She wheeled sharp toward the fire, leaped into the flames without hesitation and disappeared. She may have survived the flames of the fire-front with nothing worse than a singeing, but there was at least a mile of hot smoking burned-over ground to cross. She could never have crossed it without scorching her hooves. If a deer scorches a hoof, it means a crack in the skin at the hoof-line, flyblowing of the crack, and slow but cruel death."

Any deer managing to survive a forest fire with burned and scorched hooves is undoubtedly worse than dead.

While some deer become increasingly alarmed and stampede and consequently are scorched and burned alive, most deer seem to evade fire in a cool and collected manner. Archibald Rutledge, a keen observer of deer behavior, once had the unique opportunity to study deer behavior in response to fires for two weeks as widesweeping fires moved through the pine country, bay thickets, and swamplands of the Carolinas, leaving ashen desolation and havoc in their wake.

One afternoon, just about sundown, Rutledge encountered a spike buck encircled by a ring of crackling flames. He documented the deer's response in his field journal.

"The buck appeared not the least disconcerted by the ring of fire surrounding him, but moved steadily forward in that eerie, effacing way peculiar to deer. He reached the fire, and with one great bound and a sudden show of his regimental flag, he crossed the menacing circle, and was lost to sight in the smoky woodland. He handled himself in its presence as if it was nothing unusual for him to be caught by a ring of flames."

Several days later, he came across a large buck serenely bedded within 100 yards of a fiery blaze. The entire area around the animal contained acrid and blinding smoke. Rutledge believed that when lying close to the ground the buck avoided the full effects of the smoke. The buck paid no attention to the fire until Rutledge literally chased him from his covert.

"Not until then did the old stag make off in long, graceful leaps, his course taking him parallel to the high sheets of flame. His lithe rocking away betrayed not the least dismay or doubt."

Lowland deer, in particular, often come to smoke for protection from gnats and other insects. The Apache Indians knew about this behavioral response and consequently set forest fires during periods of heavy fly infestations in order to decoy deer to their hunters in ambush.

While lightning sets many forest fires, it occasionally kills deer immediately. In one rather bizarre situation, lightning struck a black oak in the woodlot of the Lloyd Straus farm three miles west of Rockford, Illinois. The lightning bolt tore off a splinter of oak eight feet long and four inches thick and hurled it forty yards through the woods, where it struck a buck and killed him instantly.

In another lightning strike, District Ranger William Finley, while investigating a lightning fire in the Kaibab National Forest in Arizona, discovered a doe and two fawns at the base of a thirty-inch ponderosa pine. Unmistakable evidence of electrocution existed: Lightning had stripped bark from the tree in three streaks and scorched streaks of hair existed on each of the animals.

Sanfred Olson, a Marquette, Michigan, bow hunter, also came across three dead deer struck by lightning in a field one October day—a buck and two does. All three deer showed the scorched streaks on their bodies indicating the course of electricity.

Researchers do not consider deer to be accident-prone animals. But they are very susceptible to mishaps and accidents during periods of stress, such as severe lightning storms, being chased by dogs and predators, severe weather such as deep snow and windy and icy conditions, as well as during unusual events, such as tornadoes, hurricanes, floods, wildfires, volcanoes, and when greatly pestered by insects.

Notwithstanding their great muscular agility, many die as a result of simple accidents. Yet, accidental mortality, like disease mortality, often goes unnoticed and for the same reason: Injured deer, like sick deer, often hide in the thickest cover shortly before dying, and predators often consume them so promptly that their demise goes unnoticed.

The story of woodland tragedies teaches us two things: (1) The variety and extent of accidental deaths may take a greater toll on deer populations than scientists generally believe, and (2) deer exhibit an amazing ability to recover from injuries that would decimate any other living being. Despite the wide credence accorded these two

Causes of accidental deer deaths in Missouri.		
Cause of Death	Number of Deer	Percent of Total Deaths
Highway Accidents	1571	54.7
Illegal (Poaching)	324	11.3
Undetermined	281	9.8
Dogs	169	5.9
Miscellaneous	137	4.8
Fences	133	4.6
Disease	98	3.4
Trains	85	2.9
Not Specified	75	2.6
Total	2873	100%

—Dean A. Murphy. 1959. "Cause of Death—Accidental." *Missouri Conservationist.* 20(9):3.

ideas in traditional deer hunting lore, neither idea is yet accepted as scientific fact. The more I study the scientific literature and the diaries and journals of deer hunters, the more I am convinced that non-hunting mortality represents a very significant unknown parameter in deer population modeling and monitoring and, when inaccurately accounted for, it can seriously inhibit the setting of hunting regulations.

In studying the magnitude and timing of accidental deaths of deer in Missouri, deer biologist Dean Murphy examined 2873 dead deer. (See accompanying table.) He found the highest mortality in adult deer at 61 percent. The age composition of accidental deaths was 28 percent for yearlings and 11 percent for fawns. Murphy's data showed a nearly even sex ratio for accidental death. During the rut, however, twice as many males as females died from accidents—reflecting their extended movement patterns and aggressive behavior. Acciden-

Miscellaneous deer mortality (i.e., non-hunting mortality) for whitetails in Virginia during a one year period.

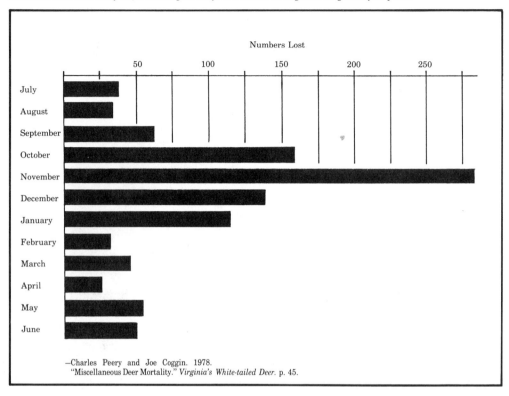

—Charles Peery and Joe Coggin. 1978.
"Miscellaneous Deer Mortality." *Virginia's White-tailed Deer.* p. 45.

tal deaths also seem to increase during periods of dispersal. Murphy's study revealed a maximum accident loss of less than 10 percent of the legal harvest.

After examining 912 deer that had died from miscellaneous causes in North Carolina and other southeastern states, wildlife researcher Frank Barick attributed 73 percent of them to cars, 12 percent to fences, 5 percent to trains, 2 percent each to falling off cliffs and tick bites, 1 percent each to drowning and disease, 3 percent to unknown causes, and a trace to cold water shock.

Many deer biologists attempt to tabulate woodland losses, although many of them remain incalculable. Researchers in Virginia, like Murphy, found a very dramatic increase in accidental deaths from September through December. (See accompanying figure.) They attribute many of these accidental deaths to hunter activity and dogs, which tend to force deer into hazardous situations. Yet, little information exists on the relationship between hunting and non-hunting mortality. Whether natural mortality increases or decreases under heavy hunting pressure remains an unanswered question.

In most areas, very few deer die of old age; the prospects of hunting and non-hunting mortality are simply too great. Those that escape hunters meet their deaths as a result of being hit by automobiles, planes, and trains. Some lose their legs to farm machinery and others perish from trying to eat bones and bearded grains of wheat. Some get caught in traps set for other animals. They die from chemical poisoning and herbicides and from such devastating diseases as epizootic hemorrhagic disease (a contagious infection) as well as from rumen overload and enterotoxemia (excess acorn ingestion). They die from starvation, predation, and malnutrition. They break their bones and hooves. They develop hoof rot, dermatitis, eye trouble, warts, rheumatism, and rickets, and they contend with tapeworms, lungworms, ticks, mites, screwworms, blowflies, bots, deer keds, mosquitoes, biting flies, sucking lice, chewing lice, and fleas.

And yet, they survive exceedingly well without any medical assistance — a remarkable phenomenon. One rugged Missouri white-tailed buck carried an entire arsenal of shooting supplies in his body — two arrow heads, several bullets, and a sprinkling of shotgun pellets — before falling dead to the forest floor after taking on a third broadhead.

We must realize, as Ernest Thompson Seton once remarked in a lecture, "that trouble is not exclusively the lot of man, but that our brethren of hoofs and horns have their full share of aches and pains, and without the human mind to point the way to comfort, or to aggravate the ills by dwelling on them."

Chapter 9

In the Wind

One of the least understood phases of deer hunting is wind, wind in all its manifestations — thermal winds, prevailing winds, storm winds.
— Francis E. Sell, *Art of Successful Deer Hunting,* 1980

A strong wind rustling the leaves of a stand of quaking aspen on an Indian Summer day produces one of the most beautiful sounds of nature. Add the subtle reality of black-capped chickadees pouring out their clearly whistled two-note phrases — fee-bee, fee-bee — the sound of insects, distant cows, a random crow, a baying hound in the distance, and the sudden snort of a white-tailed deer, and the effect gives the bow hunter in his swaying oak tree an instant, long-lived vacation.

Whether on vacation or not, the bow hunter studies wind in his deer hunting turf in an in-depth manner; he studies its velocity, its basic patterns, its predominant direction, eddies, and thermal air currents. The subject remains an eternal motif in the dialogue of American deer hunting. Some deer hunters even dream about the problem. Indeed, if the bow hunter hopes to approach white-tailed deer while stand hunting or still-hunting with any kind of consistency, he must acquire a basic knowledge of wind in all its manifestations and know how deer respond to it.

Although erratic and ethereal in character, wind is a purely physical phenomenon and as such follows definite physical laws of nature. Meteorologists generally define wind as a large-scale movement of the atmosphere generated by differences in air densities. They tell us that wind results as warmer air rises and cooler air moves in to take its place. Wind exhibits at least two basic attributes that greatly affect man and the white-tailed deer: direction and velocity. Patterns for wind directions exist but they vary with the seasons of the year. Wind velocities also vary with the seasons, reaching their maximum velocities during the winter months. They vary with the time of day as well. (See the accompanying figure.)

While analyzing the effect of wind on white-tailed deer in his *Biology and Man-*

agement of Wild Ruminants (1985), Aaron Moen, a professor of wildlife ecology at Cornell University, describes two basic patterns of wind velocity that most deer hunters and whitetails contend with on a regular basis. The first of these patterns, pattern A, exhibits little or no wind at sunrise. (See the accompanying figure.) In the morning and early afternoon, the wind increases in velocity and reaches its maximum velocity by mid to late afternoon. It then decreases its velocity in the evening hours with little or no wind shortly after sunset. This pattern reflects a stable, high pressure weather system with clear or partly cloudy skies. The second pattern, pattern B, results in a constant wind velocity throughout the day with gusts occurring at frequencies and with magnitudes characteristic of atmospheric turbulence. (See figure.) This pattern results from transient weather conditions.

The deer hunter quite often confronts one or the other of these two basic patterns, although a myriad of patterns exists, including everything from calm winds on one day to howling winds on the next day. I prefer pattern B to A for still-hunting and stand hunting, because it provides the deer hunter with a known, consistent, steady wind direction, especially at the peak hunting times during the early morning and late afternoons.

When pattern A prevails, the deer hunter often experiences a brief, calm period when the wind almost ceases just at

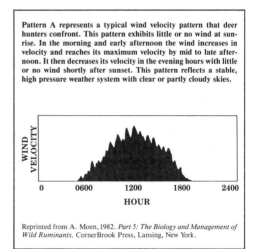

Pattern A represents a typical wind velocity pattern that deer hunters confront. This pattern exhibits little or no wind at sunrise. In the morning and early afternoon the wind increases in velocity and reaches its maximum velocity by mid to late afternoon. It then decreases its velocity in the evening hours with little or no wind shortly after sunset. This pattern reflects a stable, high pressure weather system with clear or partly cloudy skies.

Reprinted from A. Moen, 1982. *Part 5: The Biology and Management of Wild Ruminants.* CornerBrook Press, Lansing, New York.

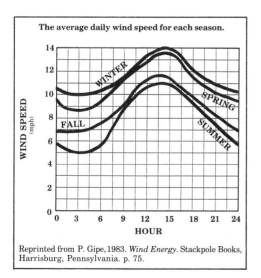

The average daily wind speed for each season.

Reprinted from P. Gipe, 1983. *Wind Energy.* Stackpole Books, Harrisburg, Pennsylvania. p. 75.

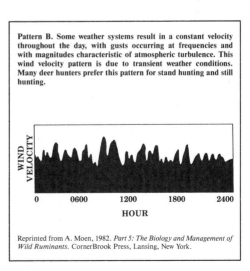

Pattern B. Some weather systems result in a constant velocity throughout the day, with gusts occurring at frequencies and with magnitudes characteristic of atmospheric turbulence. This wind velocity pattern is due to transient weather conditions. Many deer hunters prefer this pattern for stand hunting and still hunting.

Reprinted from A. Moen, 1982. *Part 5: The Biology and Management of Wild Ruminants.* CornerBrook Press, Lansing, New York.

gray dawn well before the first rays of the rising sun activate the thermal air currents and again in the late afternoon after the sun sets at dusk. Shooting remains illegal during these short gray periods of overwhelming silence in many states. During these mystical moments of calm, deer activity increases dramatically as whitetail-images gradually appear from the shadows. As master analysts of wind and thermal air currents, white-tailed deer remain doubly cautious during these intriguing periods of calm, especially at dusk.

Most deer researchers agree that the wind plays queer tricks on man as he tries to approach deer. The vagaries of wind in mountain country, for example, remain incalculable. Flying eddies of air in mountain country, comparable to the dust-devils of the desert country, often become one of the hazards of the deer stalker. Flying eddies of air as F. F. Darling describes them in his classic book, *A Herd of Red Deer* (1937), "can be heard racing through the grass a few inches up to two feet in height, causing almost a scream of sound, and if conditions are favorable their erratic course can be watched by the grass bending before them." These eddies often explain the sudden departure of deer from an area for no apparent reason to the hunter.

In his deer research, Darling found that a slight north wind in summer provides the best conditions for closely approaching deer for observational purposes. It usually means a dry atmosphere, low humidity, and clear skies. Wind, he argues, should never be considered by the hunter apart from other atmospheric conditions, the season of the year, and the particular piece of terrain being watched. Wind, according to Darling, "is the chief factor a stalker has to watch in approaching deer. Deer are always conscious of wind, and it is obvious to anybody who has watched them for any

length of time that they depend on it and utilize it as a vehicle of sensory information."

While watching whitetails during periods of various wind speeds, Edwin Michael, a Texas deer researcher, noticed that deer prefer the company of others during high winds, indicating an apparent increased dependency upon each other to detect danger. But they obviously do not rely on each other for warnings of danger. Michael found that wind speeds of fourteen m.p.h. or more coincide with a marked decrease in deer activity.

Professor Scott Hyngstrom, a deer researcher at the University of Nebraska, also reached similar conclusions after examining data from more than 33,000 hours of observations on deer by readers of *Deer & Deer Hunting* magazine: Deer activity decreased as wind velocity increased. Calm and light winds, Scott reports, produced an increase in deer sightings while moderate, gusty, and strong wind reduced deer sightings. Yet, most interestingly, Scott noticed that buck movements deviated from this overall pattern. The data revealed a decrease in buck movements during calm winds and an increase in buck movements during strong winds. Unable to explain this unusual deviation, Scott admits that while he doesn't like to explain why bucks move when they do, this inconsistency should be of some interest to the deer hunter.

I know of only one other report in the literature on deer and deer hunting that mentions this buck-movement deviation. While dealing with wind direction and speed, David Morris, an outdoor writer from Georgia, writes in the November 1980 issue of the *Georgia Sportsman,* "I have, for reasons known only to deer, seen bucks run into open fields as though frightened on very windy days. Maybe the noise from the wind spooked them and they sought relief in open country." Maybe? Morris's data on deer hunting success and wind direction at the Burnt Pine Plantation in Georgia's Old South Plantation Country indicates a clear relationship between winds from the northwest and a higher hunter success average. In my own deer hunting territory, I prefer a light, steady, northwest wind to winds from any other direction. This wind direction usually brings cool, clear days, low humidity, starry nights, crisp leaves, frost on my deer stand, and an increase in deer sightings.

While studying wind direction and white-tailed deer movements on the George Reserve, a two-square-mile fenced area in southeastern Michigan, deer researcher Steve Newhouse observed that the mean wind direction for the day represented the most significant relationship to the percentage of adult bucks sighted. Newhouse discovered that the percent of adult bucks observed during east winds over a one-year period of time was significantly higher than those observed during any other of the seven wind directions by at least 35 percent.

The most interesting phenomenon of Newhouse's study occurred on every occasion when a northeast wind prevailed: All of the deer groups he observed contained no adult bucks. According to Newhouse, "I cannot explain this finding in any biological, evolutionary, or behavioral context." A possible explanation might involve the fact that northeasterly winds often bring quickly changing weather conditions and sharply reversing trends in barometric pressure. Perhaps mature bucks sense the weather changes more quickly than young, antlerless deer and hold tight.

In any event, Newhouse also reported that the interaction of wind velocity and microclimate wind noise had a major effect on the excitability of deer. He noted that as the wind velocity increased from four m.p.h. to eight m.p.h., excitability increased most dramatically—the greater the wind noise, the greater the excitability-value.

When trying to photograph whitetails during high winds, wildlife photographer Lennie Rue says, "high winds make deer extremely nervous, because the clashing of the wind-lashed trees and branches covers almost all sounds and the eddying and reversal of air currents makes scenting impossible. With the whole world in motion, deer almost panic." During such conditions deer lose their ability to locate either the scent or the source of the scent as well as their ability to either hear or pinpoint the location of any foreign noise. The movement of leaves, branches, and grass becomes confused with predator noise and motion. I have only shot one white-tailed deer with my bow under such blustery conditions and that through a stroke of graceless luck. The casual observer who encounters a white-tailed deer on a calm, windless day may conclude that they are tame, while the same person encountering deer on a very windy day may conclude that an army of redcoats is harrassing them to death to cause them to act so wildly.

While studying wind speeds and mule deer movements in New Mexico with radio telemetry, Wain Evans, a deer researcher with the New Mexico Department of Game and Fish, found that movement activity levels associated with wind speeds fluctuated between three periods of time: (1) sunrise and sunset, (2) daytime, and (3) nighttime. The highest deer activity occurred at wind speeds of six to fifteen m.p.h. and the lowest activity at wind speeds above thirty m.p.h. (See figure.)

In examining wind velocity and deer movements, Charles Loveless, a Colorado deer biologist, detected a noticeable relationship between deer activity and high

The effect of wind speed on mule deer activity based on radio telemetry.

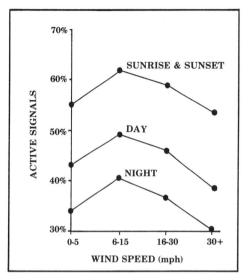

Reprinted from W. Evans, 1976. "Deer on the Move." *New Mexico Wildlife* 21(1):23.

wind velocities of twenty-five m.p.h. or more. Under these conditions deer generally avoided open slopes and other exposed areas and sought shelter on the lee side of rock outcrops, in stands of conifers, or in drainage channels. In measuring seasonal wind characteristics, Loveless recorded higher wind velocities in the late fall, winter, and early spring than during the summertime.

Other deer biologists believe that winds exceeding twenty-five m.p.h., usually referred to as a gale with whole trees in motion, induce deer bedding in thick cover. Most researchers agree that high, gusty gales, particularly in winter, cause deer to seek shelter on the lee slopes of hills and in dense, coniferous woodlands since conifer stands reduce wind velocity by as much as 50 to 75 percent. While deer seek shelter from high winds in winter, on hot summer days they take advantage of such condi-

tions by resting on ridges in high winds to cool themselves and escape annoying insects.

Deer learn to utilize wind direction and velocity for their advantage and so must the deer hunter, if he is to succeed. He must constantly test the wind while in the field. Tossing leaves into the air will sometimes indicate the direction of the wind, depending upon the velocity. A long thread tied to the upper limb of your bow may help in this regard. Even the gentlest draft can be detected with a child's bubble kit. Some deer hunters watch pipe smoke while others wet their fingers. One deer hunter I know carries a little Bull Durham tobacco sack full of powdered chalk. When in doubt, he shakes the sack to watch which way the chalk dust drifts. Others use cattail fuzz.

Regardless of the methods, judging wind speeds in the field remains very difficult. Consequently, portable weather-band radios, windmills, and low-cost anemometers are becoming standard equipment at some deer shacks. Professional meteorologists, however, give us some hints about land signs to watch when trying to determine wind speeds. Calm winds of less than one m.p.h. cause smoke to rise vertically but fail to stir leaves on trees. Some meteorologists suggest that quiet winds in the morning often mean quieter winds in the evening. Light winds of one to three m.p.h. cause smoke to drift but solicit no response from wind vanes.

A gentle breeze of seven to ten m.p.h. will extend flags and keep leaves in constant motion. A moderate breeze of eleven to sixteen m.p.h. moves small branches and raises dust and loose paper. A breeze of seventeen to twenty-one m.p.h. causes noticeable motion in the tops of tall trees and sways small trees in leaf. A strong breeze of twenty-two to twenty-seven m.p.h. puts large branches in motion and creates whistling noise along wires. Gale winds of twenty-eight to forty-seven m.p.h. or more will take the tar paper off your deer shack, place whole trees in motion, and create an inconvenience for your hunting partner when he attempts to nail the tar paper back on. Deer kill statistics indicate that bow hunters kill few deer during tree-bending gales. During such conditions, deer lay low and hold tight and so should we. How can we accurately shoot an arrow in strong winds while perched in a swaying oak tree?

Obviously, while hunting we must move as much as possible in an upwind direction, although a crosswind is acceptable if strong and steady. The stronger the wind, the more liberty we can take when still-hunting. Light winds often remain variable and frequently and unexpectedly spoil a good still-hunt. Still-hunting with light winds remains tricky because numerous variations in the height and density of adjoining tree plantations at different stages of growth tend to cause changes in wind direction. We only learn to anticipate these pitfalls as our knowledge of our deer hunting terrain grows—a knowledge that requires a life-long learning process. Experienced hunters keep track of wind directions, velocities, and prevailing winds at all times of the year.

When forced to, whitetails will move downwind. With the wind tailing them, however, they seem to prefer open terrain so that they can see well into the distance. *Leonard Lee Rue III photo*

If you're trying to stalk this old boy with your bow, forget it! He has already detected your presence. Deer hunters seldom find mature bucks in an unfavorable wind position. *Leonard Lee Rue III photo*

Remember that wind direction forecasts can be wrong, whether they are your own, based on your own primitive equipment, or that of the local weather station forecaster, a telephone pre-recorded forecast, a TV forecast, a radio forecast, or a newspaper forecast. When the wind conspires against you, be prepared to change your hunting strategy.

We know that most deer selectively move directly into the wind. As one hunter from Lake Placid, New York, wrote, "If a strong west wind is blowing, you can bet your best rifle that deer will approach their feeding area from the east side. And when a south wind whispers, they will come in from the north." Don't worry about the exceptions. After analyzing more than 10,000 deer sightings with the computer, Scott Hyngstrom reached the following conclusion, "Deer move directly into the wind for all eight primary compass directions proportionately more than moving directly with, perpendicular to, quartering with or quartering into the wind."

Yet, in areas of high hunting pressure, deer hunters frequently force whitetails to run downwind for short distances. Antlerless deer in non-hunted areas or in prairie country will also move downwind from time to time. But, in general, the deer hunter seldom sees trophy bucks in an unfavorable wind position even during the rut. Whenever the wind is not in a white-tailed buck's favor, he will travel downwind, if necessary, but when forced to do so, they seem to prefer open fields, so they can see well into the distance when the wind tails them. Gun hunters often get mature bucks who cross fields in this way under heavy hunting pressure on the opening weekend of the season; but don't plan your next hunt around this idea.

The most important element of wind to watch while still-hunting or stand hunting whitetails revolves around thermal air currents — that is, wind currents set in motion by temperature changes. These thermal wind currents occur in all latitudes where ridges and valleys exist and they greatly affect deer movements and hunting strategies under stable weather conditions. These thermal air currents move upslope after the sun comes up and begins to warm the air. Late in the afternoon, as the air cools, these air currents move downhill. These upward and downward air currents across deer country remain so slight and gentle that the hunter is seldom conscious of them, but these air currents exist under stable conditions and they carry human scent with them.

The perceptive hunter will still-hunt into these thermals by hunting downward in the early morning even in the absence of a readily detectable breeze and then reverse the procedure in the late afternoon by still-hunting upslope. If you want to watch deer trails along a ridge or a valley, place your stand upslope and look down in the morning; place your stand downslope and look up in the afternoon. Remember that on cloudy overcast mornings, the thermal reversal occurs later in the morning than on clear sunny days.

The Iroquois Indians always took advantage of these thermal air currents by

bow hunting at higher altitudes in the morning and lower ones in the evening. We find the best advice with regard to taking advantage of these thermal air currents in Allan Macfarland's *Modern Hunting with Indian Secrets* (1971). "If you are hunting in the early morning, it's often best to walk quietly along ridges or take a stand on a high point. Your scent will be lifted high above you by the thermal current. In the evening, keep to the low areas between hills and ridges, but look upward toward the slopes and crests for bucks. The downward-moving air on a still day prevents your scent from rising. In some areas, though, the ground itself shapes and focuses these air currents. You can't always depend on these air currents, but high hunting in the morning and keeping low in the late afternoon usually is best if there is no wind."

Quickly changing weather conditions affect thermal air currents: Clearing weather after a storm sends them upslope and a storm in progress or approaching sends them to the lower ground. Often these thermal winds exist in such a mild manner that they remain scarcely perceptable, but under stable and calm weather conditions they exist, working for you or against you. Strong prevailing winds, however, cancel out these thermal air currents and force deer to change their bedding sites as well, allowing them to travel nose-to-wind to reach their feeding areas. Deer beds directly relate to wind direction. Bucks, in particular, often bed on the lee side of slopes and ridges with the prevailing wind on their back while watching their backtrack.

Whitetails bed on slightly higher ground when the terrain permits. Consequently, when they move downslope toward their feeding area in the afternoon, they experience good wind coverage on their trails with the thermal air currents still moving upslope. (See figure.) When returning to their bedding area in the morning, they again experience good wind coverage with the downwind thermals holding from the high to the lower ground. (See figure.) During heavy hunting pressure, white-tailed deer often circle their feeding area to obtain the wind drift in their favor before venturing into open terrain. In flat country, these thermal air currents move outward from the forests toward the open country, swamps, lakes, or ponds in the late afternoon and hold in that direction until early morning under stable weather conditions. In the late morning, these air

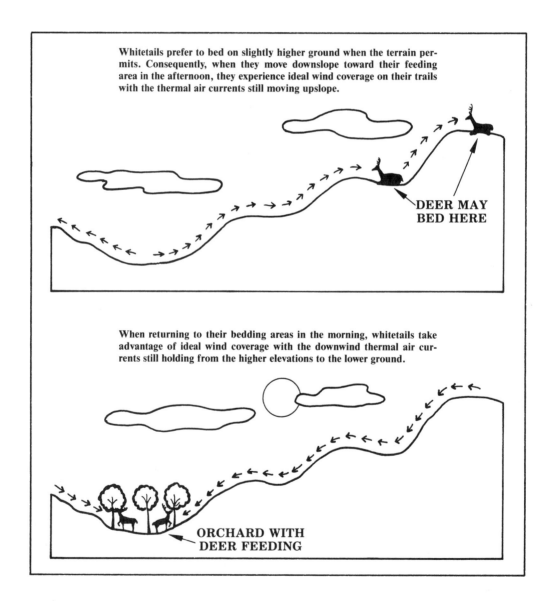

Whitetails prefer to bed on slightly higher ground when the terrain permits. Consequently, when they move downslope toward their feeding area in the afternoon, they experience ideal wind coverage on their trails with the thermal air currents still moving upslope.

DEER MAY BED HERE

When returning to their bedding areas in the morning, whitetails take advantage of ideal wind coverage with the downwind thermal air currents still holding from the higher elevations to the lower ground.

ORCHARD WITH DEER FEEDING

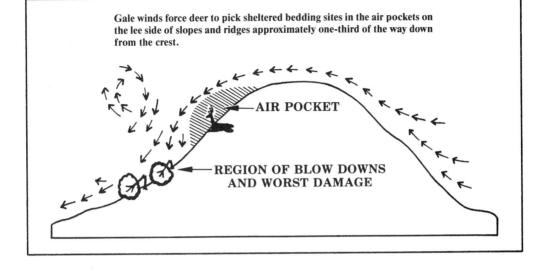

Gale winds force deer to pick sheltered bedding sites in the air pockets on the lee side of slopes and ridges approximately one-third of the way down from the crest.

currents in flat country reverse themselves and move back in toward the forest from the open terrain. "Hunting deer without taking these thermal wind drifts into consideration," Francis Sell, a famous Oregon backwoodsman, once remarked, "is a very profitless undertaking."

If you examine deer trails in your hunting area over time, you will notice that the deer trails closely match the prevailing wind direction and traditional wind changes, prevailing winds and traditional wind shifts directly shape deer trails. You may observe, for example, a deer trail being heavily used for weeks in duration with a southwest wind. Under stable weather conditions, the morning and evening thermal air currents regulate the traffic. But when a north wind suddenly begins to blow, the deer react by abandoning the trail and immediately selecting another trail that affords them better wind coverage under the changed weather conditions. Changing winds send bucks in a roundabout fashion as they move into the air currents, as these air currents follow

the contours of the land. Deer trails often appear to be purposeless wanderings, but once understood, you'll see their relationship to wind directions and thermal air movements.

Gale winds force deer to pick sheltered bedding sites in the air pockets on the lee side of slopes and ridges approximately one-third of the way down from the crest. (See the accompanying figure.) Deer hold tight in these quiet air pockets until gale windstorms pass. When gale winds strike a ridge, air currents deflect up and over the ridge. After creating an air pocket, these air currents turn downward and often double in velocity, striking the forest on the lee side of the ridge several hundred yards from the point of original deflection. The region of greatest damage occurs just ahead of the sheltered area where deer frequently bed.

There's something deeply exciting about a windstorm howling through the deer forest. During a windstorm the pines, in particular, become exceedingly visible to deer and man alike. Bedded beneath them, whitetails interpret their singing, wind-music and fragrant odors and have done so for centuries. Bedded in the pines during an intensive windstorm, listening to the passionate wild tones of the wind, white-tailed deer exist in all their grandeur. In their beds they listen to the varying wind-tones of the individual pines and the rustle of the needles near their hooves. The singing of the pines as they bend and swirl back and forth creates a glorious effect known only to the whitetail as they feel the quick, tense vibration of pine needles raining off their backs. There is nothing somber about a windstorm in the pines in the heart of deer country.

More than likely, whitetails see wind as visible as flowing water. Man can too, if he exercises his imagination. "When we look around over an agitated forest," John Muir, the wild man of the mountains, writes in his essay "A Wind-Storm in the Forest," "we may see something of the wind that stirs it, by its effects upon the trees. Yonder it descends in a rush of water-like ripples, and sweeps over the bending pines from hill to hill. Nearer, we see detached plumes and leaves, now speeding by on level currents, now whirling in eddies, or escaping over the edges of the whirls, soaring aloft on grand, upswelling domes of air, or tossing on flame-like crests. Smooth, deep currents, cascades, falls, and swirling eddies, sing around every tree and leaf, and over all the varied topography of the region with telling changes of form, like mountain rivers conforming to the features of their channels."

The other night, while listening to a windstorm howl through the uplands, an editor sat beneath the roof of his study next to his wood stove, unlike John Muir, who would have rushed into the forest to mount the nearest white pine to ride the storm out with all its whistling and bend-

ing vibrations. The wind whistled down the chimney and fired the split oak. As wind waves hissed through the oaks, they rattled the windows, sent woodsmoke back into the study, and struck battering blows against the woodshed. The fire became wind-blown by the gusts; dead oak limbs fell to the forest floor.

The editor sat in his favorite recliner reading a research paper, "Turbulence and the Visualization of Wind Flow," by a learned deer doctor who described the effect of wind on the temperature of bedded deer. When encountering the equation $U_z = (U_*/k) \ln (z/z_0)$ where U_z = wind velocity at height z, u_* = friction velocity, k = von Karman constant = 0.4, z = height in centimeters, and z_0 = roughness parameter of surface, the height at which velocity tends toward zero, the editor's head bobbed immediately as he dozed off into the corridors of our deer hunting heritage to escape biological complexity.

While dozing, he thought he heard voices in the grog room. Yes, he most certainly did. He went to investigate. When he opened the grog room doors, he found that a group of deer hunters, some of the giants in the field, had assembled after a deer shoot in the uplands. He entered the grog room and sat down unnoticed. A still-hunter from southern California named Van Dyke was holding forth on the virtues of still-hunting during heavy winds. With his vast cargo of deer hunting knowledge afloat in the hold and with the undivided attention of those present, he described how his partner, Dr. Belville, a young physician from San Francisco, gunned down a magnificent buck in a windstorm late that afternoon.

"Bang! goes the rifle," Van Dyke declared, "as the buck sweeps through the shrubbery, and the ball, whizzing through the place he has just left, hisses harmlessly

away over the great canyon far below. *Bang!* goes another shot aimed to catch him as he rises; but he never rises twice alike, and as he clears a bush with slanting spring the ball splashes itself to pieces against a rock by his side.

"Vainly Belville tries to hold the rifle on the point where the buck will touch ground; for now he springs fifteen feet ahead, slinking out of sight among the bushes and rocks; now ten feet ahead and five to one side; now five feet ahead and five to the other side; now going down behind some rocks, from the top of which the ball sings over the depths beyond; now flashing full on high with his whole shining body in the bright sun, clear above the brush and rocks, falling as the ball spins over him, and glancing up again from the hard ground as he strikes — all the time fast nearing the top of the ridge.

"Over he goes in a high curve, clear-cut in outline against the western sky, a beautiful mark if it only stayed long enough. The rifle cracks as the figure clears the climax of its bound, a plain *whack!* is borne back on the heavy breeze, and a foreleg dangles useless on the buck.

"Thanks to the light moccasins, which never slip, Belville skipped along the tops of the boulders and reached the farther edge in about a minute. A wild mass of steep confusion, chaotic with rocks and scraggy brush, lay before him, and the buck — stopped? Yes, as the rocket when it is once fairly started stops when the stick breaks. Fast as before, but more erratic in his twist, he went down the rocky slope, smashing through brush like a circus rider through papered hoops, bounding as high as if he had gained another leg, instead of losing one.

"*Bang! whang! bang! whang!* went the swift repeater with desperate energy. The bullets sank glancing from the rocks into the bluish-green abyss below, or spattered into leaden spray against their granite sides.

"*Bang! bang! bang!* in quick succession sounds the rifle; and at last a faint *spat* is heard; the bound changes to a lumbering canter; the buck no longer clears the brush, but smashes headlong through it with his momentum; he still steers clear of the rocks and bushes, crashing onward for several yards, when suddenly he lunges, staggers, rolls heavily through a bush, which is crushed beneath his weight, and the dust rises into the breeze from his scuffling feet as he turns a somersault on the dry ground among the rocks."

Before Van Dyke ever finished his wild, windy discourse, the editor wondered to himself why no deer hunter ever sent him such high-blown verbiage as that for publication. Several other hunting editors were also present and secretly asked themselves the same question.

A solo deer hunter from northern Wisconsin named George Mattis sat at the card table. While listening intently to Van Dyke's oration, the blue-eyed, short and stocky deerslayer with the ruddy cheeks and white hair stared at the buck in Ned Smith's picture titled "Through the Pines," that hangs in the grog room, as if he desired to raise his cherished 30/30 and make the one clear perfect shot that Dr. Belville's smoking repeater failed to accomplish. In thinking about whitetails and high winds, Mattis calmly said in his quiet and unassuming manner, "Strangely enough, the whitetail often leaves his bed to forage or lounge about in the dense thickets during the days of extremely high winds. Some men prefer such days to all others for deer stalking. The woods are noisy with falling branches and both deer and hunter are somewhat handicapped in the game of hide and seek."

Jack O'Connor, the highly opinionated and outspoken gun editor, took off his wire-rimmed glasses and asked Belville to promptly bring forth the rifle for his examination. Not a surprising request coming from a man who missed few shots and once shot two running coyotes in a row—one at 220 paces and another at about 300. Belville's shooting gave O'Connor the vapors. Peering out from under his old beat-up cowboy hat, the spell-binding raconteur looked at Mattis and said, "The worst type of wind for either still-hunter or stalker is the unsteady, shifting, eddying wind. Shifting, unsteady winds are bad and so are hard, gusty winds that rattle the branches and blow everything around. I do not like to still-hunt on such days. The deer are jittery. They tend either to move out wildly or refuse to move at all. If you have plenty of time, such days are good ones to spend in camp."

Another gun editor present named Wootters disagreed and argued that strong winds make still-hunting productive by covering man's sounds, "I know hunters who are so convinced that wind puts deer down and keeps them inactive that they'll hardly go out in windy weather. I think this depends upon the prevailing weather in the individual region under discussion. In some areas wind is a routine condition, and still days are the exception. In such country, the deer are accustomed to wind, whether they *like* it or not, and seem to keep pretty much on schedule regardless of wind. The kind of wind whitetails *don't* like is the wind from an unusual direction (for that season), the gusty, variable treacherous breezes which signal unsettled weather."

The debate continued with several hunters emphasizing the complex nature of wind, how wind swirls around the ends of ridges, draws up the valleys, and generally changes its course as guided by the basic contours of the terrain. One hunter from Colorado noted that wind in the West is particularly tricky. "The abrupt slopes, sun-heated pockets, and irregular stands of timber combine to play tricks with wind currents. The wind is very likely to be puffy, uncertain, blowing in one direction one moment, in the opposite direction the next."

Another deer hunter from the Adirondacks agreed. "Have you ever tried to get out of the wind on a blustery day? It seems as though you can't escape it. Winds on such days are likely to blow back in great eddies. A northwest gale will often blow from the southeast on the very next ridge, or southwest up one draw and northeast down the next. Then in the next breath it may stop altogether, for a moment."

"I know for a fact," said a ridge-running buck hunter from Vermont dressed in green-checkered wool and looking like he just stepped out of the evergreens, "that in the mountains the wind will blow four ways at once. I also know that if you get on the track of a trophy buck, you are going to follow that track and not stop because the wind is blowing the wrong way."

An Indian descendant named "Spud" Sell listened intently as he cleaned his favorite 257-caliber wildcat rifle, which he had developed for deer shooting in heavy cover. A Coquille Indian named Tom Two Ridges had taught Sell to read the wind and to listen to the voice of the wind.

"A north wind," Sell remarked, "may be channeled in a score of different directions, even though the set of the air currents is from the North. It may come spiraling around a ridge, moving east for some distance, south if the contour of the hills is favorable, west—just about any direction except north. This changes deer-trailing habits. The successful deer hunter must feel the pulse of the wind at all times. But this is an oversimplification of a rather complicated problem. Actually, you must tie *all* hunting to *deer habit,* which is greatly controlled by the wind."

Van Dyke, as usual, added the final salute to the subject by saying with his characteristic wit and humor, "Few things are so fatal to ultimate success as an early germination of the idea that you are a pretty smart chap on deer and wind. With whatever proficiency in still-hunting any mortal ever reaches with all the advantages of wind in his favor, many a deer will in the very climax of triumphant assurance slip through your fingers like the thread of a beautiful dream!"

With that final amen the editor suddenly awoke, left his recliner, and went to bed thoroughly saturated with wisdom about wind as a basic element of woodcraft and white-tailed deer hunting. The dialogue, however, continued in the grog room until the early hours of the morning as their voices finally faded into the memories of the past. . . .

Chapter 10

Whitetails and the Forest Opening

Many hunters choose stands in or near forest openings simply to gain a better view for sighting deer. Forest openings unquestionably serve as landmarks for hunters; they also help define areas for making deer drives. All things considered, openings help make the deer woods more "huntable."
— Keith McCaffery and William Creed,
*Significance of Forest Openings to
Deer in Northern Wisconsin,* 1969

The first buck I ever shot, I shot as the animal attempted to cross a one-acre forest opening. With the normal sense of "trigger itch" and with an extended sense of shaking excitement, I burned more gunpowder than was necessary. But when the 8-pointer finally fell to the forest floor, he nearly collapsed on my feet. The memory of that buck crossing the forest opening and ultimately collapsing in a heap in front of my shaking legs will burn on in my mind forever. While studying forestry and conservation as an undergraduate in the mid-1960s, I began to study and hunt forest openings. I often returned to that same forest opening in hopes of repeating the incident, but soon learned that, when

deer hunting alone, stand hunting the deer trails leading to the forest openings usually produces better results. Nonetheless, I still set up stands on the edges of forest openings for the purposes of preseason scouting and studying deer behavior.

Deer biologists generally define a forest opening as an area dominated by herbaceous vegetation (non-woody plants, grasses, legumes, and forbs) an area generally devoid of tree canopy cover. They have long considered these forest openings an important tool in the management and hunting of the white-tailed deer. Originally called "agricultural clearings," as time progressed deer biologists used them to provide supplemental food for deer and consequently renamed them "food plots." During the 1960s, the food plots became known as forest openings to reflect a broader ecological framework. We now think of them in terms of their herbage value, plant diversity, edge and cover effect. Their main attraction for whitetails revolves around food—food in the form of herbaceous vegetation. Their main attraction for deer hunters consists in their providing man with contact with the animal. By 1965, more than 30,000 acres of forest openings existed in twenty-two states. Today, hundreds of thousands of them dot the terrain of deer country.

Forest openings greatly benefit man and the white-tailed deer in at least three significant ways. First of all, the "edge effect" and the subsequent network of trails that openings create enhance deer/hunter contacts and increase hunter satisfaction and deer kill statistics. Second, the low-lying herbaceous vegetation of these openings probably increases deer productivity in spring and survival rates in winter, although a dearth of scientific documentation exists in this regard. Third, and perhaps most important, forest openings increase the esthetic values of the landscape for everyone—hunters and nonhunters alike.

Most hunters realize that the white-tailed deer is an animal of the edge. It resides where its preferred food and thick cover come together: where the edges meet. That's why the deer hunter, as Aldo Leopold writes in *Game Management* (1933), "follows the *edge* between the oaks of the south slope and the pine thicket of the north slope." While we are only beginning to understand the whitetail's preference for edges and openings, "it usually harks back," Leopold insists, "either to the desirability of *simultaneous access* to more than one environmental type or to

the *greater richness* of border vegetation, or both."

Deer hunters often report that whitetails, especially antlerless deer, frequently remain very reluctant to leave the edges of openings even after being shot at repeatedly. Indeed, why would the animal want to leave the edges that provide them with the heaviest desirable cover and the greatest amount of available food? The reality of this "edge effect" becomes obvious to anyone who spends much time in deer country. As you tramp through extensive uniform forests, they seem lifeless; when you suddenly emerge at a forest opening, you become amazed at the rich variety and abundance of all wildlife. In other words, deer density seems directly proportional to the amount of edge.

Hunter density, on the other hand, seems to be inversely proportional to the distance to the nearest paved road, unfortunate though it may be. After studying the location of hunting pressure in the central Adirondacks, New York deer biologist Bill Severinghaus reported that although some deer hunters kill bucks more than seven miles from the nearest road, most hunters kill deer relatively close to roads and deer hunting camps.

In a similar study dealing with the relations between deer-kill statistics and hunter access in North Carolina, wildlife researchers note that hunters kill very few deer more than 2400 feet from the nearest road and in many areas the optimum balance between deer populations and forage is not maintained because of an inadequate distribution of the annual kill. The mean distance from kill to the nearest road approximated only 750 feet. North Carolina researchers found that well-constructed trails and openings serve well to distribute successful hunting pressure and disperse hunters away from roads.

"I'm convinced that openings, while maybe not absolutely essential from a behavioral standpoint, serve deer a very special purpose in autumn. When interspersed throughout forested habitat, openings permit deer to gather, socialize, and visually communicate. Open areas void of predators serve as arenas where bucks can display, spar with one another, engage in serious fights to decide dominance, if necessary, and communicate their social status to prospective mates and competitors. Does and fawns, the wide-eyed spectators naturally drawn to such spectacular pre-rut exhibitions of male showmanship, seem to function as sentinels to warn the preoccupied males of approaching danger." — J. J. Ozoga. *Mike Biggs photo*

Without extensive trails and openings, deer hunters seem reluctant to penetrate the deer woods. Milt Stenlund, a wildlife biologist in northern Minnesota, tells us that hunters killed 90 percent of all deer harvested in one management unit of the Superior National Forest, less than three-quarters of a mile from access roads. Few hunters ever ventured more than a half-mile from the nearest point of access. Researchers in Virginia also conclude that deer hunters seldom carry their deer more than a half-mile to a vehicle. One researcher found that deer hunters in the Gila National Forest in New Mexico seldom go beyond a mile from the nearest road and hardly ever penetrate wilderness areas with slopes greater than 15 percent.

Joseph Larson, a wildlife scientist at the University of Massachusetts, believes that forest openings greatly affect hunter distribution. In emphasizing the positive aspects of openings for deer hunters, Larson states that "openings and clear vistas in an otherwise closed forest present good opportunities to observe deer from concealed vantage points. Where otherwise lacking, clearings and their attendant access roads provide avenues of hunter use. Bow hunting may be nearly excluded where clear openings frequented by deer are absent."

It's not surprising that bow hunters, in particular, rely heavily on openings and trails and that many bow hunters who own land create planted openings in an attempt to increase antler development and concentrate and hold deer to enhance deer hunting success and to minimize the excessive movement of "their" deer to other areas. Some hunters even try to encourage immigration, although the maximum radius of an opening's influence remains quite small in this regard.

As a result of deer hunting leases, landowners want more deer, bigger deer, and easier hunter access. Consequently, we see an increase in the acreage of planted openings on private lands nationwide as well as in our national forests.

After creating forest openings and constructing and maintaining clover-seeded trails to these openings in the Nicolet National Forest in northeastern Wisconsin, wildlife biologists not only succeeded in discouraging road hunting but received a very favorable public response and favorable deer hunting results as well. "Archer success," according to researcher Ed Wilder, "was reported especially good in and adjacent to the clover-seeded openings." A hearty influx of bow hunters and gun hunters used the trails and openings and field checks by forest service personnel indicated that the area served more deer hunters with better harvest per square mile than did forest lands in adjacent areas.

Seven major criteria governed the selection of openings to be retained along trail developments in this particular experiment: "(1) a size from one-half to ten acres; (2) location at the juncture of two or more timber or soil types; (3) presence of areas of varied low herbaceous vegetation, areas of dense grasses, areas with a variety of brush and clumps of cover trees; (4) indicators of frequent white-tailed deer use; (5) location on or near an existing or planned woods trail; (6) locations adjoining swamp conifers, low-land brush, upland conifers or hemlock cover, and (7) irregular shape with numerous pockets extending into the timber."

In the selection of forest openings, wildlife managers encourage landowners to take advantage of existing conditions and current timber-cutting practices. They emphasize using abandoned homesites because they often contain high quality deer food species such as honeysuckle, grapes, plums, blackberries, and oaks. They also recommend planting utility right-of-ways, firebreaks, and roadsides with herbaceous vegetation as part of the opening system.

While studying the influence of forest land characteristics on the spatial distribution of deer hunters, Jack Ward Thomas and his colleagues of the USDA Forest Service found that well-developed forest trails associated with clearings and openings influenced hunters more than trails without clearings. According to Thomas, "hunter distribution and satisfaction could be influenced more, at a given cost, by changing the trail layout than by any other kind of land management practice."

While game managers use forest openings to better distribute hunting pressure, whitetails use them primarily as a source of herbaceous vegetation. In studying the use and acceptability of herbages by white-

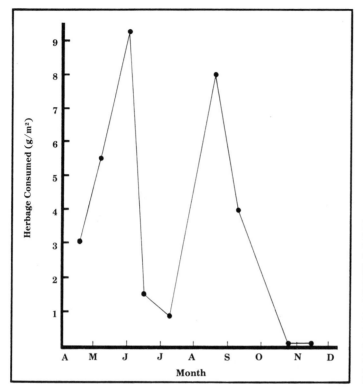

Herbage consumed by white-tailed deer in forest openings in Pennsylvania. This figure illustrates that whitetails consume their greatest amounts of cool-season grasses and legumes in spring and fall when these herbaceous species also provide their highest nutritive value.

Reprinted from Daniel A. Devlin and Walter M. Tzilkowski. 1987. "Use and Acceptability of Herbages by White-tailed Deer in Relation to Forest Openings." *Proceedings: Deer, Forestry, and Agriculture.* p. 93.

tails in forest openings in Pennsylvania, deer researchers found a direct relationship between herbage use by deer and herbage growth patterns. Dan Devlin, a wildlife biologist with the Pennsylvania Bureau of Forestry, observes that the highest use of such cool-season grasses and legume mixtures as orchard grass-ladino clover and Kentucky bluegrass-white clover correspond with peaks in the grasses' growth potential in the spring and fall. The chart illustrates the pattern of herbages of forest openings by white-tailed deer in Pennsylvania. The two peaks in herbage consumption in spring and fall match those of the growth potential of the herbage involved.

Since two of the most critical physiological periods for whitetails occur in spring and fall, deer biologists encourage land-owners to provide desirable herbage in openings for deer during these two periods of time. High-quality spring nutrition helps deer recover from the stress of winter and measurably improves fawning success; high-quality fall herbage helps them to accumulate body fat to prepare for winter.

Devlin recommends the following procedures and strategies for landowners wishing to improve their deer habitat. "New forest openings, such as log landings, haul roads, and gas well sites should be seeded to cool-season grass and legume mixtures as opposed to being permitted to revegetate naturally. Natural revegetation favors the establishment of warm-season herbage.

"Established forest openings should be maintained as grass and legume mixtures. Soil amendments, as per soil test results, should be added to maintain desirable herbage. To stimulate regrowth in fall and increase nutritive value, established openings could be cut in summer."

The criteria that deer use to find plants, grasses, and forbs acceptable, be it nutrition, taste, succulence, smell, or whatever, still remain unknown. We do know, however, that herbaceous material, which researchers associate with high nutritive value, is more acceptable to deer during its rapid growth stage.

Because the food habits of deer vary considerably depending upon season, location, habitat, sex, age, and population size, the literature remains scant with regard to the whitetail's general preference for herbaceous material. Despite the variability, whitetails use herbaceous foods as an important year-round food item in their diet. The accompanying table summarizes the species of herbage in descending order of preference by whitetails as indicated by the average percentage eaten of the amount available in Albany County, New York.

While studying the herbaceous food preferences of whitetails in New York, John Tanck of the New York Department of Environmental Conservation observed a fawn one day feeding on Canada bluegrass, aster, hawkweed, and strawberry. The next day he watched the fawn eat oldfield cinquefoil, fleabane, red clover, and goldenrod. Several days later, he viewed the fawn eating knotweed, tall yellow wood sorrel, catnip, buckhorn plantain, and butter-and-eggs. Yes, it seems that deer will eat all types of herbaceous materials known to man.

In studying whitetail preferences for herbaceous materials in the forest openings of Pennsylvania, wildlife researchers at Pennsylvania State University consider red fescue, tall fescue, orchard grass, Kentucky bluegrass, meadow foxtail, and deertongue as the best species to plant. In their opinion, birdsfoot trefoil, crownvetch, and flatpea represent the best legumes to plant in mixture with these grasses.

The preference of white-tailed deer for herbaceous plants in descending order.

Species

Joe-pye weed	Buttercup	Common St.	Liveforever
Early goldenrod	Fleabane	John's-wort	Wood sorrel
Spotted jewelweed	Agrimony	Oldfield cinquefoil	Yarrow
Woodland goldenrod	Selfheal	Pussytoes	White snakeroot
White wood aster	Aster	Vetch	Ragweed
Giant goldenrod	Red clover	Speedwell	Indian Jack-in-
Elecampane	Sheep sorrel	Common plaintain	the-pulpit
Sensitive fern	Hop clover	Fowl mannagrass	Thistle
Virgin's bower	Bluegrass	Sedge	Small purple fringed
Bracken fern	Butter-and-eggs	Avens	orchid
Whorled loosestrife	Grassleaf goldenrod	Virginia bugleweed	Rush
Goldenrod	Wild geranium	Bulrush	Indian tobacco
Water averns	Canada bluegrass	White wood sorrel	Bugleweed
Timothy	Clover	Bedstraw	Blackseed plantain
Oxeye daisy	Wild oat grass	St. John's-wort	Purple milkwort
Wrinkled goldenrod	Sweet vernalgrass	Panic grass	Arrow leaved
Redtop grass	Strawberry	Pearly everlasting	tearthumb
Hawkweed	Common wintercress	Field horsetail	Dock
Buckhorn plantain	Wild carrot	Blueflag iris	Silver goldenrod

Reprinted from Peggy R. Sauer, John E. Tanck and C.W. Severinghaus. 1969. "Herbaceous Food Preferences of White-tailed Deer." *New York Fish and Game Journal* 16(2): 150-151.

Since crownvetch and flatpea tend to dominate the sites very dramatically, they recommend sowing them sparingly in bull-dozed hummocks or in rocky and erosion-prone sites.

In their research they found that the greatest growth of the deer fetus takes place in the last third of pregnancy, which coincides with the period of utilization of these cool-season grasses and legumes, a period when these forages are at their highest crude protein levels. They suggest that landowners should select herbaceous forage for deer on two equal criteria: (1) the ability to provide growth during cool seasons, especially spring, and (2) toler-ance to less favorable soil conditions.

In evaluating white-tailed deer use of forest openings in the Arkansas Ozarks, Charles Segelquist, a deer researcher from Oklahoma State University, found that white-tailed deer consumption of cool-season grasses and legumes in the fall re-lates directly to the availability of acorns. Deer consume the greatest amount of her-baceous materials in openings during pe-riods of low acorn availability and the least during periods of high yields of mast. As acorn consumption ended, the white-tails moved back to the forest openings where they greatly relished Japanese hon-eysuckle.

Most of their feeding activity in the openings took place between 1600 to 0400 hours. Deer would appear in the openings shortly before dusk, feed heavily for a time, and then leave. Throughout the night they would move back and forth from opening to opening. Segelquist observed little activity in the openings during the daylight hours.

Radio telemetry studies also confirm this apparent tendency toward noctural use of forest openings. James Kroll, for exam-ple, a trophy deer biologist, notes that while does are highly attracted to forest

openings in spring and summer, "bucks show little daytime interest in them during *any* season." He observes, however, that bucks use openings during the nighttime hours in the Pineywoods region of east Texas. Larry Marchinton in his telemetric study of deer movement in the southeast also concludes that a common movement pattern of radio-tagged deer involves feed-ing in forest openings at night and return-ing to wooded areas at dawn.

One of the most fascinating aspects of the whitetail's use of forest openings re-volves around the animal's marked prefer-ence for smaller openings as opposed to larger ones. In the Arkansas study, Segel-quist observed five times as many deer per acre on the smallest clearings as on the largest ones and concluded that an inverse relationship exists between the size of the clearing and the number of deer sight-ings. Jesse Overcash, a forest researcher, reached the same conclusion while docu-menting deer utilization of forest openings in the Shawnee National Forest in southern Illinois. In a paper presented at the Mid-west Fish and Wildlife Conference in De-cember of 1987, Jesse reported that in pine-dominated areas he found more deer beds and deer trails in isolated openings as op-posed to clustered openings and that in general whitetails more intensively utilized small openings (0.2–1.2 acres) than larger ones. In his study of forest openings in northern Wisconsin, deer biologist Keith McCaffery also concludes that whitetails more readily utilize smaller openings of less than five acres, or five chains in width, than larger ones. If you intend to construct forest openings on your land, make them one or two acres in size or smaller; you do not need large openings to meet the re-quirements of deer.

According to McCaffery, the whitetail even exerts an influence on the mainte-nance of forest openings. "Quite by accident," Keith writes, "deer contribute much to their own welfare in maintaining openings. Where deer densities are high, browsing pressure alone is sufficient to kill invading woody species. Unpalatable species and saplings often become targets for belligerent bucks in the fall. Rare is the opening that doesn't exhibit trees and shrubs scarred or killed by buck rubs. Openings concentrate deer in fall, and obviously much of the rutting activity is also concentrated there."

The presence of does in openings during the fall of the year provides bucks with a bigger attraction than available herbaceous material. In the upland herbaceous openings that Keith studied, bucks used the openings for purposes of courtship and venting their frustrations on shrubs and saplings. By mid-November, McCaffery found the deer trails entering the openings and interconnecting nearby openings worn to bare soil. Bow hunters quickly employed stands overlooking these trails. "These trails," Keith writes, "plus the tracks which are readily apparent in the lodged grasses, are mute testimony to the use of openings by deer."

To evaluate the human use of forest openings, Keith mailed a questionnaire to owners of vehicles parked in their vicinity and found that gun deer hunting and bow deer hunting ranked high on the list of activities pursued (See table.) A similar questionnaire in West Virginia listed improved hunter access and bow hunting op-

White-tailed bucks use forest openings for purposes of courtship and venting their frustration on shrubs and saplings. Hunters frequently find scrapes on the edges of openings. This buck smells and chews the licking branch above a scrape at the edge of an opening. *Len Rue Jr. photo*

Human activities pursued in forest openings.	
Activity	**No. respondents pursuing activity***
Deer gun hunting	67
Ruffed grouse hunting	62
Sightseeing	44
Berry picking	40
Fishing	40
Deer bow hunting	34
Hiking	26
Seeking solitude	23
Working (timber harvest, mineral exploration	21
Snowmobiling	21
Bird watching	10
Trapping	8
Photography	7
Picnicking	7
Woodcock hunting	7
Skiing	6
Mushroom picking	6
Predator hunting	5
Firewood gathering	5
Trailbike riding	4
Rabbit hunting	4
Waterfowl hunting	2
Horseback riding	1
Bicycle riding	1
Camping	1
Minnow trapping	1
Jogging	1
*100 respondents provided 454 responses.	

Reprinted from Keith R. McCaffery, James E. Ashbrenner and John C. Moulton. 1981. *Forest Opening Construction and Impacts in Northern Wisconsin.* Madison, Wisconsin. Technical Bulletin –120. 28 pp.

portunity as the primary human benefits of forest openings.

In June 1987, I traveled to Warren, Pennsylvania, a small picturesque town on the edge of the Allegheny National Forest and the hometown of the great Pennsylvania deerslayer Philip Tome, to attend a deer symposium, "Deer, Forestry and Agriculture," sponsored by the Allegheny Society of American Foresters. After years of listening to deer hunters ask me what they can do to improve white-tailed deer habitat on their small parcels of land, I listened with particular interest to Steve Weber, a district wildlife biologist for the state of Vermont, present the paper "White-tailed Deer Habitat Management Guidelines in Vermont." While discussing how hunters can provide lush, green her-

baceous material during March, April, and early May for deer as they leave their winter range, Steve recommended two major practices for improving spring habitat in a primarily forested area.

The first practice entails mowing and/or brush hogging abandoned farm fields to prevent them from reverting to woodlands. These areas should be mowed at least once, every three years. If possible, these areas should be planted with a mixture of early season grasses such as Kentucky bluegrass, orchard grass, and tall or red fesque and legumes such as clover, alfalfa, and birdsfoot trefoil. A no-till seeder works well in spring.

The second practice consists of planting log landings and forest roads with a grass/legume mixture. These kinds of openings, Steve reports, "represent the most economically feasible method to develop spring habitat because they are usually cleared down to mineral soil during logging operations and herbaceous cover is easy to establish. Forest roads should be daylighted before planting and landings be at least one acre in size and be cleared of woody debris (bark and sawdust). The soil should be tested to establish lime and fertilizer requirements before seeding. If soil testing is not possible, the following recommendations should be followed: (1) Apply lime at two tons per acre. (2) Seed an early season grass/legume mix at 25 pounds per acre. (3) Fertilize with 15-15-15 fertilizer at 200 pounds per acre. (4) Mulch with hay at forty bales per acre." For the excellent pamphlet, "Model Habitat Management Guidelines for Deer, Bear, Hare, Grouse, Turkey, Woodcock and Non-Game Wildlife," contact Steve Weber, District Wildlife Biologist, 111 West Street, Essex Jct., VT 05452.

Costs for creating and maintaining forest openings greatly vary depending upon techniques, access, soil type, and desired result. In 1985, Minnesota wildlife researchers estimated the cost of maintaining forest openings from $20 per hectare (1 hectare = 2.47 acres) for burning to $277 per hectare for mechanical maintenance. The construction of new openings, including the cost of seed, averaged $445 per hectare.

Many deer hunters, like the white-tailed deer, continually return to the same location each year and establish an area as a home range for hunting. In many cases these home-range hunters see and kill more deer than transient hunters. More and more deer hunters, in maintaining their deer-hunting territory, purchase the land or lease the land and ultimately participate in habitat improvements with their own sweat, time, and dollars. The words of Robert Ardrey in his *The Territorial Imperative* (1966), give particular meaning to deer hunters who like to reflect throughout the year about their cherished, often-used deer-hunting turf and who physically construct or reconstruct the landscape of their deer-hunting territory to better suit the needs of both the hunter and the animal.

"It is a matter of surpassing remark, when you come down to think about it, what a change in the landscape occurs when you have made a place of your own: how the shape of an oak tree emerges in the darkness to take on that definition which can only be oak; how stars shine brighter, and those of fifth or even sixth magnitude become apparent; how the sound of some running brook . . . chants its quiet cadence; how smells rush at you . . . the smell of leaves, green leaves dampened by dew, but of other leaves also, old leaves, last year's fallen leaves, that sweet soft odor of death's decomposition. And then there is that muskiness. There is an animal somewhere."

In addition to their significance for the animal, forest openings create a rich and varied landscape by adding esthetic values to our woodland environment. "They provide scenic overlooks," as deer hunter Keith McCaffery tells us, "panoramas of seasonally changing colors and opportunities to stretch one's legs as well as one's imagination." They eliminate the closed-in, monotonous character of vast timber; they provide man with the opportunity to view autumn in all its splendor and color. In spring, the forest openings freshen the landscape with the flowers of fruit bearing shrubs. And in summer, orange hawkweed often sets these open vistas ablaze.

Many hunters have their favorite forest openings where they return each year to observe and hunt deer, grouse, woodcock, turkeys, and black bears, where they hike and observe man's historic past, and where they pick blueberries and blackberries as well. Hugh Fosburgh, an Adirondack deer hunter, returned to his favorite opening at Baker's Clearing near North Creek, New York, each year to do these things and to observe the ways of the white-tailed deer. Whenever he would leave the clearing for an extended period of time, he did so with foreboding and a sense of guilt.

"Something sinister will surely happen while I'm gone!" he would think to himself. "So I make a quick, surreptitious departure. And when I come back, after months, it is always a small miracle—Baker's Clearing is just as I left it."

I suspect that every deer hunter has a special place in deer country he loves best. Baker's Clearing, an opening cut from the wilderness more than 100 years ago by pioneer farmer-hunter-lumberman Thomas Baker, provided Fosburgh with a sense of well-being, of belonging, that never failed to produce the utmost in "quiet excitement." He tirelessly tramped this clearing where Winslow Homer created his famous deer paintings, hunted it, logged timber around it, and fished its ponds and brooks. He lived in Baker's Clearing much of the time. His stories about white-tailed deer at Baker's Clearing are priceless.

After deer hunting at Baker's Clearing for many years, he came to realize that the very essence of deer hunting revolves around a paradox: You love the particular species you chase and you maintain an enormous respect and consideration for the animal you kill.

"The practical application of this essence," Hugh writes in his deer hunting journal, "is knowing when to shoot and when not to shoot. You shoot to kill, and when you're not sure you can kill, you don't shoot. To me, the perfect way to kill a deer is to trail it to its bed and come upon it lying down twenty-five yards away, or maybe less; then you shoot it in such a way that it never knows you were there, or what happened to it. When you've done that, you've hunted well and made a perfect shot and done more to be pleased about than all the fantastic shots, put together, that you ever made in your life."

Fosburgh spent a great deal of time watching and hunting whitetails at this famous opening in the remote central Adirondacks. He reports in his outdoor journal, *A Clearing in the Wilderness* (1969), that whitetails used the clearing all year but especially during the autumn rut for rubbing, scraping, and courting. "One November afternoon I saw a big doe bust out of the beeches and careen across the clearing into the alders, then seconds later a buck followed in belching pursuit, then a second buck raced out, and finally a third—a monstrous grunting animal—came pounding along. By the time everything was quiet again, I was shaking with excitement." Indeed, forest openings can be exciting places for man to hunt and observe white-tailed deer behavior. If we allow them to revert to timber, we will have to be satisfied with fewer whitetails and a more monotonous deer woods.

In a detailed study of the urban deer hunter in Maryland, James Kennedy, a forest researcher, reached the conclusion that the wildlife manager's fetish with the deer herd's size and condition may be of less consequence in providing deer hunter satisfaction and enjoyment than such efforts in habitat management as creating new forest openings, improving sight distances, and improving roads and trail access. Instead of arguing that more deer necessarily equals better deer hunting, Kennedy stresses habitat improvements that reflect the changing attitudes and values of today's urban deer hunters.

"Let me suggest that we also consider investment in a decent hunter map of the forest, that forest roads be named and well signed, that trails be laid out and marked to disperse hunting pressure, that forest openings not be strung along forest roads but placed back in dense brush to create more shooting breaks and encourage hunter dispersion, and other alternatives to help the present deer population and hunters interact more often. One might also consider investments that would increase the pleasure of extra-hunt rewards such as scattered group-hunting campsites."

While not all wildlife managers will agree with Kennedy's assessment, many urban deer hunters in Maryland apparently do. Indeed, wildlife managers remain divided on the significance of forest openings, as we learn from the article "Economics of Forest Openings for White-tailed Deer" in the Winter 1987 issue of the *Wildlife Society Bulletin*. The author, Mark Lenarz, a wildlife researcher with

All whitetails consume the varied and rich herbaceous vegetation of forest openings. These openings may also be preferred fawning sites that dominant does defend. *Leonard Lee Rue III photo*

the Minnesota Department of Natural Resources, remains unconvinced. "Although forest openings have been maintained for deer since the 1930s, it has never been demonstrated that deer populations benefit from this management."

While the scientific proponents of planted forest openings may not have proven their ultimate value beyond empirical doubt, neither have the skeptics of openings proven them worthless. The numerous and conspicuous deer sign found in these openings—deer beds, droppings, tracks, trails, nipped vegetation, rubs, scrapes, and shed antlers—and the weight of the scientific evidence that I have seen convince me of the ultimate value of the forest opening for the white-tailed deer. Current research, furthermore, suggests that forest openings may be preferred fawning sites that dominant does defend. I cannot imagine the deer forest without them.

PART III

THE DEER HUNTING MYSTIQUE

Four of Seton's thirty-five journals from 1893 to 1901. *Top right:* head and hooves of a Colorado buck he downed. *Bottom right:* Alberta mulie racks.

"Whether or not I really want to kill the buck, I am not yet willing to forego the company of men who hunt." — James Kilgo, *Deep Enough for Ivory-bills,* 1988.

CHARLES J. ALSHEIMER

"No other creature of the forest seems more a shape of the moonlight than does the white-tailed deer." — Archibald Rutledge.

RICHARD P. SMITH

By using the spotlight method to study the nocturnal movement patterns of white-tailed bucks, some biologists report increased nocturnal activity during the full-moon period; other researchers, however, reach the opposite conclusion. One deer researcher notes that the eyeshine of the whitetail appears white from the frontal view and red-orange from a profile view. The greater distance between the eyes of bucks causes their eyeshine to be wider than that of does.

Many dedicated hunters believe that when the moon rises in the sky during daylight, white-tailed deer activity and movement increase during daytime hours. Scientific studies, however, do not substantiate this widely held belief.

A favorite time for feeding forays: when the sun sets in the west and the moon rises in the east.

Early in the rut, bucks frequently engage in unusual scraping behavior; they hurriedly paw the ground and consequently create scrapes that are small and hardly noticeable without overhanging branches. During this scraping behavior, the animal becomes aggressive, the hair on its back stands erect, and it often digs its antlers into the exposed soil. These unusual pawings should not be confused with scrapes made for the express purpose of breeding and establishing dominance.

Search out the early scrapes and pay close attention to them because many of them will become breeding scrapes during the peak of the rut.

As you can see from the expressions on their faces, the editors of *Deer & Deer Hunting* magazine—Al Hofacker, Rob Wegner, and Randy Schwalbach—would rather be hunting deer than working at the Wisconsin Deer Classic.

White-tailed bucks nibble, chew, lick, sniff, and thrash the overhanging branch above the scrape. They grasp it with their teeth and pull it down. They twist it and rake their antlers over it. They rub their preorbital and forehead scent glands on it. The process is *careful and deliberate* and borders on pure ecstasy. Deer researchers believe that bucks may lick their tarsal glands in order to transfer scent to the overhanging branches.

MARK S. WERNER

Rub-urination—This behavior, which combines urine with secretions from the tarsal glands and is associated with scrapes, apparently serves as an olfactory signal. Since the behavior is performed in a variety of social contexts, ranging from mild alarm among fawns to threat behavior in rutting bucks, its function remains obscure. It is always performed with the hind legs together while the animal rubs the tarsal glands up and down and urinates on them.

Flehmen—This posture, also termed "lip-curl," occurs after a buck sniffs the ground where a doe has recently urinated. The buck stands with his nose elevated and his upper lip pulled back for about five seconds, apparently testing the urine for estrus status. Much remains to be learned about this chemosensory detection of estrus and the exact role of flehmen behavior in white-tailed sexual interactions.

Quality deer management offers some very real and desirable benefits for the whitetail. Buck fawns born earlier in the year under this type of management program carry better antlers at 1.5 years of age and probably for the rest of their lives. Fawns born earlier in the year maintain a definite advantage over those coming later. They exhibit greater body weights as yearlings and maintain a greater resistance to disease and parasites. The fawn on the left was born on August 8 and the fawn on the right on April 8. Which fawn would you prefer to see in the deer forest?

Shakespeare once wrote, "Thou know'st 'tis common; all that live must die, passing through nature to eternity." But must all yearling white-tailed bucks die by the age of eighteen months?

Death by starvation in the deeryard is one of the most pathetic sights of nature.

"They are likely to die in March. And they die unmourned, untended, unnoted." — Curtis Stadtfeld.

The bone marrow test. When the bone marrow becomes jelly-like and turns red instead of its normal rich creamy color, all the fat cells have been absorbed — proving the animal died of starvation.

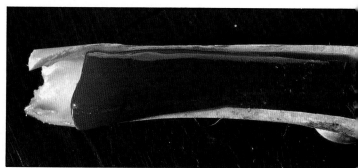

While wolves do not easily catch yarding white-tails, their success rates increase when spring green-up comes late in mid-April with white-tails in an emaciated condition.

In their weak and emaciated condition many whitetails in the deeryard fall prey to free-running dogs.

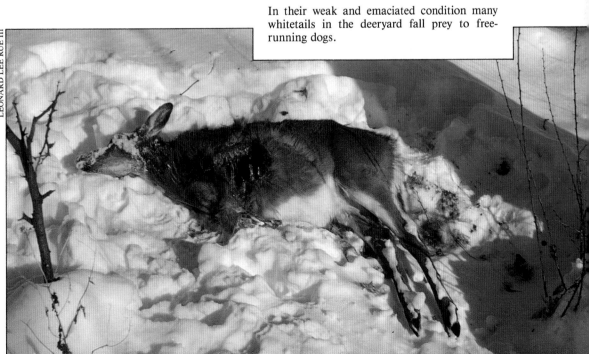

WISCONSIN DEPARTMENT OF NATURAL RESOURCES

Free-roaming dogs ate parts of this deer before its death. The deer kept right on fighting until the last drop of blood — an ignoble death for a noble deer. I used to think that all dogs seen running deer in areas where hounding deer is illegal should be shot immediately. The more I think of it, however, the more I am inclined to believe that we would do much better if we directed our ammunition towards the owner. I can hear the owner already. "Just a little pet dog who wouldn't . . ." but he did!

Deer may develop a severe fibroma problem as the animal tries to rid its body of such foreign objects as sticks and branches.

TIMOTHY C. FLANIGAN

A bobcat-kill in its white oak tree cache.

Under normal circumstances most bucks resolve their conflicts by a retreat of one of the antagonists. These two bucks chose instead to slug it out to the finish — both dying with interlocked antlers.

Len Rue Jr. found this white-tailed buck attempting to bathe its wounds in a low-lying ditch after being injured in a buck fight. Accidental mortality goes unnoticed because injured deer attempt to hide in dense cover before dying or because predators consume them so promptly that man fails to notice their demise.

A white-tailed buck accidentally trapped in barbed wire and caught in the fork of a tree.

The almighty buck rub!

CHARLES J. ALSHEIMER

The quality of the hunt is important, not the size of the rack.

MAREN LEA WEGNER

More deer drives than the hunter cares to admit merely result in "the great escape." *The Great Escape* by Don Kloetzke.

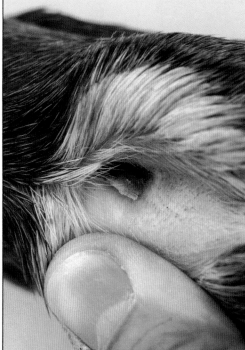

The interdigital gland showing the scent wax of a 3.5-year-old white-tailed buck.

White-tailed deer reflection: a magic moment.

Bucks will frequently check their scrapes with the wind in their noses from the secure location of a downwind position.

One of the most enduring and unresolved mysteries in the world of the white-tailed deer revolves around the ultimate meaning and significance of those indelible, well-formed, heart-shaped deer prints left in the middle of scrapes. They are obviously placed there with the utmost deliberation and attention to detail. But why? What do they signify? To which sex does the track belong?

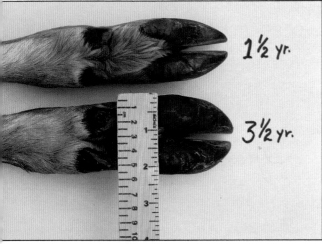

1½ yr.

3½ yr.

The difference in the hooves of a 1.5-year-old buck and a 3.5-year-old buck.

A very unusual white-tailed deer hoof on the right.

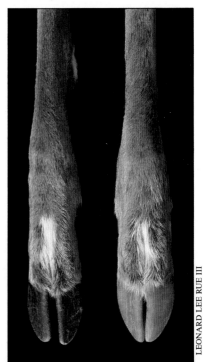

Chapter 11

Meat Fit for a King

A lot of them old bastards won't eat deer meat until it's been cooked to a frazzle. Gray right through. They never did learn how good it could taste.
— A Backwoods Deer Poacher, 1990

This republic came of age eating venison, and yet as this rather illiterate remark by a backwoods deer poacher in the woods of Maine indicates, some people still think that we need to kill deer twice: first in the deer woods and then in the kitchen with rich, heavy marination, hot fomentations, cooking wines, bourbon, and gunpowder for seasoning. For some reason, American cooks seem reluctant to appreciate the remarkable qualities of this excellent meat — the very best of meats, meat fit for a king — due no doubt to the historic tales of venison haunches returning to civilization by rail, rank with the rut when the meat started its journey and partially decomposed on final arrival after a long, dusty, hot journey from the heart of deer country. Venison, when so ill-treated in the field, obviously becomes as inedible as Missouri mule even if drowned and steeped in a witch's brew, given a prolonged bath in hot marinade, and prepared with a battery of spices, herbs, and sauces.

In today's highly diet-conscious world, more and more people are gradually discovering the ultimate value of venison. High in protein, low in fat, venison as a meat source improves the nutritional properties of human food for hunters and non-hunters alike. Because white-tailed deer meat has a lower fat content than other red meats, it is becoming especially attractive to health-conscious Americans. Today, countries such as England, New Zealand, the United States, Japan, and China market venison as a health food for people who don't like fat and who need to limit their energy intake and lower their saturated fatty acid intake while still being able to enjoy a hearty meal of red meat. Consumer interest in dietary fat, saturated fat, and cholesterol grows steadily. According to the American Meat Institute,

Total amino acids in the longissimus muscle (the loin) for white-tailed deer.

Amino Acid	mg/100g Fresh Tissue Mean	Standard Deviation
Aspartic Acid	2.23	0.12
Theronine	1.13	0.09
Serine	1.02	0.06
Glutamic acid	3.49	0.23
Proline	1.24	0.21
Glycine	1.23	0.11
Alanine	1.50	0.13
Cystine	0.27	0.04
Valine	1.12	0.08
Methionine	0.59	0.09
Isoleucine	0.95	0.09
Leucine	2.04	0.11
Tyrosine	0.85	0.06
Phenylamine	0.98	0.06
Histidine	1.19	0.09
Lysine	2.10	0.15
Arginine	1.73	0.10
NH_4	0.46	0.03

The nutrient composition of white-tailed deer and standard grade beef.

Nutrient	Whitetail Mean	Standard Beef Mean
Moisture %	73.5	73.2
Protein %	24.4	23.3
Fat %	1.4	2.8
Ash %	1.2	1.1
Energy[a] (kcal/100g)	149.0	154.0
Cholesterol[a] (mg/100g)	116.3	70.9

[a]Wet weight basis
[b]N=20

Reprinted from M. J. Marchello, et. al. 1985. "Cutability and Nutrient Content of White-tailed Deer." Journal of Food Science (7):271.

Reprinted from M. J. Marchello and P. T. Berg. 1983. "Cutability and Nutrient Content of White-tailed Deer." North Dakota Outdoors 46(4):11.

consumers whose red meat usage is influenced by health factors grew from 33 percent of all consumers in 1983 to 50 percent in 1985.

Comparative tests on the nutrient, mineral, and fat content of venison to beef, scientific research on the biochemistry of the aging process, fast freezing and electrical stimulation, and detailed studies of the factors influencing its palatability as well as its monetary value and the current volume of consumption are most revealing. Several scientific studies suggest that as the data base on the nutrient value of white-tailed deer meat grows and as deer farming practices become more systematic, venison may become the principle meat source for many individuals in the United States and in some of the developing countries as well.

One of the most revealing studies on white-tailed deer meat conducted at North Dakota State University by Martin Marchello, an avid deer hunter and proponent of venison in the family diet, indicates that deer meat contains a unique balance of protein, fats, and minerals that provides man with a complete food item in a very concentrated form. After analyzing fifteen white-tailed deer shot by hunters and examining the loin eye muscle for protein, moisture, fat, calories, cholesterol, amino acids, and minerals, Marchello found that venison, like other lean meats, contains a complete complement of essential amino acids (see table), thus giving it a high biological value. When comparing it to beef, Marchello found deer meat higher in protein (24.4 percent), higher in moisture (73.5 percent) and lower in fat (1.4 percent) and gross energy (149 kcal/100g). (See the accompanying table.)

While studying the cholesterol level, Marchello, a professor in the Department of Animal Science, discovered a notable and significant difference between venison and beef. In an article published in the *Journal of Food Quality,* Marchello re-

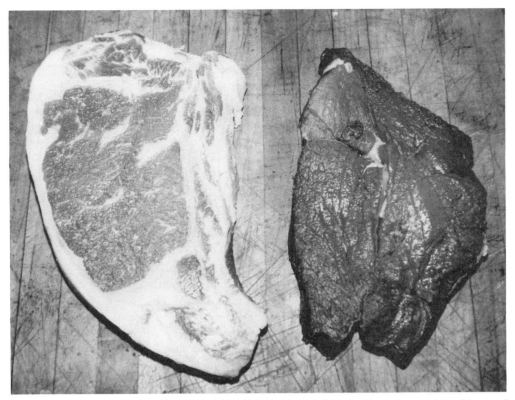

A typical beef steak *(left)* **and a venison steak** *(right).* **Knowing that the beef steak contains more fat and bone and less protein than the venison steak, which one would you prefer?** *Dennis Walrod photo*

ports that the cholesterol content of venison is *more than half again as high as beef* (116.3 mg/100g as opposed to 70.9 mg/100g). This finding will probably surprise many deer hunters, for most people confuse fat with cholesterol. While venison contains less intramuscular fat (marbling) than feedlot-fed USDA Choice beef, or typical pork, Marchello's study shows that venison from both whitetails and mule deer contains a substantially higher level of cholesterol (50 to 60 percent) than beef.

Researchers at the University of Wyoming also report that venison from mule deer contains a higher level of cholesterol than beef, but by only 10 percent. In discussing the cholesterol content of venison,

Dennis Buege, a professor in the Department of Meat and Animal Science at the University of Wisconsin, Madison, agreed with these findings. "Overall, it seems safe to report that venison is higher than beef and pork in cholesterol content, but some uncertainty currently exists in the extent of these differences."

Since venison, beef, and pork all vary in their fat and cholesterol levels, deer hunters frequently ask how these meats compare in their potential effect on the serum cholesterol level, one of the risk factors in cardiovascular disease.

When asked this question, Professor Buege tells us that the medical recommendations to reduce serum cholesterol by diet include such factors as (1) reduction in total calories, (2) reduction in total fat, (3) reduction in saturated fat, and (4) reduction in dietary cholesterol.

"On the positive side," Buege reports in a University of Wisconsin news release, "venison tends to be lower in fat and calories. On the negative side venison remains higher in cholesterol. Venison and beef fats contain about the same proportion of saturated fatty acids. From a practical standpoint, venison, beef and pork should be quite similar in their potential overall effect upon serum cholesterol. It is likely, however, that a greater potential effect on serum cholesterol results from the methods of preparation, accompanying foods in the diet and the quantity of food consumed."

Not only is venison lower in calories than beef, but boneless deer meat from does contains even fewer calories per 100 grams than deer meat from bucks — another reason for shooting antlerless deer, although seldom advocated.

With regard to fatty acids, Marchello observes that venison and beef contain about the same level of saturated fatty acids. (See table.) Venison, however, remains lower in monounsaturated fatty acids and higher in polyunsaturated fatty

Comparison of the mean mineral content of the loin muscle in white-tailed deer and beef carcasses.		
Mineral	Whitetail Mean	Beef Mean
Potassium	2.84	3.13
Phosphorus	212	170
Sodium	51	53
Magnesium	23	20
Calcium	3.84	5.04
Iron	3.60	1.74
Zinc	1.90	3.64
Copper	0.28	0.09
Manganese	0.04	ND

[a]100 mg/g wet tissue
[b]N=13 for whitetails and 16 for beef
[c]Beef used for analysis contained 71.7% moisture, 23.2% protein and 4.5% fat
ND=Not detectable

Reprinted from M. J. Marchello and P. T. Berg. 1983. "Cutability and Nutrient Content of White-tailed Deer." North Dakota Outdoors. 46(4):11.

acids. The higher content of polyunsaturated fat remains consistent with scientific observations that venison fat becomes rancid more rapidly than beef fat.

In his study of deer meat, Marchello discovered with regard to the mean mineral content of white-tailed deer meat that venison loin contains slightly more phosphorous, magnesium, iron, copper, and manganese than beef loin but lesser amounts of potassium, sodium, calcium, and zinc. (See the accompanying table.) The amounts obtained in a 3.5-ounce serving of meat are expressed as mg/100g. These differences, Marchello maintains, probably result from feed sources and the ages of the animals. His beef samples came from animals fed a commercial fattening ration and slaughtered at approximately eighteen months; his deer were older and he obviously lacked control over their food sources.

While estimating the meat yield from white-tailed deer carcasses remains quite

The relative percentage of the types of fat within the loin tissue of various mammalian species.			
Species	% Fatty Acids		
	Saturated	Monounsaturated	Polyunsaturated
Beef	46.3	45.5	8.2
Buffalo	43.2	45.0	11.8
Mule Deer	48.0	31.8	20.2
White-tailed Deer	45.6	30.6	23.9
Elk	48.4	26.6	24.9
Antelope	41.2	27.1	31.6
Moose	36.6	24.3	39.1

Reprinted from Urban Gaida & Martin Marchello. 1987. Going Wild. Minnesota: Watab Marketing, Inc. p. 229.

difficult, Marchello believes that if you shoot a deer with a field-dressed weight of 140 pounds, you can expect to obtain approximately eighty-two pounds of boneless lean meat, providing you made an excellent killing shot and did not dirty the carcass in the process of removing the animal from the woods. The average lean edible tissue from whitetails in his North Dakota study equaled sixty-seven pounds. The potential for human food consumption through systematic hunting of deer remains enormous. In 1982 alone, North Dakota deer hunters killed 31,149 white-tailed deer that provided more than two million pounds of lean meat. "This amount of lean meat at twenty-four percent protein," Marchello says, "represents the yearly protein requirement for almost 11,500 adult males."

Using venison as a basic source of food gives the sport of deer hunting a sound, utilitarian foundation. We must remember that the non-hunting public does not accept deer hunting for either recreational purposes or antler collecting; the non-hunting public, however, accepts hunting when it is done to put deer meat on the table.

As an old buck hunter once exclaimed: "If you don't eat it, don't shoot it."

While many factors determine the tenderness of venison such as age, sex, diet, concentration of deer in an area, severity of the winter, parasites, shot placement, immediacy and skill of field dressing, aging (time, temperature, and humidity) and hanging, how you cut the steaks and roasts, method of packaging, freezing and duration of storage, and length and manner of cooking, deer hunters frequently ask whether stress creates a detrimental effect on the quality and tenderness of venison. Animal scientists without exception say "yes." The National Meat Institute of Canada, for example, reports that a deer downed with one shot in the heart and/or lung area will invariably be more tender than a badly wounded and intensively tracked animal. They believe that deer shot while still-hunting will be more tender than driven, panicky, and nervous deer.

Nutrition specialists at Utah State University also tell us that the immediacy of death, wound location, and physical stress represent the greatest significant factors on the flavor of venison. In their study, "Factors Influencing the Quality and Palatability of Venison in Utah," they indicate that deer running considerable distances under wounding stress provide relatively tough meat for the palate that scores venison consistently low in consumer satisfaction tests. A panel of judges considered some of the meat from heavily stressed animals as unfit for human consumption.

In studying the effects of stress at time of death on the quality characteristics of white-tailed deer meat, Joyce Hosch, a food technology researcher, notes that stressed animals enter rigor mortis at a faster rate, which causes a decrease in tenderness. Her data indicate that deer meat from stressed animals (animals shot through the stomach and pursued in a marathon tracking session), exhibits higher levels of acidity, a darker color, and coarser texture. Deer meat from stressed deer in her study scored consistently lower in flavor by a taste panel of eight judges.

In subjecting deer to very severe levels of stress and agitation prior to slaughter, English researchers also observe that as a result the venison exhibits a darker color (a brownish-red to a purplish-black) and contains high levels of acidity with an increased rate of bacterial spoilage. The meat from stressed animals may be sticky and gummy in texture as well.

John Stransky, a research forester with the U.S. Forest Service, provides the deer hunter with the best explanation of the effects of wounding and stress on cooked venison.

"Wounding or even the threat of danger will instantaneously trigger the release of adrenalin, which accelerates the animal's heartbeat and constricts visceral blood vessels. This chemical-physiological chain reaction then floods the deer's muscles with blood—the fuel for defense or flight. The sudden and exaggerated metabolism of extra blood in muscle tissue produces a build-up of lactic and pyruvic acids, both metabolic waste products. Adrenalin in blood-engorged muscles, in combination with uneliminated metabolic wastes, is the principal cause of strong- or gamey-tasting cooked venison."

Excellent tasting venison depends upon many factors besides animal stress at the time of death. As one would expect, the older the deer, the tougher the meat. Deer less than one year old tend to be extremely tender and need not be aged at all. Deer meat from yearling animals consistently scored higher in the category of flavor in consumer tests at Utah State University than did meat from older animals. Once deer reproduce, according to the National Meat Institute of Canada, the meat becomes considerably less tender. Their research indicates that bucks over the age of two years produce tougher meat than does of the same age—another reason for shooting antlerless deer, although mentioned only infrequently.

Many backwoodsmen choose their deer with great care. They don't want trophies—you can't eat antlers—but prefer instead young, fat bucks, does, and yearlings in prime condition. The backwoodsman shoots it near his deer shack and, as deer hunter John Madson fondly insists, "hog-dresses it in as little as ten minutes,

and has the deer cooled, skinned and aging in the woodshed while the novice hunter is still stoning his knife."

The question of whether one should age deer meat or not remains a point of endless discussion among deer hunters, a question for which hunters seldom reach an agreement. This is not surprising since the microbiology of deer meat is only in its infancy and the literature remains sparse on the subject. While some scientific documentation exists on the biochemistry of the aging process, it is contradictory in nature.

Some animal scientists, such as Martin Marchello, view aging as impractical because so many people lack the proper facilities, and unfortunately so much deer meat winds up in sausage anyway. Aging skinned deer meat all to frequently results in excessive weight loss, dehydration, and discoloration of the lean tissue because of the lack of fat cover. Under improper conditions the meat becomes susceptible to deterioration by bacteria and mold growth. Since hunters shoot a large number of young animals with naturally tender meat (most deer shot today average only 1.5 to 2.5 years old), aging seems unnecessary in the opinion of some animal scientists and meat processors.

In surveying meat processors, Dennis Buege found that they did not agree on whether venison should be aged or not. "Most processors felt that aging was not beneficial to venison. One processor thought that old bucks could be improved by five to six days of aging, but young deer didn't require any aging. Another processor did feel aging was helpful in improving the quality of venison and recommended two to three days for lean carcasses and five to six days for those with some fat cover."

Most meat processors readily admit the difficulty of properly aging venison without a refrigerated cooler, for when we rely on the weather, we often encounter temperatures below 30°F that freeze meat and prevent the aging process from taking place, or temperatures above 40°F that dehydrate and spoil the meat. Cyclic freezing and thawing, meat processors generally agree, produces poor quality venison.

Animal scientists define the aging of meat as the practice of holding the carcass at temperatures of between 34° to 37°F with a relative humidity of 88 percent for seven to nine days. They recommend that the hide remain on the carcass to prevent excessive loss of moisture. They stress that aging allows the enzymes in the meat to break down some of the complex proteins, a process that usually improves flavor and tenderness.

While some deer hunters believe that leaving the hide on during the aging process causes an "off flavor," little scientific information or proof supports this belief. In a study on the quality and quantity of meat from elk carcasses at the University of Wyoming, Ray Field, a professor of meat science, reports in the *Journal of Wildlife Management* that "aging elk with the hide on or with the hide off did not affect the tenderness or flavor of the meat." Field warns hunters that carcasses of stressed animals should not be aged at all because the meat from stressed animals remains more susceptible to bacterial growth. He also reminds hunters that immediately after death (from twenty-four to thirty-six hours) all deer meat decreases in tenderness as the muscle fibers shorten and harden as a result of rigor mortis. Professor Field does not recommend processing your deer during the short process of rigor mortis, if you can avoid it.

In his research on deer meat at the University of Wyoming's Meat Science Laboratory, Field learned that aging venison for fourteen days at 34°F represents the optimum time and temperature combination for deer carcasses. If the temperature remains higher, Field suggests that the aging period be shorter. If you intend to grind or chop your venison, the meat, according to Field, does not need to be aged.

In a rather bizarre experiment conducted under Field's supervision, one researcher tried to transfer the characteristic flavor of deer meat to beef roasts. Wrapping the beef roasts in deer hides overnight and cooking the beef roasts with deer fat, deer bone sawdust, and metatarsal glands, researcher Franklin Smith placed the deer-treated, "venisonized" beef roasts together with untreated beef roasts on preheated china. He served the two types of roasts to an eight-member, trained panel of meat judges. According to Smith, the characteristic flavor of venison could not be transferred to the beef. "In each case when the treated beef roast was compared to a similar control roast from the same animal," Smith says, "a flavor difference due to the particular treatment was not noted."

The conclusion of this experiment might suggest the demolition of the commonly-held belief that venison's "gamy flavor" results from the deer hide, deer fat, deer bone sawdust, and deer glands. Maybe Lennie Rue is right when he argues that deer glands do not taint the meat while the animal lives and they won't taint the meat after the animal dies. This white-tailed deer hunter, however, continues to remove the deer hide as quickly as possible, eliminates all deer fat and deer bones, and avoids contact with the deer glands while processing venison.

One wonders why Smith didn't add a second step to his experiment by roasting beef and deer meat together to see if the beef would acquire the distinct flavor of venison. One also wonders why he didn't use the tarsal glands in his experiment. In any event, no scientific researcher to my knowledge has been able to duplicate the unique flavor of deer meat. Beef, as this experiment seems to indicate, cannot be venisonized.

The increasing interest in venison and the advent of deer farming throughout the world has led to dramatic changes in the processing methods of venison. Deer researchers in New Zealand note that electric stimulation of deer carcasses hastens rigor mortis and ensures the development of a tender product and significantly reduces the time needed to produce tender venison by enabling rapid cooling and freezing to be carried out soon after death. Although we can obtain favorable results in home freezers, animal scientists believe that "blast freezing"—a rapid process at −20°F—freezes deer meat best by preventing the formation of ice crystals in the meat fibers.

According to the Wildlife Management Institute, American deer hunters annually take home more than 128 million pounds of boneless venison. If one assumes that deer meat at least equals the price of beef, the deer hunters' yearly harvest equals a monetary value of more than $185 million. While deer hunters kill approximately 4.5 million deer annually in the United States, not a pound of their deer meat can legally be sold to stores or restaurants.

Where available, from sources licensed to sell deer meat, choice venison commands a relatively high price. As the worldwide venison export market increases, so does the market price for this choice, lean, sweet, and tender meat. While tracking down the market value of venison in the meat markets of the Washington, D.C. area, Pat NcNees, a reporter for the *Washington Post,* found the following prices for domestic deer meat (i.e., deer meat from game farms, not wild venison): boneless venison for $13.99 per pound, leg of venison for $8.99, bone-in venison for $6.98, ground venison for $5.45, and as much as $9.99 per pound for other various cuts.

Given the high monetary value of venison and the interest in promoting it as a low-fat, high-protein health food and as a fashionable meat in gourmet restaurants commanding high prices, it's not surprising that we're beginning to see the conquest of a new frontier: deer farming in North America.

If you drive through the rolling hills of upstate New York near Chaumont and the Thousand Islands, you will find the Lucky Star Ranch, the first and largest fully operating fallow deer farm in North America. On this 5000-acre deer farm, Josef von Kerckerinck, the owner and founder of the North American Deer Farmers Association, keeps 1500 head of fallow deer. The owner, called the "Baron of Venison" by *Connoisseur* magazine, exercises extreme care in the feeding and handling of his deer to ensure a healthy and chemically free herd; he does not expose his deer to growth hormones, herbicides, pesticides, or antibiotics.

Through Kerckerinck's pioneering deer farming initiatives, new markets in venison have been opened in this country; the Lucky Star Ranch provides many of the East Coast's finest restaurants with fresh, superlative quality venison that sells for an outstanding price. The Lucky Star Ranch operates under an inspected handling facility under the guidelines of the United States Department of Agriculture.

Encouraged by the success of the Venison Baron and his thriving operation, deer farming is becoming a new and fast-growing industry. These new deer farms meet the increased demand for domestic, legal venison in the United States. Many of them buy their breeding stock from the

Lucky Star and rely on Kerckerinck for help and advice.

In promoting the idea of deer farming throughout the United States and Canada, Kerckerinck remains convinced that deer farming can become a new source of income for many American farmers and can help small farmers in particular overcome their financial problems. The North American Deer Farmers Association now numbers forty members.

"If you examine the facts," the Baron of Venison argues in his *Deer Farming in North America* (1987), "it is almost unbelievable that nobody in this country has ever before thought of deer farming in the way other countries have. Thousands of farmers in Europe and New Zealand are making a living from deer farming while people in this country still think of venison as an exotic meat that is normally consumed illegally.

"When did you last see an agricultural product for which the demand exceeded the supply? Legal venison is such a product. As far as I know, it is one of very few.

"Farmed venison has a great future in the United States because fresh, legal venison is not readily available, and hunted venison cannot be bought legally."

On the flag flying above the Lucky Star Ranch, the owner emblazoned his business and obsession with the seven-point palmate antlers of a male fallow deer. Fallow deer, Kerckerinck believes, provide man with the best-tasting, top-quality venison. Many connoisseurs of deer meat agree. "Joe von Kerckerinck's venison is beautiful stuff," says Jean-Jacques Rachou, the famous chef of La Cote Basque, in New York City. Indeed, venison for the table from fallow deer maintains a high and ancient authority. In *Deuteronomy* we read: "The beasts which ye shall eat are the hart, the roebuck, and the fallow deer." It

almost seems that the name of Josef von Kerckerinck zur Borg should appear in that verse.

As founder and president of the North American Deer Farmers Association, Kerckerinck believes that fallow deer are the most suitable deer species to farm for venison because they adapt well to management and confinement. Moreover, they maintain a much higher conversion factor from grass to meat than most other farm animals.

"Another advantage of fallow deer," he insists, "is that young deer can be fed to appetite for maximum weight gain up to the age of fifteen to eighteen months without putting on fat, unlike sheep, which become fatty just over six months of age. Modern consumers don't want fat; why spend extra money to produce something that nobody wants? It takes twice as much feed to produce fat than to produce lean meat."

As a recent German immigrant to this country, Joe Kerckerinck likes to quote the words of Thomas Jefferson: "The most useful service we can render a culture is to add a new plant to its agriculture." Whether Kerckerinck succeeds in his conquest of the new deer farming frontier only time will tell. I suspect that he will, given the sweet taste of prime venison. I can already envision the first issue of *The American Deer Farmer,* a slick, four-color, specialty magazine for the pioneer deer farmers of the future.

Yet, the opposition to trafficking in venison remains fierce, for as my friend Val Geist, the leading opponent, argues, the commercialization of venison endangers conservation because it creates a retail market in dead wildlife and it endangers our indigenous deer herds with disease, crossbreeding, and genetic pollution by the release of exotic species, accidental or

Healthy, tasty, savory, and most digestible, the distinctive taste of venison tenderloins adds pleasure to life whether prepared over oak coals in the deer forest, on the Coleman stove at the deer shack, or enjoyed at th elegant Fox & Hounds in downtown Boston. *Leonard Lee Rue III photo*

otherwise. Geist rightly fears that trafficking in venison will bring out the villians in all of us. After all, even William Shakespear poached deer meat for the pot.

Court records, not surprisingly, indicate that highly trained professionals from all walks of life often revert to the unorthodox procedures of venisonivorous deer poachers to satisfy the almighty palate for high-quality venison, sweet and prime.

Venison stands out as one of the luxuries of the dinner table—"The Monarch of the Table," as Nicola Fletcher, a connoisseur

of venison, calls it. I have eaten venison all my life; I can't imagine life without this rich, red meat that contains no artificial flavor, dye, growth hormones, preservatives, or chemical additives. Aromatic, tender, juicy, healthy, tasty, and most digestible, its unique taste adds pleasure to life, whether prepared over oak coals in the forest, on the Coleman stove at the deer shack, or enjoyed at the elegant Fox & Hounds in downtown Boston.

In May 1987, the managing editor and the editor of *Deer & Deer Hunting* Magazine traveled to Boston to receive an award from the Northeast Section of The Wildlife Society. After attending the award presentation aboard the ship "Discovery" in the Central Wharf, the two country editors went to the elegant Fox & Hounds for dinner. The managing editor ordered fish; apparently he shares the concerns of Val Geist. The editor ordered "Filet of Venison St. Hubert" garnished with walnut crepes and apples and served with a Calvados Sauce. I never tasted such exquisite deer meat. The six tenderloin filets were scarcely seared on the outside and pink and juicy on the inside. I always prefer fast cooking to marinating deer meat into sur-

render, mortifying it for weeks on end and finally drowning it with fruity sauces. No "therapeutic soaking" for me. I want to taste the flavor of venison.

I asked the waiter where the venison came from. He said he thought it came from Joe's ranch in upstate New York. The sweet taste of that meat seemed like it could hardly come from this side of the Happy Hunting Grounds.

As we dined, classical hunting music played in the background. As I listened to the hunting call of the horns in Haydn's "The Hunt" symphony, my mind wandered back into time when venison provided meat for noblemen and poachers alike.

Prime venison roast might just help the deer hunter live forever. *Dennis Walrod photo*

The illustrious tradition behind its preparation for the table came to mind. I remembered reading somewhere about Magdalen Venison, one of the really great venison recipes, and how it was handed down traditionally from generation to generation for almost two and a half centuries and served annually at the Magdalen College dinner. Chefs marinated a saddle of venison from the College's own herd for days; braised it in Chateau wine; garnished it with glazed onions, chestnuts, and sauteed mushrooms; and served it with a heady port wine sauce.

As the horns of the huntsmen repeated their call in the background music, I could see Leopold cooking venison tenderloins on oak coals in front of his deer shack and knew why he dreamed of oak thickets alive with bounding bucks. I could hear Horace Kent Tenney's Hunting Call: "Twilight falling, heed the calling, / Rouse and hunt the deer!" I understood what he meant when he explained in his classic *Vert & Venison* (1924) how venison tenderloins accept the ministrations of oak coals and transform themselves from mere flesh into venison viands worthy of those who know what it means to kill deer and cook venison in forested terrain. I could see him tending the venison tenderloins in the firelight of the Huron Mountain Club.

As the hunting horns poured out their famous, irresistible, harmonious call, I understood why one deer hunter from Ohio insisted that the very thought of prime venison would help him live forever. I knew what John Woolcot had in mind when he said, "One cut from venison to the heart can speak stronger than ten quotations from the Greek." And I knew why one meat hunter wrote in his *Deer Tales and Pen Feathers* (1975), that . . .

Of all the pleasure I enjoy
  In serving friends good food,
I must admit the greatest thing
  That always lifts my mood
Is when I hear them all exclaiming
  As they smile with bliss,
"I never knew that venison
  Could ever taste like this!"

Indeed, the ultimate value of deer meat manifests itself in the acceptability of the product on the consumer's plate.

With the last ounce of *Clos Du Bois* (1984) drained, we walked out into the mindless noise and reality of St. James Avenue, where thoughts on vert and venison seemed remote.

Chapter 12

Twentieth Century Blue-Chip Deer Books

I'm at that stage in life when I find greater pleasure in rereading good, old titles than risking disappointment on unproven, new books.
— George Reiger, *The Wings of Dawn,* 1980

For the past twenty-five years I have been collecting, reading, and annotating books on deer and deer hunting. My collection of books on the subject consists of more than 800 volumes, and is probably the largest collection of its kind in the world. The books divide themselves into several basic categories: literature, science, popular science, how-to, anthologies, record books, humor, diaries, journals, and coffee table extravaganzas. I will share with you several selections that I consider to be the best deer books of the 20th century. If you only want to buy a limited number of books on the subject, buy these blue-chip deer books. If you plan on building a complete library, plan on spending tens of thousands of dollars, for most of the best books are out of print, rare, and very expensive. For a detailed discussion of the

great books on deer and deer hunting during the 19th century, see *Deer & Deer Hunting: Book 2* (Stackpole Books, 1987), pp. 195–206.

On the literary side, five authors come to mind: Rutledge, Faulkner, Ruark, Bass, and Kilgo. The favorite of most Archibald Rutledge fans would probably be his classic *An American Hunter* (1937), but I would choose *Those Were the Days* (1955) because it contains more splendid deer hunting tales than *An American Hunter.* The book is out of print and will probably cost approximately $100. When it first appeared, the *New York Times* commented on Old Flintlock:

"Mr. Rutledge loves the pleasures of the hunt, but shares none of the mere lust to kill. He is one of those hunters who, wit-

Five blue-chip deer books under the category of literature. *Robert Wegner photo*

nessing an absorbing drama or incident in the field, is likely to forget entirely the gun in his hand in the greater interest of the observer.

"The wildlife of the Carolinas is the richer, not the poorer, for such a hunter as Mr. Rutledge, and our stock of knowledge of nature is measurably the gainer."

If you want to learn about nature and natural history, read this volume of superb deer hunting tales, tales that added luster to Rutledge's fame when they originally appeared in magazines. In this collection of his best stories, the seventy-two-year-old master huntsman-narrator sums up a lifetime of deer hunting in charming, beauti-

ful prose. Since I dealt extensively with Rutledge in chapter one, I will say no more.

If you have not read William Faulkner on hunting, you have missed the best literature of our sport. You will find his hunting stories collected in a handsomely illustrated volume entitled *Big Woods* (Random House, 1955), which is out of print. In this volume of unforgettable deer hunting tales in the dense thickets of the Mississippi River Delta, Faulkner ultimately defines deer hunting as "the best game of all, the best of all breathing and forever the best of all listening." In it he presents a moving and memorable tribute to the hunter and hunted and provides us with a brilliant and penetrating examination of the hunter's paradox: How can man kill the object he loves?

Like Hemingway, Faulkner subscribed to an idealistic conception of hunting and lamented the destruction of our wildlife habitat by decadent civilization. Through the hunting initiation of Isaac MaCaslin ("Uncle Ike"), Faulkner documented his passion for the ideal deer hunt. In his story "The Old People," Ike shoots his first deer under the tutelage of Sam Fathers and graduates from rabbit shooting to big game hunting and manhood. Who will ever forget that great opening scene?

"At first there was nothing. There was the faint, cold, steady rain, the gray and constant light of the late November dawn, with the voices of the hounds converging somewhere in it and toward them. Then Sam Fathers, standing just behind the boy as he had been standing when the boy shot his first running rabbit with his first gun and almost with the first load it ever carried, touched his shoulder and he began to shake, not with any cold. Then the buck was there. He did not come into sight; he was just there, looking not like a ghost but as if all of light were condensed in him and he were the source of it, not only moving in it but disseminating it, already running, seen first as you always see the deer, in that split second after he has already seen you, already slanting away in that first soaring bound, the antlers even in that dim light looking like a small rocking-chair balanced on his head."

If that dynamic and powerful scene doesn't hook the reader into the story, nothing will. Later in the story, Ike realizes the importance of his kill that morning, even though he was only a boy of twelve . . .

". . . that morning something had happened to him: In less than a second he had ceased forever to be the child he was yesterday. Or perhaps that made no difference, perhaps even a city-bred man, let alone a child, could not have understood it; perhaps only a country-bred one could comprehend loving the life he spills."

The deer hunt for Faulkner was ancient, tribal, wild, and bloody with buckshot and howling hounds eating the viscera; whiskey followed the hunt once the gunfire stopped echoing throughout the woods. Like Rutledge and Seton, Faulkner viewed deer hunting as a school for manhood; so did Robert Ruark, as we learn in his classic story "Mister Howard Was A Real Gent," published in *The Old Man and the Boy* (Random House, 1957), which is still in print. This first-rate portrait of a deer hunt in the woods of North Carolina represents one of the finest essays ever written in American outdoor literature. Its insights and in-depth feelings warrant the reading and rereading of it each year when the deer season begins.

The story deals with the outdoor education and experiences of a young boy who is always called "the boy" (Robert Ruark), under the tutelage of his grandfather, Ned Hall, who is always called "the Old Man." Ruark's description of how the boy killed his first deer with the help of his two deer hounds, Bell and Blue, will forever live in the mind of the American deer hunter.

The dogs started to growl and bark, just letting off a *woo-woo* once in a while, and I could hear a steady swishing in the bushes.

Then I could see what made the swishing. It was a buck, a big one. He was running steadily and seriously through the low bush. He had horns—my Lord, but did he have horns! It looked to me like he had a dead tree lashed to his head. I slipped off the safety catch and didn't move. The buck came straight at me, the dogs going crazy behind him.

The buck came down the water's edge, and when he got to about fifty yards I stood up and threw the gun up to my face. He kept coming and I let him come. At about twenty-five yards he suddenly saw me, snorted, and leaped to his left as if somebody had unsnapped a spring in him. I forget he was a deer. I shot at him as you'd lead a duck or a quail on a quartering shot—plenty of lead ahead of his shoulder.

I pulled the trigger—for some odd reason shooting the choke barrel—right in the middle of a spring that had him six feet off the ground and must have been wound up to send him twenty yards, into the bush and out of my life. The gun said *boom!* but I didn't hear it. The gun kicked but I didn't feel it. All I saw was that this monster came down out of the sky like I'd shot me an airplane. He came down flat, turning completely over and landing on his back, and he never wiggled.

The dogs came up ferociously and started to grab him, but they had sense and knew he didn't need any extra grabbing. I'd grabbed him real good, with about three ounces of No. 1 buckshot in a choke barrel. I had busted his shoulder and busted his neck and dead-centered his heart. I had let him get so close that you could practically pick the wads out of his shoulder. This was *my* buck: Nobody else had shot at him.

Nobody else had seen him but me. Nobody had advised or helped. This monster was mine.

And monster was right. He was huge, they told me later, for a Carolina whitetail. He had fourteen points on his rack, and must have weighed nearly 150 pounds undressed. He was beautiful gold on his top and dazzling white on his underneath, and his little black hoofs were clean. The circular tufts of hair on his legs, where the scent glands are, were bright russet and stiff and spiky. His horns were as clean as if they'd been scrubbed with a wire brush, gnarled and evenly forked and the color of planking on a good boat that's just been holystoned to where the decks sparkle.

I had him all to myself as he lay there in the aromatic, crushed ferns—all by myself, like a boy alone in a big cathedral of oaks and cypress in a vast swamp where the doves made sobbing sounds and the late birds walked and talked in the sparkleberry bush. The dogs came up and lay down. Old Blue laid his muzzle on the big buck's back. Bell came over and licked my face and wagged her tail, like she was saying, "You did real good, boy." Then she lay down and put her face right on the deer's rump.

This was our deer, and no damn bear or anything else was going to take it away from us. We were a team, all right, me and Bell and Blue.

I couldn't know then that I was going to grow up and shoot elephants and lions and rhinos and things. All I knew then was that I was the richest boy in the world as I sat there in the crushed ferns and stroked the silky hide of my first buck deer, patting his horns and smelling how sweet he smelled and admiring how pretty he looked. I cried a little bit inside about how lovely he was and how I felt about him. I guess that was just reaction, like being sick twenty-five years later when I shot my first African buffalo.

Like Ruark, James Kilgo, a professor of English at the University of Georgia, also agonizes over killing white-tailed bucks in the Low Country of South Carolina and in the process gives us a blue-chip deer book

in the literary tradition of Hemingway, Faulkner, Ruark, and Rutledge. Since I deal with the book in the next chapter, I will merely mention it in passing. When *Deep Enough For Ivorybills* (Algonquin Books of Chapel Hill, 1988), appeared, Paul Schullery, an historian of hunting, wrote as follows in the *New York Times:*

"*Deep Enough For Ivorybills* is a book as deep in meanings and questions as the 'riverswamps' Kilgo wanders. The title refers to patches of country so wild it seemed to the young Kilgo that they still might hide a few last ivorybill woodpeckers, long believed extinct in that part of the South. It takes hunting and its complications ('I wondered what virtue there was in killing a deer, if no one understood what it meant') as seriously as ever Ruark or even Faulkner did, and leavens that intensity with finely wrought dialogue and refreshing humor."

Delightful humor also pervades the last blue-chip deer book in this category. If you cherish humor and the family tradition of deer hunting, you will want to read Rick Bass's *The Deer Pasture* (Texas A&M University Press, 1985). The Deer Pasture, like many American deer camps, becomes a cherished place to gather, to spin campfire stories, listen to grouse, bake camp biscuits, and watch the marvelous behavior of white-tailed deer. But more important, the Deer Pasture furnishes a place to recharge emotional and spiritual energy and ultimately to renew family ties while hunting whitetails.

Of the more than 800 books that exist on the subject of deer and deer hunting, *The Deer Pasture* has no counterpart; it's unique, original, fresh, and witty. It emphasizes traditions and values. In celebrating the habits of deer, the author reveals the close relationship between man, nature, and deer in the modern age. I have never read a book that so deeply penetrates the depths of the universal bond that links

If you are interested in the scientific aspects of deer, read these five great books. *Robert Wegner photo*

together man, deer, family, and the deer hunting tradition; you will want to read this special book each year before leaving for deer camp.

Under the category of science, five books stand as giants on my bookshelves. The first one, and one of my favorites, is Walter P. Taylor's *The Deer of North America* (Stackpole Books, 1956). I refer to this exhaustive and scholarly volume more than any book in my library. Long out of print, this standard reference work sells for $90 to $120 on the out-of-print book market. In it a panel of America's foremost animal scientists provide the reader with a detailed picture of the world of the white-tailed, mule, and black-tailed deer. This copiously

illustrated volume remains one of my favorites because it relates directly to the deer hunter. It was written at a time when deer research was less esoteric and more related to hunting, and when more deer biologists were deer hunters.

As a hunter and historian, I particularly enjoy two chapters: "The Deer, the Indians, and the American Pioneers" by Stanley P. Young and "Hunting the Whitetail" by Harry D. Ruhl. When the book first appeared, *The Journal of Wildlife Management* called it "the most comprehensive monograph on North American game."

The next reference volume that I would label a blue-chip deer book is *Producing Quality Whitetails* (Fiesta Publishing Co., 1975), by Al Brothers and Murphy E. Ray, Jr. Written by two Texas deer biologists with thirty-six years combined experiences in deer management and biology, this is a first-rate book for the layman and private property owner. It includes an excellent chapter on breeding and a common-sense explanation on the buck/doe ratio, and contains more than 100 superb pictures and illustrations, some dating back to the early 1900s. Few publications on management have had a more profound impact throughout Texas and the southeastern United States than this book. The book is unfortunately out of print and I have never seen it listed in an out-of-print book catalogue. Where are the outdoor book publishers when you need them?

The next great book on deer, *The George Reserve Deer Herd* (University of Michigan Press, 1979), by Dale R. McCullough, is still in print and will likely remain so since it's a publication of a university press. This book represents a necessary addition to the serious deer hunter's personal library. It's a must for game managers, deer hunters, and all those interested in the population biology of deer.

The book presents details of the long-term population dynamics of white-tailed deer on the Edwin S. George Reserve, a two-square-mile fenced area in southeastern Michigan where six whitetails were introduced in 1928. Six years later, in 1933, the same year Aldo Leopold's classic *Game Management* appeared, the first drive census indicated that the initial population of six deer had increased to 160. The phenomenal growth of this deer population became a landmark in the field of wildlife ecology. The author reassesses the conclusions of previous studies on this deer herd and reports at length on his own studies done over a twelve-year period. The book focuses primarily on one basic question: how deer population characteristics are related to density in ways that result in population regulation and changes in the number of deer that are available for hunting.

While the book is not intended for the layman, there is no reason why the intelligent deer hunter cannot comprehend the material. The information it contains is highly relevant to the perennial battles waged over deer management. Unfortunately, the so-called "barber shop biologists" and the "old buck hunters" who think they know everything will not, as usual, read this volume. They apparently do not want the facts to get in the way of their frivolous arguments. On the other hand, those serious hunters who take the time and effort to study this volume will be greatly enlightened about the many complexities of managing the white-tailed deer.

In addition, the book is interspersed with "golden nuggets" for the hunter. Consider, for example, the George Reserve's regulations governing deer shooting: "Deer were to be shot either in the neck or the heart. No shot was to be taken at distances greater than seventy-five yards, and only standing or slowly moving deer were

to be shot." Or consider the following observations: "There is a very human tendency among hunters to regard the failure to kill a deer as due to few deer or bad luck, while success is attributed to skill. . . . One need not search long to discover that the single most important criterion of the hunter as to the satisfactory state of the deer herd is the number of deer seen in the field. If tracks and droppings are abundant and deer are seen regularly, the hunter is satisfied. If few deer are seen, even the successful hunter is likely to be disgruntled."

Ultimately, this book examines what scientists call the "K-selected species"—those species such as the whitetail, "which have been adapted to live in relatively stable habitats at population densities at or near carrying capacity. . . . Certainly of more than passing interest is the fact that man, himself, is numbered among the K-selected species of the earth." Finally, the book is likely to force some deer managers to drop their buckskin breeches, for it contains a number of statements that are likely to stir their emotions to the very foundation. Take the following two as examples: (1) "Wildlife management is, and always will be, an art." (2) "Left alone (managers) tend to become deer farmers, trying to put the maximum amount of venison on car fenders."

The *Journal of Mammalogy* calls it "one of the best books that exists for population ecology of a large animal," and *The Journal of Wildlife Management* refers to it as "a curious blend of ecological theory and practical wildlife management."

Deer Antlers: Regeneration, Function, and Evolution (Academic Press, 1983), by Richard J. Goss, a professor of biology and medicine at Brown University, is a technical book written in a popular style that anyone with a keen interest in deer will want to read. For the deer hunter, as the author observes in the introduction, "antlers are prized trophies. To the animal lover, they are magnificent ornaments adorning one of the world's most graceful animals. To the zoologist, they are fascinating curiosities that seem to defy the laws of nature. To the deer themselves, they are a status symbol in the competition for male supremacy. Antlers are an extravagance of nature, rivalled only by such other biological luxuries as flowers, butterfly wings, and peacock tails. The antlers of deer are so improbable that if they had not evolved in the first place they would never have been conceived even in the wildest fantasies of the most imaginative biologists."

While this comprehensive account of antlerology might not answer all your questions about these unique appendages, it will surely arouse your curiosity about the many unsolved problems of how antlers grow, die, and are shed in the course of a year. Indeed, this book addresses the following provocative questions: From what kinds of tissues do antlers develop? What morphogenetic mechanisms regenerate them every year? What social functions prompted their initial evolution? How are they influenced by hormones? How do seasonal day-length fluctuations regulate their annual replacement?

The mechanism by which antlers grow and develop into such magnificent structures is a source of constant wonder. The entire specialized subject of antlers has diverse ramifications far beyond its own apparent limits. Not since William Macewen's *The Growth and Shedding of the Antler of the Deer* (1920) and A. B. Bubenik's *Das Geweih* (*Antlers,* 1966), has a better book been published on the subject. A highly recommended blue-chip deer book.

White-tailed Deer: Ecology and Management (Stackpole Books, 1984) authored by seventy-three people and written over a period of ten years, represents a remarkable undertaking and a monumental blue-chip deer book with no equals. It clearly stands as the most complete and informative volume ever written on the subject. We can now place Caton's *Antelope and Deer of America* (1877) and Taylor's *The Deer of North America* (1956) back on the bookshelf, and indulge in this newest classic.

This book, beautifully illustrated by Cindy House, chronicles everything from natural history, biology, and ecology to the animal's behavior, physiology, and population dynamics; it deals with the cultural history of the animals as well as the hunting of them. The color plates of the great deer and deer hunting paintings from the past greatly enhance the text, especially the romantic paintings of deer and deer hunting in the Adirondacks by Arthur F. Tait. The book contains a fantastic discussion by Richard and Thomas McCabe on how the American Indians hunted the white-tailed deer.

The graphs, charts, and illustrations, particularly those on anatomy, will greatly enhance the hunter's knowledge of his quarry. Larry Marchinton's detailed discussion of rutting behavior, especially signpost communication, adds a new dimension to our bow hunting adventures with rutting whitetails. The volume also contains the finest collection of deer photographs ever assembled in one book, together with an excellent chapter on photographing whitetails co-authored by Leonard Lee Rue III, the nation's leading wildlife photographer.

The volume ends on a very sober note with regard to the future of American deer hunting: "Hunters themselves are having to adapt to change, and the outlook for them signals more discipline, not less. As hunting regulations become more complex in certain areas to achieve more precise deer population management objectives, compliance will require a high level of cooperation and understanding. Hunters must never forget that hunting is a privilege that can be lost; it is not a right and cannot be taken for granted."

There are twelve million deer hunters in this country. If they bought and read this book en masse, the sport of American deer hunting would be ensured and the white-tailed deer would be better for it. If you want to own your own *library* on the

Some of the all-time giants under the category of popular science or natural history. *Robert Wegner photo*

white-tailed deer, buy this splendid, blue-chip deer book, for this comprehensive and attractive volume literally consists of a library in itself. The bibliography of over 2300 sources reads like a card catalogue of a major university library under the subject heading of *Odocoileus virginianus.* This incredible consolidation of information is a must for every deer enthusiast!

Under the category of popular science or natural history, I would list Seton's *Lives of Game Animals* (Doubleday, Doran & Company, 1929) as one of the classic books on the subject. Since I dealt with Seton in chapter three, I will only add here that this eight-volume work is extremely rare and seldom listed for sale in the out-of-print book market. Try to find it through the interlibrary loan system or a major university library.

In 1989 Outdoor Life Books published an updated and greatly expanded edition of Leonard Lee Rue III's *The Deer of North America.* The book greatly resembles Seton's study on deer, for Rue read all of Seton's work and patterned his own study of deer in the Seton tradition. I agree with Professor Dave Samuel of West Virginia University, who writes as follows: "It is amazing that a self-taught individual, utilizing field experience and independent research could write a book on deer that can be used by the professional wildlifer as well as the layman! I use Leonard Lee Rue III's *Deer of North America* as a textbook for my graduate classes in wildlife ecology." For a discussion of Rue, the man, and his contribution to our knowledge of deer, see chapter six in *Deer & Deer Hunting* (Stackpole Books, 1984) titled "An Affair With Deer," pages 62–76.

Under the category of popular science I would also add Dr. Frederick Weston's *Hunting the White-tailed Deer in Texas*

Two great anthologies of deer hunting stories, two excellent coffee table extravaganzas and two volumes containing detailed, annotated bibliographies of hundreds of books on deer and deer hunting. *Robert Wegner photo*

chapter two of this book, and William Monypeny Newsom's *White-tailed Deer* (Charles Schribner's Sons, 1926), discussed in chapter two of *Deer & Deer Hunting: Book 2* (Stackpole Books, 1987), stand as giants in this category. With regard to a detailed annotated bibliography of all books found in these various categories, I refer the reader to my annotated bibliographies (1838–1990) in my three-volume work, *Deer & Deer Hunting.*

In the early 1980s, Amwell Press of New Jersey produced two great anthologies of deer hunting stories. The first richly bound volume is titled *The Deer Book.* This custom-bound volume in bonded leather with ribbon place mark, contains many of the best articles on deer hunting ever assembled. Thanks to Lamar Underwood, the former Executive Editor of *Sports Afield,* we now have perhaps the best — and surely the largest — anthology of North American deer and deer hunting. If you enjoy the rich treasure of prose on deer hunting, you will enjoy this book. These great stories and reflective essays by Jack O'Connor, Ted Trueblood, Theodore Roosevelt, John Madson, Larry Koller, Archibald Rutledge, Gene Hill, Sigurd Olson — to mention but a few names — will allow your mind to slip into the enchanting world of deer hunting as you read in front of the fireplace. As Gene Hill observed, the book "fulfills all our needs for understanding ourselves as hunters and the deer as an extraordinary lure for us." This remarkable volume is a real blue-chip sporting book . . . with a blue-chip price of $60. Highly recommended for the connoisseur of deer hunting stories and articles.

The second great anthology of deer hunting stories is John Howard's *North American Big Game Hunting in the 1800's* (Amwell, 1982), which collects the classic

(privately printed, 1954), a rare book based on forty years of deer hunting experiences. In this volume Weston, a game biologist for the Texas Game and Fish Commission, provides us with a brilliant explanation of what makes a deer hunter tick, of the individualistic characteristics of deer hooves, and an excellent analysis of deer beans. This superbly illustrated volume remains extremely rare. I have seen it listed only once in all my years of collecting books.

Paul Brandreth's *Trails of Enchantment* (G. Howard Watt, 1930), discussed in big game hunting tales of such giants as Philip Tome, Meshach Browning, J. J. Audubon, William Elliott, Frank Forester, George Oliver Shields, Theodore Roosevelt, and many others. If you buy this jewel, you will never regret it, for this splendid memorial to an era that we will never see again provides the modern deer hunter with basic and essential reading. I consider it to be one of the finest books in my library. In reading through this anthology, one soon realizes that nothing changes. Here is how John Howard describes the timelessness of these men and their hunting adventures.

I did not know these men.
But they were alive once, you know.
They were real. They did live.
They laughed. They talked. They felt.
They knew joy. And I suppose sorrow.
And they loved. Most of them anyway.

They shimmer across the pages almost like
    ghosts.
We read of years long past and we can't really
    understand.
1800−1820−what do these numbers mean?
A time so long ago that it isn't really real.

But these men lived once.
They climbed the same hills we climb today.
They wondered at the same sky.
They dreamed the same dreams.
And they followed the same tracks,
Several generations removed,
That we follow today.

Nothing changes.
Only the actors in the drama. The plot
    remains the same.
The deer roams the hills. The man follows it.
Only the name of the man changes.
The deer changes too. But only the individual,
    not the species.

Nature cares not for the One, be it man or
    deer.
Nature cares only for the Whole. Only for the
    survival of the total.
Only that the Life Force continue.

It is Man who idolizes the individual. Nature is
    not concerned.

So the drama never ceases.
As it was−it is−and so shall it continue to
    be.

These men then are ourselves.
They did yesterday what we do today.
What our son's sons will do lo those many
    tomorrows.
Follow them then through their yesterdays.
    And follow them in awe.
For I tell you friend,
These are not the stories of strangers.
These are the stories of you.

When we read these classic stories, we get to know ourselves more intimately as hunters, and the sport of hunting is better for it. Only an enthusiastic, diehard hunter with a dedicated passion for collecting books on the natural history and hunting lore of American big game animals could have produced such a magnificent book. The physical appearance of the book itself is of a blue-chip nature: This limited edition of 1000 copies contains excellent line drawings by Irene Bowers, comes in a custom slipcase, and is custom-bound in bonded leather with a raised band on the spine, gilded page edges, moiré silk endpapers, and a gold ribbon.

The book needed to be done, and John Howard did a great job. Jim Rikhoff, founder of Amwell Press, says, "John Howard has put together a book that needed to be collected and he has done it well−a rare combination in this modern world of expediency and short-sighted goals." As hunters we owe John Howard a great debt. I give this one five stars.

I also give five stars to *The Bucks Camp Log, 1916–1928* (Willow Creek Press, 1974) for the diary category. Found in a dusty attic nearly half a century following its last entry, this deer camp diary reveals the true and ageless spirit of the deer hunt and includes exciting hunting adventures, tragedy, rare humor, woodsmanship, as well as philosophical reflections on the sport. The diary also contains poetry, and satirical extemporaneous dissertations by one camp member known as "The Stump Fire Ranger," who presumably wrote most of the diary. Here is one of my favorites.

IN MEMORIAM

The Bucks are dead; please call the hearse.
They long have been cold; it couldn't be
  worse.
Once they stood like strong and virile men,
But that is a story of what might have
  been.
They discarded their guns for lipstick red.
  Why wonder then that their souls have
  fled?
Once they were active and together were
  strong.
But with powder and puff they all went
  wrong.
Their interest and action gave way to
  words,
And they twittered away like sparrow
  birds.
They deserted the places and things they
  loved well,
To follow a trail that they thought more
  swell.
These poor old Bucks who once held sway,
With foible and fashion they fell by the
  way.
Like David of old they lay without heat,
Nor all of the virgins could e'en warm their
  feet.
So step gently, friends, and pull the
  shroud,
For in Life these Bucks were very proud.

This unique book also contains historic photographs and a detailed, hand-drawn map of their cherished bailiwick from the original Log, which preserves the authentic flavor of the camp located in the Blue Hills of northern Rusk County, Wisconsin. Publisher Tom Petrie sums it up best when he writes, "*The Bucks Camp Log* represents the spirit of the American deer camp,

be it located in the Blue Ridge Mountains, the bayous of the Mississippi or the north-woods of the upper Midwest, be it 1898, 1928, or today. The modern deer hunter will find much in this diary that might have been written just last deer season, and will recognize many of the personalities—with different names, from a different time—of his own hunting partners."

The group that hung out at the Bucks Camp ate baked beans and prune pie, and whether the bucks ran crooked or not they claimed they could "shoot the whiskers off a woodtick by way of pastime," as the Stump Fire Ranger put it.

This diary was originally found in the possessions of the late Glenn H. Williams, a member of the camp. When Petrie discovered the old, leather-bound ledger book, he immediately recognized its universal character and extraordinary spirit and captured that spirit in publishing this blue-chip deer book.

One does not usually find blue-chip deer books under the category of how-to books, but Larry Koller's *Shots at Whitetails,* published by one of America's finest publishing companies, Alfred A. Knopf, in 1948 and republished in 1970, is undoubtedly a deer hunting classic of wilderness lore that stands in the company of T. S. Van Dyke's *The Still-Hunter.* Shortly after its original publication it became the "deer hunter's Bible." I well remember the day I first found a copy of the 1970 edition in Harry Schwartz's Bookshop in Milwaukee, Wisconsin. Returning to Madison, I found myself spending three straight days with the book; reading, rereading, and underlining significant passages until the whole book appeared to be underlined and I could quote many passages by heart. Several years later I replaced that copy in my library and have not laid a pencil to the new one.

This instructive, practical, and invaluable book, written by one of the old masters from the Catskill Mountains, deals with all aspects of deer hunting—from the woodcraft of hunting to equipping the deer camp itself. Koller's keen interest in deer hunting, as with all his outdoor skills, came from a profound curiosity in natural history and the ways of the wild. As a result, *Shots at Whitetails* acquires a value far beyond its distinct practicality, making this all-inclusive guide a blue-chip deer book.

Koller grew up in the Catskill Mountains and hunted there from his boyhood days. Early in his life he became a guide, an excellent gunsmith, flytier, rodmaker, and bowyer who loved to bow hunt. He did it all and wrote eloquently about his experiences.

He spent a great deal of his time in the Oakland Valley section of the lower Catskills with a small group of old-time deer hunters at a comfortable camp on a mountainside above the Neversink River Gorge south of Monticello, New York. Members of the Eden Falls Rod and Hunt Club sometimes relied on a five-gallon demijohn of red Italian wine to beef up their morale, and in *Shots at Whitetails* we read about their delightful adventures.

Koller dedicated *Shots at Whitetails* to his wife, Alma, "whose great fund of tolerance and wisdom befits her admirably for existence with a hunter and angler." The book contains excellent line drawings by Bob Kuhn, and my favorite painting of a jumping buck by Kuhn graces the dust jacket. Jack O'Connor wrote the introduction to the second edition and made these comments.

"I read and enjoyed *Shots at Whitetails* some years before I ever met the late Larry Koller. I liked the book because it was practical, well organized, and clearly and interestingly written from a wealth of practical experience and a great deal of enthusiasm, intelligence, and common sense. All too many books about guns, shooting, and hunting are hasty jobs by people who are shy on experience and have little common sense. But this book was solid. As I read it I realized that this was the best book on deer hunting since Van Dyke's *The Still-Hunter.*"

Koller's early death of a heart attack while hunting in the Bavarian Alps at the age of fifty-six stunned the world of outdoor publishing. He was one of the most respected writers and editors in the outdoor field. He wrote in a friendly and easy style with wit, humor, and sincerity. He loved a humorous tale and was fond of a drink. When he died the *New York Times* referred to him as "a famous outdoor writer who can shoot as well as he can write and write as well as he can shoot." *Shots at Whitetails* is unfortunately out of print.

In the category of coffee table extravaganzas we find two exquisite volumes: *Erwin Bauer's Deer In Their World* (Outdoor Life Books, 1983) and *Whitetail Country* (Willow Creek Press, 1988) by Daniel J. Cox and John J. Ozoga. *Erwin Bauer's Deer In Their World* is a beautiful book filled with spectacular photos of deer, plus sound information on capturing them with a camera. Written by a master photographer, the book also contains an interesting discussion on using deer decoys.

One gripping photograph follows another in *Whitetail Country,* a photographic odyssey of a year in the life of the whitetail. The perceptive text is written by one of this country's finest deer researchers, John J. Ozoga. In it Ozoga raises one very important question, a question that needs to be answered: Does intensive trophy hunting (taking the very best, prime specimens) seriously affect the genetic make-up of white-tailed deer herds? In addressing the question, Ozoga writes as follows.

"Whether continuous intensive cropping of the best whitetail specimens contributes to serious social disruption and genetic degradation and is eventually detrimental to the healthful existence of whitetails, as some investigators suggest, has not been demonstrated to the satisfaction of most wildlife managers."

This blue-chip deer book goes well beyond the typical lavish coffee table book. In his review of the book for *Deer & Deer Hunting* magazine, historian James Casada notes that "words do not suffice to convey this work's visual impact. . . . A true hunter strives to be one with his prey. *Whitetail Country* comes about as close to succeeding as any book I know. That is its ultimate achievement and a testament to its importance."

More books and magazine articles have been written about deer and deer hunting than all other hunting activities combined. One wonders why the deer hunting experience brings out the emotional side of the hunter. Why the deer woods and the whitetail etch themselves so indelibly into our hearts and minds. Read these blue-chip deer books for the answer, and you will discover that deer hunting, like trout fishing, tends to turn men into boys and problems into solutions.

Since a good number of these blue-chip deer books are out of print, haunt the used books stores and get your name on the mailing lists of the out-of-print booksellers. (See the Appendix.) Devour their catalogs; hunt your books from home by ordering them through the mail. Collecting books in the out-of-print market is where the action is. These out-of-print booksellers will also conduct special searches for specific titles. Collecting books on deer and deer hunting can be compared to hunting deer: It takes the patience of the still-hunter and the endurance (financially) of the stand hunter. Bagging a mint copy with a dust jacket of *Shots at Whitetails* or *Producing Quality Whitetails* can be just as exciting as taking a trophy 10-pointer. Here is how outdoor book collector Bryan R. Johnson describes hunting the trophy books in an article entitled "Collecting the Classics," published in the October 1986 issue of *Sports Afield*.

"It's a rare man, indeed, whose love of books hasn't led him to want to own them, to build a collection of books that are old friends. For some, any copy will do as long as it holds together while being read. Others delve deeper and become collectors, hunting the trophies that live on shelves."

Chapter 13

The American Deer Camp

Whether or not I really want to kill the buck, I am not yet willing to forego the company of men who hunt.
— James Kilgo, *Deep Enough for Ivorybills,* 1988

Each fall twelve and one half million white-tailed deer hunters take to the woods for their annual pilgrimage to that sacred place in the heart of deer country we call "deer camp," in pursuit of slightly more than twenty million whitetails. Each year they kill approximately two million whitetails, many of them from remote deer camps in the bush. While I have never seen any actual statistics on the number of deer camps, I suspect that the number runs into the hundreds of thousands nationwide.

Most die-hard buck hunters, as James Kilgo points out in his classic book on deer hunting, seem reluctant to forgo the company of men who hunt. In fact, the American deer hunter, like the white-tailed deer, maintains a very strong fidelity to a core area, to a very special place, a magical and mystical place, where the hunter shares the company of others who hunt. The place

might be called the Messinger Creek Camp, The Deer Pasture, the T. Huntington Abbot Rod & Gun Club, or Camp 17, but regardless of its name, deer hunters return to this special place each year and they maintain a very deep psychological commitment to their "briar patch."

Studies in various states indicate that 70 percent of all deer hunters surveyed spent the opening day of deer season in the same place for the past five years. In a study of Michigan deer hunters, researchers learned that even in areas where the buck kill dropped to eight bucks per square mile and where hunters reported a very low level of enjoyment, 70 percent of the hunters returned to the same area the following year. In surveying 1000 New York deer hunters in 1988, human dimensions researchers Daniel Decker and Nancy Connelly of Cornell University concluded that this strong fidelity to a core area, to a special deer camp, over time prevents deer managers from promoting or effecting shifts in hunting pressure from one area to another. This strong psychological commitment to one particular place often becomes a major obstacle for initiating any change in deer hunting regulations.

Contrary to some views, the deer hunter is not a solitary figure. Most deer hunters hunt in a group. According to rural sociologist Tom Heberlein, "the deer camp is an enduring sociological characteristic of gun deer hunting. Deer hunters think of themselves as a member of a hunting party rather than solely as an individual. They share in the successes and failures of their cohorts."

In his survey of Wisconsin deer hunters, Heberlein reached the conclusion that deer hunters are unique in terms of *not* having other activities that serve as an active substitute for deer hunting: Sixty percent of those he surveyed indicated that they had *few* or *no* substitutes for the deer-hunting experience. A partial explanation for this strong commitment, Heberlein suggests, "may be due to their social environment, for deer hunting is a family-oriented activity that is passed from generation to generation with certain aspects of the hunt centering on social companionship and camaraderie. For the deer hunter, this social network extends beyond the field to everyday life, as more than 65 percent said that most or all of their friends also hunt deer."

In his study of white-tailed deer hunters in Maryland and Virginia, researcher James Kennedy also learned that few deer hunters hunt alone. He found that 73 percent of the deer hunters he surveyed preferred to hunt with friends in an area with only a 10 percent chance of killing a deer rather than to hunt alone in an area with a 50 percent chance of killing a deer. Deer hunters from urban areas, in particular, showed a distinct tendency to hunt in groups.

Indeed, deer hunting in many instances becomes a social event. Mention the very name of the deer camp, whether it be Jake's Rangers, The Horn Hunters, The Sawyer Swampers, Buckshot Inc., Camp 17, The Homestead, The Backtrackers, The Adirondack Neck Shot Club, The Catskill Trophy Killers, The Deer Pasture, or The Mosquito Lake Culture Club, and the respective members of that camp begin to pack their hunting bags and anticipate hitting the road.

While the mystique of the deer camp may remain an enigma to many hunting widows, the deer hunter knows why he prefers to be at "The Deer Pasture," as deer hunter Rick Bass calls it, rather than anywhere else in the world when the rutting moon rises in the eastern sky, for there only does he taste the real rewards of the deer-camp experience: freedom, solitude, camaraderie, ritual, and tradition.

How important is the deer-camp tradition for the white-tailed deer hunter? Ask Texas deer hunter Rick Bass. He will tell you, "On an opening-day Gillespie County whitetail-hunt, tradition is as important as anything, perhaps even more important than the deer. . . . I firmly believe that my crowd — and they are a bunch of deer hunting sons-of-guns — would hold opening day deer camp in the J. C. Penney's parking lot if that's what it took to get us all together."

For more than a half century, the Bass bunch, a close-knit group of quiet, conservative folks, has maintained a 956-acre deer hunting lease in the Texas Hill Country of Gillespie County. They call their camp "The Deer Pasture." There, in its rustic beauty, in the land of ravines and hollows, they hunt such places as "Buck Hill," "The Water Gap," and "Camp Creek." After making only three trips to The Deer Pasture, Rick Bass and his cousin Randy already made plans for the 100th anniversary of this family tradition. How important is deer camp for Rick Bass? In his marvelous book on the deer-camp tradition entitled *The Deer Pasture* (1985), the hunter explains,

"Things, like lives, take on significance in deer hunting country, perhaps because they are lived so squarely and simply, and they are stronger and more basic than lives in the city, and they stand the eroding tests of time better. Things, memories included, last longer in deer hunting country."

For Bass, The Deer Pasture takes on the flavor of the pioneer days, of arrowheads and wagon wheels. He defines deer camp life as "a closed system—oblivious to blunder, immune to disharmony." But like most well-managed deer camps, The Deer Pasture adheres to a system of rules and regulations. Bass' Rule Of The Deer Pasture No. 4 reads as follows: "No yelling at another member of one's family is allowed while in camp. Absolutely none. No matter what." I particularly like the camp's rule against shooting at running deer. "I understand that's not the way it's done in some places," Bass admits, "but then we don't lose many deer, either. Not many at all. Got to brag, even: like four in forty-nine years. One per hunter's career. The rule works."

Most deer camps boast about some particular viands or other and the Bass camp is no exception in this regard. Bass's Wonder Biscuits represent their camp-house specialty. According to Bass, they contain a super amount of energy: "Each biscuit has about 300 calories and fifteen grams of protein. It's all there—vitamins A, C, B1, B2, B6, B12, niacin, calcium, iron, phos-

phorous, magnesium, zinc, copper—the deer don't have a chance." During the closing days of the deer season, the Bass boys frequently use them for poker chips at the card table while giving the deer more of a chance.

Pranks in the deer woods frequently occur amongst the Bass family. One foggy evening, unbeknownst to Granddaddy Bass, Cousin Randy built a trophy buck to end all trophies out of plywood. He painted it gray and wired a set of antlers with thirty-two points to the head. When the fog gradually lifted the following morning, Granddaddy Bass spotted it on the other side of the meadow. Rick tells us what happened in *The Deer Pasture*.

"Granddaddy got very excited. He adjusted his glasses, eased up on his blind, and fired twenty-four times.

"You could hear the gunshots all over The Deer Pasture, but also you could hear cousin Randy's hoots of laughter, a good half-mile away, all the way over on the backside of Buck Hill."

Rick Bass, Cousin Randy, and Old Granddaddy would surely agree that deer camp provides much for mankind. Actually, the cure for many of humanity's ills may be found in these humble settings. As a matter of fact, Bass insists that we "catch the buzz-laughter in a bottle, take it back to the cities, and sprinkle it from door to door."

Like many deer hunters, Rick Bass almost consumes himself with the atmosphere of The Deer Pasture. When he finds himself back in the world of plastic-fantastic, he plants cedar trees outside his office window so he can smell The Deer Pasture. In his desk drawer, he keeps a map of his cherished deer hunting turf—the Texas Hill Country, sometimes called the deer hunting capital of the world. Nowhere in the literature on deer and deer hunting have I ever encountered a young man's greater love for a special piece of deer hunting turf.

Each November when the hickories drop their leaves in the creeks and carpet the rocky soil between the oaks and the granite outcroppings, the Bass men return to The Deer Pasture to relive the family tradition of hunting white-tailed deer, to retell campfire tales, to renew family ties, and to recharge their spiritual energies. There in the Texas Hill Country, the Bass family establishes as close a relationship as can exist between man and nature in the modern world. Some of the more free-spirited members of this group will even quit their jobs, if need be, or schedule their marriages at another time to be able to hear the happy hoots of the Bass camp and to pursue big bucks in the Texas Hill Country.

Each deer camp needs a monster buck of mythic proportions to terrorize the dream world of the hunters. Sometimes these "unhuntable" creatures receive names such as Old Mossy Horns, The Swamp Buck, Old Sludge Foot, The Rocking Chair Buck, or just plain Old Charlie. These shadowy monsters continue to haunt the deer camps of this land from opening day to the end of the season.

Rick Bass chased one for two years before concluding that the animal was "unhaveable." Despite the gunfire, they're always back next year. The eternal recurring motif of the American deer camp sounds something like this, "Charlie's still here! Saw his tracks on the ridge road."

Many deer camps actually exist, if for no other reason, for hunters to establish a one-to-one relationship with a trophy buck. For more than forty years, Lew Dietz, a well-known New England novelist, traveled impassable, abandoned logging roads along the Maine-Canadian border to reach a backwoods deer camp to pursue Old Charlie, the mythic buck everyone talked about in his camp. Old Charlie, however, became more of a friend than a quarry for Lew Dietz, an obligatory myth that all of the hunters in his deer camp savored and perpetuated.

For men who repeatedly hunt the same territory, Dietz explains, "there is always a Charlie, a big and wise buck, a patriarch that proves too smart for mere men." The essence of the deer camp often centers on hunting Old Charlie with men in the wilderness. Like many hunters, Dietz went to deer camp not only in pursuit of Old Charlie, but for a healing respite as well.

"I find my interludes in the Big Woods restorative and cleansing. It is a form of escape, perhaps. We live in a neurotic time, beset by exploiters, wasters, and plunderers. A few brief days with men at ease with the wilderness and at peace with themselves is a healing respite."

Dietz never suggested that Old Charlie reigned supreme as the most intellectual animal in the wilderness, but only that Old Charlie tended to be smarter than Lew Dietz when it counted. Old Charlie didn't care much about deer-kill statistics, but he did seem interested in making Dietz feel like a second-class hunter in the woods.

Lew Dietz missed his chance at Old Charlie one day when he turned to watch a partridge drop into a spruce thicket behind him. When he turned around again to watch the deer trail he was covering, he saw Old Charlie staring at him at point-blank range. Before Dietz could even raise his rifle, the buck took one horrendous leap, "and it was good-bye Charlie!"

But did Dietz and his coterie really want to kill Old Charlie? In an essay entitled "Whitetail Challenge" published in *Yankee Magazine,* Dietz explains:

"For all of us Charlie would be there so long as that piece of wilderness we shared with him remained inviolate. To preserve the myth of his immortality was an article of faith, a putting off of the day when the last of wildness would be civilized off the face of the earth."

Many deer hunters find just as much joy in coming out of the cold deer woods to a warm fireplace, easing out of their hunting boots with the likely prospect of soothing whiskey and branch water, as hanging Old Charlie on the meat pole. But that attitude

only comes with hunting maturity, with developing an appreciation and understanding of the many things that constitute the total deer camp experience.

All deer camps, whether the ficticious Buck Busters Hunting Club trying to figure out the antics and sly movements of Old Sludge Foot or Dietz' gang in Maine trying to determine how Old Charlie so successfully rides the thermals, need that mythic buck to add spice and flavor to deer camp camaraderie, to deer hunting yarns and lore.

Billy Claypoole (Hilburn Hillestad) and Jim Kilgo agree that it's not the size of the rack that counts, but the quality of the hunt. *Jim Kilgo photo*

Members of the T. Huntington Abbot Rod & Gun Club. *Jim Kilgo photo*

Nowhere in deer country do we find a finer example of deer camp camaraderie than at the long pine table of the T. Huntington Abbot Rod and Gun Club at Groton, a plantation in the bottomlands of the Great Pee Dee River in South Carolina, where deer hunters assemble to participate in what Jim Kilgo calls "the songfest." A proper songfest consists of three parts, according to Kilgo. The hunt itself consti-

tutes part one, the ultimate experience — chasing bucks through the bottomlands of the Great Pee Dee River provides occasion for the second part: the singing about it, telling others about what happened. Part three takes place at the pine table with the sweet taste of venison, flickering firelight, and sourmash whiskey.

The members of the deer hunting club, founded in 1975, hold a songfest every

The cabin of the T. Huntington Abbot Rod & Gun Club at the Groton Plantation in South Carolina. *Jim Kilgo photo*

night during the deer hunting season. After tramping the bottomlands all day, the members greatly anticipate returning to camp to hear the inevitable remark, "Well. Tell me about it!" At these post-hunt celebrations the hunter reenacts the events of the day before an audience of men who care and understand. At this deer hunting club the members expect the hunters to behave themselves as well in the telling of the story as in the actual deer hunt itself.

"The songfest, done well," Jim Kilgo, writer, painter, deer hunter, and professor of English, insists, "is at once an act of contrition and celebration, a way of coming to terms with the blood one has spilled and an occasion for rejoicing in the opportunity to spill it." At Groton, they tell the story not for the glory of the deer hunter, but in tribute to the deer. When a hunter kills a deer—buck, doe, or fawn—the animal deserves the honor of a story, even if the story entails the hunter admitting some failure or mistake on his part. Members of the club remain critical of hunters who refuse to share the details of a successful hunt. They compare keeping silent about killing a buck to burying the animal in the woods.

The men who hunt at Groton believe that it's not the size of the rack that matters, but the quality of the hunt. When the hunter shoots his first deer, others present bathe the beginning hunter's face with the animal's blood as a rite of passage, believing with the primitive hunters that if the hunter kills the deer in the right spirit, the animal will live again to confront the hunter at someplace in the future. When a hunter misses a buck, others cut off a piece of his shirttail. And when a hunter unfortunately makes a bad shot, he reveals the whole dilemma in all its agonizing detail.

Here's how deer hunter Jim Kilgo revealed his story about the blood trail of a wounded buck to his friend and club member Billy Claypoole in *Deep Enough for Ivorybills* (1988).

"Billy, he had a tremendous rack. It was dark and heavy at the base, and I could see all those little knobby gnarls, and the tines were real high and looked like polished ivory.

"He took two steps forward, not toward me but not away from me either, and stopped with his head behind this little forked tree. I didn't think he could see me so I brought my rifle around about three-quarters, and then I saw that his head was *between* the forks and he was looking straight at me.

"I froze and he did a complete turn around; then he took two or three steps. It happened so fast. I had an impression of that large, wild eye passing in front of me, and then he just stopped and stood still, and I had him in the scope, just a blur of hair, and I knew he was mine. It began to feel like it was ordained or something. I know this sounds strange, but I had the feeling he was being given to me.

"When I shot he leapt straight up and turned completely around, almost like he was dancing against the sun in the blast of the rifle, and then he was gone.

"I had a glimpse of him barreling away through the trees, sort of listing to one side, and that was it. I kept telling myself, *Don't panic. Just sit down and smoke a cigarette.* He's not going far. But that didn't work. I knew I'd made a bad shot.

". . . I found some hair. Just a pinch. It was white. That's the sickest feeling I've ever had. I didn't see any way I could have missed that deer. Not at that range. Still don't. Anyway, I started out after him, and in about 100 yards I found blood. Once he started he really painted the ground. For the next fifty yards it looked like somebody had sloshed a bucket of red all over the leaves.

"You know that strange feeling you get when you're following a blood trail? You feel sick because you've made a bad shot and you think you've lost the deer, but on the other hand the blood proves that the deer has actually been at that very spot. I mean, it's like you can't believe the buck was really true, but the blood is definitely true. The way it's splattered on the leaves. And you're thinking that no matter where he goes he's leaking this vitality and all you have to do is follow it far enough and there he'll be. I was so confident for awhile there that I kept looking up, expecting every second to see him, to see his white belly shining in the sun, and then the blood began to run out and I started getting scared.

"He had run down that open flat maybe 300 yards, then swung hard toward the river through an opening in the cane. The trail was still fairly easy to follow there when he turned to the west, so I stopped and smoked a cigarette. Told myself not to push him and get his adrenaline pumping again, but I guess I really wanted the comfort of the blood while it was still strong.

"Beyond that point it just stopped. I mean, like all of a sudden. I spent thirty minutes on my hands and knees. Finally found one little drop and it was no more than a daub, like a smear of lipstick on a leaf. I could tell from where it was that the buck had gone into a thicket, so I followed him in and came on an opening like a little room in the cane. Soon as I stepped into it I saw a wet place in the leaves. I knelt and touched it and my fingerprints came away red. The ground was soaked, Billy, the leaves all matted together. I figured he must have stood there like he saw me coming. But that was it. I never found another sign of him — no blood, no tracks, nothing."

The men who deer hunt at Groton frequently engage in tailgate-philosophizing about everything from blood trails to the ultimate meaning of this blood sport. It is not uncommon for two wildlife biologists, a professor of English, and a lawyer all dressed in camouflage to discuss those special moments of intense awareness while hunting that ultimately lead men to believe in their own senses again. Or to debate among themselves whether the hunter's spirit ensures the rebirth of the animal. How do we explain that moment that ultimately leads to death, consumption, and rebirth as energy in a new form, Billy Claypoole, Walter Cabin, and Charlie Creedmore ask themselves? Should we challenge the validity of the basic myth we live by, which is a kind of covenant between man and the whitetail in which the animal gives its life willingly, with the understanding that man will not only preserve the species, but that the animal's life will transcend its physical entity and return to the spiritual world through some kind of ritual restoration?

During the years that Kilgo has hunted at Groton, several members of the club changed professions; one died, the red-faced Jack Bass, gospel singer and teller of crude tales; seven members got divorced; and three dropped out of the club. "But the Savannah River Swamp remains the same," Kilgo writes in *Deep Enough For*

Ivorybills, "observing the changing light from one season to the next, year after year." As each season ends, Kilgo wonders whether he will return to Groton again next year. But, like Lew Dietz and Rick Bass, he always does, if for no other reason than to stand by the fire with his comrades Billy Claypoole, Walter Cabin, and Charlie Creedmore and to talk about shooting white-tailed bucks. Or as he so eloquently admits, "to watch the reluctant summer give way to autumn and to smell once more the stirring musk of a rutting buck."

The evening storytelling ritual as hunters come in from the field at this private deer hunting club in the Low Country repeats itself all across America — whether it occurs in Hampton County, South Carolina, or in the land of Hiawatha. Fortunately, many deer hunters take the time to document these evening storytelling rituals in their deer camp diaries, histories, and privately printed publications. In one such publication, *Deer Trails and Camp Tales* (1983), "Pete" Mer-

Pete Merrill believed that the American deer camp has no business being new. This was Pete's Messinger Creek Camp — a real jewel of prefabrication, 1942. *Bernice Merrill photo*

Pete Merrill, the sage of the Messinger Creek deer camp, who hunted in the Deer Lake area in the Upper Peninsula of Michigan for more than thirty-five years, 1946. *Bernice Merrill photo*

rill, who loved to hunt deer at his Messinger Creek Camp in the Deer Lake area of Michigan's Upper Peninsula, sums up the essence of deer camp as mostly just a lot of talk:

First you take a pound of spoof
Then stir in a fillet of hoof,
Then add a cup of old swamp water,
buck lure and a pinch of laughter.
A bit of hair, an empty shell,
A piece of horn mixes well.
Some apples and a big salt block,
But mostly just a lot of talk.

Just a lot of talk, indeed. The whole Merrill family got involved in his annual pilgrimage to the Messinger Creek Camp.

At this camp north of Amasa, Michigan, four of the "shot-n-beer boys" have gathered to hunt deer for more than thirty-three years. Deer camp for the Merrill family and the other families involved took on the significance of birthdays, Christmas, and the Fourth of July; they talked about deer camp throughout the year.

Their camp, located seven miles from any well-traveled road, first consisted of an old office building of a logging camp built from scrap lumber and black tar paper. In its one-room structure stood a massive stove that measured four feet in length, twenty-three inches wide, and twenty inches high, with four two-foot legs supporting it above the floor. This "super

"These bucks were shot in the woods — not in camp!" *Bernice Merrill photo*

heater" often required two part-time helpers working throughout the night to keep the fire burning and the temperature above 40°F.

At this old logger's shack, Pete Merrill, a welder on a maintenance crew in a papermill; Art Johnson, his brother-in-law; Carl Erickson, a lumber businessman; and Ed Faver, another blue-collar worker, assembled each year to hunt deer, tell stories, play smear, and drink Ten High.

On one of their October trips to the camp for pre-season scouting and partridge hunting, they arrived at their old campsite well after dark. Pete pulled into

the regular parking spot as usual and shut the engine off. All of them felt something was wrong as they stared into the eerie darkness. Ed grabbed a flashlight and started to shine the area.

"Where is the camp?" he asked Pete, suggesting that Pete parked in the wrong spot.

But Pete had parked in the right spot all right. When the light finally hit the place where the old shack stood, all four hunters stared at the only thing left of the first Messinger Creek Camp: a few rotted floor joists and some well-decayed pieces of flooring. Someone apparently needed a stove and some lumber. While Pete does not tell us much about the construction of the next Messinger Creek Camp, his wife Bernice does:

"We think that Pete, Art, Carl, and Ed were the inventors of the first prefabricated building, because they built this camp in sections in Menominee, Michigan, and hauled it up to Amasa where they put it together. There must have been a rule that nothing new was to go into the construction of this gem, as they all followed that rule to the letter. Whatever building material someone had discarded, they would use. We wonder how it ever survived one good windstorm."

Pete Merrill and his boys believed that a deer camp should not be new, for anything new lacks tradition.

When their first "can" filled to capacity, instead of digging new holes and moving it, they tried dynamite to do a nice quick job, so that they could get back to the more serious and delightful job of hunting. Not being demolition experts, they used five sticks of dynamite to accomplish their purpose. After Pete lit the fuse, a large fireball reflected itself off Messinger Creek. Pete documents the memorable event that some of us have threatened to do, but failed to accomplish in his *Deer Trails and Camp Tales.*

"Suddenly, all hell broke loose! A loud bang and we saw our old friend, the two-holer, disintegrate in midair. The roof disappeared completely, and the west wall and seats (one I had upholstered for myself) were last seen heading out over the swamp with a speed faster than sound. The back wall disappeared into the spruce trees and the east wall, what was left of it, landed in the driveway; the front flew halfway to camp and landed in the path we used going to and from our old, now departed. Then it started to rain a combination of crap, pages from Montgomery Ward's catalog, more crap, and pages from Sears and Roebuck's catalog. In fact, this storm continued for a long five minutes. The pages from the women's lingerie landed on the roof over the sleeping quarters, the women's ready-to-wear covered the roof over the sink, and the hardware department covered the roof over the kitchen table. Art and Carl had taken off for parts unknown and needless to say, Ed lost his silly grin."

These deer camp boys were now ready to build a new outhouse. After a few "nips" to calm their nerves, they began to draw up the blueprints for their new two-holer. They never finished this prime project to anyone's satisfaction because they decided to wait for someone to throw away a used door.

To this humble, backwoods abode, the same old gang headed each year to shoot bucks. And they shot a good number of them each year. Like the Bass men and Lew Dietz and his boys, they too chased Old Charlie, but in their camp they called him "The Blue Buck," because his hide seemed to blend to a dark blue. They referred to The Blue Buck as the smartest deer that any of them ever hunted. Like Dietz and his gang, they never did catch up with the Old Boy.

The Messinger Creek Camp enjoyed good homemade cooking, and after supper they would settle down around the fire to see who could be the biggest liar. "I will always remember how the Old Man said his gun jammed when two bucks walked past single file, not twenty feet away," a visiting deer hunter from Wisconsin recalled one night. "And how we rationed his grog until he promised not to tell tales like that again."

At the smear table each night, Ed and Pete, the factory workers, opposed Art and Carl, the so-called capitalists who owned their own businesses. Before the smear game ended, deer hunters from other camps wandered in; sometimes bringing a case of beer and a quart of Ten High. As the game wore on, Norb Brenner, a mail carrier from Lansing, Michigan, usually played his guitar and strains of "The Wabash Cannon Ball" drifted over the landscape. As they drained the Ten High, they began to sing "My Wild Irish Rose." Like many bathroom baritones, Old Pete admitted that he couldn't carry a tune in his lunch bucket, but he gave it a whale of a time nonetheless.

The demise of this deer camp occurred in the early 1970s as a result of arthritis and old age. After Art Johnson and Ed Faber passed on and Carl Erickson retired, Old Pete realized he was one of a vanishing breed. On his last trip to the Messinger Creek Camp to hunt partridge, Pete felt the full impact of going alone to deer camp. When he turned onto Deer Lake Road, it was dark and raining hard. His mind reflected back to the many years when he made this same trip with Art, Ed, and Carl—the nucleus of the camp.

When he reached the shack, it seemed cold. Only memories of the good old days of deer hunting in the Deer Lake area remained. After a restless night of sleep, he made an attempt to hunt partridge, but the effort failed; his mind continued to return to the early days of the deer hunting camp. His interest in partridge hunting vanished. Instead, he decided to walk to Art Johnson's deer stand. As he stood there motionlessly, he could hear Carl, Art, and Ed singing "The Wabash Cannon Ball." He returned to camp, packed his meager belongings into his Scout and left Messinger Camp for the last time.

Yes, Pete, wherever you are, having to forego the company of men who hunt is difficult. As more deer hunters reach their forties and think more about why they hunt deer, many of us realize that it's really the companionship of a few good old trusted buddies in the outdoor setting. Even the late Edward Abbey agreed that the essence of deer camp consists of being able to flee the crowds and concrete and live beyond civilization, if only for a few days.

Judy Stone, Pete Merrill's daughter, best explains what deer camp meant for her father and what deer camp means to all of us: "Dad loved this place so much. It was a haven for men to meet one another, form new and lasting friendships, exchange tales of experiences in this beautiful and vast wilderness and to eat good food, drink homemade brew, and know they were, for

Mer Speltz was the founder and keeper of the records of Camp 17 Inc., located in Pine County, Minnesota. In 1984 he wrote *Camp 17,* an excellent, privately published history of this deer camp. *Tom Speltz photo*

a couple of weeks every year away from the maddening crowd and having the time of their lives. How satisfying it was to know that my hard-working dedicated father had, indeed, found his Shangri-la."

Finding his Shangri-la in the heart of deer country is exactly what Merlin Speltz, a Minnesota deer hunter, set out to do in December 1956. Because of the trespass law and problems with access to good deer hunting land, "Mer," his brother Tom, and a friend, John Balint, bought Section 17, Township 44, Range 21, in Pine County, Minnesota. As a result, each of his clan, Speltz tells us, "can walk out of camp, rifle in hand, independent of the others with access to 600 acres so that he can hunt his own style, at his own pace, and for any period of time. And where no man can tell you to get off of his property!"

After forming a non-profit corporation for deer hunting purposes, they named their camp after the section number. In May 1957, Camp 17 purchased an eight- by fourteen-foot shack in North St. Paul and hauled it to the section. In October of that year, they added a fourteen- by sixteen-foot platform for a large tent which they used for sleeping.

During the first two years of this deer camp's existence, Mer spent most of his weekends from fall through spring mapping the woods, selecting stand sites, and developing trails. In the spring of 1958 and 1959 they planted 5000 jack pine and spruce seedlings in an attempt to convert eighty acres east of their camp into a yarding area for deer.

Better housing followed in the fall of 1961, when members of the camp moved a boxcar on a flatbed trailer to the camp site. They then attached the shack to the car and added a porch. As the membership increased to eighteen deer hunters, the sec-

A familiar landmark — the official outdoor crapper at Camp 17. *Tom Speltz photo*

ond generation members gradually completed the expansion of the camp's housing and parking facilities; in addition they built roads, dams, ponds, and improved the deer habitat in the area. They originally paid $1 per acre for Section 17. Today the real estate taxes exceed the original price by 71 percent.

During the first twenty-six years of the camp's history, Mer never missed a deer season. He even went to Camp 17 for three weeks when the Minnesota DNR closed the season in 1971. During his stay at deer camp, Mer kept very detailed records of the camp's activities and concludes that the patient hunter who remains on his stand

Members of Camp 17, Inc. *Tom Speltz photo*

has the best opportunity to fill his tag. Mer summarizes the statistics for the first eighty-four deer shot at Camp 17:

75 percent of all deer were taken on opening weekend.

76 percent of all bucks were taken on opening weekend.

72 percent of deer shot on opening day were bucks!

71 percent of all deer taken were shot in the morning.

70 percent of all deer were shot from stands while trail watching.

15 percent of all deer shot were driven.

15 percent of all deer shot were jumped.

As the keeper of the records, Mer Speltz proudly notes that his gang maintains a 93 percent success ratio. As of 1984, Camp 17 reports wounding and not recovering only six deer. Mer's twenty-eight years of recording camp events culminates in his privately published history of the camp titled *Camp 17* (1984). In this detailed account of deer camp life, he documents many lesser notations, everything from the "Chicken-Shit Ridge" issue to bucks sniffing the rifle barrel of Tommy Speltz, to the "hearing of Joe Stein rip off a real doozy of a fart on October 19, 1967 at 3:17 A.M."

But in this privately printed document, Mer also records his own attitude about Camp 17 and deer camp life in general. In his opinion, deer camp provides an opportunity to get away from everyday routine and to observe the wonder of wildlife in the stillness and quiet of the deer forest.

In his beautiful prologue, "The Silence," Mer eloquently describes the many things that mean so much to the deer hunter: the endless line of headlights in the rear mirror all heading toward deer country, the pungent aroma of a snapping wood fire, cleaning up mice berries from the table, stepping out into the black silence of the still woods encircling the camp, dozing off to the scampering sounds of field mice as they resume their normal activities, seeing the flickering lights of your companions disappear into the endless black void of the opening morning, and finally being alone in the dark silence of your selected stand site as you wait for the sunrise. There you learn to love the silent solitude of the winter woods and the woodsmoke as it drifts straight up from the old brick chimney of the deer shack.

"It is this total silence," Mer writes, "that stirs your very soul with a deep sense of eerie loneliness. The absolute stillness brings back vivid memories of past hunts, and you fully realize that it is this very solitude that keys your anticipation and lures you back year after year."

Like Pete Merrill, Mer Speltz went back year after year until health problems intervened. The opening day of each deer season for such deer hunters as Mer Speltz,

Rick Bass, Pete Merrill, and Lew Dietz is a significant calendar event that marks the passing of time. Mer never forgot the freedom and solitude of those early morning hours of the predawn darkness.

"Before your ever-staring eyes the leafless timber slowly distinguishes itself from the pre-dawn darkness. You watch as your frosted breath dissipates in the cold silence, and you wait. The expectations of having a ghost-like buck suddenly materialize before your very eyes is extremely acute during this seemingly timeless period as daybreak gradually penetrates the depth of the silent forest. You listen intently for any interruption of that crisp silence with strained concentration. Then the sudden explosion of a rifle report not too distant reverberates through the still timber and you instinctively grip your cold rifle just a little bit tighter and all your senses are keyed to full alert! There's a buck in the neighborhood!"

As access problems continue to plague the American deer hunter and as the deer hunting population in this country continues to grow older, more and more deer hunters buy or lease larger blocks of land and organize deer hunting clubs like Camp 17. Like Mer Speltz, an ever-increasing number of us prefer the beaver lodges of the backwoods to our cracker box houses in suburbia. Indeed, the appeal of the deer hunting club continues to grow with each passing deer season and seems to represent the wave of the future. It's not surprising that the main theme of the 1989 Southeast Deer Study Group Meeting revolved around managing deer on private deer hunting clubs.

Many of these deer camps, like Camp 17, evolve from small, family-oriented tent camps to highly-organized, non-profit corporations set up for the exclusive purpose of hunting deer. In South Carolina, for example, the average deer hunting club controls approximately 1500 acres of land with twenty-five members participating in camp activities. While the actual sizes of these clubs greatly vary, deer hunter Chapman Milling defines the "ideal club" in his classic text on the deer hunting club, *Buckshot and Hounds* (1967). "A good working rule is not more than one member per 100 acres of land. Personally, I feel that the ideal club would be one of between fifteen and twenty members deer hunting on a tract of ground 3000 acres or more." Fifteen hunters on 3000 acres, or one hunter per 200 acres, should provide a quality deer hunt.

The state of Georgia now registers more than 6000 deer hunting clubs. The members of many of these clubs want quality deer hunting experiences and quality deer management. Some of these clubs maintain well-defined organizational structures in which the members become actively involved in censusing deer populations, creating food plots and supplemental feeding stations, and keeping detailed records of all deer killed—that is, dressed body weight, age, antler measurements, and whether the does were producing milk when shot. Some professional deer biologists in the Southeast view these hunting clubs as viable management units. In East Texas, more than 2000 deer hunting clubs already form the basis for deer management units.

Some of these modern-day deer camps contain everything from Aaron Moen's Deer CAMP population model to Jim Applegate's "Oh, My Deer!" and the latest issue of *Deer & Deer Hunting;* everything from weathervanes, weather band radios, barometers, anemometers, logbooks, aerial and topographical maps, soil survey maps, aging charts, jawbone spreaders, and liability insurance policies to frayed Xerox copies of William D. Harper's "Articles of Partnership for The Deer Shack." The deer don't have a chance, as Rick Bass once concluded with regard to Bass's Wonder Biscuits.

Four scientific studies currently exist on the social and psychological aspects of deer camps and deer hunting clubs. The findings of these research studies tell us a great deal about ourselves. In the first of these scientific studies, "The Sociology of Deer Hunting in Two Pennsylvania Counties" (1953), rural sociologist William Lefes studied the membership status of deer hunting clubs in Potter and Monroe counties, the traditional deer hunting meccas of that state, and found that slightly more than 50 percent of the deer hunters he surveyed held memberships in deer hunting clubs. Less than one-third never held a membership and about 17 percent reported holding a membership in the past.

In his survey of more than 2600 Pennsylvania deer hunters, Lefes discovered that buck hunters (those hunters traditionally choosing to shoot bucks only) represented a very high proportion of club memberships. He also learned that the traditional buck hunter not only tends to be the most active club member but tends to be the most avid and enthusiastic outdoor magazine reader as well. White-collar workers in his study maintained the highest proportion among present deer club members.

The most interesting finding of Lefes's deer hunter survey revolves around hunters' negative opinions about deer hunting clubs owning and controlling large tracts of land—a finding which seems to undermine the very basic function of hunting clubs in the first place, which is to own and control large blocks of land. Approximately 16 percent responded favorably toward clubs controlling large tracts of land. Twenty-five percent said they were not too favorable, and fifty percent expressed an unfavorable opinion about clubs controlling large tracts of hunting land. Slightly less than 8 percent reported no opinion on the matter. White-collar workers constituted the highest proportion among those favoring deer hunting clubs controlling large blocks of land, while blue-collar workers maintained the highest proportion among those being least favorable.

Hunters voicing favorable opinions on the matter gave the following reasons in support of their opinions: (1) clubs aid in the protection and propagation of deer; (2) sportsmen have the right to post their own land as do other landowners; and (3) restricted areas promote good sportsmanship and safer hunting.

Those hunters not favoring clubs controlling large blocks of land gave a wide range of reasons in support of their opinions. They are listed in the order of their importance as determined by the proportion of hunters who mentioned them: (1) non-club members are deprived of hunting areas; (2) hunters who purchase a license should have the privilege to hunt wherever they please; (3) many hunters are financially unable to join clubs and may be limited in the area they hunt deer; (4) restricted club land demonstrates poor sportsmanship, selfishness, and is not fair to other hunters; (5) state game land is public property and should not be restricted; (6) controlling large blocks of land creates ill feeling among other sportsmen when land is reserved for a select few; (7) members tend to hunt on other land not posted, therefore they should not post their own land; (8) commercializing hunting in this manner is not in the best interest of the sport; (9) poor sportsmanship among club members is practiced under the guise of legal organizations; (10) most hunters are not likely to be among hunting club members; (11)

clubs usually gain too much authority and too much "pull" and become powerful interest groups; (12) hunting clubs do not aid in propagating deer; and (13) the farmers feed the deer and as a rule do not post their land.

When we compare the proportion of persons who are members of hunting clubs and the proportion who favor hunting clubs, we must logically assume that most members of deer hunting clubs do not agree with the policies of their organization or other organizations that control and post large blocks of land during deer hunting season. The whole question continues to be argued from both sides without arriving at any acceptable conclusions.

In Jim Kennedy's case study of deer hunters in Virginia and Maryland, mentioned earlier, deer hunters indicated that they derived six basic benefits from group hunting in the traditional deer camp setting in decreasing order of importance: (1) companionship, (2) an increase in their success chances, (3) a safer environment with the group, (4) an increase in the group's success chances, (5) help with dead deer, and (6) the sharing of expenses. Companionship clearly emerged as the most preferred group reward in this study.

Only 6 percent of the deer hunters in Kennedy's survey hunted alone. Sixteen percent hunted with a buddy and 78 percent in groups of three or more. Ninety-four percent of them hunting in a group have been together for a median of three years. Regardless of their reason for choosing group hunting in the traditional deer camp setting, their reluctance to trade the group for a 50 percent increase in their chances of success, if they hunted alone, testifies to the overall importance of hunting with one's buddies in a group setting or as part of an organized club.

In a 1984 survey of deer hunters in South Carolina and Mississippi, Fred

Bush and Dave Guynn of Clemson University found that hunters ranked safety (81 percent), fellowship (76 percent), and higher quality hunting (70 percent) as the most important reasons for forming deer hunting clubs and leasing hunting rights. As quality deer hunting in this country becomes more scarce and as the demand far exceeds the supply, organized deer hunting clubs such as The Deer Pasture, the T. Huntington Abbot Rod & Gun Club, and Camp 17 grow in popularity even in areas traditionally known for their open-land hunting. If you want quality deer hunting experiences, you must make your own. The days of the Mountain Man are gone.

While clubs can provide the answer for some of our hunting problems today, whether we view them as an asset or a liability to the sport remains a debatable question as the research studies of my friend Bob Jackson clearly suggest. For the past decade, Jackson, a professor of psychology at the University of Wisconsin-LaCrosse, has been studying the social and psychological behavior of Wisconsin hunters. In his study of deer camps and deer hunting clubs, Jackson concludes that "the classical deer camp has tremendous power over its members. Its cohesiveness and productivity build group bonds that demand conformity to group standards for good or bad."

Unfortunately, as Jackson's research indicates, too many deer camps sometimes measure their worth in terms of "filling up." He interviewed one camp where one individual shot twelve of the fifteen bucks killed by the entire group. In his interview, the hunters of the camp boasted about "filling up," but before the interview ended several members of the camp muttered their dissatisfactions about the greedy behavior of the individual they referred to as "The Killer."

The kind of groups that assemble each year to hunt deer affect one's hunting behavior. The same individual who hunts with an all-male group will behave quite differently when he deer hunts with his family.

Some deer hunters told Jackson that they felt used by other hunters; some said they were sought out because they had access to good deer hunting land. One hunter exclaimed, "I think they just saw me as providing them with another tag they could fill." Another hunter confirmed that motive when he told Jackson "that he always invited one or two poor shots to camp so he could get more shooting himself."

After countless home and field interviews and mail hunter-surveys, Jackson believes that deer hunting clubs "usually exert pressures that hold the hunter back at a lower stage of development. The individual has to assert himself, even rebel a bit, to reach beyond the club standards into the sportsman stage. Put another way, most hunting parties are still at the limiting-out or trophy stages in their development. The hunters that we interviewed who achieved true sportsman status strike me as individualists; they are men and women who have sorted out their own values and experiences and know who they are and why they hunt. They don't let others determine this for them."

Jackson's in-depth research leads him to believe that among all types of hunting, deer hunting attitudes and behavior are the most difficult to change because of the influence of the group. His research unfortunately shows that deer hunting groups seldom maintain clearly defined rules or practices with regard to violations. Many deer hunters told Jackson that if a hunter violates, "he is on his own," a statement that leads Jackson to conclude that "violating, if not by definition then by lack of definition, is either acceptable or a matter of indifference." In his opinion, few deer camps seem to come to terms with violators. When asked in one of his surveys whether game law violations were permitted in their camp, 41.9 percent of the hunters surveyed indicated that they were indeed permitted.

When Bob Jackson asks whether deer hunting camps and clubs represent an asset or a liability to the sport of deer hunting, he asks a very difficult question. Do they? They can provide the deer hunter with freedom, with being "alone with others" as one hunter paradoxically expressed it, and with camaraderie; they can solve the access problem for some and provide quality deer hunting experiences for others. But the dictates of group behavior can often lead to blatant ethical violations, as a good amount of the human dimensions research indicates; and the rise of the second generation in its membership can lead to conflicts and breakups. Most important, however, the traditional return each year of large numbers of hunters to the same spot can sometimes hinder needed rules and regulation changes in the interest of maintaining proper deer herd and deer hunting densities.

Jackson suggests that if your deer camp creates a meaningful social experience for all people involved, you will be able to count its longevity in terms of decades of time. The Messinger Creek Camp created such a meaningful social experience that it lasted for thirty-five years before disappearing as a result of arthritis and old age for both the shack and the boys. The Deer Pasture has been in existence for half of a century, and the Bass boys look forward to its 100th anniversary. Camp 17, founded in 1956, and the T. Huntington Abbot Rod & Gun Club, founded in 1975, also continue to provide us with excellent models of hunter ethics and social responsibility and with fine examples of what the modern-day deer camp should look like.

In the final analysis, the modern-day deer camp looks quite different physically from the weather-beaten, antique hermitages of the past few decades, but man still returns to the deer camp regardless of its physical dimension each year to rejuvenate himself in some mysterious way so he can face civilization for yet another year. Each year, these unique social institutions are reborn in the big timber of the North, in the southern swamps, in the farm country of the Midwest, and in the western mountains and deserts. Many deer hunters, myself included, consider deer camp to be the very heart and soul of the hunt — whether it be located in the Texas Hill Country, the deer forests of Maine, the bottomlands of South Carolina, the Deer Lake area of Michigan's Upper Penninsula, or in Section 17 of Pine County, Minnesota.

PART IV

THE DEER HUNTER

Chapter 14

The All-American Deer Drive

There is still another mode of deer hunting which remains to be described. It is called "driving," and is the one in general practice, and the favourite pastime among the hospitable planters of the southern states. We have . . . joined in these hunts, and must admit that in the manner in which they were conducted, this method of deer hunting proved an exciting and very agreeable recreation.

— Audubon, "Deer Hunting," 1831

During the early years of our sport, deer hunters employed the deer drive primarily in the South and Southwest. This method of deer hunting descends partially from the English stag hunt and partly from the hunting methods of the American Indians. The English part of the tradition introduces us to the use of horses and hounds; the Indian component gives us the line of standers towards which man drives the quarry. The deer drive as practiced in the deep South since Colonial times requires not only a quick hand with the double-barreled shotgun, but a firm seat in the saddle. As Judge Caton once remarked, "If the deer hunter returns with a sound horse and a sound body he may consider himself fortunate." Once the hounds start the deer, the hunters follow them on horseback. Using their knowledge of the white-

tail's habits, the hunters strive to gain ground on the deer. By cutting corners and following shortcuts, the hunters thus come to within shooting distance of the fleeing animal.

Audubon found great excitement in this form of deer hunting and considered it a very agreeable form of outdoor recreation. While we do not generally characterize Audubon as a giant among deer hunters, he greatly enjoyed deer hunting as a sport for many years, particularly the deer drive as customarily practiced in the Low Country of South Carolina with hounds, horns, and horses, an activity that Audubon considered the height of sport. Little doubt exists that deer hunting remained an essential part of Audubon's stock-in-trade as an artist and naturalist, for his cherished, deeply-engraved, long, double-barreled

John James Audubon, 1785–1851. *The American Museum of Natural History*

shotguns spoke often to the sight of fleeing deer in punctuation to the clamor of baying hounds, hunting horns, and galloping horses.

In his essay "Deer Hunting," written in 1831 and published oddly enough in his *Ornithological Biography,* Audubon argues that the deer drive to be practiced successfully requires great energy and activity, expert rifle shooting, a thorough knowledge of the forest, plus an intimate acquaintance with the habits of deer and how they respond to human pressure. While driving deer, Audubon noticed that

whitetails frequently retreat from their home range but soon return to their original haunts after the drive has ended. In Audubon's day, as in ours, hunters designated the drives with names such as Crane Pond, Gum Thicket, The Pasture, The Oak Swamp, and so on. To his great mortification, his colleagues named one bay after him, a bay where Audubon missed several deer.

In his essay on deer hunting, Audubon reports that man still-hunted, drove, firelighted, called, grunted, and decoyed deer for recreational purposes as early as the 1830s. In his essay, he gives us one of the most picturesque and enthusiastic descriptions of the deer drive ever penned.

Now, kind reader, prepare to mount a generous, full-blood Virginian horse. See that your gun is in complete order, for hark to the sound of the bugle and horn, and the mingled clamor of a pack of harriers! Your friends are waiting for you, under the shade of the wood, and we must together go *driving* the light-footed deer. The distance over which one has to travel is seldom felt when pleasure is anticipated as the result; so galloping we go pell-mell through the woods, to some well-known place where many a fine buck has dropped its antlers under the ball of the hunter's rifle. The servants, who are called the drivers, have already begun their search. Their voices are heard exciting the hounds, and unless we put spurs to our steeds, we may be too late at our stand, and thus lose the first opportunity of shooting the fleeting game as it passes by. Hark again! The dogs are in chase, the horn sounds louder and more clearly. Hurry, hurry on, or we shall be sadly behind!

Here we are at last! Dismount, fasten your horse to this tree, place yourself by the side of that large yellow poplar, and mind you do not shoot me! The deer is fast approaching; I will go to my stand, and he who shoots him dead wins the prize.

The deer is heard coming. It has inadvertently cracked a dead stick with its hoof, and the dogs are now so near that it will pass in a moment. There it comes! How beautifully it bounds over the ground! What a splendid head of horns! How easy its attitudes, depending, as it seems to do, on its own swiftness for safety! All is in vain, however; a gun is fired, the animal plunges and doubles with incomparable speed. There he goes! He passes another stand, from which a second shot, better directed than the first, brings him to the ground. The dogs, the servants, the sportsmen are now rushing forward to the spot. The hunter who has shot it is congratulated on his skill or good luck, and the chase begins again in some other part of the woods.

I hope that this account will be sufficient to induce you, kind reader, to go *driving* the light-footed deer in our western and southern woods. . . .

Audubon's spirited account of driving whitetails through the interior of tangled woods and across hills, ravines, and morasses induced many a hunter nationwide to take up the chase, to drive the whitetailed deer from the woods. The preceding account narrates what some of the most illustrious deer drives and famous deer drivers, or infamous—depending upon your point of view—have accomplished since following Audubon's inducement.

One of the earliest Dixie deerslayers to respond to Audubon's inducement was William Elliott, a contemporary of Audubon's and a planter of the noblest South Carolina breed, who carried the deer drive, Southern-style, to its ultimate climax. In his letters to the *Charleston Courier* signed "Venator," Elliott described his deer driving adventures; and when he collected these hair-splitting yarns in *Carolina Sports by Land and Water* (1846), the book became one of the classic accounts of the subject, one of the very few outdoor books to remain in print ever since the date of its original publication.

Elliott drove deer along the banks of the Chee-ha River, one of South Carolina's best deer hunting grounds of its time, with the enthusiastic gusto of starry-eyed generals engaged in sylvan warfare. With hounds and drivers ("whippers" he called them) moving the deer, he spurred his horse on until gaining a position near the deer's flank. If the deer was wounded, whether shot with the double-barrel or struck in the head with the armed heel of his boot, Elliott would often fling himself upon the struggling animal and bury the fatal blade of his knife into the whitetail's throat.

Elliott referred to deer drives as "*raids* against the deer!*" in which the hunters would marshal their forces for a week's campaign and use "all the appliances of destruction at their beck." Those "sleek-skinned marauders," as Elliott called them, had to be eliminated, for they were

William Elliott (1788-1863), a Harvard-educated deerslayer who drove deer with the enthusiastic gusto of starry-eyed generals engaged in sylvan warfare.

ruining his crops—the beginnings of our modern-day pest-control policies with regard to deer management. Consequently, Elliott waged havoc against deer in general and bucks in particular, especially old, overgrown bucks that had the insolence to baffle Elliott and his boys.

Once spotted, a buck had to be pursued until its death; killing deer, he viewed as a habit to be developed to the utmost. After watching one of his hunting buddies, a backwoods ruffian named Geordy, finally kill a deer after wounding six, Elliott cried out in one of his wild utterances, "Done like a sportsman, Geordy, one dead deer is worth a dozen cripples. I remember—once, your powder was too weak; and next, your shot was too small; and next, your aim was somewhat wild; and one went off bored of an ear; and another nick'd of a tail. You are bound to set up an infirmary across the river, for the dismembered deer! You have done well to *kill*—let it grow into a habit."

"Go, thou fool, no better than Napoleon, hast thou known the fitting time to die! The *devil* take thee, for thou hast needlessly kicked and thrust myself beyond the reach of *a blessing!*"—William Elliott, *Carolina Sports by Land and Water*, 1846. *Leonard Lee Rue III photo*

Driving deer became an intense habit of mind: The noise of the shotguns, the aroma of gunpowder, the baying of the hounds, and the echoes of the huntsmen's horns set his heart to pounding and his mind to the issuance of wild utterances as he galloped on through the deer forest. Although he loved his hounds and horses as well as the deer, when the hounds lost the trail, he cursed the laggards of the pack, the cold of nose, and the slow of foot. When one wounded buck miraculously escaped into the depths of a rapidly flowing stream, after fleeing the hounds and evading buckshot, Wild Willie stood along the shoreline and vented his frustration by hollering at the buck, "Go, thou fool, no better than Napoleon, hast thou known the fitting time to die! *The devil* take thee, for thou hast needlessly kicked and thrust thyself beyond the reach of *a blessing!*" And with that grotesque verbiage, the Harvard-educated deerslayer spurred on his horse and disappeared from the scene of ultimate disappointment only to find partial consolation later over venison steak at the campfire, where Elliott decried all bucks as "luxurious rogues and the greatest epicures alive!"

After reading about Elliott's spirit-stirring incidents of driving deer to their deaths, Thoreau responded by calling the whole affair bloody, wild, and barbaric, although he readily admitted that driving deer proved to be the top-ranked field sport of the Old South. One thing seems certain: It's hard to compare Elliott's deer drives to anything that occurred before or since. Yet in terms of effectiveness and blood they do remind us of the bloody deer drives of "Black Jack" Schwartz, who reportedly drove an area near the Upper Mahantongo Creek in Pennsylvania with a radius often running in excess of thirty miles. When the shooting stopped and the smoke cleared from the drives that "Black Jack" masterminded, it was not uncommon for as many as 198 deer to lay slain on the forest floor.

Many deer also fell to the forest floor as a result of the grandiose deer drives of Walter Winans, one of the most bizarre characters in the history of deer hunting, for his massive operations around the turn of the century required a small army of brush beaters. One photograph in his deer hunting journal records the illustrious presence of seventeen horses, thirty-five deerslayers, and twenty dead stags. His dramatically staged deer-shooting photos and deer driving illustrations have to be seen to be believed. Looking somewhat like a retired general of the Boer War, we see this infamous deer driver in formal hunting attire blazing away at deer at point-blank range with his rifle often being fired from the hip. In the photos of his deer driving journals, we see dying deer suspended in mid-air, while clouds of gun smoke ascend from his highly polished 275 Rigby-Mauser.

After a lifetime of deer driving, Winans reached the conclusion that the very term "deer driving" represents an unfortunate combination of words to describe moving deer toward the shooters.

"Deer will not be *driven;* if they think they are being forced they will break back, however thick the beaters are.

"The only way to force deer up *to* the guns is to make them think you want them to go *in the opposite direction*.

"Instead of being called deer driving it ought to be called (coining a word in the German manner) deceiving-deer-into-going-where-you-want-them-to."

Winans frequently posted his gunners behind the beaters with great success and stressed variation in the methods of driving. If the drive would succeed in one way, that was reason enough for Winans for *not* doing it that way the next time. He soon learned that an old doe often leads the deer out of danger and often "gets too clever and has to be killed," if the drive in her bailiwick is to succeed.

Old Walt prepared three different ways of driving each tract and planned them out to the minutest details to suit different wind directions. When the wind changed, the drive changed immediately. He did not like noise in the deer forest. Consequently, he used a series of signals with flags and gave his instructions by using the Morse Code. He frowned upon the German idea of using small flags on cords or nets *(Lappen)* as a legitimate way of preventing deer from going where they were not wanted. The big drives that Winans presided over often yielded as many as thirty stags in one drive, with every gun getting one or more deer.

This type of strategic success in moving deer must have been what George McCormick, a leading sportsman of Flagstaff, Arizona, had in mind when he assembled fifty-five cowboys on horseback and seventy Navajo braves on foot in an attempt to drive 8000 deer off the Kaibab, across the Grand Canyon, through the Colorado River, and on to the South Rim. This stupendous effort—led by famed outdoorsman Zane Grey himself and known as the "Great Kaibab Deer Drive"—resulted in the biggest deer drive ever attempted in the history of this country. The idea inherent in this drive revolved around moving deer off an overbrowsed range instead of controlling the population through legitimate deer hunting. Apparently the organizers of this drive figured that the only way to deal with the irrupting Kaibab deer herd was to turn the animals over to the cowboys.

The planners of this deer drive studied their maps, invited Paramount Pictures to film the event, got permission from the U.S. Forest Service and the National Park Service, elicited the help of cowboys and ranchers for miles around, and erected drift fences in strategic positions. Early in the afternoon of December 16, 1924, the members of this deer drive took their positions—125 strong. Loaded down with cowbells, tin cans, and other noisemakers, the drivers formed a line on foot and horseback. When forest ranger Thad Eburne dismounted and fired his rifle, as Zane Grey recalls in his book *The Deer Stalker* (1924), "the great deer drive was on."

With noise that sounded like claps of thunder, the line moved forward with the *Riders of the Purple Sage* hollering cattle-driving calls and the Navajos shouting their chants and clanging their noisemakers. In responding to the jangle of cowbells and the melodious Indian yells, big bucks with wide-spread antlers appeared in the open terrain to investigate. Hundreds of does and fawns started running up the hillsides, but it soon became evident to ranger Eburne that they were traveling in every direction except the one desired by the drivers. Fawns soon began to run right into the Indians. Eburne took to the high ground so he could see everything with regard to the drive as a whole.

"The deer are moving, but not forward," one cowboy hollered.

More and more deer began to show up in increasing numbers as the drive continued. In one grand spectacle, forest ranger Eburne could see as many as 500 deer at a time.

"Bucks, does and fawns, trios and sextets of deer, lines and groups, began to close in on one another," Zane Grey tells us in *The Deer Stalker.* "The riders responded with a daring and speed that for a few moments augured well for the success of the movement. But the fleetness of the deer outdistanced the horsemen. Two-thirds of that herd of deer streamed up the slope, one long bobbing line of gray and white, to pass beyond the riders; and wheeling back along the ridge, they flashed, leaped, darted in magnificent silhouette against the pale sky."

The drivers soon saw thousands of deer stampeding up and down the canyons. Eburne, as Zane Gray recalls, "drank his fill of that beautiful wild spectacle, because he knew he would never see it again. He doubted if such a sight would ever be seen by any man again. Another winter would find most of those deer dead of starvation."

As the drive progressed, the line gradually wavered, becoming disorganized and irregular. To make things worse, a threatening snowstorm soon became a reality. The cowboys now had to fight snow-laden limbs and brush and could not keep up with the running Indians, who quickly outdistanced them. As the deer reversed themselves and ran through the line of Navajos, they soon ran directly into the horsemen. In reversing themselves again, Eburne could see Indians, cowboys, and deer running in all directions. Many of the drivers soon lost their way and wandered around looking for familiar landmarks and a way out of the forest. Others, in realizing the failure of the whole fiasco, quit and turned back as the temperature approached zero.

According to one observer, no deer were spotted in front of the drivers, but thousands of deer milled around behind them. Out in front of the drivers, the shivering and frustrated cameramen from Paramount Pictures waited in vain to film fleeing deer in a blinding snowstorm, as did the standers who were acting as official counters of the number of deer moving out of the North Kaibab. When the counting

crew tallied their numbers, they recorded zero deer successfully moved. Before the drive ended and the high-pitched cowboy yells dissipated, six inches of snow had fallen.

As is the case with deer hunting in general, this unique deer drive included people from all walks of life: game wardens, deputy marshals, sheriffs, tourists, ranchers, wild horse hunters, cattlemen, traders from an Indian reservation, strangers from Utah, and last but not least, a Hopi truck driver.

This infamous deer drive sounds more like fiction than fact. Thad Eburne, the main protagonist of Zane Grey's classic *The Deer Stalker,* summarizes the colossal failure of this drive when he says, "Looks to me like they just won't drive!" It was a hard lesson learned: Surplus deer cannot be driven off their home range to prosper elsewhere.

Not all deer drives end as colossal failures. As more and more state legislatures gradually prohibited driving deer with hounds and horses, large man-made drives became the order of the day and proved more and more successful in Yankeeland. The ghost-like single files of flashlights twinkling along the deer trails in white-tailed deer country in the predawn hours became a standard fixture of the annual deer hunt. Many of these large deer drives proved to be very successful. "The Chilson Bunch," for example, that hunted the old Van Wegan farm and places thereabouts in the hills of Pennsylvania reportedly bagged thirty-seven bucks for forty-two hunters during one season alone, after four days of methodically driving an area of less than 500 acres!

The big drives of H. O. Lund and his boys at their deer camp called "The Homestead," a two-story log cabin near Iron

River, Wisconsin, also proved highly successful, because old man Lund scheduled and planned them to the nth degree well before the game ever started. "If General Ludendorf had planned his big drive against the Allies in World War I as carefully as H. O. Lund laid his plans for our big drive," his son Wigs Lund once remarked, "he might have won the war."

Old man Lund planned the same drives year after year: "The Camp 20 Drive," "The Little Trout Lake Drive," "The White Way Drive," and "The Rye Patch Drive." With fresh snow on the ground and the wind in the right direction, his crew consisted of about fifteen to sixteen guns. The old man's instructions to the greenhorns were explicit:

"Keep the wind in your right ear. Walk slowly and keep your eyes peeled. There are bucks in these woods with horns the size of rockin' chairs!"

Lund insisted that the drive be slow, methodical, and quiet until the final shootout. He had it all figured out. "Why bang away at a spooked deer, high-tailing it like the hammers of hell for the next county, when you could connect with one that was loping along."

The windup of an H. O. Lund deer drive took only about ten minutes. With final landmarks coming into view, the drivers knew that all hell would break loose. Wigs Lund saw it many times.

"The rifles of the men posted would open up from all sides and the cannonading would sound like the siege of Vicksburg. We connected and hung up many's the buck on The Big Drive."

The results of the shoot-out would frequently appear in the Iron River newspapers. According to one newspaper account, young P. O. Lund finally shot his first deer after thirty days of deer driving and 200 rounds of ammunition. This item,

however, should not denigrate the shooting abilities of the many twenty-one carat "buck-hunters of the first water" that hung out at The Homestead.

Deer hunters all across this land will do whatever is necessary to enhance the success of deer driving beyond mere strategic planning. As a last resort, some deer hunters will even try to scare 'em to death with the use of scarecrows. When Henry Milliken, a tall and lanky deerslayer from the woods of Maine, failed to shoot deer in Moose Swamp on his annual deer hunts, he would employ a one-man drive with three standers posted at strategic spots in the half-mile-long and quarter-mile-wide swamp. On the east side of the swamp, where deer frequently gave the standers the Houdini-slip, he placed a line of cedar scarecrows dressed in red hunting clothes and red bandanna handkerchiefs laced with a strong dose of Wild Root hair tonic. The whole line of deer-scaring contraptions looked unusual and ludicrous, but the tactic worked in keeping deer away from their usual escape routes up the eastern ridge and often resulted in Dick McGraw being able to unlimber his old 38/55 on 'em, as they approached the western side of the swamp.

Henry Milliken loved the one-man deer drive and so did Gordon MacQuarrie, the famous outdoor editor of the *Milwaukee Journal* and his hunting buddy "Hizzoner," the salty-witted outdoor expert known to MacQuarrie fans as the President of the Old Duck Hunters' Association, Inc., or more simply as the Old Man. While Mac did the footwork, the Old Man usually sat on a pine stump somewhere in the Norway country of Bayfield County in northwestern Wisconsin.

On the day before the opening of Wisconsin's only "split-season" (four days of buck hunting followed by four days of

"The drive is the thing. . . . We were brought up with deer hunters who drive. Still-hunting? Grand sport, indeed, but the rules are upset when 100,000 hunters go into the woods."—Gordon MacQuarrie. *Wisconsin State Historical Society photo*

antlerless hunting), Mac left Milwaukee in a light snowstorm for his log cabin on Middle Eau Claire Lake, a 460-mile journey across Wisconsin's deer country. The snowstorm eventually forced him to stop and, while lying in a foot of snow, put chains on the tires of his vehicle. Arriving at his cabin six hours behind schedule, he opened the door of his lean, modest, backwoods retreat, tired, cold, and unsteady on his feet.

"This is the worst storm to ever hit this country before the opening day of deer season," said the wiry redhead to the Old Man, who was already there dozing and warming himself before Hank Koehler's

natural-rock fireplace. "Guess we'll just hold up, and enjoy the fire, as long as we can't hunt," he added.

"Can't hunt," growled the Old Man as a horrendous cloud of pipe smoke ascended up and against the warm cedar walls. "We'll be hunting all right, and at the crack of dawn!"

"I'm not tramping around out there in several feet of snow," Mac replied.

The Old Man pointed to the snowshoes hanging next to the fireplace. "All you've ever done with those snowshoes is to varnish 'em! Tomorrow, you're going to wear off a little of that varnish."

That was the last statement Mac heard until waking the next morning, which dawned clear, bitter cold, and near zero.

In dressing that morning, the Old Man put more clothes on than usual. While putting on his sheep-lined aviation boots, he vowed that the only way a hunter could do in a buck "was to do a little personal freezing. You've got to suffer," he insisted.

Heading for his favorite stand at the top of Norway Hill, he could hardly walk, as he was swaddled so tightly in underwear, sweatshirts, and outer garments. But the Old Man had it figured out: Mac would circle to the south and west of him and drive up through the thick slashing near the edge of the opening of the Norway grove. When the antlers came through, as they usually did, he would have shooting at the buck as it hit the open grove.

The snowshoes creaked as Mac began his long journey upslope toward Hizzoner. As he snowshoed along, he noticed many old deer tracks made after the storm. But he soon found a large, fresh track—"a virgin white scar of a hoof in the snow, so unlike the settled, stiffened track of twelve hours before," as MacQuarrie so aptly described it. The deer track was big and brand-new, with the maker of it moving straight toward the Old Man's stand and an obvious rendezvous with his 30/30 carbine.

The deer kept just far enough ahead of Mac so he couldn't get a glimpse of it. "You wonder at such times," MacQuarrie wrote in his essay, "You've Got to Suffer," one of the greatest deer hunting stories ever written, "where the rascals get the wisdom to know that a man in snow cannot move rapidly. That critter had me figured out so well that sometimes it even stopped to browse. It would pay for that. . . . Contempt of court, that's what it was! Just wait until the old goat moved out from the thick stuff and started ambling through those open Norways! The Old Man has killed a half dozen bucks from that stand."

Finally, however, Mac got a glimpse of the animal — a large 10-pointer with wide beams and tall tines. He could have taken a quick shot but why chance it; instead he chose to push the animal into the open grove before the Old Man and continued to follow the track as it headed straight toward the stander.

"Pretty soon there would be a shot," he thought to himself. "Just one shot, it ought to be. That would be the Old Man's 150 grains of lead and copper going to its destination. Then silence — the sort of quiet after one shot that means so much to a deer hunter."

The Old Man's plan seemed to be working all right. Mac could already visualize the buck walking out into the open grove and the Old Man squeezing off the 30/30. He thought about how he would prepare the venison steaks for the next night's supper and whether he would drag the buck out one mile to the cabin or borrow Hank's toboggan to do so.

Minutes ticked by. "Shoot!" he said to himself. The buck must surely be in the open grove by now, but all he heard was the "kra-a-a-ak" of a raven overhead.

Finally, Mac saw the buck for the second time — right out in front of the Old Man. Mac took one quick shot but knew when he squeezed the trigger that he shot too high.

At the crack of his gun, the Old Man hollered, "Did you hit 'em?"

"Never speak to me again!" Mac replied.

The Old Man came clean: "Dammit, I had too many clothes on! I must have dozed here against this downed log for several hours until you shot!"

Mac stared at the Old Man and thought to himself, "He wasn't the Old Man of other deer drives, chilled and lean and ready, with a drop on the end of his nose. He was swathed and cluttered in a sleep-producing, separate, steam-heating system."

The Old Man had committed a major breach of ethics. He had violated a cardinal principle of the deer driving fraternity: He fell asleep while on stand, while Mac tirelessly wore the varnish off his snowshoes.

Most deer camps seem to have an Old Man who by virtue of wisdom, woodcraft, and endowed leadership assumes command of the camp and its drives. Usually, they exercise their authority without undue sternness. But when need be, they can verbally take the skin off the deer camp simpletons. The Old Man unquestionably knows the terrain well. He knows all the members of his deer camp as well as many of the members of the neighboring deer camps. But above all, the Old Man knows the white-tailed deer and its habits and how they respond to deer drives.

The Old Man loves people, especially serious deer hunters, but dislikes the "bitchers," those few who gripe about everything. The Old Man obeys the law and considers the rights and feelings of others. He is warm, friendly, and generous; he demonstrates those qualities of mind and soul that constitute the essence of the gentleman-sportsman. If that sounds like your Old Man, it probably is.

It also sounds like the grand Old Man of the deer drive himself, Archibald Rutledge, who presided over the famous drives known as "The Hampton Hunts" in the low country of South Carolina. Rutledge, known as "Old Flintlock" to those who hunted with him, taught his boys Arch, Mid, and Irv to drive deer in the tradition of Audubon and Elliott — to ride 'em up . . . to roll 'em.

When called upon to defend this type of deer hunting, Flintlock would point to the famous picture of Audubon holding his double-barreled shotgun of awesome proportions and recite Audubon's invitation. Like Audubon, Flintlock saw many a deer run in his time; they showed him some mighty "breezy capers" and some extraordinary escapes in the swampland of South Carolina, although many bucks fell when his Parker double-barreled, twelve-gauge shotgun with the thirty-inch barrels blared forth.

To this day, Flintlock remains the American deer hunter's buck hunter. He taught his boys and his drivers Gabriel and Prince and Prince's three sons, Prince, Will, and Samuel, and old Steve and Richard one basic fact of deer hunting that they never forgot nor should we:

"A true hunter of the whitetail will forego every other pleasure on earth for that rarest one of pursuing and taking an old roughshod, long-flanked, many seasoned buck, whose antlers, as he moves are likely to make an amateur hunter imagine the woods have suddenly been set in motion."

But taking such bucks on drives is never easy. After planning and executing thousands of deer drives, Rutledge explains why a wary old white-tailed buck, despite the noise behind him and the silence and apparent security ahead, will often deliberately choose to run back through the drivers.

"He understands man's tricks. He knows something about this set-up of drivers and standers. Experience may have taught him that there is more real danger in the silence ahead than in the noise behind. On many occasions I have known bucks to run back when natural sanctuaries lay ahead. Since wild creatures know the geography of the woods much better than we do, such behavior has led me to believe that, although we know something about the deer we hunt, they also know a lot about us. The more I hunt deer, the more I believe this is true."

The more I study and observe whitetails, the more I believe that the wisest and wariest bucks know more about us than we know about ourselves! You might drive such bucks from their favorite sanctuary in a certain direction, if that happens to be the direction they want to take, but if it isn't, you best count on them going back through the drivers or around them and slipping past everyone involved in the drive.

Small, midday drives, however, frequently produce some outstanding trophy racks, as Mark White and Butch and Harold Cole of Dallas discovered one cold and windy Saturday afternoon in December 1985, after driving a bullrush thicket in Talbot County, Georgia. Like many deer hunters, this threesome prefers to drive deer during the later part of the season. On their three-man drives, they usually walk slowly — about sixty or seventy yards apart — through thick hollows.

On that late-season drive, Mark walked down the middle of a draw with Butch and Harold fanned out on both sides of him some distance ahead. Shortly after the drive got underway, Mark jumped a huge buck at point-blank range in a bullrush thicket. He fired two shots at the disappearing buck. Butch also got a broadside shot before the massive buck disappeared from his view. From a higher vantage point near the rim of the hollow, Harold saw the massive 11-pointer fall. But the buck suddenly got up and came running straight toward Harold, who then killed the animal with a neck shot. This late-season team effort resulted in a field-dressed, 180-pound 11-pointer that scored 174-6/8 typical Boone and Crockett points. In examining the carcass, the three hunters discovered that all of the four shots taken hit what Duncan Dobie calls "the awesome Talbot County monarch," in his *Georgia's Greatest Whitetails* (1986).

The story of the American deer drive contains more unusual events and colorful characters than almost any other aspect of our sport. It's filled with odd situations, strokes of graceless luck, and humorous anecdotes. It represents a rich slice of our deer hunting heritage.

While most of us have probably participated in a deer drive in one form or another, not all of us would probably agree with Audubon's interpretation of the drive as an exciting and very agreeable form of recreation. In fact, some states today prohibit deer drives. According to the 1987/88 hunting and trapping regulations of Maine, "It is unlawful to drive deer or take part in a deer drive."

While most states allow hunters to participate in deer drives, more and more states are imposing restrictions on this method of hunting for safety reasons. Pennsylvania's 1988/89 digest of hunting and trapping regulations requires that if five or more persons hunt together from a permanently established deer camp and cooperate in deer drives, they must keep and post a roster with the following information: the hunting license year, name of camp or party, location, township, county, name of each party member, dates of arrival and departure, caliber of firearm, type of deer killed including the sex, weight, number of points, and date of kill.

Even in states where one can't imagine deer hunting without deer drives, more and more regulations are being imposed. In South Carolina, manmade deer drives are *only* permitted between 10:00 A.M. and 2:00 P.M. on wildlife management area lands, and drivers must not carry firearms. According to South Carolina's 1988/89 hunting rules and regulations, "Man-drives are not permitted on either-sex days on wildlife management area lands except during the last two either-sex days scheduled in December."

With all these rules and regulations, one would suspect a decline in the popularity of this method of hunting. When we surveyed the readership of *Deer & Deer Hunting* magazine in 1983, we found that gun hunters only spent 7.5 percent of their time driving deer and sighted 18.4 deer per 100 hours. Our survey indicated that bow hunters spent only 1.8 percent of their time trying to drive deer with sightings of 26.1 deer per 100 hours. But other surveys indicate that deer drives are not only popular and avidly practiced in white-tailed deer country all across America, but prove to be very successful. In fact, of the more than 4.5 million whitetails shot annually in this country, 20 to 40 percent are shot on drives. Some researchers estimate that 60 percent of the total take of white-tailed deer in some areas in the East results from deer drives.

In talking with deer hunters, it seems to me that as the success rate of killing deer declines in heavily hunted areas, the popularity of the driving method increases.

As one deer hunter from the Catskills put it, "The most successful method of killing white-tailed deer is by driving — that is, it produces the most uniform end-results. Intelligent deer driving will kill more deer in any given heavily hunted area than any other method. In many sections it is the only practical way that deer can be taken in any satisfactory number."

Or as MacQuarrie often said to the Old Man, "There are a hundred bucks back in those hills. A little drive — nothing to it. We shouldn't settle for anything less than one today. It's opening day!"

Chapter 15

Deer Movements Revisited

Even during the deer season, they're closer than you think!
— A Backwoods Buck Hunter, 1987

In the October and December 1986 issues of *Deer & Deer Hunting* magazine, two feature articles were published on white-tailed deer movements titled, respectively, "Buck Movements and Hunting Pressure" and "Buck Movements During the Rut" in an attempt to summarize the current scientific information on the subject (reprinted in *Deer & Deer Hunting: Book 2,* Stackpole Books, 1987). Deer researchers in such states as Wisconsin, Missouri, Colorado, Virginia, Montana, and Mississippi continue to radio-track deer in order to evaluate the effects of intensive hunting pressure on deer movements and home ranges and to evaluate white-tailed deer distribution, activity, and habitat use. The conclusions and implications of these scientific studies greatly interest the die-hard buck hunter who constantly tries to monitor and decipher deer movements in the back forty.

In the first of these movement studies, Tim Lewis, a wildlife researcher from the University of Wisconsin, spends most of his time trapping deer, radio-tracking them, collecting and analyzing deer droppings, and observing deer behavior at feeding stations near Clam Lake in the Chequamegon National Forest in northwestern Wisconsin. His three-year study is designed primarily to evaluate the effects of supplemental feeding on deer movements, population dynamics, and habitat selection.

Clam Lake lies between the towns of Glidden (where hunter Ed Hall shot that bizarre 10-point buck which contained the head of a 19-pointer with a 19.5-inch spread locked in its rack) and Hayward (where buck hunter and antler collector J. Widmer Smith still scores non-typical bucks "on the Richter Scale"). County roads and endless Forest Service dirt roads branch off from Clam Lake and lead northwest to the resort area of Namekagon and northeast to the lumbermill town of Mellen, where white-tailed deer aficionado

Martin Hanson goes to pick up his copy of the *Wall Street Journal* and corn for his deer feeders.

All of these places are set deep in the North Woods country dominated by pines, birch, oaks, and endless pole stands of maples and laced with deer trails leading to deeryards, which Tim follows on a daily basis. His old, green, rusted-out '77 Plymouth Fury with its ten-foot Yagi antenna and Clover deer traps draped on top has become a familiar sight to year-round residents, hunters, off-season tourists, snowmobilers, and skiers of Clam Lake.

How far do deer travel to use Martin Hanson's corn feeders? Tim wonders. How often do they use them? How long do they stay at them? Will Martin's deer feeding operation create a resident deer population that no longer traditionally travels to the Spider Lake deeryard eleven miles away? How do corn feeders affect deer movement patterns? In trying to answer some of these questions, Tim leads a life most deer hunters would envy, as this entry in his February 1988 journal indicates, written in a picturesque, isolated cabin on Spider Lake in Deer Management Unit 6.

The 5th of February was like most days. Ruth and I got up and checked our ten deer traps by eight A.M. Every morning the traps have to be baited and checked for squirrel damage. Red squirrels and snowshoe hares seem to enjoy chewing on netting and it's rather frustrating to have a deer enter a trap, eat some corn or white cedar, trip the trigger wire dropping the netting door, and then slip out a hole in the netting created by a squirrel with nothing better to chew on.

After breakfast we usually leave the cabin and start the day by locating radio-tagged deer. Using a ten-foot Yagi antenna mounted on our '77 Plymouth, we can detect a deer's transmitter from up to four miles away. My notes for the 5th of February indicate we were to locate eleven deer fifteen miles from our trapping site. We drove east on this day from Clam Lake and located the deer near the community of Glidden. The trip lasted until nearly two in the afternoon of that day. We drove about fifty miles on snow-covered forest service roads and stopped at least three times to get the location of each deer.

This day was clear and calm with an afternoon temperature of 35°F. The winter had been unseasonably warm and dry, but there was about a half-foot of snow on the ground. During one short break, we sat on the hood of the car and soaked up a few minutes of the sun's warmth. The tall stems of the balsam fir, spruces, and cedars near Torrey Lake were as solid as a wall around us. The chickadees and chattering red squirrels filled the air with sweet sounds, muffled by the carpet of snow. No office in any building is as conducive to work as that which we had around us. We felt certain we had the best office in the country for our work.

We arrived at our cabin on Spider Lake by 4:30 P.M. Before entering we checked all the traps by listening for the beeping of the transmitters. All were working fine. We went inside the cabin and got set up, piling our coats and boots by the door, putting binoculars by the window, and deciding who would watch for deer on the first shift. We watched three corn-filled feeders to collect data on the frequency of deer use. Despite the mild winter, we had some regular deer who fed nearly every night, taking in food from a feeder even though there was plenty to be found elsewhere. During past winters these feeders attracted twenty or more deer at a time. But this winter three to five were more typical.

At the cabin, Ruth and I traded observing chores every half-hour or so. While it is exciting to watch deer for long periods of time at very close range, as any bow hunter or photographer will admit, straining to read letters on collars or tags in ears can become tedious. Sometimes we traded on the hour, but depending on the other tasks at hand, and the number of deer present, the time varied. Every half-hour or so we would check the traps for captures by listening for their signal. This was accomplished from the cabin using a smaller antenna than the one described on our car.

About an hour after we started observations that night, we began cooking dinner. Soon a spike buck showed up and fed for awhile. Perhaps it was due to the mild winter, but the buck still retained his antlers. Each buck's rack tends to be different, and since we had observed this buck several times before, we knew who he was. We can only wonder what untagged deer do, and where they go. He left after twenty minutes for places known only to him. Shortly afterwards, a doe and a buck fawn came in from across the lake. They were daily visitors, with visits around sunset. Today's visit must have been delayed by the buck's presence. The air was rapidly cooling and steam left their noses with each breath.

Our stew on the stove inside was steaming as well. I checked the traps via frequency once more before dinner, and noticed one had stopped beeping indicating the trap had likely been set off. We huddled close to the receiver, staring at the eerie green glow of its dial. The frequency was dialed in correctly, but no matter how hard we strained, we heard no beeping from the trap transmitter. Each of our iron-framed, netted Clover traps had a transmitter on the door to notify us if the trap had been sprung. On a clear night we could receive the signal from all individual traps using the small antenna in the cabin at the study site.

I turned off the stove, and we put on our coveralls and boots. The trap in question was one of the closest, only 100 yards from the cabin. The routine from here is second nature. At night the deer's instinct is to hide, so we can approach fairly closely before the situation gets intense.

Before leaving we put on headlamps and grabbed the trapping kit, an army surplus bag with every tool today's trapper needs to tag and radio-collar deer. Since it was a clear night, we headed off down the trail without aid of light. We had walked only halfway to the trap when the deer decided we were close enough. The captured animal tried to bolt away, but was retained by the netting. With my light I scanned up the trail to the trap. While I couldn't quite make out the trap, there was no mistaking

the glow of the eyes set three feet off the ground and staring at us, or the grunting and kicking.

I sprinted toward the trap, no easy task in Sorrel boots and sixteen inches of snow. Our Clover traps are designed to fold, pressing the deer between the sides, much like a cattle chute. I started cutting supporting lines to the trap as Ruth got to the far side of the trap. In seconds the trap was collapsed and the deer immobilized. It was only then that we realized who we had just caught. The spike buck from earlier this evening seemed none too pleased with being trapped. In another minute or two, Ruth had snapped in the solar ear transmitter. Into his ear I snapped a tag with an identification number and instructions. This helps people notify the university of where and when the deer is found or shot in the future.

We released the buck, reset the trap, and headed back to the cabin. Our stomachs reminded us that the dinner hour was long gone, and the cold stew offered no immediate relief. But the thrill of that buck, and the chance to track his movements in the future, made it all worthwhile. We would soon discover where that buck lives, and where he goes on the many days he's not at the corn feeders. We will know next fall if he becomes a trophy, or eludes the hunters.

I can't think of a more picturesque place to study deer movements—to participate in the game of "catch and release" with whitetails—than the area around Clam Lake with its "rolling glacial ridges and crater-like depressions, its granite boulders and outcroppings," as Edward Lueders immortalized it in his *Clam Lake Papers* (1977).

Early in January of 1989, I visited Clam Lake with Orrin Rongstad, the principal investigator in this study, for an in-depth interview with Tim and a firsthand look at the Adopt-A-Deer Program, a program funded in part by Whitetails Unlimited in which individual deer hunters contribute $300 for detailed information on the sea-

A familiar sight at Martin Hanson's corn feeder and one of the many participants in the Adopt-A-Deer Program.
Martin Hanson photo

sonal movements and activities of their adopted deer.

We found Tim and his wife, Ruth, in their temporary field station, a cozy log cabin located on Highway 77 across the road from Ray and Evy Swaggerty's Irish Inn, sifting through their field notes and observations on deer behavior and studying their more than 3500 locations on eighty-nine radio-tagged deer.

"This buck number 17," Tim said while pointing to the screen of his computer which outlines the buck's home range and seasonal movements, "I captured as a buck fawn at the Holtz cabin on Spider Lake on December 26, 1986."

Tim often studied this buck at the corn feeders where the animal aggressively

chased other adults away, earning him the name of "Porker." He wintered on the west side of Spider Lake and remained there until spring of 1987. In late spring, the buck disappeared. Tim relocated the buck by an air search seven miles west of Spider Lake near Lake Namekagon. There, a resident with a deer feeding station confirmed the aggressive nature of the animal. Like many yearling bucks, buck number 17 only experienced a short life; a bow hunter shot buck number 17 during the last week of October 1987, south of Grand View on County Trunk D, eleven miles from his original trapping site. Buck number 17 proved to be eighteen months old.

While checking his radio transmitters during the deer hunting season, Tim dis-

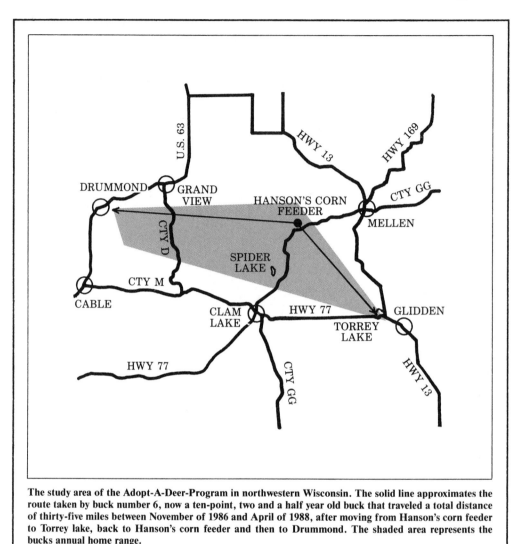

The study area of the Adopt-A-Deer-Program in northwestern Wisconsin. The solid line approximates the route taken by buck number 6, now a ten-point, two and a half year old buck that traveled a total distance of thirty-five miles between November of 1986 and April of 1988, after moving from Hanson's corn feeder to Torrey lake, back to Hanson's corn feeder and then to Drummond. The shaded area represents the bucks annual home range.

covered a dramatic decrease in deer movements. Mature bucks, in particular, tended to stay on private land where hunting access was limited. But in studying the movements of radio-tagged buck fawns, Tim found that buck number 6, which he captured on November 9, 1986 at Martin Hanson's corn feeder, moved to Torrey Lake for the 1986–87 winter, a distance of fifteen miles. In the spring of 1987, the buck returned to Martin's corn feeder for about two months. Tim then lost his signal. On May 26, Tim took an airplane up to search for the missing deer and found that the buck had moved twenty miles west to an area south of Drummond, thus moving a total distance of thirty-five miles. Buck number 6 then roamed around in an area of six square miles before establishing a new home range. This 10-pointer survived the 1987 bow and gun deer seasons and then moved several miles southwest in December of 1987 to a deeryard near Porcupine Lake. In early April 1988, Tim again lost the signal from his weak transmitter and now has no idea of the animal's current location.

As part of his field work, Tim began a series of tests to determine whether deer prefer shelled corn, processed pellets (essentially cattle feed), or calf feed. His preliminary results indicate that whitetails will eat deer pellets as readily as corn once they become accustomed to them, but they do not accept calf feed when given the choice. Tim soon learned, as many other deer feeders have, that corn costs about half as much as commercial deer or cattle feed, and does not break down when wet.

In studying the home ranges of the deer using his corn feeders, Tim discovered that deer do not travel great distances out of their established home ranges to use the feeders. Those deer that use his corn feeders are resident deer within the area of the feeders. The collective home ranges for the deer using his feeders form an ellipse one mile in length and a half-mile in width. The most interesting aspect of this ellipse is that this area becomes a preferred habitat for does especially during fawning, a conclusion I also reached after six years of feeding free-roaming whitetails. Later in the fall, this area then becomes the focal point for breeding activities.

During spring and summer, bucks avoid this area occupied extensively by antlerless deer except for nocturnal feeding. Instead, they tend to search out what some deer biologists call a "buck habitat" in the outlying area or on the immediate periphery of the does' preferred habitat. This buck habitat, which groups of bachelor bucks search out for spring and midsummer activity, usually consists of a more open habitat such as pole stands of hardwoods adjoining open fields. This more open habitat enables bucks to see one another and size up one another for the establishment of social dominance; it also allows them to avoid antler injury from densely wooded cover.

Although hunter density and the buck kill per square mile remain very low in Deer Management Unit 6, some very large antlers turn up in the area around Glidden in northwestern Wisconsin, as deer hunters Donald and Susie Bay of Milwaukee will tell you. In early November 1988 they found two locked bucks while preseason scouting on their land in the Town of Shanagolden. At the scene of the buck fight, they also discovered the carcass of a dead 8-pointer picked clean by coyotes. While locked bucks remain quite common, what sets this unique pair apart (a 9-pointer and a 13-pointer) revolves around the massiveness of their racks. The 9-pointer's antlers measure twenty inches on the inside spread and seven inches in circumference at their bases. The 13-pointer has a seventeen-inch inside spread and has several forked tines similar to those of mule deer bucks. One tine measures fourteen inches in length.

Deer Management Unit 6 remains unique in that it sported one of the highest numbers of deer per square mile in America during the 1930s, but now has one of the lowest deer densities in Wisconsin. As I snowshoed through the deeryards of Unit 6 with Tim, Ruth, and Orrin, helping them to set up deer traps, widening the deer trails leading to the traps with my snowshoes and placing broken cedar branches on the trails in an attempt to en-

Although hunter density and the buck kill per square mile remain very low in Deer Management Unit 6, some very large antlers turn up in the area around Glidden in northwestern Wisconsin, as deer hunters Donald and Susie Bay will tell you. *Steve Heiting photo*

tice the deer into the Clover traps, I kept thinking of the difficult questions these deer researchers pose:

Why have densities of white-tailed deer declined in northwestern Wisconsin over the past forty years? Can we attribute the gradual decline ultimately to the maturation of the northern forest? How does the aging of the forest limit the deer popula-

tions? Has there been a decrease in the quantity or quality of the summer food? Has the supply of winter food or cover declined? Are there now too few forest openings for adequate fawning sites? Has predation from coyotes or black bears increased? Has the deer density been too high in the past, causing an elimination of preferred food species? Has hunter density and hunting pressure been too high historically?

Interesting questions. But most of these questions still go unanswered, necessitating the need for more deer studies.

In one of the most interesting deer studies from the point of view of the deer hunter and deer hunting pressure, deer researcher Brian Root from Missouri quantifies the movement responses of white-tailed deer to intensive hunting pressure on the Deer Ridge Wildlife Management Area in northeastern Missouri, an area consisting mostly of oak-hickory stands with old fields, row crops, food plots, hayfields, and pastures interspersed throughout.

Rolling topography with steep drainages characterize much of his 3900-acre study area.

Each year in early November for a period of two years, Root intensively monitored twenty-four radio-collared white-tails (eight yearling females, ten adult females, four yearling males, and two adult males), for three nine-day periods: pre-season, firearms deer season, and the post-season. These three periods provided him with a basis for comparing deer movements before the firearms deer season, during, and after. He relocated each deer every two hours during this time while traveling through the study area in his "infamous" 4X4 Dodge truck. Hunter density

Professor Rongstad and Tim and Ruth Lewis trapping deer in the Spider Lake deeryard in northwestern Wisconsin. *Robert Wegner photo*

during the nine-day firearm season averaged 42.7 hunters per square mile per day.

While comparing his telemetry data for the three different periods of time at "The Cabin" at Deer Ridge, Root reached some interesting conclusions. When he examined the movements of white-tailed does subjected to hunting pressure, he discovered a significant increase in their movement during the firearms season, as most hunters would expect. In an article published in the *Missouri Conservationist* entitled "Deciphering Deer Movements," Root summarized his telemetry data with regard to hunting pressure and white-tailed doe movements:

"Does that had been traveling about two to 2.5 miles every day were suddenly moving well over three miles per day, or about 25 percent more than they were before the firearms season. Does that were not hunted (those that resided within the boundaries of a refuge) did not show this increase in movement. However, even with increased movement, does stayed within an established home range and did not wander into areas unfamiliar to them. From this information we determined that when there are hunters in the woods, does will not go far but will be moving around more than usual and may be more vulnerable to harvest."

Root expected bucks to react in a similar manner to intensive hunting pressure, but his data surprised him and will surprise most deer hunters.

"Instead, we found that bucks moved very erratically. Their movement showed no relationship to changes in hunting pressure, ranging from four to five miles per day regardless of whether hunters were in the woods or not. Bucks, like does, were not driven from established home ranges, even when hunting pressure exceeded 100 hunters per square mile. However, the sizes of the bucks' home ranges were more than three times larger than those of does — one adult buck covered an area of over five square miles. (See accompanying figures.)

"Bucks seemed to have a one-track mind during the rut, which is at its peak during November, and did not alter movements when hunters were around. This isn't to say that bucks won't hide in good cover for a short while to avoid a nearby hunter, but distances traveled by each buck did not change due to hunting pressure. As an example, one evening during the 1984 firearms season we watched a disgruntled hunter, trudging back to his car, pass within twenty feet of an eight-point, radio-collared buck lying in a brushy fence row. The buck stayed hidden for about ten minutes after the hunter passed, but two hours later he was over one-half mile away, probably still chuckling about the incident."

In his study, Root found no pattern in the daily movements of bucks during the intensive monitoring period. While the home range sizes of bucks exceeded those of does by three times, Root detected no significant changes in home range size for bucks between the pre-season, firearms season, and the post-season. In other words, bucks did not expand their home range during the nine-day deer hunt as most hunters would think. Their activity centers did not change significantly during the three periods of time.

While some deer researchers suggest that movements and home range sizes of bucks increase when subjected to intensive hunting pressure, others indicate that they decrease. Since most deer hunting seasons coincide with the rut, data supporting either alternative must be carefully analyzed before drawing any conclusions.

Although many hunters swear that all "their" deer head to refuges when the shooting starts, Root found no evidence at

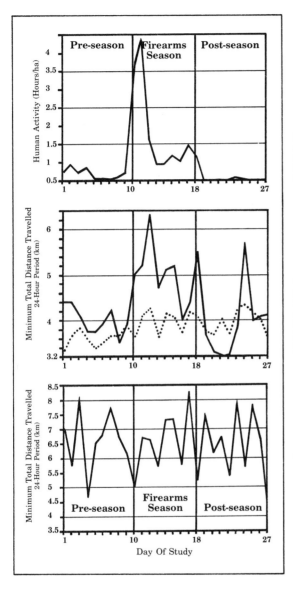

Daily human activity values nine days before (pre-season), nine days during (firearms season) and nine days after (post-season) the firearms deer hunting season on the Deer Ridge Wildlife Management Area in northeastern Missouri. Data pooled from 1984–1985.

The daily movement indices for seven non-refuge (solid line) and eleven refuge (dashed line) female deer nine days before (pre-season), nine days during (firearms season) and nine days after (post-season) the firearms deer hunting season on the Deer Ridge Wildlife Management Area in northeastern Missouri. Data pooled from 1984–85. Unlike bucks, does exhibited a significant increase in their movement patterns during the firearms deer season.

The daily movement indices for six male deer nine days before (pre-season), nine days during (firearms season) and nine days after (post season) the firearms deer hunting season on the Deer Ridge Wildlife Management Area in northeastern Missouri. Data pooled from 1984–85. Unlike the movements of does, buck movements showed no relationship to changes in hunting pressure even when hunting pressure exceeded 100 hunters per square mile.

Reprinted from Brian Root. 1986. "Movements of White-tailed Deer in Northeastern Missouri." M.S. Thesis. University of Missouri–Columbia.

Deer Ridge to support this rather errone-ous conclusion.

"Deer with home ranges outside the ref-uge did not move there when hunting pres-sure increased. Instead, they stayed within their established home ranges, contending with hunters as best they could. Thus,

hunting right along the refuge boundary, which is a very common practice at Deer Ridge, probably is no more effective than hunting anywhere else on the area."

What advice, then, do we as deer hunters get from the scientists with regard to deer movements? Root explains, "Don't worry about deer moving into areas closed to hunting — most deer will stay right where they are. All you have to do is find the right spot. And be patient.

"The next time you're in the woods and it seems that deer have become nearly extinct, remember — the deer are still around. If there are other hunters in the woods, does may be moving around even more than usual; bucks will be active anyway, responding to their increased hormone levels."

Some bucks, however, especially yearling bucks, will not always stay within their established home ranges, as Root himself discovered. In his study of deer movements on Deer Ridge, Root followed two yearling bucks that dispersed in a very dramatic way from their established home ranges during the fall. One young buck left his established range on October 10; a hunter shot that buck seventy-six miles northwest of his core area on November 10. The other young buck left his core area on October 21 and maintained a home range eleven miles south of his original home range before a hunter shot him on November 17.

In the Deer Ridge study, hunters shot 84 percent of the total kill on the first two days of the firearms season when estimated hunter densities exceeded ninety hunters per square mile, which leads me to believe that if you hunt in an area with such high hunter densities and you fail to shoot a deer during the first two days of the season, you better take a second look at the price of beef.

With hunter densities as high as 10.6 hunters per square kilometer at the Lory State Park in the Horsetooth Mountain area west of Fort Collins, Colorado, wildlife researchers with the Colorado Division of Wildlife also reached the conclusion that hunting pressure does not cause deer

movement in terms of distance or cause deer to leave their normal home ranges; it merely causes deer to move into more adequate cover.

In this Colorado study, researchers placed radio collars on seventeen adult female mule deer. After studying approximately 1500 locations and tabulating 250 hours of twenty-four-hour activity data, Roland Kufeld, a wildlife researcher with the Colorado Division of Wildlife, and his colleagues learned that all seventeen deer stayed within the interior of their minimum convex polygon home ranges during the deer hunting season. (A convex polygon home range consists of a closed plane figure placed on a map bounded by three or more line segments. Its boundaries curve or bulge outward and contain all the observed radio locations of a deer.) During the hunt, hunters often complained to the officers working at the check stations that they were not seeing any deer. "Since the deer did not leave the area," Kufeld notes in the January 1988 issue of the *Journal of Range Management,* "they apparently adapted quickly to hunting pressure by moving into nearby patches of heavier escape cover."

While trapping deer for radio instrumentation in the Rocky Mountain foothills, Kufeld discovered that eared corn remained the most effective trapping bait. Kufeld found apple pulp, deer-elk wafers, oats soaked in molasses, and corn silage less effective as a bait in decreasing order.

In studying the daily activity patterns of deer, Kufeld noticed that his radio-collared deer spent more time bedding on cloudy, full moon nights (when cloud cover exceeded 50 percent) than when the sky was clear on full moon nights. However, he found no difference in the percentage of time deer spent feeding or bedding on clear, full moon nights versus new moon nights—a finding that runs contrary to the popular belief held by many deer hunters, myself included, that deer hunting remains more difficult when the moon is full because deer feed at night. "During our study," Kufeld says, "deer fed heavily at night regardless of moon phase."

In a significant study of white-tailed deer movements in the Shenandoah National Park in Virginia, wildlife researchers John Scanlon and Michael Vaughan quantify seasonal and annual movements of deer along Skyline Drive and in a more remote "backcountry" area of the park. Their telemetry data indicates that when we try to determine the movements and activities of white-tailed deer we need to think in terms of greater distances than we usually do. In their study, does along Skyline Drive maintained a mean total home range of 1110 acres and 2198 acres in the backcountry; bucks along Skyline Drive occupied a mean total home range of 4615 acres and 3965 acres in the backcountry area.

Overall, bucks in the Blue Ridge Mountains of Virginia moved a maximum distance of 3.8 miles, although one doe moved a distance of twenty-five miles. Here today and twenty-five miles from your tree stand next week. Scanlon and Vaughan found no consistent pattern to range areas for bucks in either area of their study over the seasons. Some adult bucks established well-defined breeding territories within core areas of their home ranges, while others continued to utilize their entire home range areas for rubbing and scraping activities. (See accompanying figures.) "Of three radio-collared males (two adults and one yearling) captured in the backcountry," Scanlon reports, "one adult roamed widely during the rut while the second adult and yearling established restricted breeding territories." Bucks in their study repeatedly moved from 1.2 miles to 1.8 miles per day during the rut. Does also occasionally engaged in long-range movements from their core areas, but always returned to the same localized areas within twenty-four to seventy-two hours.

In their deer movement study, Scanlon frequently observed deer in areas receiving intense human use. Yet, according to Scanlon, "some deer of both sexes hardly ever, or never, used areas of human activity. It seems there is a gradient in deer distribution and movement from close association with human activity to little or no such association."

While studying deer movements and activity patterns on the bottomlands of the lower Yellowstone River in eastern Montana, deer researcher Jim Herriges also learned that human activities and disturbances do not adversely affect white-tailed deer distribution and movement. He often located one deer in an ash stand immediately adjacent to a river road and frequently found one radio-collared deer within fifty-five yards of heavily-traveled Montana Highway 16 and within 165 yards of an occupied farmhouse with dogs. Yes, deer often reside very close to man, the hunter, and at all times of the year.

Like other movement studies, Herriges noted a distinct fidelity for a small core area of intense activity. However, the home range sizes for individual whitetails in his study varied widely from 0.18 square miles for one adult female to 6.24 square miles for one adult male that used upland draws and agricultural fields. Yearlings of both sexes and adult males clearly exhibited more variable movements than adult females. "They were likely to move to two or more alfalfa fields in one night," Herriges reports, "change fields between nights and

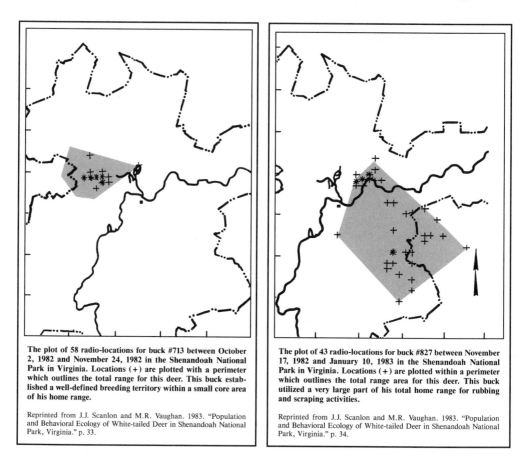

The plot of 58 radio-locations for buck #713 between October 2, 1982 and November 24, 1982 in the Shenandoah National Park in Virginia. Locations (+) are plotted with a perimeter which outlines the total range for this deer. This buck established a well-defined breeding territory within a small core area of his home range.

Reprinted from J.J. Scanlon and M.R. Vaughan. 1983. "Population and Behavioral Ecology of White-tailed Deer in Shenandoah National Park, Virginia." p. 33.

The plot of 43 radio-locations for buck #827 between November 17, 1982 and January 10, 1983 in the Shenandoah National Park in Virginia. Locations (+) are plotted within a perimeter which outlines the total range area for this deer. This buck utilized a very large part of his total home range for rubbing and scraping activities.

Reprinted from J.J. Scanlon and M.R. Vaughan. 1983. "Population and Behavioral Ecology of White-tailed Deer in Shenandoah National Park, Virginia." p. 34.

move in an unpredictable pattern. They were also less likely to return to the previous day's bedding area."

The most distinct feature of daily movements for whitetails on the lower Yellowstone River revolved around travel to agricultural fields. Herriges found that whitetails that used the same general areas of riparian habitat (habitat along the banks of rivers) for bedding during the day tended to move to the same agricultural fields at night. Deer that traveled to agricultural fields on a given night spent an average of 4.5 hours in the field. According to Herriges, "deer typically made only one

trip to fields in a night. More than one trip between riparian cover and agricultural fields was common only among individuals with daytime bedding sites in close proximity to agriculture."

Herriges noticed that nighttime movements did not follow any distinct or consistent pattern. However, he discovered one exception in this regard: Whitetails typically followed drainage ditches in their travels to reach agricultural fields. In his study, deer showed a marked preference for alfalfa in summer and ungrazed alfalfa, sugar beets, and winter wheat in winter. When trying to determine the number of deer using agricultural fields, Herriges rec-ommends shining from one to two hours after sunset until midnight, when maxi-mum numbers of deer can be expected. "Spotlight counts made in late summer," Herriges tells us, "will best represent num-bers of deer using a field because deer tend to stay longer as the summer progresses."

In a similar study of the distribution and movements of white-tailed deer in re-lation to agricultural fields on the Marion County Wildlife Management Area in southern Mississippi, wildlife researchers Carol Burns and Harry Jacobson conclude that deer do not shift their home range to take advantage of a food source that may be close by. In their study in the longleaf pine habitat of southern Mississippi, they detected no consistent relationship be-tween annual home range size and the availability of 200 planted food plots. Like Herriges, they observed that whitetails maintain a tremendous fidelity to their home range and that tradition and learning play a crucial role in determining field use and movement patterns.

The distribution of the home ranges of their twenty-one radio-collared deer did not change significantly with respect to availability of plantings; deer with ranges on the unplanted side of the study area did not shift ranges to the planted side. Their preliminary analysis, however, indicates that deer did shift their activity centers or core areas *within* their home ranges when they had access to both planted and un-planted plots, when their home ranges bi-sected both the planted and unplanted areas. In other words, man can manipu-late the location of a deer's activity center or core area through the strategic place-ment of food plots *within* or on the periph-ery of the animal's home range, but he can-not pull deer out of their traditional home ranges by creating food plots.

In the creation of their food plots, Ja-cobson and Burns chose oats, wheat, rye, rye grass, yuchi clover, subterranean clo-ver, crimson clover, ladino clover, fescue, and vetch for cool season plantings. They chose four species for summer plantings: corn, pea, soybean, and joint vetch. I mention the species because an increasing number of deer hunters now plant food plots for deer on private land, leased land, and on property belonging to deer hunting clubs and frequently query me about what they should plant. A 1988 survey of south-ern white-tailed deer hunters indicates that 37.3 percent of those surveyed plant food plots to attract deer. In the Mississippi study, deer most readily utilized rye grass, rye, wheat, ladino clover, and crimson clover.

During the 1985 and 1986 hunting sea-sons, Dr. Jacobson and his students sur-veyed the hunters using the planted and unplanted areas in their study area and discovered that hunter success rates (num-ber of deer harvested per hour spent in the field) and observation rates (number of deer observed per hour in the field) were significantly higher on the areas planted with agronomic food plots than for the ad-jacent areas containing an equal number of fallow food plots. "Hunter density and the number of deer harvested," Jacobson reports, "were also significantly higher for the planted areas than for the fallow areas for both the 1985 and 1986 deer hunting seasons. These data indicate that the planting of agronomic food plots can sig-nificantly increase deer hunter success rates, and concentrate, at least locally, both the deer and the hunter."

While monitoring the home range sizes and distribution of their twenty-one radio-collared deer, Burns and Jacobson, like Herriges, found the greatest variation and inconsistency in movement patterns for yearlings and adult males. Bucks in their study from 1984 to 1987 moved their home range centers or core areas an average of 1291 yards and displayed a wide variation in the seasonal and annual home range estimates, which varied from 909 acres to 4205 acres. These home ranges may seem quite large to most deer hunters, but other deer researchers also report very large yearly home range estimates in the South, especially for mature bucks. Steve Demarais of Texas Tech University, for example, reports that the convex polygon home ranges for fourteen bucks averaged more than 3000 acres during 1986–87. The ages of these bucks averaged 6.2 years.

Despite all the hype in the popular literature about how to "pattern your buck," these scientific studies once again demonstrated that no clear-cut movement patterns exist for radio-collared deer whether in Wisconsin, Missouri, Colorado, Montana, or Mississippi, and that deer biologists seldom agree on any aspect of deer movements and how the animals respond to hunting pressure.

Yet, behavioral responses of deer to hunting pressure and heavy hunter density have important management implications, and wildlife managers and deer hunters need to understand how hunting pressure influences deer movements and distribution and how that distribution relates to vegetative cover, posted land, and refuges so that deer habitat needs can be met. If hunted deer disperse to areas closed to hunting for whatever reason, the resulting deer kill could be less than desired.

On the other hand, if deer hunting pressure remains intense, such deer movement could prevent an overkill. Where deer adapt well to their habitat and learn to make maximum use of escape cover, they may become reluctant to leave their home ranges when hunted. Consequently, they could sustain higher levels of hunting pressure. In such situations, more hunting might be needed to achieve the desired results. But man still knows little about the behavioral responses of deer to intensive hunting pressure.

Vulnerability to hunting remains relative and varies along a wide continuum. In an ideal sense, vulnerability to hunting should be a measurable parameter, if it is to be useful in the making of meaningful management decisions. But knowledge of the effects of hunting on deer movements and distribution is limited, elusive, and virtually nonexistent, especially since so much of the information is based on such small sample sizes.

It is difficult to say exactly what any white-tailed deer is doing or where it is going. It's impossible to know when or where any event in the life of a white-tailed deer starts or terminates. The human mind unfortunately confines us to realms that contain only a small portion of the information produced in an event in the life of a deer. Some critical factor could be missing and we would never know it. Although we could theoretically design and carry out thousands of deer movement studies, we can never describe any deer as the sum of these scientific experiments.

What then do we learn from science? We learn several things: (1) As deer hunters we need to think in terms of greater distances when we try to figure out a deer's home range. (2) We will not drive deer out of their established home ranges during the hunting season. (3) Deer will not travel out of their established home ranges to use our corn feeders or food plots. (4) Deer will not head for the refuge when the shooting starts unless the refuge already coincides with the animal's established home range.

(5) Yearlings of both sexes and adult males clearly exhibit the most varied, unpredictable, and erratic movements.

After six years of feeding deer, I've learned the importance of using detailed aerial photos when trying to decipher deer movements on the back forty. Sketching and plotting observed deer movements on aerial photos and placing arrows representing the predominant wind directions and how they relate to food sources helps us to establish general patterns for habitat use and deer movement. But we must remember that these patterns, if and when they exist, differ in relation to specific topographical and vegetational features, land use practices, and local weather conditions. But when established patterns emerge, they sometimes hold over time in a specific deer hunting region. "Year to year changes in deer use of agricultural areas appear to be slight," notes Montana deer researcher Jim Herriges.

What we learn from these deer movement studies might best be summarized in the words of one backwoods buck hunter from Missouri. "Even during the deer season, they're closer than you think!"

Chapter 16

A Deer Hunter's
Photo Album

Contrary to popular belief, deer jump through or go under barbed wire fences rather than jump over them.

Bucks on a frosty morn.

**Judging from their expressions and their
ammunition belts, these Michigan deerslayers took their hunting quite seriously.**

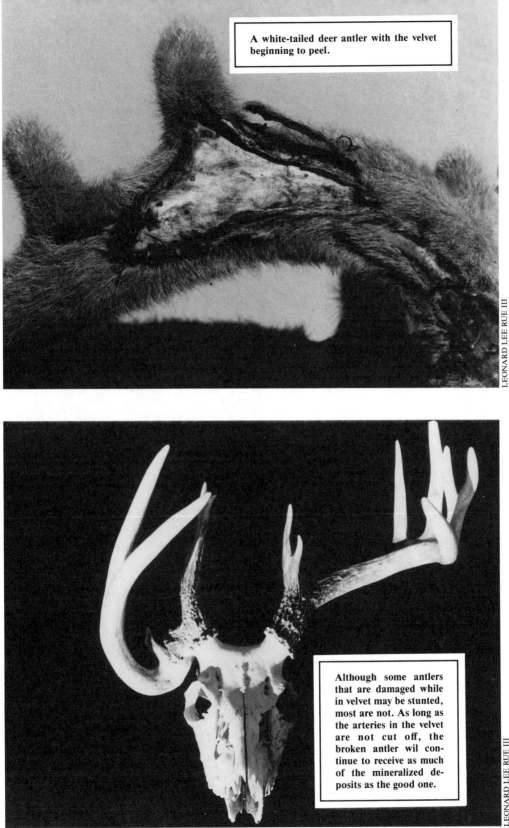

A white-tailed deer antler with the velvet beginning to peel.

Although some antlers that are damaged while in velvet may be stunted, most are not. As long as the arteries in the velvet are not cut off, the broken antler wil continue to receive as much of the mineralized deposits as the good one.

The Benoit boys, like generations before them, hold a
last minute meeting of the minds before running big
bucks on the ridges of Vermont.

Scent communication among whitetails, especially as it relates to the overhanging branch remains largely a mystery despite all the bewildering gobbledygook and mystifying hocus-pocus that we find on all the bottles of chemical juice now available in the deer-hunting marketplace. "The concept is highly complex and controversial," deer biologist John Ozoga tells us. "The exact chemistry, behavior, and physiological mechanisms involved are poorly understood and likely vary greatly from one area to the next, depending on herd density and age-sex composition, habitat characteristics, and other unidentified factors."

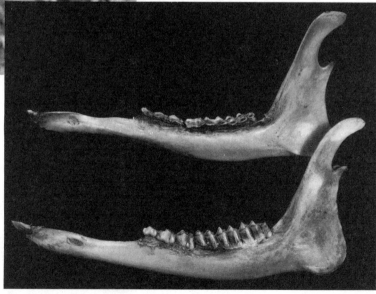

The jaw bones from two white-tailed deer. The top jaw bone is from a 11.5-year-old deer and the bottom one is from a 2.5-year-old deer.

A white-tailed doe's swollen vulva in estrus.

I have seen a lot of fawn photos in my days of editing. I give Charlie Heidecker five stars for this one.

CHARLIE HEIDECKER

"Giving Deer the Steer." When deer approach this built-in, one-way deer gate they stop, look to either side of the gate's opening, and with ears laid back aggressively jump through. They are then funneled along a 1.5-mile, eight-foot-high deer fence towards the "deer underpass" located under Interstate 70 at Mud Springs Gulch west of Vail, Colorado.

Very unusual elongated hooves.

MARILYN MARING

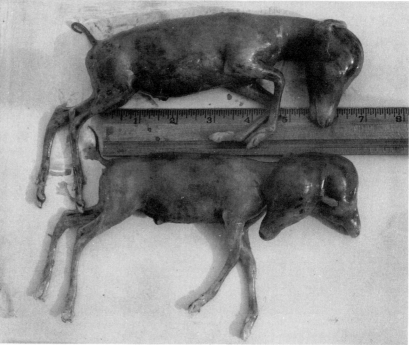

ARLOW BOYCE

In 1957, deer biologists autopsied a doe that dogs had killed on Higgins Lake in Roscommon County, Michigan. They discovered a two-headed white-tailed deer fetus. This is the only instance of dicephalism in deer that I am aware of.

RICHARD W. ROELLER

The biker and the buck. Jeffrey Morris, a New York deer hunter, shot this trophy 11-pointer two miles from his suburban Buffalo home after a fifteen minute bicycle ride.

EDWARD GRANT PHOTOS

This epic buck fight lasted for twenty-four hours on a cold, rainy day in November 1952 in Portage County, Ohio. Six men with ropes eventually lassoed the exhausted bucks, a huge 17-pointer and a 14-pointer. In the process, a main beam of one of the antlers suddenly snapped and the two giant bucks were set free, never to be seen again. Of the millions of deer photos that exist, these are perhaps some of the most dramatic.

The ideal deer camp.

Elmer Peters *(left)* **and his boys.**

Fred, I will never forget you, your Borsalino hat, and what you taught us about deer hunting!

FRED

Every deer camp has its special attraction. Shed white-tailed deer antlers hang
on a fence at a Texas deer camp.

Solidification of a white-tailed buck's antler tip.

LEONARD LEE RUE III

Heavy pearlation on a white-tailed buck's antler base.

LEONARD LEE RUE III

On November 15, 1981, Dave Beckman, a deer hunter from Missouri, found the world's new non-typical white-tailed buck dead along a fence line in St. Louis County, Missouri. It scored 325⅞, shattering the Boone and Crockett Club record that had stood since 1892. It checked in at 250 pounds (live weight). It apparently died of natural causes. Beckman reported his find to Mike Helland, a conservation agent, who holds the rack in this picture.

If a white-tailed buck is aware of the fact that you do not see him, he will try hiding anywhere.

LEN RUE JR.

It looks like Nicholas Rue is going to follow in the footsteps of his father and grandfather, two of this country's leading wildlife photographers.

RICHARD P. SMITH

"It is not essential to the hunt that it be successful. On the contrary, if the hunter's efforts were always and inevitably successful, it would not be the effort we call hunting; it would be something else. Corresponding to the eventuality or chance of the prey's escaping is the eventuality of the hunter's going home empty-handed. The beauty of hunting lies in the fact that it is always problematic." —Jose Ortega y Gasset, *Meditations on Hunting,* 1942.

LEONARD LEE RU

Wounded Deer Behavior: The Newest Research

There is five times the amount of shooting at and scaring deer than there used to be from an equal number of hunters carrying rifles that never threw "a wild ball," and that were so slow to load that every shot was fired as if it were the last ball within fifty miles.
— T. S. Van Dyke, *The Still-Hunter,* 1882

Perhaps no one subject dominates the mind of the American deer hunter more than wounding rates, crippling mortality, and wounded deer behavior. For the past decade, I have traveled around this country in an attempt to research and study these related topics from every conceivable angle. While giving a lecture entitled "The Wounded Whitetail" at Mississippi State University recently, I found myself inundated with questions from the audience about wounding rates, crippling mortality, unretrieved deer, the use of the podded arrow, the use of leashed dogs for tracking wounded deer and with questions dealing with arrow penetration, deflection, shot placement, and the reaction of the animal to hunter-inflicted wounds.

In the 1985 May/June issue of *Deer & Deer Hunting,* magazine, I summarized the latest scientific studies on some of these questions in an article titled "Crippling Losses: An Update," (reprinted in *Deer & Deer Hunting: Book 2,* Stackpole Books, 1987). Since the publication of that article, ten more studies have crossed my desk. (See the accompanying table.)

More than sixty-five scientific studies now exist on this problem. In this chapter, I summarize the newest scientific conclusions with regard to this problem. While most of these studies ultimately fail to resolve the crippling mortality question and end with the standard scientific response of "more research needed," they do provide us with a great deal of information that

Crippling loss studies, 1984–1989

WILDLIFE RESEARCHER (Or Organizations)	YEAR	TYPE OF SEASON	PLACE & TYPE OF INVESTIGATION (S) Field Search (Q) Questionnaire	CALCULATED CRIPPLING LOSS (% of legal harvest left in woods
R.W. Aho Michigan Department of Natural Resources	1984	Hunters' Choice (either sex) Archery/Shotgun	Shiawassee National Wildlife Refuge Michigan (S & Q)	Archery: 1.4 deer wounded per 1 deer retrieved Shotgun: 0.3 deer wounded per 1 deer retrieved
Ludbrook/Tomkinson Natal Parks, Game & Fish Preservation Board	1985	African Big Game	Mkuzi Game Reserve Natal, South Africa (S)	Archery: 32.7% Rifle: 7.9%
Al Hofacker *Deer & Deer Hunting* Magazine	1986	All types of seasons	Nationwide Questionnaire (Based on 2,103 wounded deer)	Archery: 56.4% Firearms: 20.8%
Boydston/Gore Texas Park & Wildlife	1986	All types of seasons	Texas wildlife management areas	Archery: 100.2% Firearms: 7%
Nixon/Hanson Illinois Natural History Survey	1986	Archery/Shotgun Either sex	Central Illinois Piatt County Study Area (Q & S of radio marked deer)	Archery: 38% Shotgun: 20%
Wescott/Peyton Michigan State University	1986	Experimental Archery Hunt	Shiawassee National Wildlife Refuge (Q based on 605 bow hunters)	1 deer wounded per 1 retrieved 100%
Todd Fuller Minnesota Department of Wildlife	1981–86	Bucks and limited antlerless seasons	Bearville Study Area Northeastern Itasca County, Minnesota (Q) and Interviews	Firearms: 19%
J.J. Robinette, *et al.* Felsenthal National Wildlife Refuge, Arkansas	1987	5-day either sex muzzleloader hunt	Mississippi, Yazoo National Wildlife Refuge (Q & S)	Muzzleloader: 23.9%
John D. Cada Montana Department of Fish, Wildlife and Parks	1988	Archery Elk Either sex	Survey of 8569 Montana elk hunters	Archery: 51%
Aaron Moen Cornell University	1989	All types of seasons	Nationwide Questionnaire based on more than 1000 responses	Archery: 68% Shotgun: 18% Rifle: 10%

Comparisons of results among such studies must be viewed with a great deal of caution because estimates of wounding rates and results can vary greatly.

should aid us in the recovery of wounded deer.

Before discussing these studies in detail, let's remember Van Dyke's advice: Shoot every arrow or shell as if it were the last one within fifty miles!

The recent and very substantial increase in the number of bow hunters leads to the inevitable comparisons between archery deer hunting and firearm deer hunting. Bow hunters, gun hunters, wildlife managers, professors of wildlife management, natural resource agency personnel, anti-hunters, and non-hunters alike hotly debate the various issues surrounding the two different forms of deer hunting. The debate, whether we like it or not, most often centers on efficiency, wounding rates, and the degree of crippling mortality. Thus far, the scientific community has unfortunately done little to either reduce the inflammatory exchanges or to resolve the complex issues.

In the first of these scientific studies, Robert Aho, a wildlife researcher with the Michigan Department of Natural Resources, set out to compare the efficiency of bow hunters and shotgun hunters in taking deer and to determine the various mortality rates for wounded deer shot with the different types of weapons. He conducted his study at the Shiawassee National Wildlife Refuge southwest of Saginaw, Michigan.

Based on field searches and 591 deer hunter surveys, Aho found that bow hunters wounded 1.4 deer for every one deer retrieved. Shotgun hunters wounded 0.3 deer for every one deer retrieved. In other words, when Aho expresses wounding rates as a ratio of deer killed, the data show bow hunters wounding deer at 4.7 times the rate of shotgun hunters.

In estimating mortality rates for wounded deer, Aho observed that the estimated mortality of arrow-wounded deer (38 percent, N = 39) appeared to be lower than that of slug-wounded deer (45 percent, N = 11), although the number of shotgun cases might be too low for a conclusive comparison. In other words, if the deer managers' objective revolves around minimizing the wounding mortality rate over time, bow hunting apparently satisfies this objective better than shotgun hunting.

If the managers' objective entails reducing the deer population immediately to reduce agricultural damage, shotgun hunting clearly appears to be the favored tool of choice, for Aho found that shotgun hunters harvested deer more than seven times as fast as bow hunters, consequently minimizing the costs of administering the deer hunts in that fewer hunters and fewer days of hunting are needed "to get the job done."

On the other hand, if the managers' objective is to maximize the hunting recreational time while minimizing the ultimate effect on the deer population, bow hunting more clearly satisfies this objective better than shotgun hunting. As you can see, any discussion of the advantages and disadvantages of bow hunting compared with shotgun hunting clearly depends upon an articulate expression of the deer managers' objectives. Aho underscores the point.

"Because objectives of deer hunting vary and frequently are not clearly conceptualized by individuals, or not clearly stated to others, interpretations and conclusions about archery and firearm deer hunting can easily clash. Clarity of objectives should stimulate mutual understanding of attitudes toward these types of deer hunting."

In the next of these studies, Tony Tomkinson, an avid bow hunter and the chief ranger at the Mkuzi Game Reserve in the Province of Natal, Republic of South Africa, set out to demonstrate in the summer of 1985 whether bow hunting proves to be a practical and ethical form of recreational hunting. Working with Ed Ashby, another enthusiastic bow hunter, Tomkinson asked five basic questions: (1) What advantages and/or disadvantages does archery equipment present us with as opposed to conventional hunting with rifles? (2) How do archery wounding rates compare with those of conventional rifle hunting? (3) At what intervals after being hit by an arrow or by a bullet does an animal become immobilized? (4) How does a big game animal react to being hit by an arrow as compared with being hit by a bullet? (5) What kinds of wounds do hunters inflict and what forms of trauma result?

In examining the data from ninety-six killed big game animals, he found that the overall wounding rate using various archery equipment far exceeded the rates for rifle hunters—32.7 percent for bow hunters compared to 7.9 percent for rifle hunters. But he observed that the wounding rates were the same, regardless of the weapon used, when the hunter hit the animal in the thorax or the spine; 0 percent.

In looking at the advantages of bow hunting, Tomkinson noticed that the meat of animals killed with rifles sustained more damage than the meat from animals killed with a bow. Another advantage of bow hunting came to light: Bow hunting caused *less* trauma not only to the target-animal but also less trauma to other animals in the vicinity of the target-animal. He also speculated that arrow wounds are less painful than bullet wounds and that the duration of fatal stress lasts only twenty seconds longer for arrows as opposed to bullets. In his study, big game animals mortally wounded with arrows traveled only thirty meters farther than animals mortally wounded with a 30/06 rifle.

Tomkinson sums up the results of his study: "The results of our study suggest that although the wounding rate of bow hunting is higher than in rifle hunting, if other considerations such as lower wounding loss, less disturbance, and immobilization times not appreciably longer than with rifle-shot animals are taken into account, bow hunting is a practical and ethical form of recreational hunting."

Like several other American researchers, Tomkinson believes that arrow wounds

sustained by animals in non-vital places most likely heal completely because of the lack of extensive tissue damage that accompanies a bullet wound and because the arrow usually comes out of the wound. In his observations, Tomkinson noted that "many bullet wounds harbour bullets or their fragmented remains, as well as bone fragments, leading to secondary infection and a lingering death of the wounded animal." In Tomkinson's study, three animals survived arrow wounds in the neck, hindquarters, and the abdomen that gun hunters subsequently shot during game control operations. In all three cases, the animals had fully recovered from their earlier arrow wounds. Tomkinson reaches these conclusions with regard to the effects of arrow and bullet wounds on big game animals:

"In the case of a bullet striking a non-vital area such as the muscle mass of the hindquarters, a large amount of energy is dissipated in a small area resulting in extensive tissue destruction. Unless a large artery is severed, hemorrhage will be stemmed by pressure from surrounding tissue and the contraction effect of the arterial intima. Death from these wounds could occur at a much later time due to hemorrhage, septicaemia, or shock from breakdown products from damaged tissues.

"When an arrow fitted with a sharp broadhead strikes a similar non-vital area, a minimum of surrounding tissue damage occurs. All the blood vessels that the blades encounter are severed and as the arterial intima is not stretched or crushed, contraction does not occur and hemorrhage is profuse causing death within seconds or minutes."

Although no hard, quantified data exist on the question of arrow-wounding mortality and surviability, some testimonials

Here's a complete skeleton of a white-tailed deer. These animals have thirteen ribs. The center of the heart rests between the fourth and the sixth rib. These ribs are wide and flat. How a broadhead penetrates the rib cage remains an interesting question with many unknowns. Arrow deflection in the rib cage can add a plus or a minus to the wounded deer story. *Robert Wegner photo*

and evidence suggest that some arrow-wounded deer do in fact survive. Several examples come readily to mind.

During the 1986 Wisconsin gun deer season, a hunter shot a yearling buck that already had a broadhead imbedded three quarters of an inch in its brain. Due to the angle and location of entry, Wisconsin DNR officials who examined the deer speculated that the deer was shot as a nubby buck and lived to approximately eighteen months of age while carrying the broadhead; the angle of entry, they believed, seemed to preclude the animal from being

shot while carrying antlers. Close examination indicated that the bone tissue began to encapsulate the broadhead, thus exhibiting the whitetail's incredible stamina and ability to recover from hunter-inflicted wounds.

When Curtis Taylor, a forty-six-year-old veteran deer hunter from Missouri, dropped a 127-7/8 point Pope and Young buck in January of 1988, at the Squaw Creek National Wildlife Refuge in northwestern Missouri, he discovered an entire arsenal of shooting efforts in his trophy buck: two broadheads, four lead slugs, and a dose of shotgun pellets. Missouri conservation officials still marvel at the 205-pound buck's capacity for survival.

One hundred years earlier, in 1888, Augustus Grimble, author of *Deer-Stalking* (1888), received this choice letter documenting the extraordinary vitality of deer. It deserves a place in the annals of deer and deer hunting.

"I was out on the 22nd of September and getting within shot of some stags, the one I wanted gave me a chance of which I at once took advantage, but hitting him low, and rather far back, the bullet cut his stomach line, and part of his insides at once protruded from the wound.

"I had a brace of deer-hounds with me, and not wishing to fire again, they were slipped at him. The stag was standing very sick, and did not see the dogs till they were close to him, and on discovering their presence he gave a tremendous bound forward; to our utter astonishment we saw the *entire stomach* tumble out like a red balloon, and fall to the ground! Notwithstanding this, the stag went top speed, and I never saw one go faster, for over half a mile before the deer-hounds pulled him down in a burn, and when we got there we found him as cleanly gralloched as if the stalker himself had performed the last rites due to a dead stag. Returning to the spot he started from, we found his stomach lying on the ground unbroken."

Without question, the vitality of a deer to survive its wounds goes beyond the proverbial vaunted life-force of the cat.

Despite this, many hunters underestimate the incredible resilience of deer. Dr. Randy Davidson, a deer hunter and a professor for the Southeastern Wildlife Disease Study Program at the University of Georgia, is one who does not, for he has inspected many white-tailed deer that have survived remarkable injuries, some inflicted by hunters.

"I recently inspected a 4.5-year-old doe that had been wounded last year, and then shot and killed this year, in Arkansas's very tightly controlled Pine Bluff Arsenal. I was doing a whitetail disease study on the area, and inspecting deer shot during a special hunt, to determine the herd's health. The hunt manager knew a bow hunter last year who had shot and 'lost' a big doe. I inspected that harvested doe this year, and what I found was remarkable.

"After having been wounded the year before, that 4.5-year-old doe was healthy enough to have bred and had a fawn this year. There was no doubt it was the same animal that had been 'lost' by the bow hunter the year before. Still imbedded in the doe were six inches of arrow shaft and a broadhead. The arrow had penetrated from the top of the animal near the rear right leg. The arrow shaft went forward through the diaphragm, penetrating the body cavity, and into the thorax. There was some inflammation around the wound, but the arrow shaft and broadhead were completely encapsulated in scar tissue, and the doe didn't seem to have had any ill-effects from the wound."

That some of these deer survive at all is amazing, but many actually thrive and lead normal wild lives! Learning more about the recuperative capabilities of deer is intriguing, to say the least.

Some knowledgeable bow hunters believe that a good number of well-shot deer not recovered after 500 or more yards of proper trailing will survive a broadhead arrow wound. Dr. Dave Samuel, a professor of wildlife management at West Virginia University, puts it this way. "The next time you wound an animal with an arrow . . . remember, if you don't find it within the first 300 yards or so, it probably is still running around the deer woods, healthy and a bit wiser." Both Drs. Samuel and Davidson agree that even a gut- or paunch-shot deer can survive, for plant eating animals such as deer have a protective lining around the stomach and intestines, called the "omentum," which plugs any holes that may puncture the stomach or intestines.

For the past nineteen years, Dr. Ward Stone has been in charge of the wildlife pathology unit of the New York State Department of Environmental Conservation. During this time, Stone has examined thousands of deer; it's his job to determine the cause of death in deer. In his opinion, "protracted morbidity caused by arrow wounds, resulting in death of white-tailed deer is rare. I have seen only two cases involving arrow wounds of the head that resulted in the death of the deer. In my experience, as a wildlife pathologist, the arrows used today by deer hunters generally cause quick kills. Wounds caused by arrows that are not immediately fatal generally heal more swiftly than bullet wounds. This is in part due to the less tissue destruction resulting in the incised wounds caused by arrows."

Thus as you can see from these numerous examples, Tomkinson's incidences of survival in the African study are not exceptions. It should be pointed out, however, that researchers at Auburn University are currently studying the broadhead wound channels of eighty-six euthanized white-tailed deer. Their findings indicate that in 100 percent of the wounds, clipped hairs are present that can lead to serious infection, thus casting doubt on this whole notion of "clean wounds" and unique survivability. Time will tell as they culture the bacteria to determine which pathogens are introduced.

No discussion of the African study on wounded big game animals would be complete without looking at one of the study's most interesting aspects: Ed Ashby's broadhead performance tests. While participating in the African field research project, Ashby had the opportunity to evaluate the effectiveness of thirty-two varieties of broadheads. In testing these broadheads, Ashby used a ninety-four-pound longbow and Tomkinson used an eighty-pound Martin Warthog compound.

While collecting data from 154 shot records, Ashby asked several very interesting questions: (1) Which angles present the most lethal shots? (2) Which shot angles offer the least chance of a lethal hit? (3) Which type of broadhead gives the greatest portion of lethal hits on the most difficult shot angles? (4) Is there a significant difference in penetration among the various types of broadheads and, if so, which broadhead provides better penetration.

Ashby and Tomkinson took twenty-five shots at animals quartering from the rear forward; twenty-four of these shots resulted in lethal hits. The quartering-away shot represented the best shot of all, for it allowed the hunter to move more freely to position himself for the shot and it gave the hunter the best probability for a quick, lethal hit. Ashby, somewhat disturbingly, found that almost 30 percent of the broadside shots into the chest-shoulder area resulted in non-lethal hits. Traditionally, the broadside shot has always been considered the "classic" shot. Based on Ashby's shot-placement records, the quartering-toward-the-archer angle with the arrow striking in the area of the neck-shoulder junction represents the worst possible shot.

When trying to determine which broadheads provide the greatest portion of lethal hits on the most difficult shot angles, Ashby discovered that 85 percent of all the hits with single-blade heads were lethal with the animal quartering toward the archer (seventeen of twenty hits) and none of the hits with multi-blade heads were lethal (zero of sixteen). According to Ashby, "when a bone of any type is hit, the single blade head offers vastly superior penetration. Even with a soft tissue hit, the single blade heads penetrate substantially better than the multi-blade heads."

One of the most striking features of Ashby's observations revolved around the fact that a large number of broadheads proved very fragile, often breaking and bending whether they hit bone or not. In his opinion, "the rigid two-blade (or more accurately, single blade with two cutting edges) broadheads appear to be significantly more resistant to damage than either the rigid, multi-blade or the replaceable blade type of broadhead." He recommends that hunters use a tough, single-blade broadhead. He names the Grizzly as his personal choice for the best broadhead tested.

"Progressively more difficult shots were taken with the Grizzly broadhead in an attempt to find the limits of its performance. It recorded a remarkable 95.8 percent lethal hits on the toughest shots I could devise, and was 100 percent lethal on the tough neck-shoulder shot (and 75 percent of those neck-shoulder shots were on the toughest animal tested, the wildebeeste)."

Many people claim that multi-blade broadheads leave a better blood trail; Ashby's broadhead performance tests cast serious doubts on this claim. After studying the results of seventy-seven shots with single-blade broadheads and seventy-seven shots with multi-blade broadheads, he believes that the claim of increased trailing ease with the use of multi-blade broadheads to be ill-founded. Actually, the amount of blood depends more on where the animal is hit and whether or not an exit hole exists than on broadhead construction.

Ashby concluded his analysis of broadhead performance with this one-liner: "As long as the very fastest of arrows travel not much over 250 feet per second and most

less than 200 feet per second, and animals move faster than the arrow, no archer can guarantee where his shot will hit."

This statement on random shot placement reminds me of what Van Dyke said a century earlier with regard to rifle shooting.

"When we come to analyze rifle shooting you will conclude that I tell the exact truth when I assert, as I do most positively, that the man who talks of placing a ball where he wishes to place it in a running deer at *any* distance, or at one standing beyond a hundred and fifty yards, is either an ignoramus or a braggart who takes his listener for a bigger fool than he is himself."

One wonders about the random patterns of our shooting. In 1986, Horace Gore, whitetail program director for the Texas Parks and Wildlife Department, analyzed the number of archery shots fired per deer killed from Texas Wildlife Management Areas and reached the conclusion that "shot placement is, for all practical purposes, random!" His data for public hunts in Texas indicated one deer killed and one deer wounded per twenty-one shots fired. (See the accompanying figure.) Nineteen of the twenty-one shots fired never hit the animal. That's a lot of indiscriminate shooting. This finding does not, unfortunately, represent an exception; researchers in Wisconsin and Michigan reached similar conclusions. Is it buck fever? These are the kinds of statistics that professional wildlife managers must deal with when trying to extend the use of archery as a management tool.

In a paper presented at the Southeast Deer Study Group meeting in Gulf Shores, Alabama, in 1987, Gore reported that his data indicated a bow hunting wounding rate of 50 percent (calculated as the percentage of deer hit but not retrieved). In

Archery shots taken per deer killed at Texas Wildlife Management areas

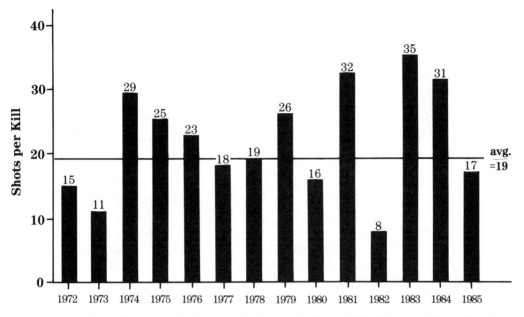

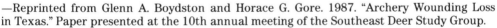

—Reprinted from Glenn A. Boydston and Horace G. Gore. 1987. "Archery Wounding Loss in Texas." Paper presented at the 10th annual meeting of the Southeast Deer Study Group.

other words, for every deer bagged, one deer is hit and not retrieved, thus equaling 100 percent of the legal harvest.

Gore rightly believes that even this high rate of wounding by bow hunters does not present a problem from a biological and management perspective. The ethical issue potentially does, however. He summarized the real problem:

"The real problem comes from the ethical-moral-humane perspective as viewed by the non-hunting public. Bow hunting and trapping have historically been the 'Achilles Heel' of hunting. This has been demonstrated over the years with both coming under attack by antihunting and humane organizations. These groups theorize that if they can win the small battles with two relatively small hunting factions, the legal foundations and precedent will help them take on hunting in general. Archery wounding loss and the lack of data open the door for legal action from these antihunting organizations."

Gore's data leads him to believe that unless a relatively low exit wound in thoracic hits exists, most bleeding is internal, resulting in poor blood trails. Many bow hunters, Gore contends, are neophytes who lack experience and knowledge in blood trails and tracking. And even worse, we all know that members of the deer family maintain an excellent blood coagulative capability. Thus, unlike Drs. Davidson, Ward, and Samuel, Gore remains a critic of the idea of "superficial" hits and subsequent survivability.

"Not all wounded deer die. Undoubtedly, many recover. However, almost all abdominally shot deer die a slow death due to peritonitis. And the concept of non-lethal, superficial hits, and subsequent survivability, has never been quantified."

Gore stresses the critical need for conclusive data on both gun and archery wounding rates and proposes three research parameters: (1) the proficiency of the hunter in hitting the vital area; (2) the efficiency of the broadheads; and (3) the proficiency of the hunter in finding a hit animal. He proposes the following research procedures.

"(1) Radio-collar a statistically valid sample of deer from any of several research facilities. (2) Use state-of-the-art archery equipment—sixty-pound compound bows, aluminum arrows, and multi-bladed, pre-sharpened broadheads. (3) Utilize bow hunters with varying degrees of experience and expertise. (4) Shoot deer as encountered in typical hunting situations. (5) Simulate standard tracking procedures. (6) Monitor deer through various means until death or recovery from wounds. (7) Collect data on the following: distance of shot, angle of shot, location of hit, penetration, initial distance traveled, total distance traveled, total time till death or recovery, deer found/not found by tracker, necropsy dead animals to determine cause of death, follow-up monitoring of wounded animals not found, calculate recovery rate, wounding rate/loss and, survival rates of wounded animals not found."

Gore believes that the use of drug-tipped arrows would significantly increase archery recovery rates, thus reducing wounding losses. But before advocating or condoning the drug-tipped arrow, he recommends that research on broadhead efficiency be conducted to determine the magnitude of the problem. He rightly argues that little data exists with regard to broadhead penetration on live deer. We know how broadheads penetrate non-organic materials such as ethafoam, Styrofoam, and wood, but not how they penetrate wild animals in real hunting situations. The fact that the general public would not accept the type of research that Gore suggests does not deny its merits.

Like Horace Gore and Ed Ashby, Buckhunter Odds—an independent concern located in Minneapolis, Minnesota—has been asking the same questions and proposes to conduct a series of broadhead penetration tests on deer carcasses furnished by the Minnesota DNR. Stu West of Buckhunter Odds wants to run a number of tests concerning broadhead penetration of white-tailed deer: (1) speed versus mass with constant kinetic energy; (2) different types of broadheads and their penetration based on the various parts of the anatomy they hit; and (3) arrow deflection. Like Gore, West realizes that the anti-hunting community will probably accuse him of "pincushion voodoo practices," but he strongly believes that we must conduct this type of research if we are to get answers for some very basic unanswered questions, "instead of letting market forces blindly create instability," as West so aptly describes the current situation.

In the next of these studies, Illinois wildlife researchers Charles Nixon and Lonnie Hansen reported that deer hit but unretrieved by hunters continued to be a major cause of loss on the Piatt County Study Area in central Illinois. They used three methods to estimate the magnitude of this loss: (1) the ratio of legal to crippling loss for radio-tagged deer; (2) the same ratio for all marked deer; and (3) the ratio of legal kills to cripples found or reported for unmarked deer.

Nixon comments on his findings. "An overall average of 38 percent (twenty-five cripples/sixty-five legal kills) or one cripple for about every three deer legally killed by archers is our best estimate of the archery crippling rate. Shotgun hunters cripple about one deer for every five legally taken. We believe that these rates represent a reasonable estimate of crippling loss experienced by deer in central Illinois under present hunting regulations (any deer hunting)."

In 1986, my colleague Al Hofacker surveyed the readership of *Deer & Deer Hunting* magazine with regard to wounding rates and unrecovered deer. His data, based on 2103 wounded deer, revealed a wounding rate of 56.4 percent for archery and 20.8 percent for firearms. Bow hunters who participated in Hofacker's survey recovered a noticeably higher percentage of the deer they wounded when they began trailing the deer either immediately or shortly after (within fifteen minutes) wounding a deer. Hofacker's data clearly

contradict the widely held belief that a wounded deer, if not disturbed by the hunter, normally runs off a short distance, beds down, and dies. Instead, his data indicate that individual whitetails react to wounds in such a variety of ways that it is impractical, if not impossible, to classify any pattern of deer behavior as being "typical" of wounded whitetails. Wounded whitetails, *simply,* do not *always* do *anything.*

Many variables and unknown factors exist in the wounded deer story as Gayle Wescott, a wildlife researcher from Michigan State University, learned in her detailed study of an experimental bow hunt conducted at Michigan's Shiawassee National Wildlife Refuge in 1986. In her study of 605 Michigan bow hunters, Wescott, like Horace Gore and Robert Aho, observed that for every deer successfully retrieved, hunters wounded one that they

Reprinted from Gayle Wescott & R. Ben Peyton. 1986. "Investigation of Reliability of Self-Reported Deer Wounding Rates and Bow Hunter Responses to Information on Wounding." Michigan Agriculture Experiment Station Project #3248.

Reported hits for retrieved and unretrieved deer in various positions during the 1984 Shiawassee National Wildlife Refuge deer hunt

	Broadside N	Down N	Heading Away N	Heading On N	Quartering On N	Quartering Away N
Hit and Wounded Deer	40 (56%)	1 (50%)	1 (100%)	2 (67%)	4 (40%)	3 (19%)
Hit and Retrieved Deer	31 (44%)	1 (50%)	0 (0%)	1 (33%)	6 (60%)	13 (81%)
Total Hits	71	2	1	3	10	16

Numbers in parentheses indicate percentage of total hits for each anatomical location.

Deer retrieved and not retrieved after being hit in various anatomical locations during the 1984 Shiawassee National Wildlife Refuge deer hunt

	Hits	Deer Retrieved		Deer Unretrieved	
	N	N	%	N	%
Head	2	1	50%	1	50%
Neck	6	3	50%	3	50%
Shoulder	22	6	27%	16	73%
Chest (thorax)	46	32	70%	14	30%
Abdomen	12	4	33%	8	67%
Hip/Thigh	10	5	50%	5	50%
Lower Legs	3	0	0%	3	100%
Brisket	2	1	50%	1	50%
Total	103	52		51	

Reprinted from Gale Wescott & R. Ben Peyton. 1986. "Investigation of Reliability of Self-Reported Deer Wounding Rates and Bow Hunter Responses to Information on Wounding." Michigan Agriculture Experiment Station Project #3248.

did not successfully retrieve. This 1:1 ratio for wounded deer to killed deer continues to surface in the hunting literature. In her study, hunters reported wounding fifty-one deer that they did not retrieve and fifty-one deer that they did retrieve. She found no indication of hunter bias in the self-reports of wounding rates.

Sixteen of the fifty-one deer retrieved showed evidence of prior wounds. Like Gore, Wescott found a great deal of random shooting: Seventy-eight percent of all shots taken missed the deer completely. In her survey, more bow hunters practiced at a bull's-eye than a deer silhouette. However, hunters spent more hours shooting at the deer silhouette than at the bull's-eye. Bow hunters according to Wescott, "who do not practice aiming at unmarked vital areas on silhouette deer targets may wound and lose more deer when faced with the *large, non-vital* area and the *small, vital* area of a deer."

Wescott conducted dead deer searches after the hunt and performed necropsies to determine shot-location mortality and to estimate potential survival. She reached these conclusions. "Shots which hit a deer in a broadside position tended to be scattered all over the deer. This supports the idea that large targets elicit a scattered pattern of shots. Regardless of where a deer was hit in a broadside position, 56 percent of those hits resulted in unrecovered deer. Eighty-one percent of the hits on deer in a quartering-away position resulted in retrieval of the animal. (See the accompanying tables.) These results support the 1983 Shiawassee National Wildlife Refuge bow hunt conducted by Ed Langenau that quartering-away shots were the most successful for deer retrieval. Chest hits and hip/thigh hits had moderate to high retrieval of deer (48 to 70 percent)." (See the accompanying tables.) Her results with regard to the quartering-away shot also support those of the African study.

Although Wescott admits that the hunting literature reveals no actual estimates of deer survival from wounding, she estimates that 61 percent of the deer reported wounded by broadheads would be the maximum to survive. Like Ashby and Gore, Wescott believes that future studies should be targeted on factors related to wounding such as broadhead penetration of live animals, arrow deflection, the ability of hunters to track wounded deer, and the extent of injury inflicted by various types of broadheads, to see if the wounding rate can be decreased.

For Wescott, the wounding and non-retrieval of white-tailed deer remains a sociological and moral issue that may or may not be a biological problem. If Michigan harvests 72,000 deer a year with the bow and arrow and we accept the 1:1 ratio of one deer unrecovered for every deer recovered, we then have 72,000 wounded deer. If we then accept Wescott's 40 percent figure for those that die of their wounds, we lose 29,000 animals as a result of wounding. Does this situation represent a biological problem? If not, when does it become one? It is definitely a subcomponent of the hunting/antihunting controversy in this country. While antihunters perceive greater numbers of wounded deer than exist in reality, hunters, conversely, tend to underestimate the numbers. Meanwhile, the non-hunters — the majority of the public — remain extremely concerned about the entire problem.

In looking at this problem from the point of view of muzzleloaders, wildlife researchers John Robinette and his colleagues conducted air and ground searches for carcasses of white-tailed deer on the Yazoo National Wildlife Refuge in Mississippi following a five-day, either-sex muzzleloader hunt. The ground and air search revealed a mortality rate of 23.9 percent of the total harvest. Hunter reports indicated a wounding rate of 23.2 percent. Like Wescott, Robinette and his

colleagues found no hunter bias in self-reported wounding rates. Both methods produced similar results with similar percentages for muzzleloaders as found elsewhere in the hunting literature.

Robinette, like Gore, also noted that the absence of exit wounds in all of the dead deer that were recovered adversely affected the hunter's ability to track the animal. The absence of adult bucks among the carcasses found suggested to Robinette that hunters intentionally abandon does, and that hunters expend less effort in retrieving antlerless deer than bucks.

At a meeting of the Northeast Deer Technical Committee, held in Rhode Island in September 1988, Dave Samuel observed that even though several studies indicate that bow hunters wound one deer for every deer killed, data from at least one other area, the Carey Arboretum in New York, reveal that hunters killed thirty-three deer while only wounding eleven additional deer, with only one carcass later found unrecovered during an intensive field search. In Samuel's opinion, the 1:1 ratio for wounded deer to killed deer needs further and more detailed study. I agree.

In a 1989 survey of the readership of *Deer & Deer Hunting* magazine on the problem of crippling losses, conducted by Professor Aaron Moen of Cornell University, bow hunters reported wounding sixty-seven deer per 100 deer harvested. Shotgun hunters reported eighteen deer wounded per 100 harvested and rifle hunters reported wounding ten deer per 100 harvested. In surveying more than 1000 deer hunters, Moen learned that regardless of the weapon used, one-half or more of hunter-killed deer die within one minute after being hit; in other words, the duration of fatal stress is very short. That's good news for all deer hunters. According to Moen, "very few deer suffer fatal stress for more than an hour regardless of the weapon used."

In 1989, wildlife researcher John Cada presented the "Preliminary Archery Survey Report" to the Montana Department of Fish, Wildlife, and Parks based on a questionnaire mailed to 15,975 bow hunters. Fifty-four percent responded. Some 2370 bow hunters reported shooting a total of 2370 elk. According to the report, bow hunters killed 1169 elk (49 percent) and wounded 1201 elk (51 percent) that they did not recover.

In the April 1989 issue of *Great Basin Naturalist,* researchers from Utah State University report that during the 1987 mule deer hunt (bucks only), "the numbers of deer that were killed (with firearms) and not retrieved were substantial, equal to about 47.2 percent of the number of legally harvested bucks, and were consistently high regardless of hunt type or area." Their report was based on more than one thousand hunter questionnaires. A majority of the hunters in this study indicated that they would prefer to reduce hunting pressure and opportunity in an attempt to kill a higher proportion of mature bucks.

The year 1989 ended with a bang for bow hunting when Adrian Benke, a deer hunter and journalist from San Antonio, published a very controversial book, *The Bowhunting Alternative,* in an attempt to deal with wounding rates and unretrieved deer as they relate to bow hunting. The book consists of a detailed, critical analysis of sport hunting with bows and arrows in which the author argues in favor of using succinylcholine chloride (SCC), a chemical frequently used by researchers to reduce the wounding and suffering of game animals, for solving the problem of wounded deer. While I do not advocate or condone the drug-tipped arrow, I recom-

mend that you read this book and draw your own conclusions.

Benke's book raises some serious questions that are not going away. We need to deal with the issues that this book addresses and stop burying our heads in the sand. "Whatever you think of it once you have read *The Bowhunting Alternative,*" Professor James Casada writes in *Deer & Deer Hunting* magazine, "it is undeniable that here is a clarion call to alertness, a warning flag we can ill afford to ignore. Written by a deep-thinking hunter, it challenges each of us to seriously contemplate a dilemma, which will not go away."

For the past fourteen years, Deer Search, Inc., a New York deer hunting organization, has been using *leashed* tracking dogs and hunter education as a way to reduce deer wounding rates. What began as a small experimental research project in 1975 has grown into a systematic program that recovers more than sixty wounded deer a year in New York State, deer that hunters were unable to recover by themselves.

In 1986, on the basis of this deer search experiment, according to Trustee and Founder Dr. John Jeanneney, "the New York Legislature passed and the Governor signed a bill which became section 11-00928 of the Environmental Conservation Law. Under this section, the Department of Environmental Conservation was authorized to license handlers to use leashed tracking dogs to recover wounded deer on essentially the same basis as during the experiment."

During the 1988/89 deer hunting season, Deer Search, Inc. recovered sixty-three wounded deer. (See the accompanying table.) Their combined recovery rates for the 1988/89 bow and gun seasons were

Recovery rates for Deer Search, Inc. and their leashed tracking dogs

Recovery rates for bow-shot deer, New York State, 1975–1989

Hunting Years	Recovery Rates	
1975	1/2	50.0%
1976–77	1/12	8.3%
1977–78	6/19	31.6%
1978–79	3/18	16.7%
1979–80	8/35	22.9%
1980–81	6/30	20.0%
1981–82	9/38	23.7%
1982–83	14/47	29.8%
1983–84	9/54	16.7%
1984–85	15/65	23.1%
1985–86	18/80	22.5%
1986–87	23/101	22.8%
1987–88	28/102	27.5%
1988–89	31/138	22.5%
Total	172/741	23.2%

Recovery rates for firearms-shot deer, New York State, 1975–1989

Hunting Years	Recovery Rates	
1975	4/9	44.4%
1976–77	6/18	33.3%
1977–78	8/28	28.6%
1978–79	5/36	13.9%
1979–80	13/31	41.9%
1980–81	6/25	24.0%
1981–82	4/44	31.8%
1982–83	14/51	27.5%
1983–84	20/52	38.5%
1984–85	13/45	28.9%
1985–86	20/67	29.9%
1986–87	23/76	30.3%
1987–88	34/73	46.6%
1988–89	32/88	36.4%
Total	212/643	33.0%

–Hans Klein, *On Track . . . News From Deer Search,* March 1989

27.9 percent (sixty-three deer per 226 sorties or tracking sessions), which was down substantially from last year's 35.4 percent (sixty-two deer per 175 tracking sessions), but .2 percent higher than their fourteen-year average of 27.7 percent. (See the table.) Since 1975, Deer Search, Inc. has successfully recovered 384 wounded whitetails and currently has the most extensive data base of information on wounded deer in North America. Jeanneney believes that a recovery in the neighborhood of 40 percent is about has high as one can expect for a leashed, trailing-dog operation.

In studying their recovery rates for bow-shot deer (see the accompanying table) as opposed to recovery rates for firearms-shot deer, one notices a distinct difference. They recover a substantially higher percentage of firearms-shot deer than bow-shot deer (33 percent as opposed to 23 percent). This might support the opinions of other researchers who argue that deer wounded with arrows have a better chance of survival than deer wounded with firearms. This difference may also result directly from a closed wound, which issues little or no blood or scent for the dog to follow. In any event, bow-shot deer represent the hardest animals for Deer Search, Inc. to recover.

Like Drs. Samuel, Davidson, and Stone, Jeanneney believes that the mortality rate for bow-shot deer remains considerably lower than for firearms-shot deer.

"Although conclusive proof is lacking, I strongly suspect that a bow hunter tends to wound more deer than a gun hunter, but that the mortality rate from these wounds is considerably lower. A broadhead can narrowly miss a major blood vessel, and yet make a clean wound that bleeds for only a short time and heals without infection. Rifle bullets and shotgun slugs smash bone and drive hair into the wound sometimes producing gangrene even when vital organs are not involved."

Dr. Jeanneney remains uncertain as to what percentage of those deer not recovered by the trailing dogs actually die later as a result of their wounds.

Bow hunters frequently shoot too high and too far forward to hit the heart. Consequently they sometimes hit the shoulder blade or scapula, resulting in an unretrieved deer. Remember that the shoulder blade remains stationary. It is attached to the skeleton with cartilage and consequently movement only occurs in the ball and socket joints of the leg. As the leg bone moves, it does not interfere with our aim at the heart or the lungs. *Richard P. Smith photo*

"On the basis of the evidence described in our trailing logs, we believe that this mortality is low. We estimate, but cannot prove, that less than 25 percent of the deer which we trail with our dogs and do not recover die in consequence of their wounds."

Several interesting working hypotheses emerge from the work of Deer Search, Inc., as I learned from talking with Don Hickman, the current president:

1. Deer frequently stop bleeding as they near collapse, thus making the dog very critical during the last stage of trailing.

2. *Badly* wounded whitetails frequently move downhill.

3. Deer that take off in a straight line and hold to it for some distance are almost never found, while deer that circle and stop are hard hit and can often be retrieved.

4. Chest hits in which an arrow penetrates only one lung present very difficult tracking problems.

5. High lung shots are difficult to track even with a dog, especially if no exit wound exists. But this situation varies with the dog's abilities and experience.

6. When an arrow passes completely through a deer, the wound tends to seal itself, especially in the thoracic area, thus preventing further blood loss and providing the hunter with little or no blood trail.

7. Deer die from "peritonitis hits" in the lower intestines. Some of these deer take several days to die while others move about for only twenty-four hours after being hit.

8. Wounded whitetails are masters of all sorts of tricks such as circling back, backtracking, and "hiding" in the best sense of the word.

9. Hard-hit deer frequently make loops and exhibit distinct circular movement patterns, especially when they are ready to bed.

10. Avoid neck shots. Shotgun slugs frequently pass completely through the neck without striking anything vital.

11. Pass up rear-end shots. Shotgun slugs seldom have enough penetration to range forward all the way to the heart and lungs.

12. Any abnormal movements, such as tucking the tail down or hunching up the back, can indicate a lethal hit. On the other hand, some mortally wounded whitetails show no visible signs of being hit at all.

13. Deer wounded with broadheads are *much more* difficult to trail with leashed dogs than deer hit with bullets, although this generalization greatly depends upon the type of hit.

14. In most cases of wounded deer behavior, by observing the deer or its hoof-prints and the pattern of travel, we can get a good idea of its condition. The hooves of wounded deer often open and exhibit a wider spread.

15. The entire lung area does not necessarily represent a reliably lethal target zone for bow hunters. The fact that many of us have dropped deer quickly with broadhead in the lungs *does not* alter this fact. More research on this topic would lead to better explanations and revisions.

Like Tomkinson, Ashby, Gore, Wescott, and other deer researchers, John Jeanneney of Deer Search, Inc. believes that further research is needed on the effectiveness of broadhead hits to the various parts of the whitetail's anatomy. "We need to get a clear picture of what happens when a wounded whitetail attempts to evade the

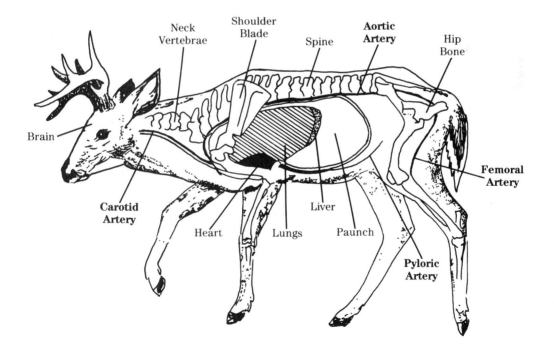

hunter," Jeanneney insists, regardless of the weapon used.

Members of Deer Search, Inc. have seen many wounded whitetails attempt to evade man and believe that many high back and neck hits result in a low rate of recovery because the animals are not seriously injured. Deer hit high frequently fall down, but they are anything but dead. By failing to place a second shot, hunters often lose their deer. Don Hickman underscores this idea in an interview with Richard Smith, field editor for *Deer & Deer Hunting* magazine.

"Year after year, we receive call after call about the deer that was on the ground and how it got up and ran away. In most cases, hunters could have easily shot them again. Unfortunately, when they see a deer go down, most hunters relax, satisfied they killed the deer.

"When we ask them why they didn't shoot again, they tell us, 'I didn't want to ruin any meat!' I then ask them, 'How much meat do you have now?' "

Most bow hunters rightly consider gut-shot deer as the most difficult to recover. When leashed tracking dogs are used, however, the opposite holds true, for a great deal of odor exists with gut-shot deer; this greatly facilitates the dog's ability to track. Indeed, Deer Search, Inc. maintains a high recovery rate for gut-shot whitetails.

No two tracking sessions are ever alike for Deer Search, Inc. John Jeanneney participated in the search for a buck shot in the liver with a shotgun slug. The buck traveled more than a mile without being pushed before going down. The trackers found only one drop of blood over the entire one-mile trail. Would you believe that the buck climbed a steep hill just before he collapsed? Other tracking sessions sometimes lead to gut piles, especially in areas

of high hunter density. Members of Deer Search, Inc. have encountered gut piles at the end of about thirty blood trails.

It is my belief as a deer hunter and a magazine editor that the sport of deer hunting in America will either flourish or be eliminated in the twenty-first century, depending primarily on how effectively we solve some of these problems and on what future scientific research concludes with regard to wounding rates, crippling mortality, broadhead efficiency, shooter proficiency, the use of SCC (a drug used to immobilize deer) and leashed tracking dogs and depending on how well hunters acquire a basic knowledge of white-tailed deer anatomy and a respectful attitude toward every, *individual* deer. A lot of changes in values need to occur if deer hunting is to truly flourish in the twenty-first century.

Two things are certain: (1) Wounding rates and crippling mortality represent major issues in American deer hunting that not only divide bow hunters and gun hunters, but hunters and non-hunters alike; and (2) As deer hunters, we can't be criticized for not trying to solve the problem.

Over the past decade, I have seen countless attempts to solve the problem: grid systems for tracking; string trackers; blood-trail games for the novice; shot-placement videos; popular books on tracking; time-of-death studies; questionnaires and hunter surveys; special bulletins; Pittman-Robertson reports; masters theses; countless magazine articles; fictional accounts; anatomy charts; deer hair posters; maps of marathon tracking sessions; letters to the editor; tables, figures, and charts on wounding rates; countless attempts to define such terms as "stiffening up," "superficial hits," "unrecovered deer," "abandoned deer," "unretrieved deer," "crippling losses," "crippling mortality"; and all sorts of computerized razzmatazz.

We are working on the problem, all right, but we need to work harder. By pooling the present knowledge of experienced deer hunters, wildlife biologists, and medical physiologists, we should be able to learn more about the probable effects of different types of wounds and how each individually wounded deer should be handled, regardless of the weapon used. We need to get beyond anecdotal tales and third-hand reports of dead deer seen and second-hand stories of the wounded buck that "got away," and instead institute some in-depth research that will provide us with some hard, concrete data.

Chapter *18*

Quality Deer Management

A revolution is needed! A revolution in deer management concepts, in range management concepts, in deer harvest and production concepts, and last but not least in importance, in methods used to disseminate research, management, and status information.

— Al Brothers and Murphy E. Ray, Jr.,
Producing Quality Whitetails, 1975

When Al Brothers and Murphy Ray issued their clarion call for revolutionary thinking in producing quality whitetails and subsequent quality deer hunting experiences in 1975, little did they know that they would have such a profound effect on white-tailed deer management. Within a decade, their original emphasis on improving nutrition, increasing the age structure of bucks, and decreasing the number and proportion of does in the population became the cornerstone for a long-term research project studying the influence of hunting on the population dynamics of white-tailed deer on the Mt. Holly Plantation in South Carolina and for quality deer management throughout the southeastern United States. Indeed, few publications on deer management have had a more pro-

found impact on managing whitetails on private lands and especially on the traditional idea of shooting any antlered buck and treating all does "like the sacred cows of India" than *Producing Quality Whitetails* (1975).

The publication of this easy-to-read, practical guide to deer management techniques for private landowners and the later 1982 paperback edition, published by the Caesar Kleberg Wildlife Research Institute, led the Southeast Deer Study Group to invite Al Brothers to deliver the keynote address on quality deer management at the 5th Annual Meeting of the Southeast Deer Study Group in Charleston, South Carolina in 1982. More than 300 people attended that meeting; more than half of them were sportsmen and/or deer man-

Al Brothers, a pioneer in quality deer management who believes that "quality deer management involves quality bucks, does, and fawns, quality habitat, and thus quality hunting experiences."

agers. (The complexion of that meeting would normally have consisted of professional deer biologists.)

In his stimulating and provocative address, Brothers, an innovator in the tech-

niques of quality deer management at the H. B. Zachry Ranches in South Texas, warned deer hunters and managers against placing too much emphasis on producing "trophy" bucks. Instead, he argued that "quality deer management involves quality bucks, does, and fawns, quality habitat, and thus quality hunting experiences." He urged hunters to stop using the term trophy buck management. "I would much rather refer to them as quality bucks."

We need to heed this warning perhaps more today than ever before for several reasons. First, trophy buck management—whether rightly or wrongly conceived—carries the bad connotation with the general public of hunters destroying the gene pool of the white-tailed deer. Second, the general public does not and will not support the idea of trophy deer hunting. In his national surveys of the American public's attitudes toward wildlife, Professor Steve Kellert of Yale University discovered that more than 80 percent of the American population disapproves of trophy hunting. Trophy hunting doesn't seem to be an idea we want to support with bumper stickers. The utilitarian meat hunter fares much better with the public.

Third, the American deer hunters themselves are not that interested in killing trophy bucks. I would suspect that less than 5 percent of all deer hunters nationwide even consider themselves trophy hunters. In his 1984 survey of twenty-seven deer hunting clubs in east Texas, Professor James Kroll of the Institute for White-tailed Deer Management at Stephen F. Austin State University found that the majority of the deer hunting clubs surveyed preferred quality deer management to trophy management programs. From his survey, Kroll learned that when faced with the real cost and difficulties of trophy management, most landowners and deer hunters opt for a quality management program. A quality buck under such a program, according to Kroll "is one which best represents the potential of its age class. It is a buck that can be displayed proudly. Most

hunters are quite happy to harvest a 2.5- or 3.5-year-old buck. Quality management programs provide greater flexibility. Few trophy-class animals are harvested, but maximum sportsman satisfaction is achieved. And isn't that what it is all about?"

Lastly, letters to this editor indicate that many deer hunters nationwide believe that outdoor magazines place too much emphasis on trophy bucks. "How do we teach Johnny to shoot antlerless deer amidst all the antler hype and antler mania?" they ask. If we don't teach Johnny to shoot antlerless deer, the American deer hunting experience will continue to deteriorate.

In his address at the Charleston meeting, Brothers warned hunters about the deterioration of the American deer hunting experience and pointed out that many good deer hunting areas "are exhibiting or beginning to exhibit symptoms of deer herd and habitat deterioration. These symptoms include lowered reproductive rates, widening buck/doe ratios, poor nutritional levels, and, in far too many instances, a buck harvest comprised mostly of yearling age class bucks."

In analyzing deer herd management as practiced by state agencies through their hunting regulations, Brothers concluded that they incur too great an expense in terms of money and labor in attempting to ensure that hunters do not kill too many antlerless deer. Worse, landowners and sportsmen also remain too conservative with respect to shooting antlerless deer—almost to the point of being overprotective.

"Yet at the same time," he declared, "the regulations allow landowners and sportsmen to literally and legally rape the antlered segment of the herd. Isn't it time we attempted to practice total deer herd management with respect to harvest by giving the antlered segment of the herd the same consideration we have given the antlerless segment?"

Many deer hunters who attended that meeting in Charleston accepted Brothers's call to give bucks the same considerations traditionally given to does. Since 1982, deer biologists throughout the Southeast have responded to ever-increasing requests from hunters for guidelines for quality deer management.

In its broadest terms, quality deer management might best be defined as the use of restraint in shooting bucks combined with an adequate harvest of antlerless deer to maintain a healthy deer population in balance with existing habitat conditions. It differs from trophy management in that the majority of the buck kill consists of 2.5- and 3.5-year-old bucks with well-developed antlers instead of trophy-class bucks 5.5 years old or older.

Numerous articles in newspapers and magazines, as well as seminars and presentations by biologists to hunting clubs, have been influential in promoting the idea of quality deer management. But the primary impetus behind the success of this program lies in changing hunters' attitudes.

Perhaps no individual has worked harder or more enthusiastically in changing hunters' attitudes and promoting the idea of quality deer management than Joe Hamilton, a wildlife biologist with the South Carolina Wildlife and Marine Resources Department. When asked about today's deer hunters, Joe Hamilton will tell you that they are much better informed about deer biology and management than ever before. "The natural progression from education to awareness to understanding and finally to respect for the quarry explains this change in attitude and the desire for quality deer hunting experiences."

Joe Hamilton pictured with the products of a four-year-old quality deer management program. These fifteen bucks and an additional sixty antlerless deer were harvested during the 1988 hunting season on a 3200-acre plantation in South Carolina's Low country. Quality deer management guidelines involving the harvest of bucks with ear-width antler spreads of fifteen to sixteen inches and a liberal harvest of females (approximately one doe per fifty acres) were initiated in 1985. Prior to 1985, this property was hunted for bucks only, and in excess of 90 percent of those bucks harvested were one-and-one-half years old. Habitat quality has been enhanced in conjunction with the change in harvest strategy. *John E. Moran photo*

Renowned for its long deer hunting seasons and liberal bag limits, South Carolina, with its large land acreage under private ownership, affords concerned sportsmen the opportunity of managing deer populations on private land to create quality deer hunting experiences. During the past five years, voluntary participation in quality deer management in South Carolina increased dramatically. More than 170 hunting clubs representing more than 750,000 acres currently participate in quality deer management guidelines.

Passing up certain categories of bucks and studying their behavior instead of shooting them provides more enjoyment for many hunters than simply counting the bucks hanging on the meat pole. "For those of you who have never faced the decision to 'let a buck walk,'" Hamilton admits, "it must be emphasized that one's emotions during and immediately following such an incident are comparable with certain other first experiences during a lifetime. To say the least, breaking the habit or 'tradition' of shooting any legal buck is a gut-wrenching ordeal. Imagine the emotional gyrations of one who is turning a loaded gun away from the traditional means of showing his prowess as a hunter. Often at the same moment his sights are lined up on a doe — the very image of motherhood — the symbol of fertility — the source of future bucks! The gunshot echoes throughout the woods, signifying that a monumental step has been taken toward total deer herd management."

The hunter's involvement in quality deer management extends the role of hunters from mere consumers of the natural resource to that of managers — it bridges the gap between hunters and deer biologists. When a small number of hunting clubs first began practicing quality deer management in South Carolina's Low Country nearly a decade ago, some people expressed a concern that this unorthodox deer hunting strategy would be short-lived. The fact that 170 hunting clubs developed a different scale of values for white-tailed deer and deer hunting provides testimony for a new, developing tradition. Participation in quality deer management and hunting continues to increase each year not only in South Carolina but in many of the other southeastern states.

When Joe Hamilton returned to South Carolina from a lecture tour to Australia in 1988, he brought back a code of ethics written by the Australian Deer management Association that now forms the basic code of ethics for a new organization known as the South Carolina Quality Deer Management Association (SCQDMA). This new organization adopts this code of ethics.

1. Members should know and obey the game and fish laws of South Carolina.

2. Members should encourage other hunters to adopt this code of ethics.

3. Members should learn as much as possible about the issues relating to wildlife management and conservation, recreational hunting, and hunter ethics and encourage other hunters to do the same.

4. Members should not act in a manner that would bring discredit to recreational deer hunting or the SCQDMA.

5. Members should foster good relations among hunters and set a good example and present a good hunter image for others.

6. Members should avoid confrontation with and not infringe on the activities of other hunters, landowners, government employees, and the general public.

7. Members should respect the rights and land use objectives of landowners and exercise proper precautions to prevent damage to their property or doing anything to interfere with the landowner's land-use objectives.

8. Members should take hunter education courses and encourage other hunters to do the same.

9. Members should adopt safe hunting practices and be competent in the use of their weapons.

10. Members must support the objectives and goals of the SCQDMA.

11. Any game law violation conviction will result in immediate expulsion from the SCQDMA.

Hamilton places the emphasis of this organization on the hunting experience, not on consuming deer as a commodity. "When a commodity is plentiful," Joe tells us, "ethics are more lax." In Australia, they've got fewer deer. But they exhibit stewardship, because the resource is more precious. Here in the Low Country of South Carolina, hunters often look at deer in piles and lose sight of individual deer. When this happens, it's difficult to savor the hunt. In Australia, a lot of ritual goes into killing one individual deer, and that animal is revered." Deer herds change more quickly than hunter's attitudes, Joe readily acknowledges, but ethics change for the better when hunters begin to understand more about white-tailed deer biology and behavior.

To obtain a quality deer hunting experience under this program, deer hunters must carefully select their targets; they must refrain from shooting too many bucks in order to keep the herd's ratio of bucks to does in balance, thus allowing bucks to reach the older age classes.

The SCQDMA is open to all deer hunters, not just members of hunting clubs. Hamilton hopes that the Association will enhance the image of the deer hunter to non-hunters and other hunters alike. He believes the Association will bring together a wide diversity of people with a common thread: a deep love of deer hunting and a deep respect for the deer themselves. This unique organization addresses deer hunters, deer herds, and self-imposed ethics and it encourages the dissemination of information to deer hunters and deer managers by promoting seminars, workshops, and other educational activities. Their quarterly newsletter, *The Signpost,* should encourage communication among deer hunters and result in a more fraternal atmosphere.

In this non-governmental, private organization, wildlife biologists offer assistance, but all officers of the Association are deer hunters not employed by the wildlife department. Hamilton views the role of the deer biologist in terms of technical guidance and coaching. For more information about the South Carolina Quality Deer Management Association, contact: Andrew Harper, President, Lower Coastal Branch, Box 98, Estill, SC 29918, 803/625-4112.

Producing quality deer herds and quality hunting experiences depends on detailed research and monitoring deer herd dynamics, on deer hunters acquiring a basic knowledge of white-tailed deer biology and learning in particular how deer population characteristics such as age structure, sex ratio, and density relate to and affect the quality of their hunting.

The production of quality whitetails and quality deer hunting in this country best manifests itself in the Mt. Holly Plantation deer herd in Berkeley County near Charleston, South Carolina. At this 6250-acre plantation, currently managed for timber, wildlife, and esthetics, a long-term research project is underway designed to study the impact of hunting on the population dynamics of white-tailed deer. Begun in 1980, this unique experiment has created a deer herd typical of quality deer management strategies. Its selective harvest has improved nutrition through reduced herd density, balanced the buck/doe ratio, and increased the buck's age structure. The primary study area consists of a 3000-acre tract located in the center of the property. In this core area, only does and

bucks with a minimum fourteen-inch inside spread can be taken.

In this case study in a quality deer management and quality hunting, the goals of four major groups coalesce into quality experience and a demonstration area for hunter education and hunter satisfaction: (1) hunting clubs, (2) an industry, (3) a wildlife agency, and (4) two universities — Clemson and the University of Georgia.

During August and September of each year, deer researchers use spotlight counts to estimate the pre-hunting density and sex ratio. In the accompanying table, Professor David Guynn of Clemson University expresses density estimates in terms of

---

Density and sex structure for the Mt. Holly Plantation deer herd, 1980 - 88.

Year	Density: (acres/deer)	Bucks: antlerless deer
1980	6	13:100
1981	14	—
1982	22	14:100
1983	19	32:100
1984	28	31:100
1985	18	36:100
1986	13	16:100
1987	15	56:100
1988	11	43:100

[a]Estimated for period of August 15 - October 1.

Reprinted from David C. Guynn, *et. al.* 1988. "A Case Study in Quality Deer Management." In *White-tailed Deer Management Seminar.* (Proceedings). Fort Jackson, S.C. p. 73.

White-tailed deer sightings by hunters on the Mt. Holly Plantation, 1982-88.

Bucks sighted/100 does sighted

Year	Season[a]	Breeding[b]
1982	27:100	28:100
1983	41:100	48:100
1984	53:100	80:100
1985	47:100	69:100
1986	44:100	61:100
1987	70:100	78:100
1988	57:100	61:100

[a]**Observations during August 15 - January 1.**

[b]**Observations during the range of conception dates.**

Reprinted from David C.Guynn, *et. al.* 1988 "A Case Study in Quality Deer Management." In *White-tailed Deer Management Seminar.* (Proceedings). Fort Jackson, S.C. p. 76.

acres per deer and sex ratios as antlered bucks per 100 antlerless deer observed. Note the dramatic improvement in the preseason sex ratio. The 1986 data, according to Professor Guynn, appears to be an anomaly, since the heavy fawn crop of that year concentrated in areas where they were highly visible due to drought conditions.

After implementing quality deer management strategies at the Mt. Holly Plantation, Guynn and his colleagues found that the buck/doe ratio as reflected by hunter sightings dramatically improved. (See the accompanying table.) During the first two weeks in October 1987, hunters observed seventy antlered bucks for every 100 antlerless deer observed. The culmina-

tion of five years of quality deer management at the Mt. Holly Plantation reflects itself in the data for 1987. During that year, twenty-two of twenty-nine bucks collected for research purposes were 2.5 years old or older. Seven of the bucks were 5.5 years old. The largest-buck weighed 202 pounds. The largest antlers measured 142-7/8 Boone and Crockett points.

Professor Guynn, an enthusiastic deer hunter himself, gives these words of advice to deer hunters and managers interested in transforming a high-density deer herd with an unbalanced buck/doe ratio into a moderate-density herd with a balanced buck/doe ratio. "Quality deer management can work on an unfenced area in the South

Carolina Coastal Plain. The key factor is control of mortality. Access control is an absolute necessity. Antlerless deer must be harvested such that habitats can provide adequate nutrition to produce deer in good body condition. Restraint must be exercised in harvesting bucks, especially 1.5- and 2.5-year-old bucks. Good nutrition and a balanced age and sex structure will lead to good body weights, improved antler development, and high reproductive rates."

During these experimental deer hunts, deer researchers discovered a very interesting and dramatic change: Quality deer management shifts breeding activity to earlier in the season, intensifies rutting activity, and thus reduces the range of conceptions. (See the accompanying figure.) Guynn believes that nutrition, the adult buck/doe ratio, and the age structure of the herd represent the major factors controlling this dramatic change. During the first year of the Mt. Holly Plantation deer hunts, the breeding season spanned a period of ninety-six days, with the peak of breeding occurring on November 11. Five years later, the breeding season shortened to fifty-one days with an obvious peak on October 22. What a dramatic change! But why? How does this change affect the animal? What does this change mean for the hunter?

In analyzing the sociobiological factors involved in the Mt. Holly Plantation deer herd, Larry Marchinton of the University of Georgia has been asking the same questions with regard to these changes. His answers, while still somewhat speculative, are most interesting and very revealing. While he agrees that nutrition is certainly fundamental to these changes, he suspects that the increased number of mature bucks plays a direct role in the earlier and shorter breeding seasons, for the increased availability of bucks to breed the does reduces the number of does remaining unbred during their first or subsequent estrous cycles. With a balanced sex ratio, estrous does more readily find bucks during their twenty-four-hour period of breeding receptivity and fewer does recycle and conceive during later estrous periods. This situation thus favors a shorter breeding season and earlier mean conception dates. But what accounts for moving the breeding season forward?

In trying to answer this question, Marchinton believes that the earlier and more synchronized breeding taking place at the Mt. Holly Plantation results from increased physiological stimulation by mature males and their signposts. In his Georgia research, Marchinton and his students recorded rub and scrape densities as high as 1400 rubs and 220 scrapes square kilometer, with the higher numbers occurring on areas with older bucks.

"On the Mt. Holly Plantation," Marchinton reports, "with its nearly even sex ratio and its much older buck age structure, there are far higher numbers. In 1987, we found an average of 2000 rubs per square kilometer, and they were *much* larger than anywhere else we surveyed. Because of this, we believe they may be having strong priming effects on the does' estrous cycles and suppressing effects on subordinate bucks' testosterone levels and that this is a factor in the shorter and earlier breeding seasons."

We know from published and unpublished sources that sociobiological factors influence white-tailed deer behavior under quality deer management programs such as the experiment taking place at the Mt. Holly Plantation and that these factors very likely include what Marchinton calls, "a complex semiochemical system," that regulates their behavior and physiology.

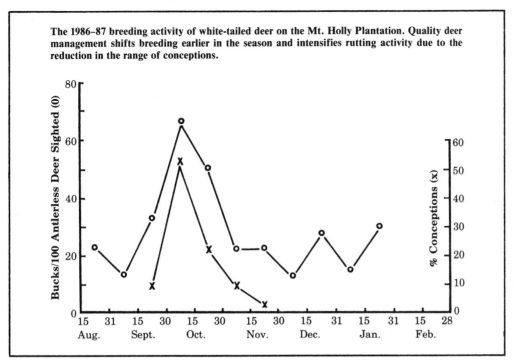

The 1986–87 breeding activity of white-tailed deer on the Mt. Holly Plantation. Quality deer management shifts breeding earlier in the season and intensifies rutting activity due to the reduction in the range of conceptions.

Reprinted from David C. Guynn, *et al.* 1988. "A Case Study in Quality Deer Management." In *White-Tailed Deer Management Seminar.* (Proceedings). Fort Jackson, S.C. p. 78.

When deer managers manipulate such things as sex ratio and age structure, they cause sociobiological changes that result in many subtle effects on the deer population that traditional deer management theory does not take into account.

We also know that quality deer management offers both the deer and the deer hunter some very real and desirable improvements. First of all, a shorter and earlier rut allows breeding bucks to enter the winter months in better physical shape. Second, a more intensified rut gives the hunter greater opportunities for practicing rattling, calling, and scrape hunting techniques. Third, bucks born earlier in the year under this management schema carry better antlers at 1.5 years of age and probably for the rest of their lives. Fourth,

fawns born by midsummer have a definite advantage over those coming later. They tend to exhibit greater body weights as yearlings and a greater resistance to disease and parasites.

Fifth, young, *non-breeding bucks grow bigger* under quality deer management as a result of what Marchinton calls the "suppressor effect." According to Marchinton, the presence of older bucks and their signposts suppress the levels of testosterone in younger bucks, thereby reducing their competitiveness and libido. Lower levels of testosterone result in a decreased loss of weight during the rut, thus allowing young bucks to grow to a greater size before assuming their role in breeding activities. It is important to remember that bucks participating in breeding can lose up to 25 percent of their body weight. A developing buck cannot lose this amount of weight, if he is to reach his potential.

Sixth, and perhaps most interesting of all, the removal of large numbers of does on the Mt. Holly Plantation created the effect of reducing the dispersal of young bucks. While deer biologists have traditionally thought competition from older males forces young bucks to disperse from an area, they now speculate that harassment from mature does causes buck fawns and yearling bucks to leave an area.

In 1986, Marchinton implemented a quality deer management program on his own 200-acre tree farm in cooperation with adjoining landowners in Jackson County, Georgia. He now believes "that harassment by too many adult does causes male fawns and yearling bucks to leave the area. If we let the number of does build up too high, a lot of those young bucks leave the area. In a few years, research information may be available to prove this pretty far-out idea."

To obtain quality deer hunting, we need to change our values. We need to shoot more adult does and fewer of our quality yearling bucks; we need to cull inferior yearling bucks and shoot big bucks. When confronted with the six yearling bucks shown in the accompanying illustration, we need to restrain ourselves from shooting the two superior yearling bucks at the bottom.

On Marchinton's farm, hunters shoot only inferior yearling bucks or bucks with a minimum sixteen-inch outside spread. How do you estimate antler spread, you ask? Look at the buck's ears. A buck's ear-spread approximates fifteen inches. If the antlers extend an inch on either side of the ears, they probably approach a seventeen-inch spread. When uncertain about antler size, don't shoot; give the buck the benefit

Examples of antlers from yearling bucks. The problem we face in developing quality deer hunting in this country revolves around the fact that we shoot most, if not all, of these yearling bucks during the first year they carry antlers. If you want quality deer hunting, don't shoot the two bucks at the bottom! We need to leave these two yearling bucks in the deer forest.

CULL

LEAVE IN THE DEER FOREST

Reprinted from Al Brothers and Murphy E. Ray, Jr. 1975. *Producing Quality Whitetails.* Texas: A Wildlife Services Publication. p. 84.

of the doubt, if you are interested in the long-term welfare of the whitetail!

"This approach is not for everybody," Marchinton admits, "but if you are a selective hunter, finding an inferior yearling buck or old doe to 'cull' becomes something of a challenge and serves the purpose of filling the freezer. Killing only the 'proper' deer will result in appreciation and admiration from your knowledgeable friends.

"I am convinced that a single hunter passing up yearlings will be improving his chances of killing quality deer if he hunts the area regularly. The more people practicing this kind of hunting obviously the more older bucks available to harvest. Sharing your changing values and enthusiasm with fellow hunters, neighboring clubs, and landowners will be a step toward enhancing the quality of hunting experiences in your deer woods and those of your neighbors as well. This is *certainly not* the only good way to manage a deer herd, but it is one that is already providing many groups of hunters both tangible and intangible rewards."

Proper deer management cannot be achieved under today's norms of shooting either trophy-class bucks or the first legal animal to present itself. Hunting regulations need to spell out not just the number of animals to be killed in a given area but the social classes of those animals. We need to determine which classes of an unbalanced population exist as "troublemakers" in a sociobiological sense and cull those animals. In too many areas, the social mechanisms of white-tailed deer herds are being dangerously stressed. In too many areas, the buck/doe ratio is way out of balance. In too many areas 85 to 95 percent of all bucks shot are yearlings. Bucks rarely reach the age of 2.5 years old. The social imbalances and the overharvesting of yearling bucks create prolonged rutting periods in which we see yearling bucks breeding most does and some doe fawns as well. If this trend continues, what will happen to the genetic base of this species?

Our hunting goals need to be guided by a more informed knowledge of white-tailed deer biology and behavior than the mere ability to distinguish between legal or illegal animals, or between mediocre and record-book antlers. We need a new kind of deer hunter in the woods. We need what deer hunter and deer biologist "Tony" Bubenik calls "an informed and selfless in-

dividual who is willing to support biologically sound management principles that may, at least in the short run, work against his or her personal desires, but which will, in the long run, strengthen the resource."

Quality deer management demands selective hunting techniques, and landowners and deer hunters must change their values, cooperate with one another, and do their homework. Unless we convince the majority of landowners in each of our hunting areas about these techniques, quality deer hunting will remain but an elusive dream. Quality deer management may not be for everyone, but as more deer hunters in this country mature, as more hunters complain about too many scrawny deer and too many yearling bucks with tiny antlers, and as deer herds continue to increase and deteriorate, the need for this type of program increases steadily. Quality deer management programs now exist in such states as Texas, Florida, Virginia, Georgia, South Carolina, North Carolina, Mississippi, and Alabama. These programs represent more than just "tinkering" with deer-kill statistics to grow big bucks; they represent a sincere attempt on the part of man to improve the social quality of deer herds and the well-being of individual deer. In doing so, they represent the ultimate expression of why men and women love deer and the values they gain from deer hunting.

While the techniques and ideas of quality deer management may be relatively new, the realization of quality deer hunting in the woods has long been reflected in the minds of deer hunters. While quality deer hunting means many things to many deer hunters, here's what it means to some members of the deer hunting fraternity.

When James Kilgo, a South Carolina deer hunter and professor of English, talks about quality deer hunting in his *Deep*

Enough For Ivorybills (1988), a classic literary book on deer hunting, the likes of which we seldom see, he emphasizes the quality of the entire outdoor experience regardless of whether one sights that elusive phantom buck or not. After spending countless hours in his deer stand, he admits that "by Thanksgiving I knew every bush, tree, and rock within sight of that tree stand. From its high perch I monitored the changing of leaves from one week to the next and even the quality of light as it changed, evening by evening." Monitoring the changing of leaves and the quality of light in the forest, savoring the scents of the hunt—"the taste of wind blowing through dead corn, mixed faintly with a musky animal odor"—take precedence over killing deer for hunters such as James Kilgo.

Like Professor Kilgo, South Carolina's poet-in-residence and avid bow/deer hunter James Dickey couldn't agree more. Whether drawing a literary image of the hunter in poetry or a bead on a 10-point buck, Dickey loves to talk about quality deer hunting and what its values mean to him and should mean to all of us.

"It's not important to kill, to make the kill. The feeling of enjoyment is in the activity itself and in being there with the animals, in their environment. They have *every* advantage over you: sight, smell, and speed. They're so well-equipped. And so quiet. A whole herd of them can run through heavy brush right by you and you cannot hear a thing. It is like an illusion. I like that; I like that feeling."

Like James Dickey, Gertrude Sanford Legendre, one of this country's most extraordinary women hunters, emphasizes the pursuit itself in her autobiography, *The Time of My Life* (1987). "When you come to the final moment, when the hunt is over and the prize is within reach, the truth

dawns on you that you don't really want what you thought you wanted at all. What matters is the pursuit of it."

In pondering why men pursue deer and the hunter's paradox of how man can kill the object he loves, William Faulkner ultimately defines the real value of deer hunting as "the best game of all, the best of all breathing and forever the best of all listening." What an unforgettable description!

In one of the most moving and beautifully written deer hunting tales, Robert Ruark, a world-famous newspaper columnist and avid deer hunter, captures the real quality of the deer hunting experience in that memorable essay, "Mister Howard Was A Real Gent." He describes what happened as he listened to the hoot of the owl in deer camp on the night before the opening day.

"I pulled off my shoes and crawled under the blanket. I heard the owl hoot again and the low mutter from the men, giant black shapes sitting before the fire. The pine-needle mattress smelled wonderful under me and the blankets were warm. The fire pushed its heat into the tent, and I was as full of food as a tick. Just before I died I figured that tomorrow had to be heaven."

In *Hunters' Verses From the High Country* (1986), a remarkable anthology of deer hunting poetry written by Australian deer hunters and published by the Australian Deer Research Foundation, Max Downes, a noted deer biologist and follower of Leopold's, insists that for the deer hunter, deer represent the very meaning of the mountains themselves.

"Deer are the numenon, the inner meaning of the mountains. Their presence or absence does not affect the outward appearance of deer country, but it does mightily affect our reaction toward it. Without deer tracks on the trail and the potential presence of the animal at each new dip and bend of the hillside, the forest is an empty shell, a spiritual vacuum."

Like many deer biologists, Downes believes that deer hunting cannot exist anywhere in the world and progress without a literature, without deer hunters communicating their innermost thoughts about the quality of the experience to each other and to the entire community of deer hunters of which they are a part. Fortunately, for all of us, deer hunters continue to communicate their innermost thoughts about the ex-

perience. And no one better expresses the ultimate meaning of deer hunting in this country than Archibald Rutledge. In his book, *An American Hunter* (1937), "Old Flintlock" compares deer hunting with going to heaven:

"Though confessing a very inferior acquaintance with things celestial, deer hunting has always seemed to me like going to heaven; the thing is undoubtedly hard, but the reward is such that if a man really arrives, he will not complain of the journey."

PART V

Where to Find More Information

Chapter 19

Deer and Deer Hunting: An Annotated Bibliography Continued, 1838–1990

Few of us have enough time to spend out in the woods observing and stalking deer, so we turn to books to find out more about these fascinating animals and to make sure, as far as possible, that we make the very best use of the few precious hours that the Red Gods provide.
— Richard Prior, *Modern Roe Stalking,* 1985

A Note About the Bibliography

This bibliography represents a continuation of "The Deer Hunter's Four Hundred," a comprehensive, annotated list of more than four hundred books published in the English language on the subject of deer and deer hunting found in *Deer & Deer Hunting,* Book 1 (Stackpole Books, 1984) and the annotated list of 185 titles in *Deer & Deer Hunting,* Book 2 (Stackpole Books, 1987). I again annotate this list of 240 book titles with the hope that readers will seek out memorable titles that appeal to their interests. An asterisk (*) indicates that the book is out of print. It will either have to be located in a used-book store or you will need to have an out-of-print-book specialist search for it. You will find a list of reputable book specialists in the field of outdoor literature in the Appendix. Most of the books without an asterisk should be available through special order from your local bookstore. Privately printed titles may be difficult to locate, however, and could be another job for the out-of-print-book specialist. For an ongoing comprehensive review of books and information pertaining to white-tailed deer and deer hunting, read *Deer & Deer Hunting* magazine, Box 1117, Department 5B, Appleton, WI 54912, telephone (414) 734-0009.

When not roaming The Uplands of Iowa County in southwestern Wisconsin or the hills of the Chequamegon National Forest in northwestern Wisconsin, the author spends most of his time editing, writing, reading, and researching the white-tailed deer and the American deer hunting experience. *Mike Fehrenbach photo*

Abbott, Henry, "The Anxious Seat." In *The Birch Bark Books of Henry Abbott.* New York: Harbor Hill Books, 1980. pp. 1–6.

An ageless tale spiced with a sense of humor about a deer stand in the Adirondacks and what happens to Henry Abbott, an Adirondack naturalist and deer hunter, while waiting for deer. Written at Abbott's Deerland Lodge at the head of Long Lake and originally published as a tiny, elusive book in 1914. The volume contains several other deer hunting tales that evoke the very smell of the deer forest.

Ahlstrom, Mark E. *The Whitetail.* Minnesota: Crestwood House, 1983. 47 pp.

Juvenile literature describing the physical characteristics, habits, and natural environment of the white-tailed deer.

Alexander, T. L., ed. *Management and Diseases of Deer.* England: Moredun Research Institute, 1986. 254 pp.

A technical book intended primarily for the veterinary surgeon.

Allen, Durward L. "Frozen Asset." In *Our Wildlife Legacy.* New York: Funk & Wagnalls Company, 1954. pp. 135–156.

One of the best reviews of the deer problem, or what Allen calls "the deer-herd wrangle," that I have ever read. Contains many references to deer and deer hunting throughout the text.*

Alsheimer, Charles J., and Larry C. Watkins. *A Guide to Adirondack Deer Hunting.* New York: Beaver Creek Press, 1987. 219 pp.

If you hunt or plan to hunt whitetails in the Adirondacks, you will want to consult this very useful guide. As my colleague Al Hofacker says, "this book captures the true essence of deer hunting in the Adirondacks."

Anderson, Julie. "Sound Shots." In *I Married a Logger.* Michigan: Avery Color Studios, 1951. pp. 223–231.

A critique of the deer hunting behavior of city slickers who return to civilization and leave in their wake unclaimed doe carcasses and cases of empty whiskey bottles.

Anderson, Tom. "The Test of a Deer Stand." In *Learning Nature by a Country Road.* Minnesota: Voyageur Press, 1989. pp. 218–220.

In this reflective essay, a wildlife biologist deals with the pains and tribulations of waiting in a cold November deer stand for the passing of a white-tailed buck.

Andrews, J. D., and Bill Molitor. *Trophy Bucks of South Dakota.* South Dakota: Staghorn Mountain Publishing, 1989. 239 pp.

A collection of accounts of how deer hunters killed their great trophy bucks from South Dakota. Contains a brief profile of the Sturm Deer Camp and an interesting story of "Old Iron Sides," a ten-year-old, 10-point buck. After shooting this buck in the heart and the stomach, Larry Nylander saw the old boy fall to the forest floor. While skinning it, Larry found several .22 slugs under its skin and a shotgun slug imbedded in its front leg. Apparently, this 238-2/8 nontypical buck not only eluded a good number of hunters but foiled a poacher or two as well.

Aragon, Jane Chelsea. *Winter Harvest: On Moonlit Snow, A Deer Waits for Us.* Boston: Little, Brown and Company, 1988.

BARREN-DOE MYTH DEBUNKED

Deer & Deer Hunting

MARCH 1990
$2.95
CDCOO655
Canada $3.95

PRACTICAL & COMPREHENSIVE INFORMATION FOR WHITE-TAILED DEER HUNTERS

SPIKE BUCKS:
SHOOT OR
PROTECT?

TURKEY TIME
DEER SCOUTING

FOOD PLOTS
NATURE'S
DEER ATTRACTANTS

DEER HARVESTERS
ANIMAL LIBERATORS

"The Northeast Section of The Wildlife Society is proud to recognize the magazine *Deer & Deer Hunting* for its unique and substantial contribution to the wildlife management profession, to the hunters who participate in management programs, and to the species that has at once been the nation's greatest conservation story, as well as the species evoking the greatest controversy. The high educational standards of *Deer & Deer Hunting* magazine are unmatched in the natural resource publishing industry, and we hereby honor the magazine and its staff with the 1987 Northeast Section of The Wildlife Society's Certificate of Recognition." — The Northeast Section of The Wildlife Society.

A description of how a child experiences deer feeding in winter. A story in rhyme for the young reader.

Arnosky, Jim. *Deer at the Brook.* New York: Lothrop: Lee & Shepard Books, 1986.

A poetic and pictorial portrayal of the natural events deer encounter at a brook. Written for children whose eyes brighten whenever they see deer.

Arsenault, Richard P. *The Maine Antler and Skull Trophy Club: 9th Annual Big Game Records Publication.* Maine: The Maine Antler and Skull Trophy Club, 1987. 104 pp.

Another fine record book by the Maine Antler and Skull Trophy Club, which continues to hum — writing, typing, recording, measuring, and conducting shows and banquets.

Audubon, John James. "Deer Hunting." In Maria R. Audubon, *Audubon and His Journals.* Massachusetts: Peter Smith, 1972. pp. 466–473.

In this unusual essay, somewhat ambivalent in its attitude toward hunting, Audubon notes that man still-hunted, drove, firelighted, called, grunted, and decoyed deer for recreational purposes as early as the 1830s. In it Audubon describes three basic modes of deer hunting: still-hunting, firelighting, and driving. He describes the deer drive as "extremely agreeable and successful on almost every occasion." Audubon admits that he wrote the essay to induce his readers "to go driving the light-footed deer in our western and southern woods." The cry of deer hounds, the sight of galloping horses, and the sound of hunting horns obviously inflamed the author's imagination when he wrote this colorful account of our sport.

———. "A Moose Hunt." In *Delineations of American Scenery and Character.* New York: G. A. Baker & Company, 1926. pp. 210–216.

A brief description of a moose hunt in the spring of 1833 in the neighborhood of the Schoodiac Lakes. This volume also contains Audubon's essay on deer hunting.*

Australian Deer Research Foundation. *Hunters' Verses from the High Country.* Australia: Australian Deer Research Foundation, 1988. 187 pp.

An anthology of humorous and serious poetry written by deer hunters for deer hunters. Readers will be surprised by the sensitivity shown by these deer hunting poets.

Back Then: A Pictorial History of Americans Afield. Wisconsin: Willow Creek Press, 1989. 143 pp. This splendid pictorial history of Americans afield contains a good number of early deer and deer hunting pictures between the years of 1870 and 1940. Includes some very interesting early deer camp scenes.

Baily, Jill. *Discovering Deer.* New York: The Bookwright Press, 1988. 46 pp.

A general introduction to deer for the young reader.

Baillie-Grohman, W. A. *Sport in the Alps: In the Past and the Present.* New York: Charles Scribner's Sons, 1896. 356 pp.

An interesting account of European deer and deer hunting written by a prominent historian of sport with special emphasis on red deer and roe deer. Alpine venery at its best. Includes some sporting reminiscences of the Duke of Saxe-Coburg — a mighty deerslayer whose favorite .450 Henry Express rifle finished off many a royal "harte of grease" and stag of ten. The author recalls how the Duke once brought down with two double shots four stags in full flight — the nearest of them over two hundred yards away. When the Duke died in 1893, his last words epitomized his profound passion for deer hunting: "Let the deer drive commence!"*

Banwell, D. Bruce. *Great New Zealand Deer Heads: Volume II.* New Zealand: The Halcyon Press, 1987. 176 pp.

Once again Banwell has produced a book that documents the truly great deer trophies of New Zealand. A first-rate record book by a recognized authority.

Barker, Elliott S. "My First Buck." In *The Great Southwest.* Missouri: The Lowell Press, 1974. pp. 36–45.

Historians of hunting know well the value of the material stored in the minds of old-timers. However, not many of these old-timers have the writing ability to provide us with firsthand accounts of their deer-hunting adventures. Barker, a well-known conservationist, was an exception in this regard. In this colorful, well-told story, Barker shares his youthful experience of shooting his first buck.

———. "Royal Bucks of Rincon Bonito." In *Smokey Bear and the Great Wilderness.* New Mexico: Sunstone Press, 1982. pp. 55–62.

A beautiful description of a New Mexico deer season high in the Pecos wilderness.

Basala, Allen C. *Official North Carolina Records of the Dixie Deer Classic: Volume II.* North Carolina: Wake County Wildlife Club, Inc., 1988. 114 pp.

In this record book, Basala points out that our deer hunting philosophy often changes: one may be a deer hunter on a trip to a high deer density county, but become a big buck hunter when hunting in a low deer density trophy buck area. Hunters entering deer in the 1982 through the 1987 Dixie Deer Classics classified their hunting philosophies into five categories: trophy hunters (11.0 percent), big buck hunters (6.2 percent), buck hunters (22.6 percent), deer hunters (59.1 percent), and other (1.1 percent).

Benke, Adrian. *The Bowhunting Alternative.* Texas: Privately printed, 1989. 110 pp.

This book consists of a detailed, critical analysis of sport hunting with bows and arrows. The author discusses the problem of wounded deer and argues in favor of using succinylcholine chloride, SCC, a chemical frequently used by researchers, to reduce the wounding and suffering of game animals. While I do not advocate or condone the drug-tipped arrow, I recommend that you read this book and draw your own conclusions.

Bentham, T. *Asiatic Horns and Antlers.* Calcutta: The Indian Museum of Natural History, 1908. 96 pp.

An illustrated catalogue of the Asiatic horns and antlers in the collection of the Indian Museum.

Biel, Timothy Levi. *The Deer Family.* California: Wildlife Education, Ltd., 1988.

An excellent summary of the deer family for the young reader.

Blacklock, Les. "I Lived With Deer." In *Ain't Nature Grand!* Minnesota: Voyageur press, 1980. pp. 71–77.

In this essay the author reminisces about his adventures while filming a deer documentary near the Cascade River, about a thousand yards inland from Minnesota's north shore of Lake Superior.

———. "The Phantom Buck." In *Meet My Psychiatrist.* Minnesota: Voyageur Press, 1977. pp. 65–66.

The story of how a famous buck gave a group of Minnesota deer hunters the slip. Who would disagree with Elmer Westholm, one of the buck's pursuers, when he says, "I'm always glad to see a famous buck get away. His legendary size and antler measurements could probably never be matched by the real thing. Besides, once you've nailed him, the fun is over; the speculative record measurements have shrunk to realistic mediocrity. And next year's hunting season is not the exciting prospect it would have been had The Phantom Buck still been out there."

Blaxter, Sir Kenneth, *et al. Farming the Red Deer.* Scotland: Crown, 1988. 169 pp.

Farming the red deer has become an accepted form of livestock husbandry. This in-depth report deals with experimental laboratory work and field investigations. Contains an excellent annotated bibliography on the subject.

Boone and Crockett Club. "The Deer." In *North American Big Game.* New York: Charles Scribner's Sons, 1939. pp. 171–224.

Contains an early account of hunting whitetails by J. Watson Webb.*

Bromley-Davenport, William. "Deer-Stalking." In *Sport.* London: Chapman and Hall, Ltd., 1888. pp. 161–243.

Includes two chapters on stalking deer, one on reindeer in Norway and the other on red deer in the Highlands.*

Brunner, Paul. *Tree Stand Hunting.* Montana: Privately printed, 1988. 198 pp.

A detailed discussion of hunting natural funnels.

Buehler, Maynard P. *Deer Hunter's Handbook, Or How to Win Your Way Through a Bull Session.* California: Privately printed, 1953. 33 pp.

A pocketbook guide that undoubtedly served to resolve the bull sessons of its time.*

Buff, Mary and Conrad Buff. *Dash & Dart.* New York: The Viking Press, 1942. 73 pp.

Life in the deer forest for children three to five years of age.*

Buffon's Natural History. "The Stag." New York: Hurst & Company, n.d. pp. 228–234.

The great French naturalist Buffon knew a great deal about deer in the eighteenth century that modern students of the deer have gone to much trouble to relearn. Characterizes the stag as being created solely to adorn the solitude of the forest and calls stag hunting the most noble of all European sports. One of the great classics of natural science.*

Cabinet of Natural History and American Rural Sports. Vol 1. "The Common Deer: Cervus virginianus." Philadelphia: J & T Doughty, 1830–1833. pp. 3–7.

In this item of a three-volume work, published in parts, the unknown author suggests that because the intellectual character of the white-tailed deer is so far from contemptible, hunting them becomes a very curious activity and must be considered an art with a set of technical techniques. Emphasizes the elegance of their form, the symmetry of their proportions, the swiftness of their movement, and the exquisite taste of their flesh. Discusses the various modes of deer hunting and amusingly supposes that whitetails live from thirty to forty years. Volume one also contains a beautiful poem by C. W. T., entitled "To A Wild Deer," that describes the death of a deer that wanders into the borough of Columbia in Lancaster County, Pennsylvania, and questions the animal's motives for forsaking the deer forest and roaming into civilization—a question that many deer managers concerned with urban deer problems are currently asking themselves as well. A gold mine of information on the earliest accounts of deer and deer hunting published in this country. Scarce and very expensive.*

Campbell, Dennis, ed. *Alabama Whitetail Records.* Alabama: Alabama Whitetail Records, 1989. 362 pp.

This state record book contains an interesting discussion on the Black Belt and trophy whitetails and notes that although the Black Belt contains only 3.5 percent of the land area of Alabama, this small area produces 85 percent of the trophy white-tailed bucks listed in the record book.

Campion, J. S. "A Fat Buck." In *On the Frontier: Reminiscences of Wild Sports, Personal Adventures and Strange Scenes.* London: Chapman & Hall, 1878. pp. 137ff.

Deer hunting experiences among the Mohave and Apache Indians in the Colorado River Valley. Old buckskin-clad Campion argued as early as 1878 that a deer hunter could determine the sex and size of a deer by analyzing the track.*

Canfield, H. S. "Following Deer Trails in the Northwestern Woods, 1904." In *Tales of the Great Lakes.* New Jersey: Castle, 1986. pp. 323–328.

A choice piece of deer hunting nostalgia illustrated with romantic drawings by Lynn Bogue Hunt. Emphasizes the point that "he only is a deer hunter who has killed his buck unaided."

Caton, John Dean. *The Antelope and Deer of America.* South Carolina: The Premier Press, 1990.

Thanks to the diligent efforts of historian Jim Casada, we now have a deluxe edition of this blue-chip deer book with an introduction by Robert Wegner.

Clutton-Brock, T. H. and S. D. Albon. *Red Deer in the Highlands.* London: BSP Professional Books, 1989. 260 pp. A rich synthesis of existing knowledge on the behavior, ecology, and population dynamics of Scottish red deer. Of great interest to the student of deer. Contains a detailed discussion of the relationship between weather variables and red deer behavior.

Colby, C. B. *Wild Deer.* New York: Duell, Sloan and Pearce, 1966. 126 pp.

An attractive introduction to the deer of the world for the young readers, grades seven to nine.*

Cook, Gary W. "Deer Hunt." In *The Old Man.* Tennessee: Pioneer Press, 1987. pp 33–34.

Everyone needs an Old Man as a hunting partner and a deer camp comrade. Gary Cook's Old Man was Sam Kenton, the hero of this deer hunting tale of ultimate solitude that originally appeared in *The Tennessee Wildlife Magazine.*

Cook, Sam. "Forgotten Stand." In *Up North.* Minnesota: Pfeifer-Hamilton, Publisher, 1986. pp. 144–146.

High-level prose about a weathered deer stand.

Cooper, Helen A. *Winslow Homer Watercolors.* New Haven: Yale University Press, 1986. 259 pp.

This splendid volume contains many of Homer's unsurpassed deer and deer hunting watercolors, especially "Fallen Deer" (1892), "A Good Shot" (1892), and "Hound and Hunter" (1892), that vividly express the anguished moment between life and death in a sensational way, while at the same time emphasizing the paradox of the deer hunter: that it's chiefly through the instinct to kill that man achieves intimacy with nature and life.

Cox, Daniel J., and John Ozoga. *Whitetail Country.* Wisconsin: Willow Creek Press, 1988. 145 pp.

In this illustrated life history of the white-tailed deer, deer biologist John Ozoga raises one very important question, a question that needs to be answered: Does intensive trophy hunting (taking the very best, prime specimens) seriously affect the genetic make-up of white-tailed deer herds? According to Ozoga, "whether continuous intensive cropping of the best whitetail specimens contributes to serious social disruption and genetic degradation and is eventually detrimental to the healthful existence of whitetails, as some investigators suggest, has not been demonstrated to the satisfaction of most wildlife managers."

Creeth, E. H. *Deerlover.* Vermont: The Countryman Press, 1987. 290 pp.

A novel in the literature of crime and suspense set against the background of the deer hunting season in northern Michigan.

Cruickshank, Helen Gere., ed. *John and William Bartram's America.* New York: Doubleday & Company, Inc., 1957. 378 pp.

These selections from the writings of two of America's earliest naturalists contain numerous references to early deer observations and a colorful short essay describing an eighteenth-century deer hunt, "Deer Hunt on the Alachu Savannah" by William Bartram, dated 1791 — undoubtedly one of the earliest essays ever written on deer hunting for sport.

Cunningham, Marci. *The Deerhunters' Guide to Success.* Pennsylvania: Backwoods Books, 1985. 48 pp.

With the possible exception of cookbooks, this self-published pamphlet on deer and deer hunting represents one of the very few books ever published by a woman of the more than eight hundred volumes that exist on the subject in the English language.

Dalrymple, Byron W. "Whitetail Deer." In *North American Big Game Hunting.* New York: Winchester, 1974. pp. 166–183.

Basic and practical information on hunting whitetails.*

Daniels, Jerry. *Hunting the Whitetail.* Texas: Privately printed, 1990. 197 pp.

Recommends that you heat your doe scent to 103 degrees to imitate the smell of a "hot doe."

Darling, Fraser. "Red Stags." In *Wild Country.* England: Cambridge University Press, 1938. pp. 60–63.

In his Highland notes, naturalist Darling asks one basic question that antihunters have never been able to answer in any sensible way: "Here is the wild red deer—how are its numbers to be kept in check except by man, the hunter, now that carnivorous enemies such as the wolf have been exterminated?"*

Deason, Wilborn J. "The Game of Deer Hunting." In *Nature's Silent Call.* Illinois: The Bunting Publications, Inc., 1925. pp. 259–283. An eloquent plea by a Chicago physician for taking up the game of deer hunting. The rule for diet in his deer camp read: "Sit six inches from the table and eat till you touch."*

Deer Research Unit. *Deer Refresher Course.* Australia: University of Sydney, 1984. 762 pp.

Postgraduate lectures on all aspects of deer by leading world veterinary authorities.

De Gouy, Louis P. "Deer." In *The Derrydale Game Cook Book of Fish and Game.* Vol. 1. Wisconsin: Willow Creek Press, 1987. pp. 188–217.

This reprint of the classic Derrydale cookbook contains some of the all-time great venison recipes.

De Nahlik, A. J. *Wild Deer: Culling, Conservation and Management.* England: Ashford Press Publishing, 1987. 264 pp.

This second, revised edition introduces a great deal of current British data. A standard volume on English deer and deer management.

Devoe, Alan. "The Deer." In *Down to Earth: A Naturalist Looks About*. New York: Coward-McCann, Inc., 1940. pp. 143–149.

An anti-hunting essay that wrongly equates deer hunting with deer poaching.*

Diehl, Scott R. "The Translocation of Urban White-tailed Deer." In *Translocation of Wild Animals,* edited by Leon Nielsen and Robert D. Brown. Wisconsin: Wisconsin Humane Society, 1988. pp. 239–249.

Deals with the problem of high population densities of whitetails throughout the surburban areas of northern Milwaukee County, Wisconsin.

Dietz, Lew. "Some Maine Deer Trails." In *Touch of Wilderness*. New York: Holt, Rinehart and Winston, 1969. pp. 95–109.

While not suggesting that the whitetail is the most intellectual animal in the world, the author acknowledges that the whitetail is smarter than Lew Dietz when it counts. Recommends avoiding the full phase of the moon when deer hunting; if you doubt his opinion, the author suggests that you consult the deer-kill statistics in your area during the full moon period.*

Diman, Jeremiah Lewis. "A Deer Hunt on the Raquette." In *Memoirs of the Rev. Jeremiah Lewis Diman*. Boston: Houghton, Mifflin, 1887. pp. 243–253.

Even though Walton recommended angling as the contemplative man's recreation, Rev. Diman views deer hunting in the Adirondacks for the ultimate in contemplation.*

Dinesen, Wilhelm. *Boganis: Letters From the Hunt: A Field Journal*. Boston: Rowan Tree Press, 1987. 147 pp.

The first English-language edition of a Danish book originally published in 1888. Contains one chapter on deer hunting in North America.

DiSilvertro, Roger L. "North American Deer." In *The Endangered Kingdom*. New York: John Wiley & Sons, 1989. pp. 19–39.

An excellent discussion of the complex relationship between deer hunters and game managers by the former senior editor of *Audubon* magazine.

Dobie, Duncan. *White Tales and Other Hunting Stories*. Georgia: Privately printed, 1989. 229 pp.

A collection of fictional material on white-tailed deer hunting.

Dodge, Richard Irving. "Black-tailed Deer." In *The Hunting Grounds of the Great West*. England: Chatto & Windus, Piccadilly, 1877. pp. 173–186.

A valuable account of western deer hunting with some detailed descriptions of wounded deer behavior. On one unfortunate day, Lieutenant-Colonel Dodge mortally wounded four bucks without bagging any of them. "On the next day I went over the same ground with my dog (which had been sick the day before), and found all the bodies, unfortunately spoiled from remaining so long after death. The best sportsman, unless he has a good dog, may calculate on losing one out of every three actually killed."*

Doll, G. Fred, S. T. Mast, and Judy Denison. *Deer Hunter Perceptions and Preferences, Wyoming 1986*. Wyoming: University of Wyoming, 1986. 48 pp.

In this survey of deer hunters, the so-called "big buck hunters" tend to be somewhat more negative than deer hunters as a whole in their perceptions of deer hunting trends during the past ten years. Big buck hunters more readily favor managing for big bucks, restricting the number of hunters and restricting hunting to every other year. All respondents felt that the total number of deer, the number of bucks, and the average size of bucks in Wyoming had all decreased in the past ten years.

Donald, Garry. *Saskatchewan's Greatest Big Game*. Canada: Privately printed, 1987. 340 pp.

Stories and pictures of trophy whitetails of this province.

Dumke, Robert T., George V. Burger, and James R. March., eds. *Wildlife Management on Private Lands*. Wisconsin: The Wisconsin Chapter of the Wildlife Society, 1981. 576 pp.

These proceedings of a symposium held in Milwaukee, Wisconsin, deal with one very crucial problem that needs to be solved if hunting is to survive in this country: How do we manage a public resource on private property?

Eiseley, Loren. "The Deer." In *Another Kind of Autumn*. New York: Charles Scribner's Sons, 1977. pp. 76–77.

A classic poem on the relationship between man and deer written by a great popularizer of science.*

————. "Never Like Deer." In *All the Night Wings*. New York: Times Books, 1979. p. 71.

A great poem comparing the clumsy departures of men to the brilliant, shadowy escapes of deer at dawn. A haunting poem by an extraordinary writer.*

Elliott, William. *Carolina Sports by Land and Water*. New York: Arno Press, 1967. 172 pp.

This facsimile of the first edition details the hair-raising deer hunts of William Elliott (1788–1863), a lifetime planter, politician, and poet and one of the most widely read authorities on southern sports during his day. These candid pieces of sylvan warfare in the Chee-ha area of South Carolina include everything from melodious music of baying deerhounds to the chilling echoes of the huntsman's horn. This volume remains one of the few early American sporting books that has stayed in print almost without interruption from the date of its first publication in 1846. Several of these deer hunting sketches were originally published in the sporting press of Elliott's day under the signature of Venator. A refreshing portrait of southern deer hunting by one of the gentleman plantation owners of the period. Roosevelt referred to it as an "excellent and trustworthy" account.

Ellis, Billy. "The Grey Ghosts of Windsor." In *Hunter to the Dawn*. Mississippi: Mississippi River Publishing Company, 1988. pp. 119–130.

Bow hunting whitetails on the Cedar Ridge Hunting Preserve.

Elman, Robert, ed. *The Complete Book of Hunting*. New York: Abbeville Press, 1980. 319 pp.

This oversized reference volume contains a fine section on the history of hunting by his-

torian John Reiger as well as a section on European deer and deer hunting.*

Errington, Paul L. *A Question of Values*. Iowa: Iowa State University Press, 1987. 196 pp.

This collection of published and unpublished writings of the internationally renowned scientist and naturalist Paul Errington contains the classic (often reprinted) hunting essay "Question of Values," in which Errington writes, "To me, with gun in hand or without, the appeal of the out-of-doors seems chiefly conditioned by the relative diversity and completeness of its native fauna and flora and the naturalness of its topography." If sport hunting must be purchased at a disproportionate cost to such outdoor values, Paul Errington, hunter though he was, did not think it was worth the price.

Eschmeyer, R. W. *Willie Whitetail*. Ohio: Fisherman Press, Inc., 1953. 49 pp.

This life history of the white-tailed deer written for children by a professional conservationist draws heavily on the research of Michigan's Ilo Bartlett.*

Etling, Kathy. *Hunting Superbucks*. Connecticut: Grolier, 1989. 444 pp.

Stories and photos of trophy buck hunters.

Fears, J. Wayne. *Hunting Whitetails Successfully*. Minnesota: North American Hunting Club, 1986. 206 pp.

The first book in the North American Hunting Club series. A basic how-to manual.

Flack, Captain. "The Common American Deer." In *A Hunter's Experiences in the Southern States of America*. London: Longmans, Green, and Company, 1866. pp. 88–117.

An early account of the natural history of whitetails and the different modes of hunting them as practiced in the south.*

Fletcher, Rich. *Chronicle of a Western Archery Season*. California: Towhee Publishing, 1988. 113 pp.

The daily journal of a western bow hunter.

Ford, Corey. "Everybody Gets Buck Fever." In *The Corey Ford Sporting Treasury*. Wisconsin: Willow Creek Press, 1987. pp. 291–294.

In a well-cast tale of the Lower Forty Shooting Club, Corey Ford emphasizes the universality of this eternal affliction by having Judge Parker proclaim, "If a feller didn't get a little mite excited once in a while, where would be the fun o' huntin'?"

Fosburgh, Hugh. *One Man's Pleasure: A Journal of the Wilderness World.* New York: William Morrow and Company, 1960. 191 pp.

This outdoor journal contains a detailed and introspective diary of a deer hunt in the Adirondacks that reaches the conclusion that "the perfect way to kill a deer is to trail it to its bed and come upon it lying down twenty-five yards away, or maybe less; then you shoot it in such a way that it never knows you were there or what happened to it. When you've done that, you've hunted well and made a perfect shot and done more to be pleased about than all the fantastic shots, put together, that you ever made in your life." Well-expressed, colorful observations.*

Freethy, Ron. "Artiodactyls: Deer." In *Man & Beast: The Natural and Unnatural History of British Mammals.* England: Blandford Press, 1983. pp. 215–234.

A guide to British deer and their relationships with man.

Gabrielson, Ira N. *Wildlife Management.* New York: The Macmillan Company, 1951. 274 pp.

This standard volume contains an excellent chapter on sportsmanship that warns us against the general tendency to relax standards of conduct in an end-justifies-the-means type of philosophy, a position too often advocated by deer hunters who should know better.

Gaida, Urban, and Martin Marchello. *Going Wild.* Minnesota: Watab Marketing, Inc., 1987. 240 pp.

An excellent guide to field dressing, butchering, and cooking venison. Contains detailed information on the nutrient and mineral content of venison as compared to beef that will surprise most deer hunters. Documents the fact that venison is *twice as high* in cholesterol as USDA Choice beef, a little-known fact in the world of deer hunting.

Gates, Jay M., III. *Bucks I Have Taken (And Bucks That Got Away).* Arizona: Privately printed, 1988. 175 pp.

A photo album of one man's trophy bucks.

Gerstäcker, Friedrich. *Wild Sports in the Far West.* North Carolina: Duke University Press, 1968. 409 pp.

Originally published in German in 1844 with the title *Streif-und Jagdzüge durch die Vereinigten Staaten Nordamerikas,* this narrative of hunting in America provides us with a portrait of the early, nineteenth-century deerslayer (1837–1843), viewed and experienced through the eyes of a young German deer hunter and popular story writer. Despite the misnomer of the English title due to poor translating, this sporting volume narrates primarily the author's deer hunting experiences and adventures in the swamps and the Ozarks of Arkansas. These wild tales of deer shooting, like those of Meshach Browning and Philip Tome, include many hair-raising incidents of fighting with wounded bucks while relying only on a knife and a die-hard deerhound named "Bearsgrease." While the author drank his share of raw whiskey out of tumblers with Indians, deerslayers, and backwoodsmen, the historic record suggests that he never lapsed from the perpendicular. This German observer realized as early as 1844 that the chase in America was on the decline, for the American hunter spared nothing in his war of extermination against deer. Episodic tales of deer shooting for the pot with a dim sense of sportsmanship rare in Gerstäcker's day. He obviously read Cooper's *The Deerslayer* (1841) while rambling around the American deer forest. Went through many editions and translations and still remains in print today.

Gilchrist, Duncan. "Short Course on Whitetail Deer Hunting." In *Successful Big Game Hunting.* Montana: Stoneydale Press Publishing Company, 1987. pp. 98–111.

An enthusiastic buck hunter offers twenty-five helpful tips.

Giles, Robert H., Jr. *Wildlife Management.* California: W. H. Freeman and Company, 1978. 416 pp.

This standard text on wildlife management contains numerous references to deer, deer hunting, deer hunters, poaching, and poachers.

Gillette, Bertha Chambers. *Homesteading with the Elk.* Utah: Privately printed, 1968. 175 pp.

A historical novel of the development of the elk refuge in Jackson Hole, Wyoming.

Gillmore, Parker ("Ubique"). "A Big Buck." In *Gun, Rod and Saddle*. London: Chapman and Hall, 1869. pp. 87–94.

The story of shooting a big buck in Illinois, written by an adventurous Englishman who traveled and hunted widely in the United States and throughout the world. Gillmore believed that deer drop their tails when hit.*

———. *Accessible Field Sports*. London: Chapman and Hall, 1869. 336 pp.

Contains two chapters on deer hunting: "First Deer in America" and "A Long Deer Hunt." An interesting mixture of fact, fancy, and romance.*

Greenwood, James. "The American Deer." *Wild Sports of the World. A Book of Natural History and Adventure*. New York: Harper & Brothers, 1870. pp. 347–382.

This description of deer hunting in America during the 1860s contains a very interesting discussion on the remarkable vitality of the white-tailed deer and its incredible capacity to recover from serious wounds that would seemingly be fatal to any other mammal. Greenwood, a journalist and novelist, documents how one buck in Virginia even survived after an elder stick penetrated its heart.*

Gregory, Tappan. *Nature Photography at Night*. Colorado: Denver Museum of Natural History, 1957. 64 pp.

Includes six of the all-time great deer photographs by one of the founders of wildlife photography.*

———. *Eyes in the Night*. New York: Thomas Y. Crowell Company, 1939. 243 pp.

More of the great deer photographs by Gregory, who spent more than thirty years snapping deer with his "Brownie."*

Grooms, Steve, ed. *Minnesota Deer Classic Record Book*. 2nd ed. Minnesota: Wildlife Heritage Foundation, 1987. 164 pp.

Another record book for trophy aficionados. Contains the story of how Curt Van Lith killed his number three Pope and Young white-tailed buck in a cornfield after a marathon tracking season lasting ten hours and covering a distance of four miles. One wonders what the "brown" deer meat tasted like.

Grzimek, Berhard, ed. "Deer." In *Grzimek's Animal Life Encyclopedia*. Vol. 13. (Mammals IV.) New York: Van Nostrand Reinhold Company, 1972. pp. 154–245.

A standard reference on the subject.

Haas, George H., ed. *Outdoor Life Deer Hunter's Yearbook, 1988*. New York: Outdoor Life Books, 1987. 185 pp.

Reprints on deer hunting from *Outdoor Life*.

Hall, Leonard. "Deer Crossing." In *A Journal of the Seasons on an Ozark Farm*. Missouri: University of Missouri Press, 1980. pp. 148–156.

Characterizes Missouri deer hunting at the Gooseneck Club in the Ozarks as *more* fun when it becomes custom and tradition with less emphasis on antlers and meat for the pot. Views deer camp camaraderie as more important than three or four white-tailed bucks hanging on the meat pole by the second day of the season. Rightly criticizes the sport of deer hunting in the 1980s for becoming too technological and too artificial, with less and less skill, hardihood, and woodcraft required for its pursuit. Ends on a very bitter note: "As each season draws to a close, I find myself feeling glad that it is over—that now these beautiful dwellers of the forest can go back to the quiet and peace of their hills and hollows, safe for another year from all but the running dog pack, the occasional poacher, and the cars that drive too swiftly on highways that run through the deer woods."*

Hamerstrom, Frances. "Swamp Buck" In *Is She Coming Too? Memoirs of a Lady Hunter*. Iowa: Iowa State University, 1989. pp. 97–104.

Dreams of shooting a large swamp buck lead to a base case of buck fever.

Hanks, Charles Stedman ("Niblick"). "Some Deer That I Have Met." In *Camp Kits & Camp Life*. New York: Charles Scribner's Sons, 1906. pp. 122–151.

In this guide to outdoor camping, "Niblick" insists that if you wound a deer and lose it, always take the time to study how you lost it, for an analysis of your errors will be far more beneficial to you than an analysis of what you did correctly.*

Harder, D. J. *Whitetail Tales.* Wisconsin: Privately printed, 1990. 56 pp. Humorous cartoons about awkward deer hunting situations.

Harrison, Jim. "Dead Deer." In *Selected & New Poems, 1961–1981.* New York: Delta/Seymour Lawrence, 1982. p. 26.

This poem, written in a deer shack in an isolated part of Michigan's Upper Peninsula by that backwoods genius Jim Harrison, captures the essence of a starved whitetail in the deeryard better than anything I have ever read.

Harrison, Mike, ed. *The Australian Deerhunter's Handbook.* Australia: The Australian Deer Research Foundation, 1986. 92 pp.

A sound summary of the Australian deer hunting scene.

Haugen, Arnold O., and Harlan G. Metcalf. *Field Archery and Bowhunting.* New York: The Ronald Press Company, 1963. 213 pp.

Written by a well-known wildlife biologist and a professor of physical education, this well-illustrated book contains many excellent old-time deer hunting photos, a "Who's Who Among Women Bowhunters," and a fine sketch of the development of modern bow hunting. A favorite book among archers and white-tailed deer hunters of the 1960s.*

Headley, Joel T. *The Adirondack, Or, Life in the Woods.* New York: Harbor Hill Books, 1982. 461 pp.

A popular and romantic account of deer hunting in the Adirondacks during the 1840s, written by a minister who went to the Adirondacks to improve his failing health and who soon became enamored with chasing whitetails. Saw a direct relationship between the croaking of frogs and the feeding of deer. Excellent descriptions of deer and deer hunting in the form of letters. Originally published in 1849.

Henderson, Robert W. *Early American Sport: A Check-List of Books by American and Foreign Authors Published in America Prior to 1860 Including Sporting Songs.* New York: A. S. Barnes & Company, 1953. 234 pp.

This excellent bibliography of early American sport lists about a dozen items on deer and deer hunting not found in Phillips' *American Game Mammals and Birds.**

Hendy, E. W. "Stag-Hunting on Exmoor." In *Wild Exmoor Through the Year.* London: Eyre and Spottiswood, 1946. pp. 125–134.

Reaches the conclusion that the opposition to stag hunting takes the form of a curious and perverted type of class hatred, described as "an urban prejudice." Notes that you cannot find a more democratic institution than a deer hunt. Indeed, nowhere do classes mix so easily as in the sport of deer hunting. The love of the sport is indigenous in the folk of all classes: they have shared in it for generations, it's in their blood. "What I enjoy besides the jolly sound of the horn, the 'tuneable cry' of hounds, the thud of horses' hooves, the gay camaraderie of the field and foot-followers," Hendy writes, "is the skill of the huntsman, the perseverance of the hounds, following their own natural instinct, in puzzling out a difficult scent and pitting their cunning against that of the deer. All these are good and healthy pleasures."*

Herter, George L., and Jacques P. Herter. *Professional Guide's Manual.* 2 vols. Minnesota: Herters, Inc., 1963.

Like Joseph Brunner, the Herters argue that in the absence of a blood trail, you can tell whether a deer is wounded by studying its track. They also insist that a wounded deer carries its tail held tightly down against its rump. They calculate the national wounding rate at 33–38 percent of the harvest.

Hingston, Frederick, ed. *Deer Parks & Deer of Great Britain.* England: Sporting & Leisure Press, 1988. 136 pp.

Deer have never been more popular in England than today. This book explains why and greatly adds to their popularity by giving deer lovers a guide to more than 170 deer parks, farms, zoological gardens, and estates arranged county by county. Includes their location, the species and numbers of deer in each herd, acreage, owner, history, description, and details of access where available. Thirty-seven owners declined to advertise their deer parks in this volume for fear of attracting the attention of deer poachers—a sad reflection of our times.

Hodges, Terry. "Border Deer Poachers." In *Sabertooth*. California: Paladin Press, 1988. pp. 79–85.

Catching big-time deer poachers red-handed in Modoc County, California, with "Old Sabertooth," a legendary game warden.

Holden, Philip. *New Zealand: Hunter's Paradise*. New Zealand: Hodder and Stoughton, 1985. 255 pp.

In this volume Holden takes up the story of New Zealand's red deer, tracing their fall from grace as farmers and foresters call for their eradication and as the government offers two shillings per tail for their destruction. He tells the story from 1930 to the mid-1950s, through the eyes of deer hunters, newspaper reports, and government documents. Deals with the problems man encounters when he introduces deer for sport hunting. Basic reading for understanding man's attempt to control deer populations. A great deer book about a country long regarded as a mecca for trophy hunters. As Robert Ruark once noted, if a deer hunter dies and goes to heaven, he will likely view the whole place disparagingly if he had first hunted deer in New Zealand.

————. *Hunter by Profession*. New Zealand: Hodder and Stoughton, 1973. 171 pp.

Describes the free and adventurous life of a full-time venison hunter at a time when the New Zealand government actually paid men to hunt deer.

Holt, Dave. "Buck Fever." In *Balanced Bowhunting*. Colorado: Privately printed, 1988. pp. 51–61.

An excellent discussion of that intermittent disease that affects hunters in the deer forest all across America and how to deal with the problem.

Hoover, Helen. "The Deer Family." In *The Long-Shadowed Forest*. New York: W. W. Norton, 1963. pp. 129–141.

Observations on deer from her remote cabin on the Minnesota-Canada border.

Hornaday, William T. "The Deer Family." In *The American Natural History*. Vol. 2. New York: Charles Scribner's Sons, 1919. pp. 55–121.

In this book, originally published in 1904, Hornaday considers still-hunting as "the true sportsman's method" of killing whitetails and views one fine white-tailed buck shot in this method as equal to two mule deer or three elk. The white-tailed deer knows well, the author writes, "that as a discourager of cervine curiosity nothing in the world equals a breech-loading rifle."*

————. "Deer as a Food Supply." In *Our Vanishing Wild Life: Its Extermination and Preservation*. New York: Charles Scribner's Sons, 1913. pp. 234–243.

While I disagree with Hornaday's extreme preservationist philosophy and his later anti-hunting sentiments, I agree with his suggestion that every pioneer should have emblazoned a figure of the white-tailed deer on his tombstone, for the white flag greatly assisted the pioneers in their westward expansion. Yet, as Hornaday asks, how many men today recall with any feeling of gratitude the significant role played in American history by the white-tailed deer? Very few!*

Hudson, David. *Highland Deer Stalking*. England: Crowood Press, 1989. 192 pp.

A practical guide to Highland deer stalking.

Huggler, Thomas. "Carl's Cabin." In *Midwest Meanders*. Michigan: Avery Color Studios, 1984. pp. 82–87.

A nostalgic look at an old Michigan deer hunting camp.

Ingraham, Joseph Holt. *The South-West*. New York: Harper & Brothers, 1835.

Historian Clark Burkett of Jefferson College calls this one of the most famous and popular books in America during the 1850s. In it, Ingraham describes a Mississippi deer hunt in the early 1830s.*

Ives, Edward D. *George Magoon and the Down East Game War: History, Folklore, and the Law*. Illinois: University of Illinois Press, 1988. 335 pp.

The adventures of a notorious deer poacher in Maine who was the hero of scores of funny stories telling how he outwitted the game wardens. It seems likely that Edmund Ware Smith patterned Jeff Coongate after George Magoon.

Jaeger, Ellsworth. *Tracks and Trailcraft*. London: The Macmillan Company, 1969. 381 pp.

Contains a fascinating account of whitetailed deer tracks and trail craft. Jaeger believes that tracks provide us with a complete autobiography of a living deer from day to day. He summarizes his great love of tracking deer in one sentence: "When we find the whitetail's beautiful petal-like tracks in the nearby woodlot we still get a thrill that only wild nature can grant."

Kellert, Stephen R. "Human-Animal Interactions: A Review of the American Attitudes to Wild and Domestic Animals in the Twentieth Century." In *Animals and People Sharing the World,* edited by Andrew N. Rowan. New Hampshire: University Press of New England, 1988. pp. 137–175.

This excellent paper contains the results of Kellert's various studies, conducted over more than a decade, concerning American perceptions of animals and the natural environment. Reaches some fascinating conclusions with regard to the public's attitude toward hunting: (1) 60 percent oppose hunting *solely* for recreational or sporting purposes, and (2) 80 percent object to the notion of hunting for trophies, but (3) 64 percent of hunting for recreational purposes *as long as the meat is used.*

Kelly, Joe, and Terry Madewell. *Joe Kelly's Tactics for Trophy Whitetails.* South Carolina: Privately printed, 1988. 140 pp.

Advice from Joe Kelly, a South Carolinian who has killed more than five hundred deer, scores of trophies, and two record book bucks. Includes ads for Northcon Teleproductions, Inc., producers of Joe Kelly video tapes, Joe Kelly's Trophy Secret Concentrated Mineral Supplement, Joe Kelly's Whitetail Deer Guide Service, and last but not least, an application blank to join Joe Kelly's Southeastern Bow and Gun Hunters Association for $250.

Kelly, Tom. "People." In *Tenth Legion.* Alabama: Wing-feather Press, 1973. pp. 1–11.

Although this book deals with the turkey hunting subculture, chapter one, entitled "People," contains a psychological digression into the mind of the redneck, Alabama deer hunter.

Kerfoot, Justine. "Deer Hunters, 1937." In *Woman of the Boundary Waters.* Minnesota: Women's Times Publishing, 1986. pp. 84–86.

A woman's deer hunting experiences at Gunflint Lodge.

Kilgo, James. *Deep Enough for Ivorybills.* North Carolina: Chapel Hill, 1988. 193 pp.

The wonderful title certainly does not indicate that the contents of this book deal with deer hunting. But they do, for its prominent theme revolves around one man's quest for antlered bucks in the wild swamps of South Carolina. Captures with keen insight and rich detail the pleasures of the deer hunt, deer camp camaraderie, and the excitement of the chase. Not many books about deer hunting rank as literature, but this one does. Five stars. Kilgo cares deeply about deer, deer hunting, and his deer hunting turf. A powerful memoir. The book, as historian Paul Schullery notes in *The New York Times Book Review,* "is as deep in meanings and questions as the river swamps Kilgo wanders."

Kinton, Tony. *The Beginning Bowhunter.* Indiana: ICS Books, Inc., 1985. 119 pp.

Covers the basics of bow hunting the whitetailed deer.

Kroeber, Theodora. *Ishi: Last of His Tribe.* New York: Bantam Books, 1981. 213 pp.

———. *Ishi in Two Worlds.* California: University of California Press, 1961. 255 pp.

Two very sensitive and remarkable accounts of the last wild Indian in North America documenting how he trailed and hunted deer with his bow and arrow and a stuffed deer head that he used as a deer decoy. Notes that Ishi preferred to lure and ambush deer rather than still hunt or drive them.

Labarbera, Mark, ed. *Wisconsin Deer & Bear Record Book.* 2nd ed. Minnesota: Privately printed, 1989. 231 pp.

In this second edition, the editor compiles pictures, records, and various articles about Wisconsin deer and deer hunting written by various authors.

Lapinski, Mike. *Radical Elk Hunting Strategies: Secrets of Calling Elk in Close.* Montana: Stoneydale Press Publishing Company, 1988. 159 pp.

A basic how-to manual.

Laubach, Don, and Mark Henckel. *Elk Talk*. Montana: Privately printed, 1987. 202 pp.

A self-published guide to finding, calling, and hunting elk.

Lawson, Larry E. *Indiana's Greatest Whitetails: Volume II*. Indiana: Privately printed, 1989. 352 pp.

Since Volume I, white-tailed deer fanatic Larry Lawson had been hard at work collecting pictures and stories of the giants shot in the Hoosierland. In this second volume he provides us with more than 240 big deer photos while keeping the fantasy of monster whitetails alive.

Leach, A. J. "Hunting Elk and Deer in Custer County." In *Early Day Stories*. Nebraska: Huse Publishing Company, 1916. pp. 111–119.

Nebraska deer hunting adventures during the 1870s.*

Leader-Williams, N. *Reindeer on South Georgia: The Ecology of an Introduced Population*. Cambridge: Cambridge University Press, 1988. 319 pp.

An in-depth study of a single species in an alien environment.

Leopold, Aldo. "Control of Hunting." In *Game Management*. New York: Charles Scribner's Sons, 1961. pp. 208–229.

One of the best statements on the theory of hunting ever penned. The book, in general, is as usable today as the day it came off the press.

Leschak, Peter M. "The Quest and the Kill." In *Letters from Side Lake: A Chronicle of Life in the North Woods*. New York: Harper & Brothers, 1987. pp. 75–96.

This reflective story of a moose hunt in the canoe-wilderness area of northern Minnesota examines the relationship between the hunt and the kill and comes to the conclusion that "we can't justify the hunt; we can only enjoy it. We need the quest and not the kill, but the way of the world is that you can't have one without the other. The best we can do is to make damn sure we don't waste the meat."

Lindsay, David Moore. "Mule Deer Shooting." In *Camp-Fire Reminiscences*. Boston: Dana Estes & Company, 1912. pp. 47–61.

Tales of mule deer shooting in the mountains of Colorado. Raises the question as to whether the Ute Indians were great conservationists or slaughterers of deer.*

Lund, Fred P. "Me, the Mighty Buckhunter." In *Iron River, My Home Town*. Minnesota: Privately printed, 1975. pp. 14–29.

A fine story of how a kid ("Wiggles" Lund) gets buck fever on his first deer hunting trip and how he associates his deer hunting experiences with those of Davy Crockett, Daniel Boone, Kit Carson, Buffalo Bill, and the Royal Mounted Police. Deals with a common problem of many deer camps: the kid who balks at using a shotgun, but then goes on to triumphantly gun down an eight-pointer with the "lowly shotgun." Also captures well the moment of utter shock when the kid sees for the first time an old timer washing his blood-soaked hands in his own urine while relieving himself.

———. "Deer Hunting Episodes of Yesterday." In *And That's the Way It Was*. Minnesota: Privately printed, 1973. pp. 96–115.

More deer and deer hunting stories of The Homestead deer camp located south of Iron River in Bayfield County, Wisconsin, by "Wigs" Lund.

McClung, Robert M. *Whitetail*. New York: William Morrow and Company, Inc., 1987. 82 pp.

Juvenile literature. This life-cycle study of a white-tailed deer introduces the young reader to the pros and cons of hunting. Narrates the story of a fawn learning to deal with such dangers of nature as cars, hunters, snowmobiles, and dogs.

McConnochie, Alex Inkson. *Deer Forest Life*. London: Alexander Maclehose & Company, 1932. 237 pp.

Interesting reminiscences and anecdotes of stalkers on the hill. Of particular interest for the naturalist as well as the deer hunter.*

McConochie, Newton. *You'll Learn No Harm from the Hills*. New Zealand: A. H. & A. W. Reed, 1966. 199 pp.

The adventurous shooting life of a New Zealand deer stalker, known as the "Grand Old Man" of the sport.*

McDiarmid, A. *Roe Deer Management and Stalking.* England: The Game Conservancy, 1987. 82 pp.

This fascinating booklet reaches one inescapable conclusion about deer hunting: "Buck fever accounts for more misses, wounded animals and bad shots than any other cause, and anyone who is keen enough to go out more than once or twice after deer is likely to have at least a twinge from time to time."

Macfarlan, Allan A. "Outguessing the Wily Deer." In *Exploring the Outdoors with Indian Secrets.* Harrisburg: Stackpole Books, 1971. pp. 65–88.

A rather superficial attempt to discuss the Indian ways of getting close to whitetails.

McFarland, David, ed. *The Oxford Companion to Animal Behavior.* New York: Oxford University Press, 1987. 685 pp.

This excellent handbook contains numerous references to deer behavior.

McIntyre, Thomas. "Remembering Blacktail." In *Days Afield.* New York: E. P. Dutton, Inc., 1984. pp. 42–49.

This essay on black-tailed deer hunting in Oregon remembers the black-tailed deer hunting of Ishi and Teddy Roosevelt but, more important, raises the fundamental question of who really cares about trophy antlers.

McManus, Patrick F. "The Case of the Missed Deer." In *The Grasshopper Trap.* New York: Holt, Rinehart and Winston, 1985. pp. 115–119.

———. "My First Deer, and Welcome to It." In *They Shoot Canoes, Don't They?* New York: Holt, Rinehart and Winston, 1981. pp. 54–61.

Two humorous tales of man against deer. His definition of that mythical first deer remains unsurpassed in the literature on deer and deer hunting: "A first deer not only lives on in the memory of a hunter but thrives there, increasing in points and pounds with each passing year until at last it reaches full maturity, which is to say, big enough to shade a

team of Belgian draft horses in its shadow at high noon."

Madson, John. "Under the Rutting Moon." In *Audubon Nature Yearbook, 1987,* edited by Les Line. New York: Grolier Books, 1987. pp. 49–52.

Illustrated with great deer photos by Erwin and Peggy Bauer, this essay concentrates on that period of time when, as Madson says, "suddenly, there are bucks."

Magie, Bill. "Depression Deer." In *A Wonderful Country.* Wisconsin: The Sigurd Olson Environmental Institute, 1981. pp. 128–130.

Poaching venison during the Depression years with one of the most colorful guides of the Quetico-Superior region.

Martindale, Thomas. "Adventures of a Deer Hunter in Maine." In *Sport Royal, I Warrant You!* Philadelphia: H. W. Shaw, 1897. pp. 133–144.

A descriptive account of a deer hunt in Maine in 1896, near a sheet of water known as Moose Pond.*

Mason, Bernard. "Buckskin." In *Woodcraft & Camping.* New York: Dover Publications, Inc., 1939. pp. 423–455.

In this splendid chapter on buckskin, Bernard Mason, a well-known authority on Indians and crafts, tells us that only those hunters who have spent long evenings beside campfires can appreciate the eternal appeal of buckskin, which he describes in the following manner: "The magic of wood smoke is in it, the most stirring of all perfumes is of it! Wherever it goes in the city world it carries with it perpetually and abundantly that matchless aromatic lure of the wilds, to fill the room with a restless urge to 'go, go, go away from here.' It is literally steeped with the incense of wood smoke."

Massie, Larry B. "Once Nearly Extinct, Whitetails Bounded Back." In *Voyages into Michigan's Past.* Michigan: Avery Color Studios, 1988. pp. 191–195.

In this historic essay, we learn that one Michigan pioneer named William Nowlin paid off the mortgage on the family farm by deer hunting as a full-time profession during the 1840s. He shipped carloads of venison to an eager market in Detroit.

Mathews, John Joseph. "Deer-Breeding Moon." In *Talking to the Moon*. Oklahoma: University of Oklahoma Press, 1981. pp. 156–174.

Short deer hunting sketches in the Osage country of northeastern Oklahoma. Like many deer hunting writers, Mathews pushes his typewriter aside when the hunting moon rises in the November sky. "If I attempt to carry on, the writing suffers; it loses so much in such a mysterious way that it is often useless and insipid."

Merrill, Lawrence "Pete." *Logging Trails and a Sportsman's Tales*. Michigan: Privately printed, 1987. 86 pp.

More delightful and humorous deer camp tales from the sage of the Messinger Creek Camp, who hunted in the Deer Lake area in the Upper Peninsula of Michigan for more than thirty-five years.

Mersfelder, L. C. "Deer or Steers?" In *Cowboy-Fisherman-Hunter: True Stories of the Great Southwest*. Missouri: Brown-White-Lowell Press, 1951. pp. 193–196.

Using trick photography, several deer hunting buddies substituted a couple of steers for two deer in an original photo, and the hunters in the photo never lived it down.*

Murie, Margaret and Olaus Murie. *Wapiti Wilderness*. Colorado: Colorado Associated University Press, 1985. 302 pp.

Two great naturalists study the world of elk. "Pure gold, every word of it," as *Natural History* reports.

National Rifle Association. *Whitetail Deer Hunting*. Washington, D.C.: National Rifle Association, 1988. 261 pp.

An introductory overview of many aspects of white-tailed deer hunting.

Nesbitt, W. H., and Jack Reneau, eds. *Records of North American Deer*. Virginia: The Boone and Crockett Club, 1987. 246 pp.

A paperback recognizing state and provincial white-tailed deer records.

New Brunswick Record Book Bucks. 2nd ed. New Brunswick, 1988. 98 pp.

The official record book of the New Brunswick white-tailed deer.

Nordberg, Ken. *The Whitetail Hunter's Almanac*. Minnesota: Privately printed, 1988. 150 pp.

Argues that you can determine the age of the buck by the size of the poop. "One-inch droppings mean SUPER BUCK!" I must admit that I have never seen anything in the scientific literature to support this intriguing notion.

Olson, Sigurd F. "Trail's End." In *The Collected Works of Sigurd F. Olson: The Early Writings, 1921–1934*. Minnesota: Voyageur Press, 1988. pp. 212–226.

A great fictional account of a wounded buck who escapes both the hunter and trailing wolves. Five stars.

Oppel, Frank, and Tony Meisel, eds. *Hunting North America, 1885–1911*. New Jersey: Castle, 1987. 480 pp.

The best literature on deer hunting remains, unfortunately, in the out-of-print back issues of such magazines as *Outing, Scribner's Magazine, The Century Magazine, Harper's New Monthly Magazine,* and others. This wonderful collection of original articles and stories from these magazines contains four blue-chip deer and deer hunting tales: "Deer Hunting on Sanhedrin" by Ninetta Eames, "Hunting the Virginia Deer" by T. S. Van Dyke, "Following Deer Trails in Northwestern Woods" by H. S. Canfield, and "The White-tailed Deer and Its Kin" by Ernest Thompson Seton. Illustrated with original artwork from such artistic giants as Seton, Rungius, and Lynn Bogue Hunt, these tales of sport and high adventure are filled with humorous anecdotes, technical detail, nostalgia, and the smell of the rugged outdoors.

Orman, Tony. *In Hind Sight: Deerstalking, A Personal Insight*. New Zealand: Inprint Books, 1987. 143 pp.

An excellent sequel to Orman's *Reflections of a Deer-stalker*. Filled with the thoughtful commentary of a thinking, deeply caring deer hunter. His words of warning with regard to trophy mania remain perhaps more relevant for America than New Zealand: "Unfortunately, too much emphasis is put on the trophy set of antlers, and this can lead to a hunter losing sight of sportsmanship. I have known of champion trophy heads which were shot by unethical means such as spot-lighting or hounding with dogs. The head adorns the wall of a home simply to satisfy a human ego. Antlers should not be a simple status symbol. They should serve as a re-minder of days spent hunting, whether it be that particular stag or the whole host of hunt-ing memories."

Ormond, Clyde. "Whitetail Deer." In *How to Track and Find Game*. New York: Outdoor Life, 1975. pp. 9–14.

Ormond summarizes well the difficulty of finding and tracking the white-tailed deer when he writes, "In his strategy to elude enemies, the whitetail ducks, skulks behind foliage, sneaks low to the ground, circles, doubles back, and lies low close to known danger—all in a canny effort to play hide-and-seek with man. His backtrack becomes a maze rather than a trail such as that left by other species."

Palliser, John. *Solitary Rambles and Adven-tures of a Hunter in the Prairies*. Vermont: Charles E. Tuttle Company, 1853. 326 pp.

Contains short sketches of western deer hunt-ing in the early 1850s.*

Pearce, Ken. *Walking Them Up*. Australia: The Australian Deer Research Foundation Limi-ted, 1987. 208 pp.

The author's respect for the quarry borders on reverence. A classic in the ever-growing literature on Australian deer and deer hunt-ing.

Pennsylvania Game Commission. *Pennsyl-vania Big Game Records, 1965–1986*. Harris-burg: Pennsylvania Game Commission, 1988. 216 pp.

A very informative record book that demon-strates that many of the white-tailed deer taken in Pennsylvania are truly of record class. Contains a good number of deer and deer hunting tales from the *Pennsylvania Game News* magazine.

Petersen, David. *Among the Elk*. Arizona: Northland Publishing, 1988. 118 pp.

A beautiful portrait of the most regal of North America's great wild deer.

Peterson, B. R. "Buck." *Buck Peterson's Guide to Deer Hunting*. California: Ten Speed Press, 1989. 153 pp.

In the interest of deer camp protocol, eti-quette, and social cohesiveness, no deer camp should be without this guide, one of the most sardonic gut piles of deer camp wisdom to appear since man first came down from the trees.

Phillips, John, and Denise Phillips. *Deer & Fixings*. Alabama: Privately printed, 1988. 186 pp.

This cookbook includes more than one hun-dred venison recipes for steaks, roasts, and ground venison.

Pope and Young Club. *Bowhunting Big Game Records of North America*. California: Pope and Young Club, 1987. 392 pp.

This third edition of the standard record book contains a short but excellent annotated list of the early books on bow hunting.

Powell, Michael. *A Waiting Game*. New York: St. Martin's Press, 1975. 175 pp.

The hunt lies at the heart of this novel—first for the deer that prowl by Brandon's Glade, and then for the dangerous and resourceful man who caused the glade to be renamed the Valley of Death.

Prior, Richard. *Deer Management in Small Woodlands*. England: The Game Conservan-cy, 1987. 116 pp.

If you are interested in deer and deer hunting in the United Kingdom, you will want to read this excellent summary of deer management principles. "Deer are beautiful animals," Prior rightly insists, "and any thinking per-son needs to assure himself of the necessity for shooting them, as well as the humanity of his actions when he does."

————. *Roe Stalking*. England: The Game Conservancy, 1987. 130 pp.

In this roe deer hunting guide, the foremost roe deer expert points out that while a child's bubble kit may look eccentric in the deer woods, it provides basic information on wind direction and velocity as it swirls through the forest.

————. *Deer Watch*. Vermont: David & Charles Inc., 1987. 199 pp.

A great book about deer, from the perspec-tive of the deer itself, for the general public—whether hunters, nonhunters, or antihunters — written by one of England's most enthusiastic deer specialists. Tells us that deer are designed to be eaten. Excellent photography and illustration. First-rate popularization of deer biology at its best.

————. *Modern Roe Stalking.* England: Tideline Books, 1985. 248 pp.

Studying, hunting, and working with deer remains Prior's basic preoccupation. In this distillation of a lifetime's observations on deer, Prior points out that if you hunt a deer forest repeatedly and at regular hours, deer merely alter their habits in order to avoid you at those critical times. The book contains an excellent section on wind and the different ways of checking wind while still hunting. Although Prior admits that plenty of practical devices exist to test the wind, he notes that the gadget-minded deer hunter can obtain a portable wind vane from Germany "consisting of a pivoted and counter-balanced feather in its own little green leather case." The author, who has made a great contribution to the deer literature of our time, divides deer books into three categories: deer books that no deer hunter can be without, reference works into which it is interesting to delve, and books on deer hunting reminiscences that lure us into the deer forest with their nostalgia. Essential reading, practical and down to earth.

Pruitt, William O., Jr. *Wild Harmony: Animals of the North.* New York: Nick Lyons Books, 1988. 180 pp.

In this classic ecological portrait of the taiga, the subarctic-zone home of caribou and moose, Professor Pruitt gives us a unique blend of sound ecology and superb prose. In his 1988 epilogue to this classic, Pruitt comments on Indian treaty rights and hunting: "The freedom to hunt at any time, claimed as a treaty right by status Indians, combined with their antagonism to reporting numbers and sexes of animals taken, means that the basic data for management and conservation of any species are lacking. In effect, there is no wildlife management in Canada today wherever treaty Indians hunt. This unrestrained, unreported and unrecorded use of wildlife by the burgeoning population of native people in Canada is without doubt the most pressing problem today affecting survival of large, northern mammals."

Putnam, Rory. *The Natural History of Deer.* London: Christopher Helm, 1988. 191 pp.

A comparative review of current knowledge of the biology and natural history of the world's forty species of deer. Of great value to the informed amateur naturalist. Argues that ever since prehistoric time man has had a close relationship with deer. Indeed, few people escape a quickening pulse when presented with the fleeting sight of a wild deer. An excellent attempt to introduce the nonspecialist to the diversity of deer throughout the world.

Randolph, John W. *The World of "Wood, Field and Stream."* New York: Holt, Rinehart and Winston, 1962. 117 pp.

This volume of dry wit contains several of Randolph's best pieces on deer hunting that originally appeared in his outdoor column in the *New York Times.* I particularly like his article entitled, "Deer Tracks May Be Exciting, but They Cannot Be Hung in the Barn."*

Rau, Ron. "A Hunting Fantasy." In *Sage Lake Road.* Wisconsin: Willow Creek Press, 1983. pp. 50–59.

A well-written, thought-provoking story about why we do not take chancy shots at deer while bow hunting. Originally appeared in *Gray's Sporting Journal.*

Redlin, Terry. *The Art of Terry Redlin: Opening Windows to the Wild.* Minnesota: Haley House, 1987. 132 pp.

If you are like me and enjoy the romantic realism of Redlin's white-tailed deer prints but can't afford them or lack wall space to hang them, you will want a copy of this marvelous book, which features four of his white-tailed deer drawings and fifteen of his celebrated white-tailed deer prints.

Reid, Captain Mayne. "Deer Hunt in a Dug-Out." In *The Hunter's Feast: Or, Conversations around the Camp Fire.* New York: Carleton Publisher, 1880. pp. 198–216.

Stirring tales of rattling and calling bucks as early as the mid-1800s and shooting them from a "dug-out," a crudely hollowed-out cottonwood tree set afloat with burning dry knots of pine trees.*

Révoil, Bénédict Henry. "Virginian Deer." In *Shooting and Fishing in the Rivers, Prairies and Backwoods of North America.* Vol. 1. London: Tinsley Brothers, 1865. pp. 136–163.

A Frenchman's interpretation of American deer hunting during the 1840s, when Révoil lived in New York for eight years. Mixes fact with fiction and draws from Audubon and Elliott to help his deer hunting narratives along. Interesting and finely detailed deer hunting stories to amuse and entertain.*

Richard, Edmond H. *Deer Production Versus Doe Reduction.* New York: Privately printed, 1951.

An attack on antlerless deer hunting by a backwoods buck hunter who doesn't believe that scientific theory can replace common sense.*

Richardson, Ernest. *Bowhunting the Prairie Whitetail Deer of the Midwest. Part 1.* Indiana: Privately printed, 1988. 117 pp.

The deer hunting experiences and adventures of an Illinois buck hunter.

Rogers, Lynn. "Walking with Deer." In *Records of North American Big Game,* edited by Philip L. Wright. Virginia: The Boone and Crockett Club, 1981. pp. 29–34.

The fascinating story of how a wildlife biologist travels with radio-collared deer during a four-year period to study their food preferences and general behavior.

Roosevelt, Theodore. *The Wilderness Hunter.* South Carolina: The Premier Press, 1987. 468 pp.

Most of what Roosevelt had to say about deer and deer hunting is contained in this new deluxe edition of one of his classic hunting books. When the book first appeared, one reviewer wrote in *The Spectator* of October 13, 1894, that "no man seems to have more brilliantly combined the functions of the hunter and the writer; it is a real pleasure to read and roam with him in the wilderness."

———. "The Whitetail Deer." In *Outdoor Pastimes of an American Hunter.* Harrisburg, Pa.: Stackpole Books, 1990. pp. 215–249.

Like Audubon, William Elliott, and Judge Caton, Roosevelt liked to chase whitetails with horses and hounds: "To be able to ride

through woods and over rough country at full speed, rifle or shotgun in hand, and then leap off and shoot at a running object is to show that one has the qualities which made the cavalry of Forrest so formidable in the Civil War." This volume also contains an excellent chapter on "Books on Big Game" in which Roosevelt reveals his admiration for two other giants among deer hunters: Judge Caton and T. S. Van Dyke.

Royston, Angela. *The Deer.* Tennessee: Ideals Publishing Corporation, 1988. 24 pp.

The life of deer for children between the ages of five and eight.

Rue, Leonard Lee, III. *The Deer of North America.* Connecticut: Grolier, 1989. 544 pp.

Everyone interested in deer will want to read this updated and expanded edition. It's loaded with facts, insights, and many surprises. Read it!

Rutledge, Archibald. *Those Were the Days.* Virginia: The Dietz Press, Inc., 1955. 462 pp.

This volume is almost exclusively devoted to the deer hunting tales of this giant among deer hunters. After its publication, The *New York Times* reported that "it is a rare thing for a book on this subject to prove so vastly entertaining through almost 500 pages." Captures the real essence of the South Carolina deer hunting tradition.*

Ryman, D. P. *Better Bowhunting.* Ohio: SBHA, Inc., 1982. 72 pp.

A pocket guide to white-tailed deer hunting for the bow hunter.

Saintsing, David. *The World of Deer.* Milwaukee: Gareth Stevens, 1988. 32 pp.

An introduction to the world of deer for the primary reader.

Sampson, Alden. "A Deer's Bill of Fare." In *Three Essays on the Wild Life.* Philadelphia: Privately printed, 1905. pp. 38–58.

A detailed analysis of what a deer eats. Reaches the conclusion that "the deer's hobby is food and it is *quality* quite as much as *quantity* that gives him delight."*

Schroder, Piffa. *Fair Game: A Lady's Guide to Shooting Etiquette.* Southampton: Ashford Press Publishing, 1988. 96 pp.

A tongue-in-cheek guide to deer shooting for the aspiring Lady.

Schullery, Paul. "Elk Watch." In *Mountain Time*. New York: Simon & Schuster, Inc., 1988. pp. 10–18.

Reaches the conclusion after intensive elk watching that elk watch us as well but that we will never know for sure what they make of us.

Scott, Jack, and Ozzie Sweet. *Moose.* New York: G. P. Putnam's Sons, 1981. 64 pp.

Juvenile literature focusing on the world's largest deer.

Seton, Ernest Thompson. "Rolf's First Deer." In *Rolf in the Woods*. New York: Grosset & Dunlap, 1911. pp. 97–103.

In this wildwood tale, Seton documents a severe case of buck fever and argues that while still-hunting the wise deer hunter never ignores the warning cry of the bluejay.

———. "Still-Hunting the Buck, or the Deer-Hunt." In *The Book of Woodcraft and Indian Lore*. New York: Doubleday, Page & Company, 1922. pp. 199–202.

A description of Seton's game to teach young boys and girls how to hunt whitetails with bow and arrow.

Shuster, William. "Field Judging Whitetail Deer." In *Field Judging Trophy Animals*. Indiana: Blue-J Inc., 1987. pp. 41–54.

Emphasizes one basic rule in field judging trophy whitetails: "The inside spread of the main beam should equate or extend beyond the tips of the buck's ears when the ears are in the alert position."

Simmons, Alan. *How to Hunt Sika Deer.* New Zealand: The Halcyon Press, 1987. 126 pp.

Underscores two basic notions: (1) Deer are where you find them and where you find them they aren't, and (2) It takes more than deer sign to make soup. Puts forth the interesting notion that you can determine the sex of deer from the shape of deer droppings: "The poop of a sika stag is pinched at one end and there is more of it." Look for pinched poop.

Smillie, Ian Scott. *A Guide to the Stalking of Red Deer in Scotland*. London: Regency Press, 1983. 137 pp.

In this guide, Smillie stresses the significance of wind and how deer depend on it as a vehicle of sensory information. He agrees with Cameron, who once said that "on his own familiar beat a deer has a cozy corner for every wind that blows." Consequently, if the hunter thoroughly knows his deer forest, he should be able to predict their location with accuracy for any given wind direction or velocity.

Smith, J. Widmer. *Widmer's Whitetail Tales*. Wisconsin: Privately printed, 1987. 19 pp.

Tales from one of this country's original antler collectors, who especially likes nontypical antlers and likes to judge them by how well they score "on the Richter scale" rather than via the traditional numerical ratings.

Smith, Ned. "The Indomitable White-tailed Deer." In *Ned Smith's Wildlife Sketchbook*. Washington, D.C.: National Wildlife Federation, 1988. pp. 44–45.

More of those incredible sketches by that great painter of the whitetail.

Smith, Ray. "The Deer on the Freeway." In *The Deer on the Freeway*. South Dakota: University of South Dakota, 1973. p. 1.

A poem dealing with deer being smashed on the freeways by autos.

Smith, Richard P. *Tracking Wounded Deer*. Harrisburg: Stackpole Books, 1988. 159 pp.

A sound introduction to a very important subject. Contains a chapter on New York State's Deer Search, Inc., and a chapter on the wounded deer trail of Curt Van Lith's record buck.

"Snaffle." *The Roedeer: A Monograph*. England: Ashford Press Publishing, 1987. 192 pp.

A new limited edition of a very important deer book, originally published in 1904, that has hitherto been an exceptionally rare book. This excellent photographic facsimile is a welcome addition to the deer watcher's library, since the original edition consisted of less than one hundred copies.

Snyder, Gary. "this poem is for deer." In *Myths & Texts*. New York: New Directions, 1978. pp. 26–28.

This poem suggests that the "dance" of the hunter and hunted ultimately leads to death, consumption, and rebirth as energy in a new form. In this poem and elsewhere, the Pulitzer-Prize-winning author explores the power-vision of solitude and invokes the shamanistic techniques of hunting in which the hunter cultivates a primitive consciousness akin to animism. While combining Buddhist thought and American Indian lore, Snyder stresses those special moments of intense awareness while hunting and emphasizes that when deer hunting man can once again "believe in his own senses." To read Snyder on hunting is to take a mythical journey into the unconscious. "To hunt," Snyder explains, "means to use your body and senses to the fullest: to strain your consciousness, to feel what the deer are thinking today, this moment; to sit and let yourself go into the animal . . . while waiting by a game trail." Hunting, in Snyder's view, represents the communion of all life forms and the participation of man in his ecosystem. Hunting means to participate directly in the lives of deer and to depend upon them. When properly undertaken with love, reverence, and full awareness, deer hunting becomes holy and sacred.

Speltz, Merlin G. "Supplement #1 to the Camp 17 History." Minnesota: Privately printed, 1984. 13 pp.

A brief addendum to his excellent history of this very traditional deer camp in Pine County, Minnesota.

Spinage, C. A. *The Natural History of Antelopes.* New York: Facts on File, 1986. 203 pp.

A standard work on the antelope that contains an excellent chapter on communication—scent, color, display, and fighting. Enriched with thirty years of personal anecdotes.

Stam, Harold H. *The Making of a Mighty Hunter (Or How Many Dumb Things Can a Man Do).* Wisconsin: Privately printed, 1987. 140 pp.

Humorous deer hunting tales, many of which took place in the heart of the Chequamegon National Forest in northwestern Wisconsin.

Stilwell, Hart. "In the Heart of the Hills." In *Hunting and Fishing in Texas.* New York: Alfred A. Knopf, 1946. pp. 136–146.

Deer hunting in the Texas Hill Country during the 1940s. Also includes a chapter on rattling entitled "Answering the Antlers."*

Street, Alfred B. "Deer Shooting." In *The Poems of Alfred B. Street.* New York: Clark & Austin, 1847. pp. 241–243.

A great poem that captures the very essence of our sport.*

Syroectikovskii, E. E., ed. *Wild Reindeer of the Soviet Union.* Calcutta: Oxonian Press, 1984. 309 pp.

A compendium on the results of scientific studies on wild reindeer in the Soviet Union.

Teale, Edwin Way. "The Deer Yard." In *The American Seasons.* New York: Dodd, Mead & Company, 1976. pp. 355–358.

A snowshoe trip through a deeryard in northern Maine. Notes that deer do not maintain any special places for resting and sleeping in a deeryard, but simply lie down wherever fancy dictates.

Thomas, Murray. "Whitetail, The Little Grey Ghost of New Zealand." In *South Pacific Trophy Hunter.* Australia: Privately printed, 1987. pp. 131–141.

White-tailed deer hunting experiences in New Zealand, where whitetails were first imported from New Hampshire in 1905.

Thornberry, Russell. *The Art & Science of Rattling Whitetail Deer.* Alabama: Buckmasters, 1988. 106 pp.

This booklet on rattling contains a section entitled "Advanced Potty Training for the Deer Hunter" as well as advertisements for Buckmasters.

———. *Bucks, Bulls and Belly Laughs.* Alabama: Buckmasters, 1989. 176 pp.

Contains an intriguing tale entitled "The Last Big Buck In Texas," in which a hunter tries to kill a buck by throwing his pocket knife at him.

Thrasher, Halsey. "Deer Hunting." In *The Hunter and Trapper.* New York: Orange Judd and Company, 1868. pp. 7–13.

Shooting deer from scaffolds overlooking salt blocks.*

Traver, Robert. "STATION D-E-E-R!" In *Danny and the Boys.* New York: The World Publishing Company, 1951. pp. 154–164.

Wild tales of whiskey drinking and an ill-fated deer drive in Mul-Muligan S-S-Swamp in the Upper Peninsula of Michigan with Old Danny McGinnis and his boys.*

Trippensee, Reuben Edwin. "Deer." In *Wildlife Management: Upland Game and General Principles.* New York: McGraw-Hill Book Company, Inc., 1948. pp. 179–232.

An early general survey of deer management in this country.

Trout, John, Jr. *Trailing Whitetails.* Maine: North Country Press, 1987. 207 pp.

This paperback concentrates on tracking wounded deer and draws heavily on material originally published in *Deer & Deer Hunting* magazine.

Van Doren, Mark. *The Mayfield Deer.* New York: Henry Holt & Company, 1941. 272 pp.

A long narrative poem written in blank verse that retells a legend about a boy who shoots the pet deer of a lonely hunter and the feud that results from that hasty action.

Van Dyke, Theodore S. *The Still-Hunter.* South Carolina: The Premier Collection, 1988. 390 pp.

A deluxe edition of that unsurpassed blue-chip deer book with an introduction by Robert Wegner.

Von Kerckerinck, Josef. *Deer Farming in North America: The Conquest of a New Frontier.* New York: Phanter Press, 1987. 225 pp.

A systematic treatise on deer farming in America by a German immigrant whom *Connoisseur* magazine calls the "Baron of Venison." If you have eaten venison in any of the elite east coast restaurants, chances are that the deer meat came from Kerckerinck's 5000-acre deer farm in the rolling hills of upstate New York. Whether the venison baron succeeds in his promotion of deer farming in America remains to be seen. I suspect he will, given the sweet taste of succulent prime venison and the changing diet of Americans.

Warren, Robert L. *Utah's Biggest Bucks.* Washington: Shields Printing, 1988. 463 pp.

The standard record book of mule deer trophies from Utah.

Waterson, H. A., ed. *Going to the Hill.* England: The British Deer Society, 1987. 48 pp.

An introduction to red deer stalking in Scotland.

Wegner, Robert. *Deer & Deer Hunting: Book 2.* Harrisburg: Stackpole Books, 1987. 384 pp.

Historian James Casada calls this volume "a seminal work that every deer hunter should read." *Gray's Sporting Journal* reports that "both volumes together form the most comprehensive modern book on the whitetail. *Newsday* calls it "the classic on deer hunting!" Professor Harry Jacobson of Mississippi State University calls them "two of the most interesting and informative books ever written on the white-tailed deer." Why would I want to argue with these folks?

Weiss, John. *Advanced Deer Hunting.* New York: Outdoor Life Books, 1987. 334 pp.

Another how-to volume from Outdoor Life Books.

Wemmer, Christen M., ed. *Biology and Management of the Cervidae.* Washington, D.C.: Smithsonian Institution Press, 1987. 577 pp.

This comprehensive volume reviews key aspects of deer biology, field studies in progress on exotic deer species, and the management of selected species. Contains several interesting chapters on deer farming and an excellent chapter by Dale McCullough that discusses the many trade-offs of white-tailed deer population management programs that managers must face when asked to be all things to all people.

Wensel, Gene. *One Man's Whitetail.* Montana: Privately printed, 1988. 218 pp.

One man's opinions on trophy hunting.

Werich, Jacob Lorenzo. *Pioneer Hunters of the Kankakee.* Indiana: Chronicle Printing Company, 1920. 197 pp.

Deer hunting incidents in Indiana in 1878. Deals with hunters who have "buckfevered" and with hunters killing deer with pitchforks.*

White, Steward Edward. "On Seeing Deer." In *The Mountains.* New York: McClure, Phillips & Company, 1904. pp. 119–128.

A great outdoor writer argues that the whole secret of seeing deer in the woods rests in the elimination of the obvious. You need to train your eye to stop on the unusual.

Whitehead, Charles E. "The Deer Hunt." In *The Camp-Fires of the Everglades or Wild Sports in the South*. London: David Douglas, 1891. pp. 55–67.

A fast-moving sketch written with grace and style on coursing deer with hounds and horses in the swamps of Florida in the 1850s. Originally appeared in *The Spirit of the Times*.*

Williams, Donald R. *Oliver H. Whitman: Adirondack Guide*. New York: Privately printed, 1979. 186 pp.

A portrait of a well-known deer hunting guide who devoted his life to the Adirondack whitetail. Based on the journals of Oliver H. Whitman, 1882–1920.

Wilson, Robert A. *My Stalking Memories*. New Zealand: Pegasus Press, 1961. 138 pp.

Recalls the golden age of deer stalking in New Zealand, when prominent deer hunters from all around the world went to that country in search of trophy heads. Emphasizes the idea that there is always a magnificent stag with a perfect rack around the next bend. Written by one of the most fervent followers of the sport.*

Winch, Frank. "Deer Hunting." In *The American Hunter*. Boston: National Sportsman, Inc., 1923. pp. 13–20.

Argues that still-hunting is the "sportiest and most scientific way" of hunting whitetails.*

Wisconsin Buck and Bear Club. *Wisconsin Buck & Bear Club Trophy Records, 1989*. Wisconsin: Wisconsin Buck & Bear Club, 1989. 54 pp.

A listing of Wisconsin's trophy records.

Wolff, Ed. *Taking Big Bucks: Solving the Whitetail Riddle,* Montana: Stoneydale Press, 1987. 169 pp.

This book focuses on hunting trophy whitetails in the northern Rockies. Based on interviews with such trophy hunters as Paul Brunner, Dick Idol, Gene Wensel, and Barry Wensel.

Woolner, Frank. "The Deerslayer." In *My New England*. Massachusetts: Stone Wall Press, 1971. pp. 149–151.

A thoughtful essay on why the author enjoys those deer hunts in which a buck is not brought down.

Zumbo, Jim. *Hunt Elk*. New Jersey: Winchester Press, 1985. 259 pp.

A how-to guide for hunting elk.

Chapter 20

The Deer Hunter's Checklist Continued

Extraordinary Sources of Information

The deer books on my shelves divide themselves easily into three categories;
books that no keen deer stalker can be without, reference works into which
it is interesting to delve, and books of stalking reminiscences, which will
waft the reader away to the green woods . . .
— Richard Prior, *Modern Roe Stalking*, 1985

A Note About the Checklist

This checklist represents a continuation of the checklist found in *Deer & Deer Hunting: Book 2* (Stackpole Books, 1987). Copies of the Master's theses and Ph. D. dissertations can be ordered and charged to your credit cards by calling University Microfilms International, toll free, (800) 521-3042. The articles in the journals and periodicals can be located at your library or through the interlibrary loan system. You can order the bulletins, reports, and miscellaneous publications, if still in print, from the respective university or state department of natural resources. For telephone numbers and addresses see the *1990 Conservation Directory,* published annually by the National Wildlife Federation, 1400 Sixteenth Street, N. W., Washington, D.C. 20036-2266.

Master's Theses and Ph.D. Dissertations

Andersen, Thomas Andrew. "Human Dimensions of Michigan Deer Law Violations." Master's thesis, Eastern Michigan University, 1987.

Anderson, David Thomas. "The Effect of Dog Harassment on Translocated White-tailed Deer *(Odocoileus Virginianus)* on the Cumberland Plateau in Tennessee." Master's thesis, Tennessee Technological University, 1979.

Bridges, Robert J. "Individual White-tailed Deer Movement and Related Behavior During the Winter and Spring in Northeast Florida." Master's thesis, University of Georgia, 1968.

Burns, Carol J. "Home Range and Distribution of White-tailed Deer in Relation to Agricultural Food Plantings." Master's thesis, Mississippi State University, 1988.

Byford, James Lloyd. "Movements and Ecology of White-tailed Deer in a Logged Floodplain Habitat." Ph.D. diss., Auburn University, 1970.

Cross, Dalton C. "The Food Habits of White-tailed Deer on the Kerr Wildlife Management Area in Conjunction with Prescribed Burning and Rotational Livestock Grazing Systems. Master's thesis, Southwest Texas State University, 1984.

Day, Benjamin W., Jr. "Winter Behavior of White-tailed Deer in North-Central Maine." Master's thesis, University of Maine, 1963.

Eyler, Philip L. "Treaty Indian Hunting Rights and the Deer Hunting System in Manitoba." Master's thesis, University of Manitoba, 1976.

Forand, Kenneth J. "Dominance Relationships in White-tailed Deer." Master's thesis, University of Georgia, 1984.

Forster, Daniel Lee. "Attractiveness of Conspecific Bladder Urine in White-tailed Deer." Master's thesis, University of Georgia, 1988.

Green, William Rodney. "Seasonal Shifts in Home Range Utilization by White-tailed Deer." Master's thesis, Stephen F. Austin State University, 1988.

Haulsee, Hada V. "Factors Affecting Deer Hunting Participation in Michigan." Master's thesis, Virginia Polytechnic Institute, 1973.

Hepburn, R. L. "Effects of Snow Cover on Mobility and Local Distribution of Deer in Algonquin Park." Master's thesis, University of Toronto, 1959.

Herriges, James Daniel, Jr. "Movement, Activity, and Habitat Use of White-tailed Deer along the Lower Yellowston River." Master's thesis, University of Montana, 1986.

Herriman, Kevin Ray. "Hunting Season Movements of Male White-tailed Deer on Davis Island." Master's thesis, Mississippi State University, 1983.

Hildebrand, Dale N. "The Isolation and Identification of Compounds from the Tarsal Tufts of Male White-tailed Deer." Master's thesis, Syracuse University, 1972.

Hood, Ronald Earl. "Seasonal Variations in Home Range, Diel Movement and Activity Patterns of White-tailed Deer on the Rob and Bessie Welder Wildlife Refuge." Master's thesis, Texas A&M University, 1971.

Hosch, Joyce Aline. "The Quality of White-tailed Deer Meat *(Odocoileus Virginianus)* as Influenced by Slaughtering and Handling Practices." Master's thesis, Texas A&M University, 1976.

Hosey, Arthur George, Jr. "Activity Patterns and Notes on the Behavior of Male White-tailed Deer During the Rut." Master's thesis, Auburn University, 1980.

Huot, Jean. "Winter Habitat Preferences and Management of White-tailed Deer in the Area of Thirty-One Mile Lake (Gatinau County, Quebec)." Master's thesis, University of Toronto, 1972.

Johansen, Karen Lynn. "Seasonal Variation in Marking Behavior of White-tailed Deer." Master's thesis, University of Georgia, 1987.

Kagel, Ray L., Jr. "Fall Movements of Male White-tailed Deer in Noxubee County, Mississippi." Master's thesis, Mississippi State University, 1984.

Kile, Terry Lee. "Physical Characteristics, Temporal Distribution, and Spatial Patterns of Rubs and Scrapes Made by Male White-tailed Deer." Master's thesis, University of Georgia, 1974.

Knox, William Matthew. "Recurrent Estrous Cycles and Reproductive Steroids in White-tailed Deer." Master's thesis, University of Georgia, 1987.

Larson, Joseph Stanley. "Wildlife Forage Clearings on Forest Lands—A Critical Appraisal and Research Needs." Ph.D. diss., Virginia Polytechnic Institute, 1966.

Licht, Daniel Scott. "Movement of White-tailed Deer in the Edwards Plateau Region of Texas and Responses to Point Attractants." Master's thesis, Texas A&M University, 1987.

Litchfield, Thomas Richard. "Relationships Among White-tailed Deer Rubbing, Scraping, and Breeding Activities." Master's thesis, University of Georgia, 1987.

Masek, Joseph Warren. "Deer Winter Concentration Areas in Southern Michigan." Master's thesis, Michigan State University, 1979.

Mattfeld, George Francis. "The Energetics of Winter Foraging by White-tailed Deer: A Perspective on Winter Concentration." Ph.D. diss., State University of New York, 1974.

Miller, Ronald Robert. "The Demand for the Colorado Deer Hunting Experience." Ph.D. diss., Colorado State University, 1980.

Moulton, John C. "Movement and Activity of Three White-tailed Deer During the Winter of 1964–1965 in East-Central Minnesota Determined by Telemetry." Master's thesis, University of Minnesota, 1967.

Newhouse, Stephen J. "Effects of Weather on Behavior of White-tailed Deer of the George Reserve, Michigan." Master's thesis, University of Michigan, 1973.

Norberg, Elmer R. "White-tailed Deer Movements and Foraging on the Cedar Creek Forest, Minnesota." Master's thesis, University of Minnesota, 1957.

Overcash, Jesse Lee. "Inventory, Classification and Management Evaluation of Forest Openings in the Shawnee National Forest." Master's thesis, Southern Illinois University, 1987.

Reeves, John Henry, Jr. "The History and Development of Wildlife Conservation in Vir-ginia: A Critical Review." Ph.D. diss., Virginia Polytechnic Institute, 1980.

Richardson, Larry Wayne. "The Acoustic Behavior of White-tailed Deer." Master's thesis, Mississippi State University, 1981.

Root, Brian Gregory. "Movements of White-tailed Deer in Northeastern Missouri." Master's thesis, University of Missouri, 1986.

Sawyer, Timothy Garrette. "Behavior of Female White-tailed Deer with Emphasis on Pheromonal Communication." Master's thesis, 1981.

Scott, Mark Elijah. "Seasonal Use of Clearcuts by White-tailed Deer in Vermont." Master's thesis, University of Vermont, 1982.

Segelquist, Charles August. "Evaluation of Wildlife Forage Clearings for White-tailed Deer Habitat Management in a 600-Acre Arkansas Ozark Enclosure." Ph.D. diss., Texas A&M University, 1964.

Thomas, Keith P. "Nocturnal Activities of the White-tailed Deer on Crab Orchard National Wildlife Refuge." Master's thesis, Southern Illinois University, 1966.

Tibbs, Arthur Lee. "Summer Behavior of White-tailed Deer and the Effects of Weather." Master's thesis, Pennsylvania State University, 1967.

Turner, Arthur David. "Seasonal Movements and Habitat Use by Deer in North-Central Missouri." Master's thesis, University of Missouri, 1973.

Visser, Larry Gene. "Deer Use of Managed Forest Openings in Northern Lower Michigan." Ph.D. diss., University of Michigan, 1988.

Weber, Steven J. "A Quantitative Analysis of White-tailed Deer Winter Concentration Areas in Northern New Hampshire." Master's thesis, University of New Hampshire, 1981.

Weeks, Harmon Patrick. "Physiological, Morphological, and Behavioral Adaptations of Wild Herbivorous Mammals to a Sodium-Deficient Environment." Ph.D. diss., Purdue University, 1974.

Woods, Grant R. "Scrape Behavior and Physical Characteristics of Scrapes and Rubs of White-tailed Deer." Master's thesis, Southwest Missouri State University, 1988.

**Conservation Bulletins, University Publications, Extension Reports,
Pittman-Robertson Reports, Proceedings of Symposiums,
and Miscellaneous Publications.**

Adams, Clark E., and John K. Thomas. "Characteristics and Opinions of Texas Hunters." *Proceedings of the 1986 International Ranchers Roundup* (1986): 255–261.

———. Characteristics and Opinions of the Texas Hunters." *Proceedings of the Thirty-Seventh Annual Conference Southwestern Association of Fish and Wildlife Agencies* (November 1983): 244–251.

Adams, Noel. "Hunting Management to Achieve Ranch Goals on the Welder and Mc-Can Ranch, Texas." *Proceedings of the 1988 International Ranchers Roundup* (1988): 121–127.

Alexander, Harold E. *Deer Problems: New to Arkansas, An Old Story Elsewhere.* Arkansas Game and Fish Commision, 1954.

Allen, Carroll. *Statewide Deer Herd Reconstruction and Population Monitoring, 1982–1986.* Georgia Pittman-Robertson Report W-47-R, 1987.

Andrews, R. D., and J. C. Calhoun. *Characteristics of a White-tailed Deer Population in Illinois.* Illinois Pittman-Robertson Report W-63-R, 1968.

Applegate, James E. "Dynamics of the New Jersey Hunter Population." *Forty-Second North American Wildlife Conference* (1977): 103–116.

Armstrong, William E. "How to Manage Deer Habitat: Edwards Plateau." *Proceedings of the International Ranchers Roundup* (1984): 316–320.

———. "Key Food Plants for Deer—Edwards Plateau." *Proceedings of the International Ranchers Roundup* (1984): 277–280.

Ball, Claudia A. "An In-Between Deer Hunting Program." *Proceedings of the 1986 International Ranchers Roundup* (1986): 262–268.

Bennet, C. L., Jr., *et al.* "Experimental Management of Michigan's Deer Habitat." *Transactions of the 45th North American Wildlife and Natural Resources Conference* (1980): 288–306.

Benson, Delwin E. "Principles of Habitat Management for Deer." *Proceedings of the 1984 International Ranchers Roundup* (1984): 302–310.

Bohley, Lou. "The Great Hinckley Hunt." *Ohio Conservation Bulletin* 18, No. 10 (1954): 11, 31–32.

Boxall, Peter C., and Lavern C. Smith. *Estimates of the Illegal Harvest of Deer in Alberta: A Violation Simulation Study.* Alberta Fish and Wildlife Division. Occasional Paper Number 2, 1987.

Bromley, Peter, and Hobson Bryan. "The Human Dimension." *Proceedings of the Thirty-Fourth Annual Conference Southwestern Association of Fish and Wildlife Agencies* (November 9–12, 1980): 530–534.

Brooks, Rob. *The Net Economic Value of Deer Hunting in Montana.* Montana Department of Fish, Wildlife & Parks, 1988.

Brown, Tommy L., *et al. Public Response to Deer Trap and Transfer in the Peripheral Adirondacks: Determination of Favorable Initial Sites for Releasing Deer.* Vol. 1. Outdoor Recreation Research Unit, Cornell University, 1977.

Brown, Tommy L., and George F. Mattfield. "The Future of Hunting in New York." *Transactions of the 52nd North American Wildlife and Natural Resources Conference* (1987): 553–566.

Bush, Frederick A., and David C. Guynn, Jr. "Characteristics of Deer Hunting Lessees in South Carolina and Mississippi." *1987 Proceedings of the Annual Conference of Southeastern Association of Fish and Wildlife Agencies* (1987): 266–270.

Byford, James L. "Telemetrically Determined Movements of Two White-tailed Deer Fawns in Southwestern Alabama." *1970 Proceedings of the 24th Annual Conference of the Southeastern Association of Game and Fish Commission* (1970): 57–63.

Campo, Joseph, Gary E. Spencer, and Brent Ortego. "White-tailed Deer Hunting with Dogs in East Texas." *Proceedings of the Forty-First Annual Conference of the Southeastern Association of Fish and Wildlife Agencies* (October 4–7, 1987): 404–409.

Cartwright, Mike. *The White-tailed Deer in Arkansas.* Arkansas Game & Fish Commission, 1987.

Colvin, Thagard R. *Deer Herd Population Modeling.* Alabama Pittman-Robertson Report W-35, 1987.

Compton, Bradley B. *Population Ecology and Habitat Relationships of White-tailed Deer in River Bottom Habitat in Eastern Montana.* Montana Pittman-Robertson Report W-120-R-16 and 17, 1986.

Connelly, Nancy A., Daniel J. Decker, and Sam Wear. *White-tailed Deer in Westchester County, New York: Public Perceptions and Preferences.* Series No. 87-5. Human Dimensions Research Unit, Cornell University, 1987.

———. *Public Tolerance of Deer in a Suburban Environment: Implications for Management and Control.* Paper presented at the 3rd Eastern Wildlife Damage Control Conference. Gulf Shores, Alabama, 1987.

Cook, Robert. *Learn about Whitetails.* Texas Parks and Wildlife Leaflet 7000-7, 1979.

Cumming, H. G., and F. A. Walden. *The White-tailed Deer in Ontario.* Ontario Fish and Wildlife Branch, 1970.

Cypher, Brian L., and Ellen A. Cypher. *Ecology and Management of White-tailed Deer in Northeastern Coastal Habitats.* Biological Report 88(15). U.S. Fish and Wildlife Service, 1988.

Davis, Ernie. "How To Manage Deer Habitat: South Texas." *Proceedings of the International Ranchers Roundup* (1984): 311–315.

Decker, Daniel J., and George F. Mattfeld. *Hunters and Hunting in New York.* HDRU Series No. 88-7. Human Dimensions Research Unit, Cornell University, 1988.

Decker, Daniel J., and Nancy A. Connelly. *Hunters' Assessment of the Deer Management Permit System in New York State.* HDRU Series No. 88-8. Cornell University, 1988.

Decker, Daniel J., and Thomas A. Gavin. *Public Tolerance of a Suburban Deer Herd: Implications for Control.* Paper presented at the 2nd Eastern Wildlife Damage Conference. Raleigh, North Carolina, 1985.

———. *Human Dimensions of Managing a Suburban Deer Herd: Situation Analysis for Decision Making by the Seatuck National Wildlife Refuge.* Series No. 85-3. Human Dimensions Research Unit, Cornell University, 1985.

Decker, Daniel J., *et al. Hunter Reaction to a Proposed Deer Management Initiative in Northern New York: Antecedents to Support or Opposition.* New York Pittman-Robertson Report W-146-R, 1983.

Deer, Forestry, and Agriculture: Interactions and Strategies for Management. Proceedings of papers presented. Warren, Pennsylvania, 1987.

Demarais, Steve, and Bob Zaiglin. "The Effect of Doe Harvest on White-tailed Deer Populations." *Proceedings of the International Ranchers Roundup* (1987): 120–124.

DeYoung, Charles A. "White-tailed buck Mortality in South Texas." *Proceedings of the International Ranchers Roundup* (1987): 108–110.

Donnelly, Dennis M., and Louis J. Nelson. *Net Economic Value of Deer Hunting in Idaho.* Resource Bulletin RM-13. USDA Forest Service, 1986.

Downing, Robert L., *et al.* "Comparison of Deer Census Techniques Applied to a Known Population in a Georgia Enclosure." *Proceedings of the Nineteenth Annual Conference of the Southeastern Association of Game and Fish Commissioners* (October 10–13, 1965): 26–30.

Duffield, John. *The Net Economic Value of Elk Hunting in Montana.* Montana Department of Fish, Wildlife and Parks, 1988.

Dusek, Gary L. *Montana Deer Studies.* Montana Pittman-Robertson Report W-120-R-15, 1984.

———. *Montana Deer Studies.* Montana Pittman-Robertson Report, 1985.

Dusek, Gary L., and Alan K. Wood. "An Evaluation of the Average Activity Radius as an Estimator of Monthly Movements of Deer." *Proceedings of the Montana Academy of Science* 46 (1986): 19–26.

Ellingwood, Mark, and Jim Spignesi. *Connecticut Deer Program Summary, 1988.* Connecticut Department of Environmental Protection, Wildlife Bureau, 1988.

Farrar, J. W. *Deer Study—Illegal Spotlighting of Deer.* Louisiana Pittman-Robertson Report W-29-29, 30, 31, 1984.

Fenley, James. *McCurtain County Deer Law Enforcement Project*. Oklahoma Pittman-Robertson Report W-104-R, 1971.

Foote, Leonard E. *The Vermont Deer Herd: A Study in Productivity*. Vermont Pittman-Robertson Report No. 1-R, 1945.

Fuller, Todd K. *Hunter Harvest of White-tailed Deer in the Bearville Study Area, North-central Minnesota*. Wildlife Report 6. Minnesota Department of Natural Resources, 1988.

Geist, Valerius. "Legal Trafficking and Paid Hunting Threaten Conservation." *Transactions of the Fifty-Fourth North American Wildlife and Natural Resources Conference* 54 (1989): 171–178.

Glover, Ronald L. "Effectiveness of Patrol Techniques for Apprehending Deer Poachers." *Proceedings of the Annual Conference of the Southeastern Association of Fish and Wildlife Agencies* (1982): 705–716.

Glover, Ronald L., Pamela S. Haverland, and Donald K. Heard. "Missouri Fifth Graders' Knowledge about Deer." *Proceedings of the Annual Conference of the Southeastern Association of Fish and Wildlife Agencies* (1987): 514–523.

Gore, Horace. "Benefits From Deer Management." *Proceedings of the International Rancher's Roundup* (1988): 128–138.

Gruell, George E. *Post-1900 Mule Deer Irruptions in the Intermountain West: Principle Cause and Influences*. General Technical Report INT-206. USDA Forest Service, 1986.

Guynn, David C. Jr. "Deer Harvest — What Percent Should Be Harvested." *Proceedings of the International Ranchers' Roundup* (1985): 438–444.

———. "Economics of Young Deer vs. Trophy Deer." *Proceedings of the International Ranchers' Roundup* (1982): 286–294.

———. "White-tailed Deer Hunting Enterprises." *Proceedings of the First International Wildlife Ranching Symposium* (1988): 218–226.

Guynn, David, C., Jr., Harry A. Jacobson, Sarah P. Owen, Edsel Cliburn, and William D. Cotton. "Involving Sportsmen in Deer Management on Private Lands in Mississippi." *Proceedings of the Annual Confer-ence of the Southeastern Association of Fish & Wildlife Agencies* (1978): 765–770.

Guynn, David C., Jr., Richard W. Whiteside, and Harry A. Jacobson. "Characteristics and Opinions of Mississippi Deer Hunters Using Public Areas." *Proceedings of the Annual Conference of the Southeastern Association of Fish & Wildlife Agencies* (1981): 167–173.

Guynn, David C., Jr., and Robert J. Hamilton. "The Effects of Adult Sex Ratio on Reproduction in White-tailed Deer." *Proceedings of the International Ranchers' Roundup* (1986): 233–240.

Guynn, David C., Jr., Thomas Michale Lowe, and Harry A. Jacobson. *Characteristics and Attitudes of Mississippi Deer Hunters*. Mississippi State University Information Sheet #1300, 1980.

Guynn, Dwight E. "Deer Census Using Spotlight and Hahn Lines." *Proceedings of the International Ranchers' Roundup* (1982): 324–330.

———. "Interpreting Harvest Records." *Proceedings of the International Ranchers' Roundup* (1983): 418–426.

———. "Put Your 'Bucks' Where the Most Profit Is." *Proceedings of the International Ranchers' Roundup* (1985): 404–416.

Hailey, Tommy L. "Producing Quality Whitetail Deer." *Proceedings of the International Ranchers' Roundup* (1983): 415–417.

Halls, Lowell K. "What Do Deer Eat and Why." *Proceedings of the International Ranchers' Roundup* (1984): 266–276.

Hamilton, Joe, *et al. White-tailed Deer Management Seminar*. The proceedings of a workshop sponsored by the South Carolina Chapter of the Wildlife Society, 1988.

Hanselka, C. Wayne. "Key Food Plants For Deer — West Texas." *Proceedings of the International Ranchers' Roundup* (1984): 292–301.

Harmel, D. E. *White-tailed Deer Growth and Development*. Texas Pittman-Robertson Report W-109-R-9, 1987.

———. *The Effects of Genetics on Antler Development and Body Size under Field Conditions*. Texas Pittman-Robertson Report W-109-R-10, 1987.

Harmel, D. E., John D. Williams, and William E. Armstrong. *Effects of Genetics and Nu-*

trition on Antler Development and Body Size of White-tailed Deer. FA Report Series No. 26. Texas Parks and Wildlife Department, 1988.

Harmel, Donnie E. "Spike Bucks—Nutritional or Genetic?" *Proceedings of the International Ranchers' Roundup* (1984): 353–364.

Harwell, Fielding, Donnie Harmel, and Jim Perkins. *A Tale of Two Deer Herds.* Texas Parks and Wildlife Department PWD-L-7100-138-5/86, 1986.

Haywood, Dennis D., Richard Miller, and Gerald I. Day. *Effects of Hunt Design and Related Factors on Productivity in Mule Deer and White-tailed Deer in Arizona.* Arizona Pittman-Robertson Report W-78-R, 1987.

———. *Migration Patterns and Habitat Utilization by Kaibab Mule Deer.* Arizona Pittman-Robertson Report W-78-R, 1987.

Horejsi, Ronald G., Dennis D. Haywood, and Ronald H. Smith. *The Effects of Hunting on a Desert Mule Deer Population.* Arizona Pittman-Robertson Report W-78-R, 1988.

Humphreys, Doug, and Amy Elenowitz. *New Mexico's Mule Deer Population/Environment/Hunt Computer Model.* New Mexico Pittman-Robertson Report W-124-R, 1988.

Inglis, Jack, M., *et al.* "A White-tailed Deer Herd Management System." *Proceedings of the International Ranchers' Roundup* (1988): 146–156.

———. *Deer-Brush Relationships on the Rio Grande Plain, Texas.* Kleberg Studies in Natural Resources RM14/KS6, 1986.

Jackson, Robert M., and Raymond K. Anderson. "Hunter-Landowner Relationship: A Management and Educational Perspective." *Transactions from the 47th North American Wildlife and Natural Resources Conference* (1982): 693–704.

Jacobson, Harry A. "Relationships between Deer and Soil Nutrients in Mississippi." *Proceedings of the Annual Conference of the Southeastern Association of Fish and Wildlife Agencies* (1984): 1–12.

Jacobson, Harry A., David C. Guynn, and Edsel Cliburn, eds. *Bibliography of the White-tailed Deer.* Prepared for the Southeast Deer Study Group Meeting, 1979.

Jacobson, Harry A., D. C. Guynn, and S. P. Mott. *Investigations to Improve the Management of White-tailed Deer in Mississippi.* Mississippi Pittman-Robertson Report W-48-24, 25, 26, 27, 1981.

Johnson, Fred. "Hunter Distribution—Studies and Methods." *Eighth North American Wildlife Conference* (1943): 392–407.

Johnson, Kenneth G. "Effects of Pine Regeneration on Vegetation, Deer Hunting, and Harvest." *Proceedings of the Annual Conference of the Southeastern Association of Fish and Wildlife Agencies* (1987): 271–278.

Johnson, Loayal J. *Reproductive Potential of Sitka Black-tailed Deer in Southeast Alaska.* Alaska Pittman-Robertson Report W-22-4 and 5, 1987.

Kammermeyer, Kent, *et al. Deer Herd Management for Georgia Hunters.* Georgia Department of Natural Resources, Game and Fish Division, 1988.

Klimstra, W. D., *et al. Florida Key Deer Recovery Plan.* Contract No. 14-16-0004-79-007. U.S. Fish and Wildlife Service.

Kufeld, R. *Winter Habitat Selection and Activity Patterns of Mule Deer in Front Range Shrubland and Forest Habitats.* Colorado Pittman-Robertson Report W-126-R-4; 1981.

Loomis, Forrest, *et al. Population Studies of White-tailed Deer.* Illinois Pittman-Robertson Report W-63-R(25), 1983.

Loomis, John, Douglas Updike, and William Unkel. "Consumptive and Nonconsumptive Values of a Game Animal: The Case of California Deer." *Transactions of the Fifty-Fourth North American Wildlife and Natural Resources Conference* 54 (1989): 640–650.

Loomis, John, and Joseph Cooper. *The Net Economic Value of Antelope Hunting in Montana.* Montana Department of Fish, Wildlife & Parks, 1988.

McCaffery, Keith R., James E. Ashbrenner, and John C. Moulton. *Forest Opening Construction and Impacts in Northern Wisconsin.* Technical Bulletin No. 120. Wisconsin Department of Natural Resources, 1981.

———. *Reinventory of Deer Range.* Wisconsin Pittman-Robertson Report W-141-R-23, 1988.

McCulloch, Clay Y., and Richard L. Brown. *Rates and Causes of Mortality Among*

Radio-Collared Mule Deer of the Kaibab Plateau, 1978–1983. Arizona Pittman-Robertson Report W-78-R, 1986.

Marchinton, R. Larry. "White-tailed Deer Dispersal: Population Regulation and Management Implications." *Transactions of the International Congress of Game Biology* 14 (1982): 81–88.

Marquis, David A. *The Impact of Deer Browsing on Allegheny Hardwood Regeneration.* USDA Forest Service Research Paper NE-308, 1974.

Mattfeld, George F., *et al. Developing Human Dimensions in New York's Wildlife Research Program.* New York Pittman-Robertson Report W-146-R, 1984.

Mech, L. David, and Patrick D. Karns. *Role of the Wolf in a Deer Decline in the Superior National Forest.* USDA Forest Service Research Paper NC-148, 1977.

Moran, Richard J., and James R. Terry. *Initial Response of Deer Populations to Experimental Forest Cuttings in Michigan.* Michigan Pittman-Robertson Report W-117-R and W-127-R, 1987.

Mott, Seth E., Randy L. Tucker, David C. Guynn, Jr., and Harry A. Jacobson. "Use of Mississippi Bottomland Hardwoods by White-tailed Deer." *Proceedings of the Annual Conference of the Southeastern Associations of Fish and Wildlife Agencies* 39: 403–411.

Murphy, Dean A. "Effects of Various Opening Days on Deer Harvest and Hunting Pressure." *Proceedings of the 19th Annual Conference of the Southeastern Association of Game and Fish Commission* (1965): 141–146.

Nelle, Steve. "How To Manage for Deer Food." *Proceedings of the International Ranchers' Roundup* (1985): 417–427.

————. "Key Food Plants For Deer—South Texas." *Proceedings of the International Ranchers' Roundup* (1984): 281–291.

Nelson, Michael E., and L. David Mech. *Deer Population in the Central Superior National Forest, 1967–1985.* USDA Forest Service Research Paper NC–271, 1986.

Nixon, Charles M., and Lonnie P. Hanson. *Illinois Deer Investigations.* Illinois Pittman-Robertson Report W-87-R-7, 1986.

Oklahoma Department of Wildlife Conservation. *Deer Hunter's Handbook and Big Game Report 1989.*

Olson-Rutz, Kathrin Maja, and Philip J. Urness. *Comparability of Foraging Behavior and Diet Selection of Tractable and Wild Mule Deer.* Publication No. 88-3. Utah Natural Resources, 1987.

Pomerantz, G. A., D. Bogan, and R. A. Smolka, Jr. *Educators' Attitudes Toward Management of Deer in Northern New York.* New York Pittman-Robertson Report, 1985.

Ryel, L. A., and C. L. Bennett, Jr. *Technical Report on the Spring 1971 Dead Deer Searches.* Research and Development Report No. 247. Michigan Department of Natural Resources, 1971.

Saskatchewan Parks, Recreation and Culture. *Guide to Winter Deer Feeding,* n.d.

Scanlon, John J., and Michael R. Vaughan. "Movements of White-tailed Deer in Shenandoah National Parks, Virginia." *Proceedings of the Annual Conference of Southeastern Association of Fish and Wildlife Agencies* 39 (1985): 396–402.

————. *Population and Behavioral Ecology of White-tailed Deer in Shenandoah National Park, Virginia.* National Park Service Research Report, n.d.

Sepik, Greg F., and Edwin D. Michael. "The Role of Access in Hunter Use of Canaan Valley, West Virginia." *The Twenty-Eighth Annual Conference of the Southeastern Association of Game and Fish Commissions* (1975): 682–686.

Severinghaus, C.W. "Relationships of Weather to Winter Mortality and Population Levels among Deer in the Adirondack Region of New York." *Transactions of the North American Wildlife Conference* 12 (1947): 212–223.

Shelton, Ross "Skip." "Fee Hunting Systems in Mississippi." *Proceedings of the International Ranchers' Roundup* (1982): 302–312.

Sheriff, Steven L., and Norbert F. Giessman. *Public Use on Deer Ridge Wildlife Area Associated with the 1985 Firearms Deer Season.* Special Report. Missouri Department of Conservation, 1986.

Shult, Milo J., and Bill Armstrong. *Deer Census Techniques.* Special Report 7/B-238-

0584. Texas Parks and Wildlife Department, 1984.

Smith, Alan D., and David Schubert. *Discriminating Degree of White-tailed Deer Travel Route Use.* Unpublished Report. Pittsburgh, Pennsylvania: Department of Quantitative and Natural Sciences, Robert Morris College, n.d.

Smith, Christian A., *et al. Predator-Induced Limitations on Deer Population Growth in Southeast Alaska.* Alaska Pittman-Robertson Report W-22-5 and W-22-6, 1987.

———. *Wolf-Deer-Habitat Relationships in Southeast Alaska.* Alaska Pittman-Robertson Report W-22-4 and W-22-6, 1987.

Smolka, Robert A., Jr., and Daniel J. Decker. *Identifying Interest Groups' Issue Positions and Designing Communication Strategies for Deer Management in Northern New York.* New York Pittman-Robertson Report W-146-R, n.d.

Smolka, Robert A., Jr., Daniel J. Decker, Nick Sanyal, and Tommy L. Brown. *Northern New York Deer Management: Hunter's Opinions and Preferences.* New York Pittman-Robertson Report W-146-R-8, 1983.

Smolka, Robert A., Jr., D. J. Decker, and T. L. Brown. *Attitudes of Key Organization Leaders Toward Deer and Deer Management in Northern New York.* New York Pittman-Robertson Report W-146-R-10, 1985.

Smolka, Robert A., Jr., G. A. Pomerantz, and D. J. Decker. *Importance of Deer to Residents' and Nonresidents' Recreational Experiences in Northern New York.* New York Pittman-Robertson Report W-146-R-11, 1986.

Spencer, Gary. *Effects of Hunting Deer with Dogs.* Texas Pittman-Robertson Report W-109-R-10, 1987.

Steffen, David E. *Mississippi Mail Survey of Game Harvest and Hunter Effort for 1986–87.* Mississippi Pittman-Robertson Report W-48-34, 1987.

Stewart, Robert R., and Wayne Runge. *The White-tailed Deer of the Crystal Beach Game Preserve: An Ecological Investigation.* Wildlife Technical Report 85-1. Saskatchewan Parks and Renewable Resources, 1985.

Strong, Karl F. *Evaluative Review of Deer Yard Management Work in New Hampshire and Maine.* New Hampshire Pittman-Robertson Report W-21-D, 1977.

Suprock, Lori H., and Pamela W. Paasche, eds. *Transactions of the Twenty-Fourth Annual Meeting of the Northeast Deer Technical Committee.* Rhode Island Division of Fish and Game, 1988.

Synatzske, David R. *Evaluation of Spotlight, Fixed-Wing Aircraft and Helicopter Censusing of White-tailed Deer in South Texas.* Texas Pittman-Robertson Report W-109-R-9, 1986.

Thomas, Jack Ward, James C. Pack, William M. Healy, John D. Gill, and H. Reed Sanderson. "Territoriality Among Hunters—The Policy Implications." *Thirty-Eighth North American Wildlife Conference* (1973): 274–280.

United States Army. *Guide to Hunting in Germany.* USAREUR Pam 28-148, 1970.

United States Department of the Interior. *1985 National Survey of Fishing, Hunting, and Wildlife Associated Recreation.* Fish and Wildlife Service, 1988.

University of Wisconsin—Stevens Point. *Deer Hunting and the Landowner Conference* (Proceedings). College of Natural Resources, 1982.

———. *Hunting: Sport or Sin?* College of Natural Resources, 1974.

Verme, Louis J. *Cooperative Studies on Penned Deer.* Michigan Pittman-Robertson Report W-127-R-5, 1986.

Voigt, Dennis. *Cooperative Deer Study Annual Report, 1985–1986.* Ontario Ministry of Natural Resources, Wildlife Research Branch, 1986.

———. *Cooperative Deer Study Annual Report 1987.* Ontario Ministry of Natural Resources, Wildlife Research Branch, 1987.

———. *Winter Feeding of Deer in Ontario: A Cooperative Deer Study Update.* Ontario Ministry of Natural Resources, Wildlife Research Branch, 1989.

Weber, Steven. "Guidelines for Deer Range Management in Vermont." In *Is Good Forestry Good Wildlife Management?* Miscellaneous Publication No. 689. Maine Agricultural Experiment Station, 1986.

———. "White-tailed Deer Model Habitat Management Guidelines." In *Model Habitat*

Management Guidelines for Deer, Bear, Hare, Grouse, Turkey, Woodcock and Non-Game Wildlife. Vermont Fish & Wildlife Department, n.d.

White-tailed Deer in Pennsylvania. Educational Pamphlet No. 6. The Pennsylvania Game Commission, 1942.

Wise, Sherry. *The White-tailed Deer.* Publ-WM-013-86. Wisconsin Department of Natural Resources, Bureau of Wildlife Management, 1986.

Wood, Alan K., Richard J. Mackie, and Kenneth L. Hamlin. *Ecology of Sympatric Populations of Mule Deer and White-tailed Deer in a Prairie Environment.* Montana Department of Fish, Wildlife & Parks, Wildlife Division, 1989.

Woolf, Alan. *White-tailed Deer Fawn Survival at the Union County Conservation Area.* Illinois Pittman-Robertson Report W-63-R(S1)-29, 1987.

Articles in Journals and Magazines

Abercombie, Lt. W. R. "A Deer Drive with Spokane Indians." *Recreation* 3, No. 4 (October 1895): 153–157.

Adams, Chuck. "Bowhunter's Broadhead Review." *Petersen's Bowhunting* 1, No. 3 (October 1989): 39–46.

Adams, Frank. "Shooting to Kill." *Maclean's Magazine* 101 (November 7, 1988): 52–53.

Aharrah, Ernest. "The Old Deer Hunter." *Game News* (August 1988): 21–23.

Alison, Robert M. "Cynegeticus – The First Book on Hunting." *Game News* (July 1983): 29–31.

Alsheimer, Charles J. "Forty Years of Deer Research (C. W. Severinghaus)." *Deer & Deer Hunting* 6, No. 3 (January/February 1983): 33–37.

———. "Dr. Aaron Moen – White-tailed Deer Visionary." *Deer & Deer Hunting* 9, No. 5 (May/June 1986): 42–49.

Altherr, Thomas L. "'Mallards and Messerschmitts': American Hunting Magazines and the Image of American Hunting During World War II." *Journal of Sport History* 14, No. 2 (Summer 1987): 151–163.

———. "The American Hunter-Naturalist and the Development of the Code of Sportsmanship." *Journal of Sport History* 5, No. 1 (Spring 1978): 7–22.

Altmann, Margaret. "The Flight Distance in Free Ranging Big Game." *Journal of Wildlife Management* 22, No. 2 (April 1958): 207–209.

Alverson, William S., Donald M. Waller, and Stephen L. Solheim. "Forests To Deer: Edge Effects in Northern Wisconsin." *Conserva-tion Biology* 2, No. 4 (December 1988): 348–358.

Anderson, Mark W., Alan S. Kezis, and Stephen D. Reiling. "Hunting in Maine – Who, What, Where and Why." *Maine Fish and Wildlife* (Fall 1981): 6–9.

Anthony, Harold E. "But It's Instinctive." *Saturday Review* (August 17, 1957): 9–10, 40.

Applegate, James E. "A Change in the Age Structure of New Hunters in New Jersey." *Journal of Wildlife Management* 46, No. 2 (1982): 490–492.

———. "And That's A Fact." *Deer & Deer Hunting* 8, No. 2 (November/December 1984): 45–50.

———. "Deer Hunting in the Shadow of Skyscrapers." *Deer & Deer Hunting* 8, No. 2 (November/December 1983): 26–33.

———. "Hunting an American Tradition." *The American Hunter* (November 1981): 14–15, 56–57.

Ashley, Richard F. "Milwaukee's Dear Deer." *Wisconsin Natural Resources* 6, No. 6 (November-December 1982): 6–11.

Atamian, Sarkis. "Heroes and Hunters." *Safari* (May/June 1982): 16–22.

Atkeson, Thomas D., Victor F. Nettles, R. Larry Marchinton, and William V. Branan. "Nasal Glands in the Cervidae." *Journal of Mammalogy* 69, No. 1 (February 1988): 153–156.

Atkeson, Thomas D., R. Larry Marchinton, and Karl V. Miller. "Vocalizations of White-tailed Deer." *The American Midland Naturalist* 120, No. 1 (1988): 194–200.

Bahti, Tom. "Is Wisconsin Ready for Trophy Deer Management?" *Wisconsin Outdoor Journal* (October/November 1987): 18–21.

Barsness, John. "Dead Deer/Late Fall." *Gray's Sporting Journal* 6, No. 1 (Winter 1981): 5.

———. "The Spirit Still Lives." *Sports Illustrated* 48 (June 26, 1978): 38-40.

Baughman, Michael. "In Pursuit of an Ancient Pursuit." *Sports Illustrated* 48 (April 3, 1978): 45-46.

Beattie, Kirk H. "Deer Hunting Accidents." *Deer & Deer Hunting* 8, No. 2 (November/December 1984): 59-65.

———. "The Influence of Game Laws and Regulations on Hunting Satisfaction." *Wildlife Society Bulletin* 9, No. 3 (1981): 229-231.

———. "Wildlife Violations: Probing a Problem." *Wildlife in North Carolina* (October 1977): 6-7.

Beier, Paul. "Sex Differences in Quality of White-tailed Deer Diets." *Journal of Mammalogy* 68, No. 2, (1987): 323-329.

Benner, J. Merlin, and R. Terry Bowyer. "Selection of Trees for Rubs by White-tailed Deer." *Journal of Mammalogy* 69, No. 3 (1988): 624-627.

Benson, Seth E. "Decoying Coyotes and Deer." *Journal of Mammalogy* (November 1948): 406-409.

Bestul, Scott. "Trail to a Dream Buck" *Gray's Sporting Journal* 13, No. 4 (Winter 1988): 49-54.

Bigony, Mary-Love. "Brush Country Deer." *Texas Parks and Wildlife* (December 1983): 3-7.

Blair, Mike. "Doe A Deer." *Kansas Wildlife & Parks* 46, No. 6 (November/December 1989): 35-38.

———. "Hunter 1." *Kansas Wildlife & Parks* 46, No. 4 (July/August 1989): 38-39.

Blaisdell, Harold F. "A Deer to Believe In." *Reader's Digest* 131 (November 1987): 25-26.

Boardman, W. H. "The Ring and the Deer." *Harper's Monthly Magazine* 102 (May 1901): 963-965.

Bodio, Stephen J. "Why We Should Hunt." *Outdoor Life* (February 1985): 58, 136-137.

Bossenmaier, E. "Ecological Awareness and Sport Hunting—A Viewpoint." *Wildlife Society Bulletin* 4, No. 3 (Fall 1976): 127-128.

Bouwman, Fred. "Lyme Disease and the Whitetail." *Deer & Deer Hunting* 8, No. 6 (July/August 1985): 64-69.

Bower, Janet Newlan. "Pere David's Deer: An Exercise in Planned Preservation." *Nature Study* 35, No. 1 and 2: 13-16, 28.

Bowers, Glenn. "Our Best Bucks of Three Generations." *Game News* (May 1988): 11-14.

Boyle, Robert H. "Hey, You Wanna Deer? Portrait of Joe Defalco." *Sports Illustrated* 58, No. 1 (January 10, 1983): 38-49.

Boyles-Sprenkel, Carolee. "Tracking Wounded Game." *Florida Wildlife* 44, No. 1 (January/February 1990): 35-37.

Brandreth, Paul. "Bucks of Cathedral Meadow." *Field & Stream* (February 1938): 30-31, 64-65.

———. "Clean Kills—Still Hunting the White-tailed Deer." *Forest and Stream* 98, No. 11 (November 1928): 669-672.

———. "Commercialism or Conservation?" *Forest and Stream* 95 (September 1925): 582-583, 639-640.

———. "Days With the Deer." *Forest and Stream* 64, (March 18, 1905): 213-214.

———. "Days With the Deer." *Forest and Stream* 64, (March 25, 1905): 234-235.

———. "Deer in Winter—Each Winter Many Deer Perish Miserably in the Deep Snow." *Forest and Stream* 99 (January 1929): 26-27.

———. "Good Luck." *Forest and Stream* 66 (May 12, 1906): 752-753.

———. "Haste Makes Waste." *Field & Stream* 39, No. 7 (November 1934): 30-31.

———. "Hints on Deer Shooting." *Forest and Stream* 80 (October 1, 1904): 281-283.

———. "Hunting the Whitetail—Long May He Live to Grace Our Forests." *Forest and Stream* 13, No. 10 (October 1923): 547-549, 599-608.

———. "Northern Whitetails." *Forest and Stream* 97 (November 1927): 656-658.

———. "Reuben Cary—Forest Patriarch—A Biographical Sketch of a Well Known Adirondack Guide." *Forest and Stream* 82 (June 27, 1914): 854-855.

———. "Still-Hunting the White-tailed Deer." *Field and Stream* 17 (March 1913): 1192-1195.

———. "The Art of Still-Hunting." *Forest and Stream* 77, No. 6 (August 5, 1911): 207-209.

———. "The Public Benefit of Private Game Parks—How the Overflow of Game Helps to

Stock Open Shooting Territory." *Forest and Stream* 96 (March 1926): 138–139, 180–182.

———. "The Silver Horn—A Forest Idyl." *Forest and Stream* (November 21, 1908): 808–810.

———. "The Sunrise Buck—A Day on a Stand and an Evening Beside the Campfire with an Adirondack Guide." *Forest and Stream* 76, (April 15, 1911): 568–571.

———. "The White-tailed Deer." *Field and Stream* 16, (October 1911): 606–614.

———. "The Wiles of the Whitetail." *Forest and Stream* 96 (October 1926): 590–591, 626–628.

Brewer, Wayne. "Undercover." *The Conservationist* 44, No. 4 (January-February 1990): 14–19.

Brooks, Rob, and John Duffield. "The Worth of Hunting." *Montana Outdoors* 20, No. 2 (March/April 1989): 6–9.

Brothers, Al, Joe Hamilton, David C. Guynn, Jr., and R. Larry Marchinton. "Spike Buck: Should We Shoot or Protect?" *Deer & Deer Hunting* 13, No. 5 (March 1990): 13–17.

Brown, Larry. "Hunting Fort McCoy." *Fins and Feathers* (November 1980): 11–14.

Brown, Tommy L., Daniel J. Decker, and John W. Kelley. "Access to Private Lands for Hunting in New York: 1963–1980." *Wildlife Society Bulletin* 12, No. 4 (1984): 344–349.

Bullis, Jerald. "Plot Your Buck." *Outdoor Life* (September 1985): 84–85, 128–131, 135–138.

Burcalow, Donald W., and William H. Marshall. "Deer Numbers, Kill, and Recreational Use on an Intensively Managed Forest." *Journal of Wildlife Management* 22, No. 2 (April 1958): 141–148.

Burden, W. Douglas. "The Still Hunter." *The Atlantic Monthly* 198 (November 1956): 55–60.

Burkett, Clark. "How the Indians Hunted." *Mississippi Outdoors* (March/April 1988): 22–23.

Burroughs, John. "A Night-Hunt in the Adirondacks." *Putnam's Magazine* (August 1868): 149–154.

Byers, John A. "Why the Deer and the Antelope Play." *Natural History* (May 1987): 54–61.

Callicott, J. Baird. "A Non-Hunter Talks about Hunting." *Wisconsin Natural Resources* (November/December 1981): 6–7.

Capel, R. E., and R. K. Pandey. "Evaluating Demand for Deer Hunting: A Comparison of Methods." *Canadian Journal of Agricultural Economics* 21, No. 3 (November 1973): 6–14.

Caro, Tim. "Big-Game Hunters Are Not Biologists." *New Scientist* (December 13, 1984): 13–15.

Carter, Art. "Anticosti—Deer Hunter's Dream." *Sporting Classics* 6, No. 5 (September/October 1987): 49–55.

———. "Judgement Day at South Fork." *Sporting Classics* 5, No. 5 (September/October 1986): 37–41.

Cartmill, Matt. "'Four Legs Good, Two Legs Bad.'" *Natural History* (November 1983): 65–80.

Cartwright, Michael E. "Either-Sex Deer Management: Does Bucking Tradition Really Help the Herd?" *Arkansas Game and Fish* (September/October 1986): 2–7.

Case, David J., and Dale R. McCullough. "The White-tailed Deer of North Manitou Island." *Hilgardia* 55, No. 9 (December 1987): 1–57.

———. "White-tailed Deer Forage on Alewives." *Journal of Mammalogy* 68, No. 1 (February 1987): 195–197.

Causey, Ann S. "On the Morality of Hunting." *Environmental Ethics* 11, No. 4 (1989): 327–343.

Causey, Keith. "Ten Pointers for Trophy-Buck Success." *The Complete Deer Hunting Annual* 8, No. 1 (1990): 4–6, 97–98.

Clarke, C. H. D. "Autumn Thoughts of a Hunter." *Journal of Wildlife Management* 22, No. 4 (October 1958): 420–426.

Clutton-Brock, T. H. "Red Deer and Man." *National Geographic* 170, No. 4 (October 1986): 538–562.

Cockerham, Maurice. "The Cult of the Whitetail." *Louisiana Conservationist* (July/August 1985): 4–8.

Cohen, James A. "Why Do You Hunt?" *The Humane Society News* (Spring 1977): 25.

Compton, Brad B. "Use of Agricultural Crop Types by White-tailed Deer." *Proceedings of* the *Montana Academy of Science* 46 (1986): 5–17.

Compton, Bradley B., Richard J. Mackie, and Gary L. Dusek. "Factors Influencing Distribution of White-tailed Deer in Riparian Habitats." *The Journal of Wildlife Management* 52, No. 3 (July 1988): 544–548.

Cook, Gary. "The Interview." *Tennessee Wildlife* 12, No. 2 (September/October 1988): 2–4.

Copp, John D. "Why Hunters Like to Hunt." *Psychology Today* (December 1975): 60–62 & 67.

Cornell, Al. "Keeping a Deer Journal." *Deer & Deer Hunting* 13, No. 1 (September 1989): 44–49.

———. "Maintaining the Shrub Component." *Deer & Deer Hunting* 13, No. 2 (October 1989): 46–54.

———. "Values of Oaks and Oak Management." *Deer & Deer Hunting* 12, No. 5 (March 1989): 42–47.

Cronin, Edward W. "Doe Harvest." *Blair and Ketchum's Country Journal* 6, No. 11 (November 1979): 100–109.

Daniel, Walton S. "Travels of Post Oak Whitetails." *Texas Parks and Wildlife* (October 1973): 21–22.

Daniels, Thomas J., and Richard C. Falco. "The Lyme Disease Invasion." *Natural History* 7 (July 1989): 4–9.

Darrow, Robert W. "Deer Hunting—Then and Now." *The New York State Conservationist* 10, No. 1 (August/September 1955): 10, 20–23.

Davis, J. W. "How We Got the White Stag." *Recreation* 4, No. 4 (April 1896): 168–169.

Decker, Daniel J., and George F. Matfield. "Beyond the Guns and the Gamehunters and Hunting in New York." *The Conservationist* 43, No. 3 (November/December 1988): 3–7.

Decker, Daniel J., and Ken G. Purdy. "Becoming A Hunter: Identifying Stages of Hunting Involvement for Improving Hunter Education Programs." *Wildlife Society Bulletin* 14, No. 4 (1986): 474–479.

Decker, Daniel J., Ken G. Purdy, and Tommy L. Brown. "Degree to Which Participants in the 1978 Hunter Training Course Subsequently Bought a Hunting License: A 6-Year Follow-up." *New York Fish and Game Journal* 33, No. 1 (January 1986): 46–50.

———. "Early Hunting Experiences: Insights into the Role of Hunting 'Apprenticeship' from the Perspectives of Youths and Adults." *New York Fish and Game Journal* 33, No. 1 (January 1986): 51–54.

Decker, Daniel J. and Nancy A. Connelly. "Deer in Suburbia—Pleasures and Pests." *The Conservationist* 43, No. 5 (March/April 1989): 46–49.

Decker, Daniel J., and Thomas A. Gavin. "Public Attitudes toward a Suburban Deer Herd." *Wildlife Society Bulletin* 15, No. 2 (1987): 173–180.

Decker, Daniel J., and Tommy L. Brown. "How Animal Rightists View the 'Wildlife Management-Hunting System.'" *Wildlife Society Bulletin* 15, No. 4 (Winter 1987): 599–602.

———. "Hunting in New York: Participation, Demand and Land Access." *New York Fish and Game Journal* 26, No. 2 (July 1979): 101–131.

Decker, Daniel J., Tommy L. Brown, and Deborah Hustin. "Comparison of Farmers' Attitudes toward Deer Abundance in Two Regions of New York Having Different Agricultural and Deer Population Characteristics." *New York Fish and Game Journal* 28, No. 2 (July 1981): 202–207.

Decker, Daniel J., Tommy L. Brown, and R. J. Gutierrez. "Further Insights into the Multiple-Satisfactions Approach for Hunter Management." *Wildlife Society Bulletin* 8, No. 4 (1980): 323–331.

Decker, Daniel J., Tommy L. Brown, and William Sarbello. "Attitudes of Residents in the Peripheral Adirondacks toward Illegally Killing Deer." *New York Fish and Game Journal* 28, No. 1 (January 1981): 73–80.

DeJong, Cornell. "A Question of Baiting." *Field & Stream* 43, No. 5 (September 1988): 57–58, 136–137.

Demarais, Steve, and Bob Zaiglin as told to Kathy Etling. "Blueprinting Big Bucks." *Outdoor Life* (October 1989): 62–63, 108–110.

DeYoung, Charles A. "Mortality of Adult White-tailed Deer in South Texas." *The Journal of Wildlife Management* 53, No. 3 (July 1989): 513–581.

Dietz, Lew. "Confessions of a Maine Deer Hunter." *Field & Stream* 73 (April 1969): 66–67, 174–178.

Disilvestro, Roger, Rex Umber, and Neil Keyes. "The Oklahoma Whitetail." *Outdoor Oklahoma* 36, No. 9 (November/December 1980): 3–11.

Downing, Robert L. "Deer Harvest Sex Ratios: A Symptom, A Prescription or What?" *Wildlife Society Bulletin* 9, No. 1 (1981): 8–13.

Driscoll, Jack. "A Short Story from the Hermit Journals." *The Northern Review* 2, No. 1 (1988): 11–13.

Duffy, McFadden. "Hunting is Her High." *The Louisiana Conservationist* 34, No. 2 (March/April 1982): 18–22.

Dunlap, John C. "In Defense of Hunting." *Newsweek* (March 7, 1983): 12.

Dunnigan, Kevin N. "Hunting, Ethics, and You!" *North Dakota Outdoors* (October 1983): 18–19.

Dunraven, Earl of. "Moose Hunting in Canada." *Appleton's Journal* 38 (August 1879): 168–179.

Dusek, Gary L. "Ecology of White-tailed Deer in Upland Ponderosa Pine Habitat in Southeastern Montana." *Prairie Naturalist* 19, No. 1 (1987): 1–17.

Dusek, Gary L., Alan K. Wood, and Richard J. Mackie. "Habitat Use by White-tailed Deer in Prairie-Agricultural Habitat in Montana." *Prairie Naturalist* 20, No. 3 (1988): 135–142.

East, Ben. "The Great Deer War." *Outdoor Life* 132, No. 6 (1963): 17–19, 111–114.

Eaton, Randall L. "The Evolution of Trophy Hunting." *Carnivore* 1, Part 1 (January 1978): 110–121.

Ecenbarger, William. "Opening Day, Potter County, Pennsylvania." *Sport* (December 1985): 84.

Eiseley, Loren. "The Deer." *Audubon* 78, No. 6 (1967): 74–75.

Elder, John. "Hunting in Sand County." *Orion: Nature Quarterly* 5, No. 4 (1986): 46–53.

Ellis, Leslie. "Aristotle's Deer." *Florida Wildlife* (March/April 1982): 30–31.

Epstein, Mark B. "The Cruel Myth." *South Carolina Wildlife* 29, No. 2 (March/April 1982): 22.

Ernst, Stanton. "The Enigma of the Whitetail." *Maryland Conservationist* 39, No. 3 (1962): 12–15.

Errington, Paul L. "A Question of Values." *Journal of Wildlife Management* 11, No. 3 (July 1947): 267–272.

Evans, Jim. "Oak Ridge: A Hot Spot for Deer." *Tennessee Wildlife* 12, No. 3 (November/December 1988): 4–18.

F. W. M. "Two Deer at One Shot." *Recreation* 8, No. 5 (May 1898): 389.

Fadala, Sam. "Either/Or Hunting: Curse or Cure?" *Petersen's Hunting* (November 1980): 26–27, 85.

Fegely, Tom. "A Deer Hunter's Thanksgiving." *Game News* 59, No. 11 (November 1988): 9–12.

Fenstermacher, Ted. "Hunter John McHenry." *Game News* (July 1983): 15–17.

Fergus, Charles. "Empty Days." *Country Journal* 14, No. 12 (December 1987): 64–69.

Flanagan, John T. "Big Game Hunter, Henry H. Sibley." *Minnesota History* (Spring 1969): 217–228.

Forand, Kenneth J., and R. Larry Marchinton. "Patterns of Social Grooming in Adult White-tailed Deer." *American Midland Naturalist* 122, No. 2 (1989): 357–364.

Forand, Kenneth J., R. Larry Marchinton, and Karl V. Miller. "Influence of Dominance Rank on the Antler Cycle of White-Tailed Deer." *Journal of Mammalogy* 66, No. 1 (February 1985): 58–62.

Fosburgh, Hugh. "The Desperate Life of the Ghetto Deer." *Audubon* (July 1972): 78–91.

Franklin, Ben. "A New Twist to Tracking Deer." *Tennessee Wildlife* 12, No. 2 (September/October 1988): 11–14.

Franklin, William. "A Roadside Technique Using Scent Lures for Measuring Relative White-tailed Deer Abundance." *Proceedings of the Iowa Academy of Science* 93, No. 2 (1986): 44–47.

Fromm, Erich. "Man Would As Soon Flee As Fight." *Psychology Today* (August 1973): 35–39.

Geist, Valerius. "Battle Scars." *Deer & Deer Hunting* 11, No. 2 (November/December 1987): 56–62.

————. "Lessons Whitetails Taught Me." *Deer & Deer Hunting* 6, No. 2 (November/December 1982): 10–15.

————. "New Evidence of High Frequency of Antler Wounding in Cervids." *Canadian Journal of Zoology* 64 (1986): 380–383.

————. "Sparring." *Deer & Deer Hunting* 10, No. 4 (March/April 1987): 42–47.

————. "Super Antlers and Pre-World War II European Research." *Wildlife Society Bulletin* 14: No. 1 (1986): 91–94.

Giffin, Tom. "Deer Hunting Fundamentals." *Kansas Wildlife & Parks* 46, No. 6 (November/December 1989): 2–7.

Gladfelter, Lee. "White-tailed Deer in Iowa — Farmers' Reactions to the Increasing Population." *Iowa Conservationist* 48, No. 11 (November 1989): 3–9.

Glassen, Harold W. "Big Game Hunting in Germany." *Michigan Conservationist* (November/December 1952): 6–9.

Glover, Ronald L. "Detecting Lead in 'Arrow' Wounds in Deer Using Rhodizoinic Acid." *Wildlife Society Bulletin* 9, No. 3 (Fall 1981): 216–219.

Goldfrank, Esther. "Notes on Deer-Hunting Practices at Laguna Pueblo, New Mexico." *Texas Journal of Science* 6 (1954): 407–421.

Gore, Horace. "Summer Bucks." *Texas Parks and Wildlife* 46, No. 8 (August 1988): 12–15.

Gore, Horace, and Fred Bryant. "No Shortcuts to Good Deer Management." *Texas Parks and Wildlife* (October 1984): 31–35.

Gottschalk, John. "The German Hunting System, West Germany, 1968." *The Journal of Wildlife Management* 36, No. 1 (January 1972): 110–118.

Grange, Wallace. "The Commotion on Balsam Ridge." *The American Gun* 1, No. 1 (Winter 1969): 62–67.

Griffith, Brad, and Berta A. Youtie. "Two Devices For Estimating Foliage Density and Deer Hiding Cover." *Wildlife Society Bulletin* 16, No. 2 (Summer 1988): 206–210.

Gutshall, Jennifer. "My King of the Mountain." *Game News* 60, No. 10 (October 1989): 29–33.

Guynn, Dwight E., and John L. Schmidt. "Managing Deer Hunting on Private Lands in Colorado." *Wildlife Society Bulletin* 12, No. 1 (1981): 12–19.

Haas, George H. "German Hunting: It's the Tradition That Counts." *International Wildlife* (November 1977): 39–43.

Hale, Robert. "My Ten-Point Buck." *New Yorker* 20, No. 4 (December 9, 1944): 78–81.

Hansen, Lonnie P., Charles M. Nixon, and Forrest Loomis. "Factors Affecting Daily and Annual Harvest of White-tailed Deer in Illinois." *Wildlife Society Bulletin* 14, No. 4 (Winter 1988): 368–376.

Hansen, Lonnie, and John Fischer. "Is This Deer Safe to Eat?" *Mississippi Conservationist* 50, No. 11 (November 1989): 23–25.

Harper, Ray. "Big Bucks — The Wealth of Deer Hunting." *Outdoor Indiana* 54, No. 9 (November 1989): 32–37.

Harrison, Jim. "Where the Chase Is a Song of Hound and Horn." *Sports Illustrated* 36, No. 12 (March 20 1972): 64–75.

Haugen, Arnold O. "Deer Hunting with Bow and Arrow." *Kansas Fish and Game* 22, No. 2: 14–15, 19–20.

Heberlein, Thomas A. "Stalking the Predator." *Environment* 29, No. 7 (September 1987): 6–11, 30–33.

Heidel, Kathy. "My Friends among the Deer." *The Minnesota Volunteer* (January/February 1988): 57–61.

Henricksson, John. "New Sport for an Old Hunter." *Outdoor America* 54, No. 1 (Winter 1989): 16, 27.

Henry, Byron. "Habitat Use and Home Range of White-tailed Deer in Point Pelee National Park, Ontario." *The Canadian Field-Naturalist* 89, No. 2 (1975): 179–181.

Herrera, Joe G. "Whitetails: The State's Most Important Game Animal." *Texas Parks & Wildlife* (June 1983): 3–4.

Hillman, Bruce J. "The Hunter in Poetry." *The Country Gentleman* (Summer 1980): 28–31.

Hirth, David H. "Mother-Young Behavior in White-tailed Deer, *Odocoileus Virginianus*." *The Southwestern Naturalist* 30, No. 2 (May 31, 1985): 297–302.

Hodges, Terry. "Stakeout at Trumbly's Still." *Outdoor California* 49, No. 1 (January/February 1988): 19–21.

Hofacker, Al. "The Lunar Cycle and Deer Activity." *Deer & Deer Hunting* 4, No. 6 (July/August 1981): 4–8.

Holbrook, Vi. "Young Hunter's First Deer Stolen." *Arizona Wildlife Views* (December 1986): 4.

Hölzenbein, Stefan, and Georg Schwede. "Activity and Movements of Female White-tailed Deer During the Rut." *The Journal of Wildlife Management* 53, No. 1 (January 1989): 219–223.

Hoskins, John D. "Searching for a Crime." *Missouri Conservationist* 50, No. 9 (September 1989): 2–5.

Hummel, Richard L. "Hunting and Fishing— But Not in Sociology." *The Rural Sociologist* 3, No. 4: 255–258.

Ingraham, John Holt. "Natchez Deer Hunt." *Mississippi Outdoors* (January/February 1988): 5, 18–19.

Ishmael, William E. "Urban Deer Problems." *Deer & Deer Hunting* 8, No. 3 (January/February 1984): 24–28.

Jackson, Robert "Hunting as a Social Experience." *Deer & Deer Hunting* 11, No. 2 (November/December 1987): 38–51.

———. "The Case for Women Who Hunt." *Deer & Deer Hunting* 12, No. 1 (September 1988): 54–61.

———. "The Making of a Hunter." *Wisconsin Sportsman* 15, No. 6 (September/October 1986): 39–41.

———. "Who Are We?" *Archery World* 33, No. 2 (1984): 16, 48–50.

Jackson, Robert, and Robert Norton. "The Last Deer Hunt." *Deer & Deer Hunting* 7, No. 1 (October/November 1983): 54–59.

Jackson, Robert M., and Stephen E. Leggans. "The Pull of the Bow." *Deer & Deer Hunting* 10, No. 2 (November/December 1986): 16–26.

Jacobson, Harry H., Joe Bearden, and David B. Whitehouse. "Artificial Insemination Trials with White-tailed Deer." *The Journal of Wildlife Management* 53, No. 1 (January 1989): 224–227.

Jameson, Dennis. "Deer Diary." *Wisconsin Natural Resources* 12, No. 6 (November/December 1988): 17–22.

Johnson, Dan. "South Carolina's Quality Deer Management Association." *South Carolina Game and Fish* No. 7 (July 1989): 29–31.

Jones, Franklin Reed. "Bruce's Buck." *Gray's Sporting Journal* 13, No. 4 (Winter 1988): 18, 21–24.

Jones, Robert F. "Slaughter on South Island." *Sports Illustrated* 40, No. 11 (March 18, 1974): 42–48.

———. "The Man With the Bow." *New York Times Magazine* (December 9, 1973): 42–43.

Kays, Margaret. "Living with Deer." *New York Conservationist* 22, No. 6 (1968): 9–10, 31.

Kelsey, Paul. "Training New York's Bowhunters." *The Conservationist* (September/October 1977): 32–33.

Kerrick, James N. "Hunting Ethics, A Sportsman's Challenge." *Virginia Wildlife* (February 1985): 15–17.

Knox, William M., Karl V. Miller, and R. Larry Marchinton. "Recurrent Estrous Cycles in White-tailed Deer." *Journal of Mammalogy* 69, No. 2, (May 1988): 384–386.

Kouba, Leonard J. "Charting Deer Hunting Success." *Outdoor Highlights* 17, No. 6 (March 20, 1989): 3–5.

Krug, Alan S. "Sociology of Hunting." *Virginia Wildlife* (February 1981): 16–17.

Kurzejeski, Adam J. "Three-Shot Buck." *South Dakota Conservation Digest* 56, No. 5 (November 1989): 16–18.

Laffin, W. Mackay. "Deer Hunting on the Au Sable." *Deer & Deer Hunting* 11, No. 1 (September/October 1987): 126–146.

Lagory, Kirk E. "Habitat, Group Size, and the Behavior of White-tailed Deer." *Behavior* 98, No. 1–4 (1986): 168–179.

Lancia, Richard A., *et al.* "A White-tailed Deer Harvesting Strategy." *The Journal of Wildlife Management* 52, No. 4 (October 1988): 589–595.

Lautenschlager, R. A., and H. S. Crawford. "Training White-tailed Deer, *Odocoileus virginianus,* for Food Habitat Studies." *The Canadian Field-Naturalist* 98, No. 4 (1984): 503–505.

Lawrence, Lea H. "Tennessee's 'Atomic' Deer." *Petersen's Hunting* (June 1987): 64–67, 98.

Lemarz, Mark S. "Economics of Forest Openings for White-tailed Deer." *Wildlife Society Bulletin* 15, No. 4 (Winter 1987): 568–573.

Lentz, W. Mac, Karl V. Miller, and R. Larry Marchinton. "How Much Do Antlers

Shrink?" *Deer & Deer Hunting* 11, No. 1 (September/October 1987): 149–150.

Leopold, A. Starker. "Meditations in a Duck Blind." *Gray's Sporting Journal* (Fall 1977): 6–10.

LeResche, Robert E. "A Time for Unity." *Maine Fish and Wildlife* (Winter 1981): 2–7.

"Lesmok." "Some Bucks I Have Known." *Pennsylvania Game News* (December 1941): 18–19, 30.

Licht, Dan. "The Dispersing Yearling Buck." *Deer & Deer Hunting* 10, No. 5 (May/June 1987): 22–29.

Logan, Tom H., and Allan Egbert. "The Florida Deer Story." *Florida Wildlife* (November/December 1981): 28–33.

McClung, Robert M. "The Deer Slayers . . . The Deer Protectors." *Defenders of Wildlife* 50, No. 3 (1975): 228–231.

McCullough, Dale R. "Evaluation of Night Spotlighting as a Deer Study Technique." *Journal of Wildlife Management* 46, No. 4 (1982): 963–973.

McCullough, Dale R., David H. Hirth, and Stephen J. Newhouse. "Resource Partitioning between Sexes in White-tailed Deer." *The Journal of Wildlife Management* 53, No. 2 (April 1989): 277–283.

Machan, Dyan. "Bambi and the Baron." *Forbes* (December 11, 1989): 298–300.

McKee, Russell. "Peregrinations and Permutations of a Contrary Eight-Toed Beast." *Audubon* 89, No. 3 (May 1987): 54–80.

McLennan, Bill. "Aransas Refuge Archery Season—Rugged Bowhunting." *Texas Parks & Wildlife* (September 1983): 22–25.

McQuarrie, Gordon. "Just Look at This Country." *Deer & Deer Hunting* 6, No. 5 (June 1983): 26–33.

Madison, Chris. "To Feed or not to Feed." *Audubon* (March, 1986): 22–27.

Madson, John. "Serengeti North." *Audubon* (May 1988): 54–65.

———. "The Genuine Deer Hunter." *Deer & Deer Hunting* 6, No. 3 (January/February 1983): 20–24.

———. "What About This Anti-Hunting Thing?" *The Conservationist* (September/October 1976): 2–4.

Maning, Ron. "The Whitetail Mystique." *Mississippi Game and Fish* 40, No. 5 (1977): 14–16.

Marburger, Rodney, and Jack Ward Thomas. "Anatomy of a Deer Hunt." *Texas Game and Fish* 22, No. 9 (1964): 10–12.

Marchinton, R. Larry. "Dogs, Deer, and People in the South." *Deer & Deer Hunting* 7, No. 6 (July/August 1984): 65–73.

Mason, Dorothy Stafford. "Private Deer Hunting on the Coastal Plain of North Carolina." *Southeastern Geographer* 29, No. 1, (May 1, 1989): 1–16.

Matthews, Bob, and Keith Sexson. "25 Years of Deer Management in Kansas." *Kansas Wildlife & Parks* 46, No. 5 (September/October 1989): 35–39.

Mech, L. David. "An Unusually Long Pursuit of a Deer by a Wolf." *Journal of Mammalogy* 59, No. 4 (November 1978): 860–861.

———. "Deer Distribution in Relation to Wolf Pack Territory Edges." *Journals of Wildlife Management* 44, No. 1 (1980): 253–258.

———. "Observations of a Swimming Wolf Killing a Swimming Deer." *Journal of Mammalogy* 65, No. 1 (1984): 143–144.

———. "Why Some Deer Are Safe from Wolves." *Natural History* 88, No. 1: 70–77.

Miller, Karl V., Kent E. Kammermeyer, R. Larry Marchinton, and E. Barry Moser. "Population and Habitat Influences on Antler Rubbing by White-tailed Deer." *Journal of Wildlife Management* 51, No. 1, (January 1987): 62–66.

Miller, Karl V., and R. Larry Marchinton. "New Discoveries about Antler Rubs." *Deer & Deer Hunting* 10, No. 4 (March/April 1987): 28–31.

Miller, Karl V., R. Larry Marchinton, Julian R. Beckwith, and Parshall B. Bush. "Variations in Density and Chemical Composition of White-tailed Deer Antlers." *Journal of Mammalogy* 66, No. 4 (November 1985): 693–701.

Miller, Karl V., R. Larry Marchinton, Kenneth J. Forand, and Karen L. Johansen. "Dominance, Testosterone Levels and Scraping Activity in a Captive Herd of White-tailed Deer." *Journal of Mammalogy* 68, No. 4 (November 1987): 812–817.

Miller, Karl V., R. Larry Marchinton, and Victor F. Nettles. "The Growth Rate of Hooves of White-tailed Deer." *Journal of Wildlife Diseases* 22, No. 1 (January 1986): 129–131.

Minch, Norm. "Quality Vs. Quantity — Trophy Deer Management." *Kentucky Happy Hunting Ground* 44, No. 6 (November/December 1986): 5–7.

Minnesota DNR. "Hunting in Minnesota: The View Ahead." *The Minnesota Volunteer* (September/October 1983): 15–20.

Moen, Aaron N. "Buck Rubs." *Deer & Deer Hunting* 10, No. 1 (September/October 1986): 54–60.

———. "Crippling Loss: How Much of a Problem." *Deer & Deer Hunting* 10, No. 3 (January/February 1987): 33–35.

———. "Crippling Losses." *Deer & Deer Hunting* 12, No. 6 (June 1989): 64–70.

———. "Deer Population Dynamics." *Deer & Deer Hunting* 11, No. 2 (November/December 1987): 102–109.

———. "Electronic Licensing." *Deer & Deer Hunting* 13, No. 4 (December 1989): 18–25.

———. "Energy Conservation by White-tailed Deer in the Winter." *Ecology* 57 (1976): 192–198.

———. "Hunter Bias: What Is It?" *Deer & Deer Hunting* 10, No. 2 (November/December 1986): 44–46.

———. "Man the Hunter, Hunting and the Hunted." *Deer & Deer Hunting* 9, No. 1 (January/February 1986): 62–76.

———. "Seasonal Changes in Heart Rates, Activity, Metabolism, and Forage Intake of White-tailed Deer." *Journal of Wildlife Management* 42, No. 4 (1978): 715–738.

Moen, Aaron N., and C. W. Severinghaus. "The Annual Weight Cycle and Survival of White-tailed Deer in New York." *The New York Fish and Game Journal* 28, No. 2 (July 1981): 162–177.

Montgomery, H. T., II. "Not As Easy As You May Think — 'Doe Season.'" *Game News* 60, No. 12 (December 1989): 18–20.

Mooty, Jack J., Patrick D. Karns, and Todd K. Fuller. "Habitat Use and Seasonal Range Size of White-tailed Deer in Northcentral Minnesota." *The Journal of Wildlife Management* 51, No. 3 (July 1987): 644–648.

More, Thomas A. "Hunting: A Theoretical Explanation with Management Implications." *Wildlife Society Bulletin* 12, No. 4 (1984): 338–344.

Moreland, A. D. "A Stuffed Deer." *Recreation* 4, No. 1 (January 1896): 29–31.

Morrissey, William J. "The Diana Hunting Club." *Wisconsin Sportsman* (November/December 1982): 24–27.

Nelson, Michael E., and L. David Mech. "Home-Range Formation and Dispersal of Deer in Northeastern Minnesota." *Journal of Mammalogy* 65, No. 4 (1984): 567–575.

———. "Mortality of White-tailed Deer in Northeastern Minnesota." *Journal of Wildlife Management* 50, No. 4 (1986): 691–698.

———. "Relationship between Snow Depth and Gray Wolf Predation on White-tailed Deer." *Journal of Wildlife Management* 50, No. 3 (1986): 471–474.

Nelson, Richard K. "Shooting A Buck." *Harpers* 274 (January 1987): 29–30.

Nesmith, Rod, and Ron Keiper. "Human Hair as Deer Repellent." *Pennsylvania Game News* (July 1982): 43–44.

Nicholson, Charles. "Hunter's Home — A Story of Deer Hunting in the Deep South." *Game Country* 1, No. 1 (November/December 1988): 74–77.

———. "Hunting William Faulkner's South: A Celtic Continuum." *Game Country* 1, No. 2 (January/February 1989): 24–27.

Nisbet, Lee. "A Deer Killing." *Deer & Deer Hunting* 10, No. 3 (January/February 1987): 6.

———. "Harvesting Deer and Liberating Animals." *Deer & Deer Hunting* 13, No. 5 (March 1990): 20–30.

———. "The Ethics of Pursuit." *Deer & Deer Hunting* 11, No. 1 (September/October 1987): 50–56.

Olson, Dennis. "Why a Naturalist Kills Deer." *Deer & Deer Hunting* 8, No. 3 (January/February 1984): 50–53.

Olson, Sigurd F. "My First Buck." *Deer & Deer Hunting* 6, No. 3 (January/February 1983): 26–32.

Ozoga, John J. "Behavior and Deer Herd Dynamics." *Deer & Deer Hunting* 10, No. 3 (January/February 1987): 52–61.

———. "Bones of Contention." *Deer & Deer Hunting* 11, No. 1 (September/October 1987): 12–25.

———. "Hunting and Deer Herd Dynamics." *Michigan Out-Of-Doors* (March 1986): 50–53.

———. "Induced Scraping Activity in White-tailed Deer." *Journal of Wildlife Management* 53, No. 4 (1989): 877–880.

———. "Predation by Black Bears on Newborn White-tailed Deer." *Journal of Mammalogy* 63, No. 4 (1982): 695–696.

———. "Super Does." *Deer & Deer Hunting* 13, No. 5 (March 1990): 72–77.

———. "Temporal Pattern of Scraping Behavior in White-tailed Deer." *Journal of Mammalogy* 70, No. 3 (1989): 633–636.

———. "The Social Role of Buck Rubs and Scrapes." *Wisconsin Sportsman* 15, No. 6 (September/October 1986): 23–27, 82.

———. "White-tailed Deer." *Michigan Natural Resources* (September/October 1985): 27–33.

———. "Winter and Whitetails." *Michigan Natural Resources* (November/December 1986): 27–33.

———. "Yearling Sires." *Commemorative Bucks of Michigan—BUCK FAX* (Winter 1986): 12.

Ozoga, John J., and Louis J. Verme. "Activity Patterns of White-tailed Deer During Estrus." *The Journal of Wildlife Management* 39, No. 4 (October 1975): 679–683.

Pacelle, Wayne. "Activists Disrupt Thanksgiving Deer Hunt." *The Animal's Agenda* (March 1987): 24–25.

———. "Saviors or Sellouts?" *The Animal's Agenda* (July/August 1988): 6–9.

Parker, Katherine. "Effects of Heat, Cold and Rain on Coastal Black-tailed Deer." *Canadian Journal of Zoology* 66, No. 11 (1988): 2475–2483.

Parks, Marshall. "Of Bucks and Men—Sparring Deer Create an Adventure of a Lifetime." *Outdoor Indiana* 50, No. 9 (November 1985): 12–14.

Pekins, Peter, and William W. Mautz. "Acorn Usage by Deer: Significance of Oak Management." *Northern Journal of Applied Forestry* 4 (1987): 124–128.

Progulske, Donald R., and Donald C. Duerre. "Factors Influencing Spotlighting Counts of Deer." *Journal of Wildlife Management* 28, No. 1 (January 1964): 27–34.

Raedeke, Jerry. "Why I Hunt." *The Minnesota Volunteer* (September/October 1977): 2–9.

Rasmussen, Gerald P. "Antler Measurements as an Index to Physical Condition and Range Quality with Respect to White-tailed Deer." *New York Fish and Game* 32, No. 2 (July 1985): 96–113.

Reardon, John. "Hemingway's Esthetic and Ethical Sportsmen." *University Review* 34 (1967): 13–23.

Reardon, P.O., L. B. Merrill, and C. A. Taylor, Jr., "White-tailed Deer Preferences and Hunter Success under Various Grazing Systems." *Journal of Range Management* 31, No. 1 (January 1978): 40–42.

Reed, Dale F. "Effectiveness of Highway Lighting in Reducing Deer-Vehicle Accidents." *Journal of Wildlife Management* 45, No. 3 (1981): 721–726.

Reed, J. D. "Sayonara Bambi." *Sports Illustrated* 40, (February 18, 1974): 78–82, 85–86.

Reiger, George. "Public Vs. Private Hunting." *Field & Stream* 91, (March 1987): 38–40.

Rhodes, Richard. "A Thin Disguise." *New York Times Magazine* (July 19, 1987): 62.

Ricciuti, Ed. "How Israel Rescued the Shah's Deer." *International Wildlife* (September/October 1981): 40–42.

Richards, Tudor. "History of the White-tailed Deer in New Hampshire." *Proceedings of the New Hampshire Academy of Sciences* 1, No. 9 (1949): 46–52.

Rohlfing, A. H. "Hunter Conduct and Public Attitudes." *The Forty-Third North American Wildlife Conference* (1978): 404–411.

Root, Brian G., Erik K. Fritzell, and Norbert F. Giessman. "Effects of Intensive Hunting on White-tailed Deer Movements." *Wildlife Society Bulletin* 16, No. 2 (Summer 1988): 145–151.

Rothwell, Reg. "Whitetail Versus Mule Deer." *Wyoming Wildlife* 53, No. 9 (September 1989): 24–29.

Ruthaven, Alexander, and Norman A. Wood. "The White-tailed Deer of Michigan." *Science* 35, No. 909 (May 31, 1912): 863–864.

Rutledge, Archibald. "Bucks Are Like That." *Field & Stream* (July 1938): 22–23, 60, 71.

———. "Certain Great Stags." *Field & Stream* (October 1927): 26–27, 62–66.

Rutledge, Archibald. "Deer Propagation on Waste Land." *The Game Breeder* 35, No. 1 (January 1931): 3–4, 23–24.

———. "Horns on the Delta." *Sports Afield* (September 1938): 14–15, 62–63.

———. "Hunting Helmetted Stags." *Field & Stream* (March 1917): 400–403.

———. "My Friend the Deer." *The Country Life* (May 1918): 45–48.

———. "My Most Memorable Deer Hunt." *Outdoor Life* 148 (July 1971): 44–45, 80–84.

———. "Riding Them Up." *Field & Stream* (August 1931): 20–21, 55.

———. "Steve and the Plateye Buck." *Field & Stream* (July 1937): 20–21, 72.

———. "Tales of Deer." *The Rotarian* 83, (November 1953): 20–22, 51–52.

———. "The Boy and the Buck." *Forest and Stream* 97, (September 1927): 530–531, 554–555.

———. "The Buck at the Secret Crossing." *Outdoor Life* (March 1965): 46, 94–95.

———. "The Buck with the Palmated Horns." *Field & Stream* (December 1941): 24–25, 68.

———. "The Christmas Eve Buck." *Field & Stream* (December 1929): 40–41, 64–65.

———. "The Deer of Coastal Islands." *Country Life* (February 1920): 70–76.

———. "The Deer of Southern Woods." *Field & Stream* (January 1915): 948–952.

———. "The Funny Side of Deer Hunting." *Forest and Stream* 95, No. 11 (1925): 646–648, 691–692.

———. "The Horn Architecture of the Whitetail." *Field & Stream* (December 1927): 20–21, 76–77.

———. "The Odyssey of Old Clubfoot." *Field & Stream* (September 1928): 34–35, 67–68.

———. "The Romance of Deer Stands." *Field & Stream* (May, 1945): 16–17 110–111.

———. "The Surprise of My Life." *Field & Stream* (April 1942): 20–21, 72.

———. "What Your Buck May Do." *The Saturday Evening Post* (October 12, 1929): 68, 70, 214.

———. "Why I Taught My Boys to Be Hunters." *Massachusetts Wildlife* (November/December 1964): 12–17.

Ryel, Lawrence A. "The Occurrence of Certain Anomalies in Michigan White-tailed Deer." *Journal of Mammalogy* 44, (February 1963): 79–98.

Samuel, David. "Biopolitics—The Smithsonian's Deer Problem." *Deer & Deer Hunting* 6, No. 4 (March/April 1983): 50–53.

———. "Bow Wounding Losses—The Big Myth." *Bowhunter* 18, No. 1 (October/November 1988): 15–18, 134–135.

———. "More Deer . . . More Hunting." *Whitetail Bowhunter* (1989): 44–47, 66.

———. "The Best Bow Shot." *Bowhunter* 14, No. 1 (October/November 1984): 34–38.

Sanz, Robert. "On the Mountain." *Colorado Outdoors* 38, No. 4 (July/August 1989): 28–30.

Sarbello, William, and Lawrence W. Jackson. "Deer Mortality in the Town of Malone." *New York Fish and Game Journal* 32, No. 2 (July 1985): 141–157.

Sasser, Ray. "Antlerless Deer Hunting—A Balancing Act." *Texas Parks and Wildlife* (September 1986): 39–42.

———. "Ruminations of a Deer Hunter." *Texas Parks & Wildlife* 47, No. 11 (November 1989): 14–19.

———. "Woodland Deer—Restocking Brings Back East Texas Whitetails." *Texas Parks & Wildlife* (November 1983): 3–7.

Savage, Will. "Wildlife Misfortunes." *Game News* (February 1983): 7–13.

Scharf, John A. "This Urgent Matter of Hunting Values and the Quality Crisis." *The Conservation Volunteer* (September/October 1968): 15–25.

Scheffer, Victor B. "The Future of Wildlife Management." *Wildlife Society Bulletin* 4, No. 2 (Summer 1976): 51–54.

Schiedermayer, David L. "The Killing Fields." *Deer & Deer Hunting* 9, No. 6 (July/August 1986): 10–11.

Schneider, Dona, and John Kuser. "Suburbia: Too Many Deer or Too Many People?" *New Jersey Outdoors* 16, No. 1 (January/February 1989): 28–32.

Schoen, John W., and Matthew D. Kirchoff. "Little Deer in the Big Woods." *Natural History* 97, No. 8 (August 1988): 52–55, 78–79.

Schoenecker, Roger. "Let's Send the Hunter Back to School." *The Minnesota Volunteer* (July/August 1973): 36–40.

Schultz, William E. "Wisconsin Deer in Dixie." *Wisconsin Natural Resources* 12, No. 1 (January/February 1988): 5–6.

Seidler, Robert. "Decoy Deer Detail." *Alabama Conservation* 58, No. 5 (September/October 1988): 13.

Seton, Ernest Thompson. "A Carberry Deer Hunt." *Forest and Stream* 26 (June 3, 1886): 366–368.

———. "A New Deerhunt with the Bow." *Country Life* 7, (February 1905): 370–371.

———. "Deer Hunting with the Bow." *Forest and Stream* 81 (November 15, 1913): 626.

———. "The Buck We Didn't Shoot." *Forest and Stream* 37 (September 1891): 143.

———. "The Revival of the Bow and Arrow." *Country Life* 7 (January 1905): 273–275.

———. "What Is a True Sportsman?" *Forest and Stream* 47 (September 1896): 245.

Severinghaus, C. W. "Springtime in New York—Another Angle." *The New York State Conservationist* (April/May 1953): 2–4.

Severinghaus, C. W., and C. P. Brown. "History of the White-tailed Deer in New York." *New York Fish and Game Journal* 3, No. 2 (1956): 129–167.

Shaw, Mike, and Rex Umber. "Oklahoma Whitetails: A Look at the Past, Present and Future of Our Most Popular Big Game Animal." *Outdoor Oklahoma* (November/December 1983): 3–7.

Shea, David S. "White-tailed Deer Eating Salmon." *Murrelet* 54, No. 2 (May/August 1973): 23.

Shelton, Ken. "Why I Hunt." *Colorado Outdoors* (January/February 1983): 27–28.

Shipman, Bert. "Dogs and Deer." *Country Journal* 14, (April 1987): 17–20.

Slaughter, Dinny. "Bambi Revisited." *Virginia Wildlife* 43, No. 5 (May 1982): 17–19.

Sloan, John. "The Making of a Bowhunter." *Tennessee Wildlife* 13, No. 2 (October 1989): 7–9.

Smith, Edmund Ware. "Jake's Rangers Hunt the Whitetail." *Deer & Deer Hunting* 6, No. 6 (August 1983): 34–44.

Smith, Hal. "Deer Ranching: Do Fallow Deer Offer Hope for Struggling Farms?" *Country Journal* 14 (November 1987): 48–53.

Smith, Richard P. "Lou Verme—Deer Researcher." *Deer & Deer Hunting* 8, No. 6 (July/August 1985): 36–43.

Sterba, James P. "Even a Real Genius Notes That Bambi Is a Relevant Factor." *Wall Street Journal* 80, No. 253 (October 12, 1989): 1, 12.

Stokes, Bill. "The Deer Dilemma." *The Chicago Tribune Magazine* (August 6, 1989): 12–16, 25–27.

Stransky, John J. "Hunting on Scrapes." *The American Rifleman* 115, No. 9 (September 1967): 112–113.

Stringham, Stephen F. "Revitalizing Vermont's Deer Herd: Who Should the Doctors Be?" *The Vermont Sportsman* 20, No. 5 (August 1989): 16–18.

Stromp, Bruce. "Enforcement." *Outdoor Oklahoma* 45, No. 6 (November/December 1989): 20–24.

Stüwe, Michael. "Flight Order and Its Development in White-tailed Deer." *The Journal of Wildlife Management* 50, No. 4 (October 1986): 699–701.

Tanck, John E. and Franklin J. Passer. "Still Hunting." *New York Conservationist* 6, No. 2 (October/November 1951): 6–7.

Taylor, James H., Jerold V. Owens, Czerny R. Newland, Reginald G. Wycoff, John Robinette, Jr., Kerney J. Sonnier, and David W. Moreland. "Good News for Deer Hunters." *Louisiana Conservationist* 41, No. 6 (November/December 1989): 22–25.

Teer, James G. "Of Nature, Deer and Man." *Texas Game and Fish* 14, No. 10 (October 1956): 4–5.

Thomas, E. Donnall. "Death By Broadhead." *Bowhunter—Special 1989 Big Game Issue* (September 1989): 67–74.

Thomas, Gary. "Whitetail Wiles." *Outdoor Highlights* 16, No. 21 (November 7, 1988): 6–9.

Thomas, John K. and Clark E. Adams. "Socioeconomic Factors Affecting Land Access to Hunt White-tailed Deer." *Wildlife Society Bulletin* 13, No. 4 (1985): 388–394.

Thomas, Jack Ward, John D. Gill, James C. Pack, William M. Healy, and H. Reed Sanderson. "Influence of Forestland Characteristics On Spatial Distribution of Hunters." *Journal of Wildlife Management* 40, No. 3 (1976): 500–506.

Tolman, Newton F. "Hunting Hunters." *The Atlantic Monthly* 204 (November 1959): 98–100.

Trabb, Harvey. "Deer Management Is Applegate's Game." *Deer & Deer Hunting* 6, No. 6 (August 1983): 75–77.

Trudge, Colin. "Custom-Built Deer Take to the Hills." *New Scientist* (April 9, 1987): 28.

Trueblood, Ted. "I Didn't Want to Kill a Deer." *Field & Stream* (October 1984): 30–36.

Verme, Louis J. "Niche Selection By Male White-tailed Deer." *Wildlife Society Bulletin* 16, No. 4 (Winter 1988): 448–451.

Verme, Louis J., John J. Ozoga, and John T. Nellist. "Induced Early Estrus in Penned White-tailed Deer Does." *The Journal of Wildlife Management* 51, No. 1 (January 1987): 54–56.

Vitali, Theodore. "Sport Hunting: Moral or Immoral?" *Environmental Ethics* 12, No. 1 (1990): 69–82.

Ward, Bill. "The Way to a Deer's Stomach." *Tennessee Wildlife* 12, No. 2 (September/October 1988): 8–10.

Wathen, Greg. "Managing Tennessee's Bumper Crop of Whitetails." *Tennessee Wildlife* 13, No. 3 (November/December 1989): 9–12.

White, Jack. "Bambi Can Kill." *Outdoor California* (May/June 1982): 19–21.

Wilder, Edwin H. "Walking-Trail Developments for Hunters on the Nicolet National Forest." *Journal of Wildlife Management* 33, No. 4, (October 1969): 762–768.

Williams, Ted. "Attitudes toward Wildlife in 2049 A.D." *ORION: Nature Quarterly* 8, No. 2 (Spring 1982): 28–33.

Woods, Grant R., Lynn W. Robbins, and Susan F. Spence. "New Scrape Research." *Deer & Deer Hunting* 12, No. 2 (October 1988): 34–43.

Wulff, Lee. "Some Personal Thoughts on Hunting." *Gray's Sporting Journal* 1, No. 7 (Fall 1976): 24–26.

Yarrow, Greg, and Harry A. Jacobson. "Can Deer Lead Scientists To Better Hunting." *Mississippi Game and Fish* 41, No. 5 (1978): 9.

Crippling Losses and Wounded Deer Behavior

Aho, Robert W. "Deer Hunting Retrieval Rates." *Michigan Pittman-Robertson Report*. Michigan Department of Natural Resources (1984). 11 pp.

Ashby, Ed. "Broadhead Performance." Unpublished manuscript (1985).

Benke, Adrian. *The Bowhunting Alternative.* Texas: privately printed (1989). 110 pp.

Bennett, Bill. "Rugged Buck." *Deer & Deer Hunting* 12, No. 1 (September 1988): 86.

Boydston, Glenn A. and Horace G. Gorr. "Archery Wounding Loss in Texas." Paper presented at the 10th Southeast Deer Study Group Meeting (1987).

Cada, John D. "Preliminary Archery Survey Report." Helena, Mont.: Montana Department of Fish, Wildlife, and Parks (1989). 7 pp.

Fuller, Todd K. "Hunter Harvest of White-tailed Deer in the Bearville Study Area, Northcentral Minnesota." *Minnesota Wildlife Report 6* (1988). St. Paul, Minnesota. 45 pp.

Grimble, Augustus. "Wounded Deer." In *Deer-Stalking* (1888): 124–133.

Jeanneney, John. "Tracking Wounded Deer with Leashed Dogs." *Deer & Deer Hunting* 8, No. 1 (October 1984): 44–55.

———. "The Use of Leashed Trailing Dogs for Tracking Wounded Deer." *Transactions of the Northeast Fish and Wildlife Conference* (1977): 143–151.

Ludbrook, J. V., and A. J. Tomkinson. "Evaluation of Bow Hunting as a Form of Recreational Hunting in Natal." *South Africa: Natal Parks, Game & Fish Preservation Board* (1985).

Moen, Aaron N. "Crippling Losses." *Deer & Deer Hunting* 12, No. 6 (June 1989): 64–70.

———. "How Long Does It Take a Deer to Die?" *Deer & Deer Hunting* 13, No. 3 (November, 1989): 83–87.

Nixon, Charles M., and Lonnie P. Hansen. *Illinois Forest Game Investigations* (September 25, 1986).

On Track—News From Deer Search. Newsletter of Deer Search, Inc. (March 1989).

Robinette, John R., *et al.* "An Estimate of Unretrieved Deer Following a Muzzleloader Hunt." *Proceedings of the Forty-First Annual Conference of Southeastern Association of Fish and Wildlife Agencies* (1987): 318–322.

Samuel, David E. "Factors Affecting Bow and Gun Wounding." Unpublished Paper for the Northeast Deer Technical Committee (1988).

———. "The Best Bow Shot." *Bowhunter* (November/December 1984): 34–38.

Smith, Richard P. "Tracking with Dogs." In *Tracking Wounded Deer.* Harrisburg, Pa.: Stackpole Books, 1988. 130–141.

Tomkinson, Tony. "South Africa's Bow Hunting Research." *Petersen's 1987 Hunting Annual.* 136–138.

Wegner, Robert. "Crippling Losses Revisited." In *Deer & Deer Hunting: Book 2.* Harrisburg, Pa.: Stackpole Books, 1987. 143–151.

Wescott, Gayle, and R. Ben Peyton. "Investigation of Reliability of Self-Reported Deer Wounding Rates and Bow Hunter Response to Information on Wounding." *Agriculture Experiment Station Project No. 3248.* (1986).

The Human Dimensions of Hunting

Belanger, Dian Olson. *Managing American Wildlife: A History of the International Association of Fish and Wildlife Agencies.* Amherst: The University of Massachusetts Press, 1988. 247 pp.

Borland, Hal, and the National Wildlife Federation. *The History of Wildlife in America.* New York: Arch Cape Press, 1988. 197 pp.

Brusewitz, Gunnar. *Hunting: Hunters, Game, Weapons and Hunting Methods from the Remote Past to the Present Day.* London: George Allen & Unwin, Ltd., 1967. 251 pp.

Campbell, Joseph. *Primitive Mythology: The Masks of God.* New York: Penguin Books, 1987. 504 pp.

———. *Renewal Myths and Rites of the Primitive Hunters and Planters.* Texas: Spring Publications, Inc., 1989. 51 pp.

———. *The Way of the Animal Powers: Historical Atlas of World Mythology.* London: Times Books, 1983. 301 pp.

Dembeck, Hermann. *Animals and Men.* New York: The American Museum of Natural History, 1961. 390 pp.

Dunlap, Thomas R. *Saving America's Wildlife.* New Jersey: Princeton University Press, 1988. 222 pp.

Gilbert, Frederick F., and Donald G. Dodds. *The Philosophy and Practice of Wildlife Management.* Florida: Robert E. Krieger Publishing Company, 1987. 279 pp.

Hobrusch, Erich. *Fair Game: A History of Hunting, Shooting and Animal Conservation.* New York: Arco Publishing, Inc., 1980. 279 pp.

Horton, Tom. *Bay Country: Reflections on the Chesapeake.* New York: Ticknor & Fields, 1987. 210 pp.

Horwood, Harold. *Dancing on the Shore: A Celebration of Life at Annapolis Basin.* New York: E. P. Dutton, 1987. 219 pp.

Jones, Robert F. *Blood Sport: A Journey up the Hassayampa.* New York: Simon and Schuster, 1974. 255 pp.

———. *Slade's Glacier.* New York: Simon and Schuster, 1981. 205 pp.

Lesley, Craig. *WinterKill.* New York: A Laurel Book, 1984. 306 pp.

Martin, Brian P. *The Great Shoots: Britain's Premier Sporting Estates.* London: David & Charles, 1987. 255 pp.

Mead, James R. *Hunting and Trading on the Great Plains 1859–1875.* Norman: University of Oklahoma Press, 1986. 276 pp.

Nash, Roderick Frazier. *The Rights of Nature: A History of Environmental Ethics.* Madison: The University of Wisconsin Press, 1989. 290 pp.

Proulx, E. Annie. *Heart Songs and Other Stories.* New York: Charles Scribner's Sons, 1988. 151 pp.

Salt, Henry S., ed. *Killing for Sport: Essays by Various Writers.* London: G. Bell and Sons, 1915. 186 pp.

Thompson, E. P. *Whigs and Hunters: The Origin of the Black Act.* New York: Pantheon Books, 1975. 313 pp.

Trollope, Anthony. *Hunting Sketches.* New York: The Gosden Head, Ltd., 1933. 103 pp.

Appendix

Booksellers Who Specialize in Out-of-Print Outdoor Literature

Kenneth Anderson Books
38 Silver Street
Auburn, MA 01501
(617) 832-3524

Aspen Hills Books
3724 Hill Lake Road
Hill City, MN 55748
(218) 697-2772

Judith Bowman Books
Pound Ridge Road
Bedford, NY 10506
(914) 234-7543

Seymour Brecher
The Woodland Gallery
P.O. Box 987
Monticello, NY 12701

Callahan & Company Booksellers
P.O. Box 505
Peterborough, NH 03458
(603) 924-3726

Gary L. Estabrook — Books
Box 61453
Vancouver, WA 98666
(206) 699-5454

Fair Chase Inc.
Box 838
Twin Lakes, WI 53181
(414) 279-5478

Colonel J. Furniss
Old Police House
Strathpeffer
Ross-shire
Great Britain

Game Bag Books
Henry S. Paul
2704 Shiprock Road
Willow Street, PA 17584

Grayling Books
Lyvennet, Crosby Ravensworth, Penrith
Cumbria CA10 3JP
Great Britain

Gunnerman Books
P.O. Box 4292
Auburn Hills, MI 48057
(313) 879-2779

Donald E. Hahn
Natural History Books
P.O. Box 1004
Cottonwood, AZ 86326
(602) 634-5016

E. Chalmers Hallam
9 Post Office Lane, St. Ives
Ringwood, Hants BH24 2PG
Great Britain

Hampton Books
Route 1, P.O. Box 202
Newberry, SC 29108
(803) 276-6870

Hartland Books
P.O. Box 1094
Woodstock, IL 60098

Morris Heller
P.O. Box 46
Swan Lake, NY 12783
(914) 583-5879

Henderson & Park
Fifth and Main
Greenwood, MO 64034
(816) 537-6388

Patricia Ledlie — Bookseller
P.O. Box 46B
Buckfield, ME 04220
(207) 336-2969

Melvin Marcher Bookseller
6204 N. Vermont
Oklahoma City, OK 73112
(405) 946-6270

Gerald Pettinger Books
Route 2
Russell, Iowa 50238
(515) 535-2239

Piece of Time
Jack Ragonese
North Stonington, CT 06359
(203) 535-1375

Pisces and Capricorn Books
514 Linden Ave.
Albion, MI 49224
(517) 629-3267

Ray Riling Arms Books Co.
6844 Gorsten St.
P.O. Box 18925
Philadelphia, PA 19119
(215) 438-2456

Gustave H. Suhm "Book-tique"
81 Llewellyn Drive
Westfield, MA 01085
(413) 568-5627

Trophy Room Books
P.O. Box 3041
Aqoura, CA 91301
(818) 889-2469

University Microfilms International
Dissertation Copies
P.O. Box 1764
Ann Arbor, MI 48106
(To order by phone and credit card, call
(800) 521-3042, toll free.)

John Valle
550 Mohawk Rd.
West Hempstead, NY 11552
(516) 887-3342

Watkins Natural History Books
Larry C. Watkins
R.D. #1
Belden Corners Rd.
Dolgeville, NY 13329-9526
(518) 568-2280

R. E. and G. B. Way, A.B.A.
Brettons
Burrough Green, Newmarket, Suffolk
CB8 9NA
Great Britain

Reflections of the Dawn

I know the whitetail. He is big and free
and this is his range.
Soon his form will break the stillness
of the dawn.
By his presence, my spirit is feverish.
By this light my bones are cold.
The sun has yet to mount the peak at my
back to warm the air.
But my heart is warm. This is my sunrise,
my day.
I am the hunter.
I marvel that I have lived to enjoy this
moment and the freedom of hunting
in a land teeming with wildlife;
A land painted by the Maker's hand.
I cherish this moment, this mountain,
this day and this life.
Where but here can a man know
such freedom?

— Anonymous

IRENE VENDERMOI

Index